SOCIAL WELFARE IN TODAY'S WORLD

Ronald C. Federico

Iona College

This text was developed for McGraw-Hill
by Irving Rockwood & Associates, Inc.

McGRAW-HILL PUBLISHING COMPANY

New York St. Louis San Francisco Auckland Bogotá Caracas
Hamburg Lisbon London Madrid Mexico Milan Montreal New Delhi
Oklahoma City Paris San Juan São Paulo Singapore Sydney Tokyo Toronto

This book was set in Palatino by the College Composition Unit
in cooperation with Waldman Graphics, Inc.
The editors were Phillip A. Butcher, Irving Rockwood, and Elaine Rosenberg;
the production supervisor was Birgit Garlasco.
The cover was designed by Katherine Urban.
Cover illustration by Jane Sterritt.
R. R. Donnelley & Sons Company was printer and binder.

SOCIAL WELFARE IN TODAY'S WORLD

1 2 3 4 5 6 7 8 9 0 DOC DOC 8 9 4 3 2 1 0 9

ISBN 0-07-020374-1

Library of Congress Cataloging-in-Publication Data

Federico, Ronald C.
    Social welfare in today's world/Ronald C. Federico.
        p.   cm.
    Bibliography: p.
    ISBN 0-07-020374-1.—ISBN 0-07-020375-X (instructor's manual)
    1. Social service—United States.   2. Social service—Cross-
cultural studies.   3. Human services—United States.   4. Human
services—Cross-cultural studies.   I. Title.
    HV91.F42   1990
    361.973—dc20
                                                89-12443

SOCIAL WELFARE IN TODAY'S WORLD

ABOUT
THE AUTHOR

RONALD C. FEDERICO is Professor of Social Work at Iona College in New Rochelle, New York. He holds a bachelor's degree from Yale (where he graduated magna cum laude in 1962), a master's in Social Work from the University of Michigan, and a Ph.D. in Sociology from Northwestern. Professor Federico is one of today's leading figures in baccalaureate social work education. He is an active member of the Council of Social Work Education and the Association of Baccalaureate Program Directors and has served as director or program chair of three undergraduate-level social work programs. In addition, he is the author of numerous scholarly articles, the coauthor (with Betty L. Baer) of the highly influential two-volume study, *Educating the Baccalaureate Social Worker* (Ballinger, 1978 and 1979), and the author or coauthor of several successful undergraduate-level texts, including *The Social Welfare Institution* (D.C. Heath), *Human Behavior: A Social Work Perspective* (Longman), and *Sociology* (Addison-Wesley).

In the final analysis, however, we must realize that social injustice and unjust social structures exist only because individuals and groups of individuals deliberately maintain or tolerate them. It is these personal choices, operating through structures, that breed and propagate situations of poverty, oppression and misery.

Pope John Paul II
San Antonio, Texas
September 13, 1987

CONTENTS

ILLUSTRATIONS

Tables

PREFACE

The following encounter was reported in a large United States city. [A man sat on the steps of a church, surrounded by his belongings.] "In his outstretched hand he held a paper cup; his plea - 'Change. Spare change?'-was addressed to all passsers-by, among them a boy of about 8 or 9.

When he heard the elderly man's request, the boy bounced off his skateboard, placed it under his arm and approached the man with concern. 'I don't have any money, but I've got some baseball cards,' the boy said. 'Would you want some of those?'

The man looked at him for a long moment. The squint into the sun turned into a smile. 'Yeah, let's see what you've got,' he said.

The boy knelt on the sidewalk, pulled some cards out of his knapsack and handed over a few. The man held them with great care, turning them over and over as if they were precious objects. When at last he spoke, he said: 'Thanks. Thanks a lot. I could use these.'

Satisfied, the boy hopped back up on his skateboard. The elderly man watched him speed off into the distance."[1]

This book is about encounters of this kind between people. It explores why people are in need, and why others choose to help - or not to help - them. It also examines what makes things valuable to people, and the formal and informal strategies through which people are linked to the resources they need. The helping impulse that leads people to share with others what is meaningful to them is at the core of this book. What is shared may be love, money, housing, counseling, or even baseball cards. Whatever it is, the quality of social life is affected by how it is shared, either informally (as between the vagrant and the skate-boarder) or formally through highly structured social welfare programs.

The book approaches these topics by posing a series of questions, each of which then becomes the focal point of a chapter. These questions move sys-

[1]Weinberg, Sydney. 1988. Metropolitan diary. *The New York Times*, July 6, B2.

tematically from a concern with the nature of social welfare and why it is needed in today's world, to more technical questions about how helping programs are designed and structured. The focus throughout the book is on social welfare in the United States, but comparative material from three other societies—Mexico, Poland, and Sweden—is also included. This material highlights major issues in the relationship between helping efforts and the political, economic, educational, and family structures of society. It should also serve to expand our thinking about alternative ways of conceptualizing and delivering help to people in need. Using a comparative perspective has the additional benefit of linking the United States with social processes and social issues that seem to be common to many industrialized societies.

Learning about organized helping in the United States can be challenging and frustrating. Its mixture of public tax-supported and private non-profit and for-profit services is unique and creative, but also complex. The very controversy over whether providing economic support to the poor and the disadvantaged actually helps or hurts them is symptomatic of the difficult decisions involved in social welfare. To study the limits and nature of our responsibilities to those who are especially vulnerable or disadvantaged brings us close to the heart of the problem. This book seeks to enable its readers to understand these issues better so that they can participate in decision making about them, either in the voting booth or through a career choice.

ACKNOWLEDGMENTS

Writing this book has been a wonderful personal experience. I have met many valued colleagues in other societies, and I have had the opportunity to learn much that I value. This project would not have come to fruition without the help of many people, only a few of whom I can cite here.

Iona College granted me the sabbatical leave that made the intensive work possible that was necessary to complete the book. In addition, Iona's commitment to basic human values and to internationalizing its curriculum as a way of helping students understand the common human enterprise in which we are all involved, stimulated and focused my own thinking.

My developmental editor, Irving Rockwood of Irving Rockwood & Associates, Inc., was a tremendous support during the formulation and execution of this book. He understood my goals, and he helped me to formulate them so that they could be made real in a book format. He also provided invaluable editorial assistance.

Many colleagues went out of their way to help me obtain data and learn more about social welfare in the United States and elsewhere. In Mexico, I would especially like to thank Lidia Proal, Rosa Maria de Castro Valle, and Jesus Ferreiros Lopez for their help, along with the social work faculty at the Universitaria Nacional Autonoma de Mexico. My work in Poland was made possible by Janet Schwartz, a valued colleague in this country, and Professor Jan Rosner and Professor Ewa Leś, who live in Poland. Professors Rosner and

Leś were tireless translators, helpful colleagues, and extraordinary hosts. To them, and all those with whom they arranged meetings for me, I am deeply grateful.

Studying social welfare in Sweden is greatly facilitated by the helpfulness of the Swedish Information Service in New York and the Swedish Institute in Stockholm. Catharina Mannheimer at the Swedish Institute was a most helpful hostess and coordinator of my study efforts in Sweden. I appreciate the cordial help of the many colleagues who met with me, especially Maria Danielsson and Sten-Ake Stenberg who shared a good deal of literature with me, and Ulf Wester, Goran Hoglund, and Ingvar Krakau, who were unusually helpful and hospitable. Through my Swedish research, I have come to know Mait Widmark and Siri Andersson who continue to expand my thinking about social welfare.

Closer to home, many of my United States colleagues were helpful and supportive. They include Graciela Castex and Dean Pierce, Alvin Sallee, Kay Hoffman, and Robert Berger. In addition, the following people who reviewed the manuscript were extremely helpful in guiding and sharpening my thinking and writing: Margaret J. Allen, Eastern Kentucky University; L. Jay Bishop, Ohio University; Eleanor Brubaker, Miami University of Ohio; J. Douglas Burnham, Eastern Kentucky University; Edward W. Davis, University of Nevada—Las Vegas; Morris D. Klass, Memphis State University; Kathleen McInnis, Marquette University; Dorothy C. Miller, University of Maryland—Baltimore County; Roscoe Y. Miller, California State University—Northridge; Elizabeth Thompson Ortiz, California State University—Long Beach; Robert P. Scheurell, University of Wisconsin—Milwaukee; and William H. Whitaker, University of Maine. I thank everyone who made this a better book because of their time, interest, and expertise. Any errors that remain in spite of their help are my own responsibility.

Finally, my friends and family have played an important role. Without their interest and support, projects like this are impossible, and I am grateful to them.

I wish that I could convey the many wonderful experiences that I have had in writing this book. I will always remember the residents of a geriatric day care center in Poland who proudly showed me their scrapbook, the loving interaction between parents and children in Mexico City's Chapultepec Park, and the father wheeling his baby in a carriage down special ramps provided in Stockholm so that families can have access to the subway. It is indeed a rich and wonderful world, and I am so grateful to have had a chance to learn more of it. I hope you share some of my joy and learning as you read further.

Ronald C. Federico

INTRODUCTION

AN INVITATION TO THE READER

If you have just acquired this book, it is quite likely you have done so because it has been assigned in one of your classes. If so, you may have mixed feelings about reading it. Will it be interesting and informative? Or will it be difficult to understand and a possible source of grade problems?

As you begin this book, I thought it might be helpful to talk to you about what you can expect. First, I want to say I am very happy you will be reading my book. Naturally I am proud of it, but I also believe that you will find it very useful.

The major purpose of this book is to describe and explain the social welfare system in the United States. Thus, it discusses our society's basic views about helping people, the resources that we allocate to helping efforts, the way we provide help and to whom, the major helping programs through which help is delivered, and what it is like to be involved in helping others.

There are a number of reasons why learning about the social welfare system is worth your time and effort.

If you choose a social welfare career, such as social work, nursing, or mental health, you will find it essential to have a working knowledge of the social

1

welfare system. Together, the programs that comprise this system supply the assistance needed to help people meet their emotional, financial, housing, medical, educational, and community needs on a daily basis. As a social welfare professional, you will need to know what services are available and how to link people with them.

Even if you choose a career in a field not directly related to social welfare, a knowledge of social welfare services is still useful. You and your family may experience needs that can be met with the help of social welfare programs. In planning for retirement, for example, most of us rely, at least in part, on "Social Security" payments in order to have a decent retirement income. All of us, too, need medical care from time to time. And if we experience emotional stress, we can profit from counseling. There are, in short, many times during most people's lives when it is useful to know what resources are available and how to make use of them.

A working knowledge of social welfare is also an important part of our obligations as responsible citizens in a democratic society. What helping services should be provided, to whom, and how are major issues of our day. A knowledge of social welfare is important in making informed decisions about these and related questions. I hope this book will help you be a more informed and active participant in the political process.

There is a final way in which an understanding of social welfare is valuable that is somewhat less concrete than the others. Part of being an educated person is having the capacity to reflect on your own thoughts in a systematic way. Social welfare raises some of the most fundamental human issues—freedom and dependence, basic human needs, personal and social responsibility, the rights of citizenship, and others. I hope that this book will stimulate your thinking about these issues, and help you clarify your own personal beliefs and commitments.

PLAN OF THIS BOOK

Each of the chapters following this introduction addresses a basic question about social welfare. These are taken up in logical order as follows:

- What is social welfare?
- Why do we need social welfare?
- How has it developed over time?
- How is it organized?
- What are the major services it provides?
- How does social welfare relate to the rest of society?
- Why is social welfare controversial?
- Who delivers social welfare services?
- What is it like to work in the social welfare delivery system?
- What does social welfare have to contribute to our society's future?

If, after reading this book, you are able to answer these questions, you will have acquired a sound, basic understanding of social welfare. In order to help you realize this objective, each chapter contains a number of features designed to make it as easy as possible to master the chapter material.

1 *A chapter overview*. Each chapter begins with a brief statement of purpose and description of the chapter's central topic. This overview, entitled ''What to Expect from This Chapter,'' will help guide your thinking as you approach the chapter.

2 *Learning objectives*. Following the overview, each chapter contains a list of specific learning objectives to be mastered by the time you have completed the chapter. As much as possible, these are stated in behavioral terms— that is, they are statements of what you will be able to *do* as a result of your reading and study.

I strongly recommend that when you have finished a chapter, you return to the learning objectives and make sure you have mastered them. If not, you should restudy the appropriate sections of the chapter. If you have difficulty with any of the learning objectives, you should speak with your instructor.

3 *Illustrations*. There is a variety of illustrative material in each chapter. Charts and tables provide statistical and empirical data. Diagrams or other schematic materials are provided to help clarify relationships between ideas or structures. Four photo essays, one on each of the four countries discussed in the text, convey something of the flavor of these four different societies.

4 *Case studies and examples*. Throughout the text, under the heading ''The Human Face of Social Welfare''—the first of which appears in this chapter—you will find a series of case studies. Focusing on real people and real cases, these case studies convey a sense of the human dimensions of social welfare issues and programs. Finally, a series of mini-essays labeled ''On the Street'' describes my impressions of people, places, and programs discussed in the text.

5 *Comparative approach*. Perhaps the single most distinctive feature of this book is that each chapter includes examples and illustrations from other societies—principally Mexico, Sweden, and Poland—in addition to our own. The purpose of these examples is to help you better understand social welfare in the United States by placing our society's experience and practice in a larger context. I also think you will be interested to see how other societies try to meet the needs of their citizens.

6 *Chapter summary*. A brief summary appears at the conclusion of each chapter. Entitled ''Let's Review,'' these highlight points of particular importance and provide transitions between chapters.

7 *Chapter outline*. An end-of-chapter outline immediately follows each summary. You will find these useful to help clarify the relationships between ideas discussed in the chapter. You might also want to use these outlines as the basis for any notes you take, filling in the outline as you read or reread the chapter.

8 *Study questions.* Questions are provided at the end of each chapter that are intended to help you review, integrate, and apply the material you have read. They focus on you and your own life experiences so that you will be able to see the day-to-day relevance of social welfare.

9 *Key terms and concepts.* A list of key terms and concepts used in the chapter follows the chapter outline. Definitions of these terms appear in the text and in the glossary at the end of the book.

10 *Suggested readings.* A short annotated list of suggested readings also appears at the end of each chapter. You will find the sources listed there especially useful for pursuing ideas in depth, or for obtaining additional information needed for special projects that your instructor may assign.

11 *References.* Each chapter ends with a list of sources cited in the chapter. These enable you to refer to the actual works cited in the event you want more information.

12 *Glossary.* A glossary containing definitions of the most important technical terms used throughout the text appears at the end of the book where you can easily refer to it as needed. The glossary also provides a convenient tool for reviewing major concepts whenever you wish.

As you read *Social Welfare in Today's World,* I hope three points will emerge. The first is that social welfare as a subject is endlessly fascinating, challenging your ability to think and reason as well as your emotions and your values. The second is a respect for how tightly social welfare is woven into societal ways of thinking and organizing daily life. Third, as I hope will become apparent, I have tried to create a book that itself exemplifies the goals of social welfare. As a learning tool, it seeks to help you by providing support, stimulation, and encouragement, and by strengthening your ability to grow and develop as a person. I hope that you will feel I have succeeded.

Now that you know how the book is organized, let's look more closely at its subject matter.

APPROACHING SOCIAL WELFARE

In discussing the existing social welfare system in the United States, the approach I have adopted is one I call *active choice.* By this I mean *that social welfare systems result from a society's decisions about what the functions and structures of social welfare ought to be.* These decisions reflect prevailing values, needs, resources, and decision-making structures and processes. In other words, the social welfare system about which you will learn is neither inevitable nor unchangeable but rather is the product of thousands of decisions made over many years.

You will soon see that decisions about social welfare are made by individuals, families, communities, agencies, governments, and others. Although none of us can predict what social welfare will be like in the future, we can be certain that we, as a society, will continue to make decisions about social welfare on an ongoing basis. We can be sure too that the choices made will continue to reflect changing values, needs, resources, and the views of those who have influence in decision-making structures and processes.

In keeping with the active choice approach, this book also employs a *cross-cultural comparative perspective,* drawing upon social welfare examples from other societies. By comparing the United States with other societies, we will see that social welfare is embedded in the particular social fabric of its own society. Every society has some type of social welfare system, but each—including our own—has created a system adapted to its own needs and social patterns. As these needs and patterns change, so will the social welfare system.

A comparative perspective can enrich your study of social welfare in several ways:

1 It can help you identify and focus on our own society's social welfare choices. As we compare the choices of other societies with our own, it will seem quite natural to examine why the United States has made the choices it has.

2 As we explore choices, we will uncover the social structures that influence decision-making. Social structure has an impact on social welfare in all societies, but the nature of that impact varies considerably. Comparing the way in which our structures function to those of other societies can give us better insight into how our society works.

3 Looking at other societies' choices can also expand our thinking about social welfare. For every problem there are many possible solutions, and other societies may well have found innovative methods of meeting social welfare needs that we should consider. The old saying that "two heads are better than one" applies to social welfare.

4 Finally, a cross-cultural perspective can increase our understanding of the wholeness of societies. We will see that choices about social welfare have to mesh with the knowledge, values, beliefs, and behaviors that characterize each society. This will make us explore these aspects of our own society more deeply and better understand their complexity. Although we want to learn from other societies, we cannot uncritically implement choices made elsewhere.

To summarize the book's approach to social welfare:

1 It employs an active choice approach that focuses on a society's choices about how to attain its social welfare goals. These often change over time.

2 It adopts a cross-cultural comparative perspective to help illustrate the wide-ranging nature of these choices, and their relationship to social structures, values, and belief systems.

3 It focuses on the United States social welfare system. This knowledge is important for daily use. However, illustrations from other societies will enable us to probe more deeply into the factors that influence social welfare in this society, to identify problems with the current system, and to consider changes for the future.

THE HUMAN FACE OF SOCIAL WELFARE 1

Choices

I witnessed an epileptic seizure for the first time in 1979, when I was 18. In the center of my college dining hall, a young man who worked in the kitchen had collapsed in a convulsion. Four students quickly piled on top of him. His arms and legs jerked violently and, in the process of trying to hold him down, the students seemed to be smothering him. The young man's face, twisted and red, made him appear to be in great pain and, somehow, inhuman. Yet I could see myself in his place—I had just found out that I had epilepsy.

I did not want to say anything, but I thought the four students, in their panic, might kill the young man. So I told the largest of them, who by then had a headlock on the kitchen worker, to let go. The student brushed off my concern and seemed irritated that I would bother him at such a time. I paused, then repeated my statement in louder tones.

The student was angry. "Look, kid," he said, "I'm a pre-med. I know what I'm doing. What makes you think you know so much?"

I opened my mouth, but no words came. Instead, I walked to a corner and leaned against the wall. As the young man's convulsions grew more violent, I whispered an apology to him and began to cry.

Just four weeks before, back home in Dallas, a neurologist had diagnosed my epilepsy. The doctor warned me—and so did members of my family soon afterward—that if I did not keep my epilepsy a secret, people would fear me and I would be subject to discrimination. Even now, seven years after that scene in the dining hall, it is difficult for me to say that I have epilepsy. Back then, it was impossible.

In the years since, I have had hundreds of various types of seizures. I have experienced the mental, physical and emotional side effects caused by changes in the anticonvulsant drugs I take each day. Yet, for the first two years, I refused to learn about epilepsy. My fears of being found out were my real concern....

Epilepsy is a condition encompassing about 20 different types of seizures, uncontrolled bursts of electrical energy in the brain. Convulsions, while among the most dramatic, are only one type of seizure.

According to the Epilepsy Foundation of America, there are more than two million Americans with epilepsy. Half have what I have, idiopathic epilepsy, meaning there is no known cause for the seizures. Of the two million, partly because of misunderstanding about the symptoms, about three-quarters of a million go undiagnosed or untreated.

By the time I arrived for my freshman year at [college] in 1979, I had already had many seizures, although my family, friends and I did not know it....

I do not remember my first major seizure.... Mostly, I remember my own stunned silence. My memory of the visit to my first neurologist, in Dallas that Thanksgiving, is sketchy, although, sitting in a hospital hallway waiting to have my first CAT scan, I recall thinking that I might have a brain tumor and could die....

The doctor gave me several warnings: Never tell anyone unless necessary, because I might be ostracized. Call it "seizure disorder," not epilepsy, because fewer people would be frightened. Try to choose a profession as free from stress as possible.

For a long time, I followed his advice, afraid that if the truth were known, I would lose my friends and never get a job....

Over the next two years I sometimes ignored the limitations on my life and sometimes did not talk to my doctor. I also asked the doctor to say nothing to my parents. I knew my condition deeply troubled my family and that made me feel guilty. Unlike the other feelings that accompanied my condition, guilt was one I could control. I stopped talking about my epilepsy....

Toward the end of the summer [following the author's second year of college], with my work at [my summer job] suffering badly, I reluctantly went home to see a new neurologist my mother had found. I had grown tired of doctors and did not want them to hurt me anymore. I was convinced I would not live to see my college graduation. I would die from accident, a stroke or by my own hand....

After tests, [my new doctor] prescribed Dilantin, another anticonvulsant. My sudden "drop attacks" stopped. Soon, with convulsions occurring only twice a month, I finally believed that my life was coming together.

In September, I returned to [college] for my junior year. I was happy, even though the medication gave me severe drowsiness and slightly changed my personality, making me more dour than I usually am. I began to tell friends about my condition, easing the burden on Carl and Franz [the author's roommates who until now had been among the few people in whom he had confided about his condition]. For the first time in two years, I walked the campus by myself....

In the first week of November, the administration of [my college] dismissed me from school because of my health. My fears from years earlier were realized. After my first eight weeks of honesty, control of my life had been taken away from me....

After I arrived back home, my dismissal triggered an intense rage. I screamed at my family, my friends, sometimes at myself....The explosion of anger was so strong that all of us worried I was losing my sanity.

My father changed. When it appeared to him that I would not be readmitted to [college], his own anger overtook him. Finally accepting my condition, he became enraged that anyone would deny me a normal life.

By December, I learned that I could not be dismissed from school because of my health under section 504 of the Rehabilitation Act of 1973, which provides rights to the handicapped. With advice from the Government's [Department of] Health and Human Services, my family and I contacted school officials and lawyers to get me back to school.

At the end of the first week of the second semester of my junior year, without going to court, I was readmitted to [college] and continued my studies as a political science major....In June of 1983, I graduated with distinction.

I found work...[and] now live in New York, where I can function without a car....I carry an emergency card with the phone numbers of people who can help. My epilepsy is under good control, although I still sporadically have convulsions. I have had to struggle with various problems, such as the difficulty of obtaining health insurance and sometimes of working with colleagues who are unsure, or wary of me. My doctor tries for better control, still making occasional changes in my medication....

I still get angry that people with epilepsy feel driven to hide their condition, but I understand why. I know now that there is discrimination and fear but have learned that the best way to address that is through educating people and, if necessary, turning to the law.

I now believe what Carl [my college roommate] once said to me: "If everybody in the world knew how to deal with epilepsy, if everybody in the world were not mystified by a seizure, if everybody in the world were willing to help out when they see a stranger have a seizure, then the life of people with epilepsy would be infinitely easier. They would be able to go everywhere and do just about anything and not worry."

Kurt Eichenwald's story illustrates the many levels at which social welfare choices are made. Knowing that he had an illness that would sometimes disrupt his activities, he had to choose whether to acknowledge his condition publicly and how to determine its impact on his life goals. His family also had to make choices, both in terms of their response to him, and the types of assistance they were willing to seek outside the family.

The choices available to Kurt and his family were affected by the help available through various components of the social welfare system, itself the product of choice. The doctors whom Kurt consulted had to choose treatment strategies that included not only medication but counseling about how best to cope with his illness. Information was available from the Epilepsy Foundation of America, a voluntary organization formed to provide information to those suffering from epilepsy and to educate the general public about the illness.

The decision of Kurt's college to dismiss him as a result of his condition was another choice that affected his situation. This attempt to solve what the school saw as a problem for itself became, for Kurt, a major and painful obstacle to overcome as he attempted to take control of his own life by making positive and life-affirming choices.

Finally, Kurt's situation was affected by society's choice to protect people with disabilities, including epilepsy, through legislation. Society's affirmation of the rights of disabled people was a critical resource for Kurt Eichenwald as he fought to manage his life and illness in a productive way.

Stories like Kurt Eichenwald's raise issues about values and choices. As his roommate said so eloquently, the choices made by individuals and organizations affect what people with conditions like Kurt's will be able to do. It is clear that fear and misinformation played a large role in the choices made by all of the actors involved in Kurt Eichenwald's case. This is very common. Our beliefs about the causes of behavior and our fears about their consequences often influence our choices, even though our knowledge may be wrong and our fears ungrounded. What, for example, would *you* do if you saw someone having an epileptic seizure?

From Kurt Eichenwald, Braving epilepsy's storm, *The New York Times Magazine,* January 11, 1987, pp. 30–36. Copyright (c) 1987 by The New York Times Company. Reprinted by permission.

---

4 An underlying assumption of the book is that social welfare is embedded in the fabric of society. What works in one society may not work in another. Nevertheless, we can expand our thinking about choices by looking at how various societies address a similar need.

It will become apparent as you read this book that there are many unmet needs in the United States. Why this should be so will emerge from our exploration of how decision-making structures work.

THE COMPARATIVE VIEW: FOUR SOCIETIES

Throughout this book, social welfare in the United States will be systematically compared with three other helping systems: those of Mexico, Poland, and Sweden. These three systems were chosen because each of the societies involved is of a type significantly different from the United States. Mexico is a developing nation that is in the midst of significant political, economic, and demographic changes. Poland is a socialist nation influenced by communist political and economic practices that come from the Soviet Union. Sweden is an advanced social welfare state with a unique commitment to social planning for meeting social welfare needs.

Each of the societies discussed in this book has created its own approach to social welfare. By comparing them we will see how decision-making about similar social issues occurs in different social environments. Sometimes the results are similar. Sometimes they are not. As you compare societies with each other, you will see how each seeks to integrate social welfare into its basic social fabric. In the process, you will come to a better understanding of our own society and its social welfare system.

A few facts about each of these four societies will provide a helpful context for understanding their social welfare systems. As you learn about each society, notice that there are substantial differences between them in such factors as land size, population size, the capacity of the economy to generate goods and services, the form of government, level of industrialization, and so forth. Some of the more important of these are summarized in Table I.1. The effect of these factors on social welfare will become clear from data presented at various points throughout the book.

Mexico

Geographic Area Mexico is part of North America, lying between the United States (Texas, New Mexico, Arizona, and California) on the north, Guatemala and Belize on the south, the Gulf of Mexico and the Caribbean Sea on the east, and the Gulf of California and the Pacific Ocean on the west. The

TABLE I.1 FOUR SOCIETIES: AN OVERVIEW

	Mexico	**Poland**	**Sweden**	**United States**
Geographic area				
Square miles	761,530 sq. mi.	120,400 sq. mi.	173,400 sq. mi.	3,615,123 sq. mi.
Relative size	Three times size of Texas	Size of New Mexico	Size of California and Massachusetts	Size of India and Australia
Population	80 million (1984 data)	36.5 million (1983 data)	8.3 million (1983 data)	226.5 million (1980 data)
Gross national product (GNP)	$163.3 billion	$170 billion	$103 billion	$3 trillion
GNP per person (1983 data)	$2,180	$4,670 (1982 data)	$12,440	$14,080
Form of government	Limited democracy with one dominant party	Communist—the majority of candidates selected by Communist party or political parties aligned with it	Democracy with limited monarch	Democracy
Economic system	Mix of socialist and capitalist—free enterprise with some government ownership of business	Socialist—government owns and controls virtually all business activities	Mix of socialist and capitalist—limited government ownership but strong government regulation of business	Capitalist—free enterprise with limited government regulation

Sources: Data on geographic area from *The Times Concise Atlas of the World,* revised edition (London: Times Newspapers Limited, 1973). Data on population, gross national product, and GNP per person from *The World Bank Atlas 1986* (Washington, D.C.: The World Bank, 1986). Supplemental data for Poland from *The World Almanac and Book of Facts 1986* (New York: Newspaper Enterprise Association, Inc., 1985) and from Tagliabue, John. 1989. Poland sets free vote in June, first since '45; Solidarity reinstated. *New York Times,* April 6, p.A1.

topography ranges from semidesert conditions in the north to mountains and fertile highlands in the central part of the country. The eastern and far southern areas are primarily tropical. Only 12 percent of the land surface in Mexico is suitable for farming without irrigation.

Once a primarily agricultural society, Mexico has in recent decades experienced a pronounced increase in its urban population as many Mexicans have moved from rural areas to the cities in response to economic opportunity and somewhat better living conditions. Mexico City, the capital, is now thought to be the largest city in the world with a population of nearly 18 million people, many of whom live in shantytowns (Eckstein, 1988). In addition to the cities of the urban area in the south central part of the country, there are several rapidly growing cities along Mexico's northern border with the United States. The growth of these cities has been spurred by industrial development in this area, as well as by the need for housing the 2 to 4 million Mexicans who live in Mexico but work in the United States.

Major Cultural Groups The area now known as Mexico was originally inhabited by several Indian groups, most notably the Aztecs and the Mayans. The arrival of the Spanish Conquistadors in the 1500s led to large-scale colonization by Europeans. The current population is primarily Indian, with significant groups of mestizos (descendants of Indians and Europeans who have intermarried) and descendants of the European invaders. Most Mexicans are Roman Catholic. Spanish is the official language, but there are also many Indian languages in common use.

Economic Characteristics Oil, agriculture, fishing, and manufacturing have been the main strengths of Mexico's economy. Most industry is privately owned, but there is some governmental ownership. Government policy has encouraged investment by outside multinational corporations. Trade imbalances in recent years have led to a huge foreign debt as well as a national debt that is among the highest in the world (Ward, 1986:23). The population living in urban areas increased from 22 percent in 1940 to about 55 percent in the early 1980s, and in 1983 the urban unemployment rate was 12.5 percent (Ward, 1986:17,25). Many Mexicans survive by selling goods and services on the street. These people usually lead a marginal existence in shantytowns on the outskirts of the major cities. They have little economic or job security and no work-related social welfare benefits (Eckstein, 1988).

Political Characteristics The current political structure dates from the Mexican Revolution (1910–1917) and the Constitution that resulted from it. Mexico has a federal government with thirty-one states and a Federal District—Mexico City—that is similar to Washington, D.C. in the United States. Each state has a popularly elected governor and legislature.

The national president and legislature are also democratically elected. However, Mexican politics has effectively been dominated by one party, the Partido Revolucionario Institucional (PRI), since the Revolution (Rudolph, 1985:xxvii). The PRI's candidates are almost always successful in elections for major offices, including the presidency—held continuously by the PRI since

ON THE STREET IN MEXICO CITY

Mexico City is the largest city in the world and it well captures the youth and vitality of the country. With an annual population growth rate of about 2.5 percent in 1984, and with nearly 55 percent of the population age 19 or younger, the presence of children is very noticeable. They seem to accompany adults everywhere, especially in Indian and mestizo families. The other very noticeable source of activity is the ever-present automobile. Many are old American cars and Mexican-made Volkswagens whose exhaust systems emit noise and smoke. But no matter how old or battered, it is common to see Mexicans carefully cleaning their cars.

In overall appearance, Mexico City resembles many other large, modern cities. It has beautiful boulevards and narrow side streets, modern high-rise buildings and elegant older structures, and a wide range of restaurants and shops. Behind the facade, however, other realities become apparent. The old downtown section near the Zona Rosa and Alameda Park still exhibits a good deal of damage from the 1985 earthquake, with a number of partially or completely destroyed buildings not yet re-built. Huddling quietly in some doorways are Indian women, a shawl completely wrapping themselves and their small children. Only an outstretched hand indicates their reason for being there. In other locations, an entire family begs quietly—beseeching passersby only with eyes, or perhaps by playing an instrument. At traffic lights, young men sell trinkets, gum, or newspapers to those in cars, or else perform what seems to be a Mexico City specialty—exhaling fire in return for a few coins.

Many of the buildings have some type of painting or sculpture on them, conveying an impression of a country that values its artistic heritage. These works of art are usually derived from or refer to the country's Indian culture, an ever-present part of daily life as evidenced in street names, decoration, and the beauty of the people themselves.

People on the street exhibit a wide range of skin color, facial features, and body types, representing the different physical contributions of the Indians and the Europeans who have shaped the country's history. Most give evidence of Indian ancestry, being brown-skinned, fairly short, dark-eyed, and with beautiful straight black hair. However, most of those in positions of power seem to be of European ancestry.

The shantytowns that house approximately 38 percent of the residents of Mexico City are well outside the area likely to be seen by visitors. They provide the only housing available to most of the poor rural immigrants who flock to the city seeking work and better living conditions. In many cases, families gradually improve their housing and the communities themselves become permanent (Eckstein, 1988). Nevertheless, amenities and public utilities are few, and most people become street vendors to support themselves. Some flavor of life in these communities can be found in the street markets adjacent to the main downtown area. At little stalls families sell fruit, vegetables, toiletries, clothing, and other necessary goods. Most startling to outsiders is the sale of meat and fish on open tables, unrefrigerated and unprotected from flies.

Mexico City, then, is a city of contrasts. It has luxurious shops in whose doorways women and their children may beg at night. It is a major world capital that is still struggling with the effects of a devastating earthquake. It is a city of youth and growth, of beautiful children lovingly cared for, along with massive traffic jams, unplanned shantytowns, and begging in the street. It is a city of deep Indian cultural roots, yet its official language is Spanish. It is a city in which American-style fast-food shops serve anything from hamburgers to spicy local and regional foods. Mexico City is an exciting city that captures the duality of developing nations. Western-style urban lifestyles and social problems coexist with centuries-old agricultural and non-Western cultural traditions.

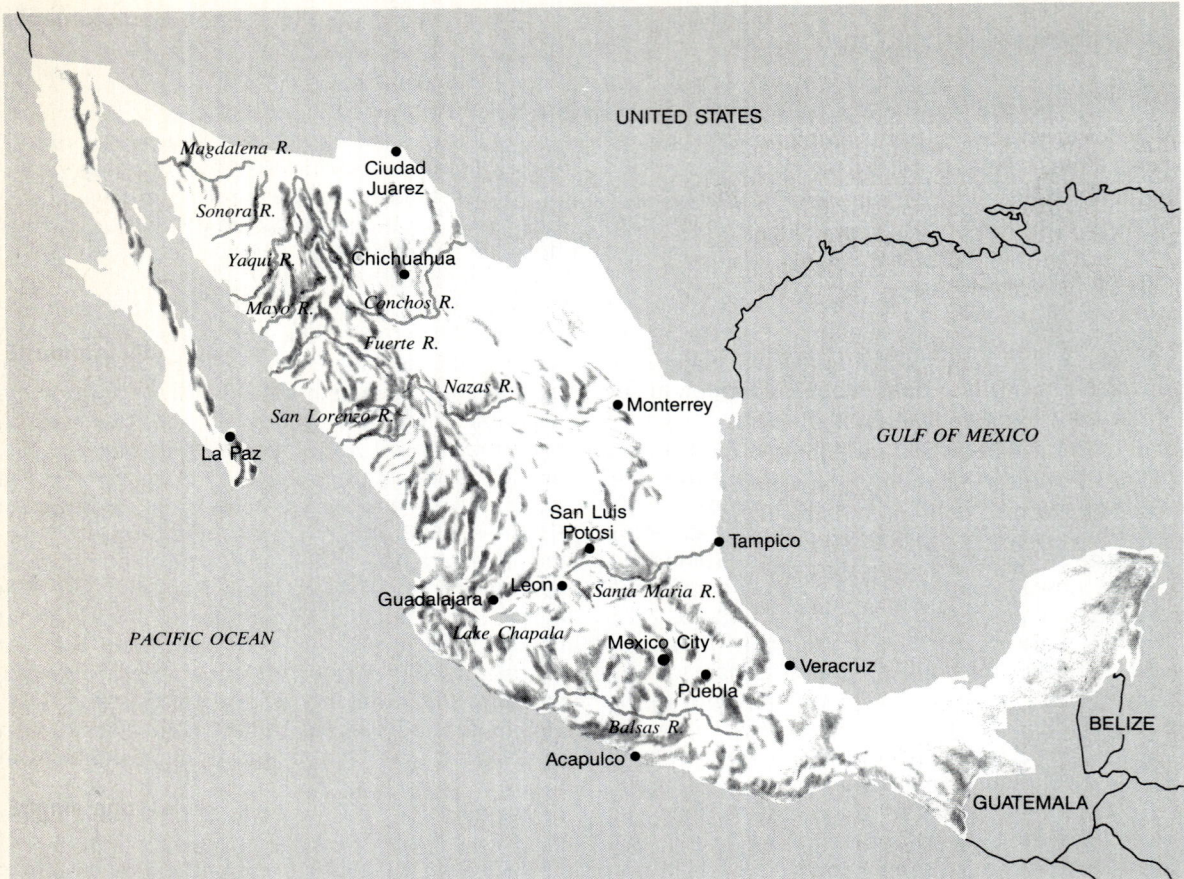

The Land at a Glance—Mexico

(Map showing Mexico with labeled cities and rivers: UNITED STATES, Magdalena R., Sonora R., Yaqui R., Mayo R., San Lorenzo R., La Paz, Ciudad Juarez, Chichuahua, Conchos R., Fuerte R., Nazas R., Monterrey, PACIFIC OCEAN, San Luis Potosi, Tampico, GULF OF MEXICO, Guadalajara, Leon, Santa Maria R., Lake Chapala, Mexico City, Veracruz, Puebla, Balsas R., Acapulco, BELIZE, GUATEMALA)

1929—although the size of the PRI's majorities has declined in recent years. In the controversial 1988 presidential election, for example, the PRI candidate received approximately 55 percent of the vote. For several days after the election, there were rumors that he had actually received less than 50 percent, although the fact that there were two major opposition candidates splitting the opposition vote would have ensured a PRI victory regardless.

The PRI's power has been maintained through a vast patronage system (Eckstein, 1988). Since presidents are elected for a single 6-year term, party favors are especially widespread toward the end of each president's term. The dominance of the PRI suggests that Mexican politics, while genuinely democratic in form, generally reflects the priorities and policies of a powerful national elite.

Poland

Geographic Area Poland is part of the Soviet Bloc in eastern Europe. It is bounded by the Baltic Sea on the north, the Soviet Union (Lithuania,

Belorussia, and the Ukraine) on the east, East Germany on the west, and Czechoslovakia on the south. Two-thirds of the country is lowland, including farmland and one of Europe's last virgin forests. There are also two low mountain ranges, the Sudetes on the west and the Carpathians on the east.

Major Cultural Groups In World War II, Poland was invaded by both Germany and Russia, ending the war under Russian control. The treaties that ended the war changed the prewar boundaries. Much of Poland's eastern half became part of the Soviet Union. In compensation, a considerable amount of land that had been German, primarily parts of East Prussia, Brandenburg, Pomerania, and Silesia, became Polish territory. Poland sustained the heaviest human and economic losses of any country in the war, so that its postwar recovery was very difficult.

Currently the largest minority groups in Poland are Ukrainians and Belorussians who comprise less than 2 percent of the population. There is also a small Gypsy population. Since virtually the entire Jewish population fled or

The Land at a Glance—Poland

was killed during World War II, nearly 95 percent of the current population is Roman Catholic.

Economic Characteristics The Polish government does not publish statistics on the gross national product, but various estimates are available. According to the *1986 World Almanac and Book of Facts,* for example, the 1982 Polish gross national product was approximately $170 billion, resulting in a per capita income of approximately $4,670. A reluctance to divulge economic statistics is common in Communist societies, whose governments consider such information sensitive. It is generally believed that if official economic data were available, they would reveal a worsening economy, something the government is reluctant to publicize. Poland has an economy that is half-agricultural and half-industrial. The main crops are various grains, fruit, and forest products, while shipbuilding, mining, textiles, chemicals, metallurgy, cement, and food are the main industries.

Approximately 77 percent of the workforce is employed by government-run businesses, and less than 1 percent of the workforce is unemployed. (The government guarantees a job to all Polish citizens who want one.) Nevertheless, many workers are unhappy with their working and economic conditions, and worker demonstrations have erupted periodically. The most widely publicized of these during recent years was the 1980 strike at the Lenin Shipyard in Gdansk, which resulted in the formation of the Solidarity Trade Union led by Lech Walesa. Although officially outlawed in 1981, Solidarity was restored as a legal entity by the accords signed in 1989.

Political Characteristics The Polish People's Republic is a socialist state with a Soviet-type constitution that dates from 1952. The Parliament, called the Sejm, is the major legislative institution of government. There is also a smaller body, the Council of State, whose chairman functions as nominal head of state. Government policymaking is dominated, however, by the ruling party, the Polish United Worker's party, a communist party based on the Soviet model and which the constitution singles out as the nation's "guiding political force in the construction of socialism." The leader of the party is appointed prime minister by the Sejm and is the most powerful government leader.

Recent Soviet experiments with *glasnost,* along with Poland's serious economic difficulties, led to changes in the structure of some aspects of government in 1989. The Parliament was changed from a one-house to a two-house body, with 35 percent of the seats in the lower house allocated to the Solidarity-based opposition to the dominant Communist party. The upper house's members were chosen in free and open elections, the first since 1945. A new post of president of the republic, to be elected by the Parliament, was also created. These changes are dramatic departures from the total control previously exercised by the Communist party, although the party still wields majority control (data from Nelson, 1984: 229–235, and Tagliabue, 1989: Al).

ON THE STREET IN WARSAW

Most of Warsaw was destroyed during World War II, so that virtually all existing buildings are either new or rebuilt. The meticulous rebuilding of the Old Town, including the Royal Castle, that today looks much as it did before the war, provides evidence of the Polish people's pride in their history. Charming cafes and shops are set in elegant townhouses, many with beautiful and elaborate paintings on their facades. In good weather, the cobblestone streets are full of people enjoying this historic area. There are, in addition, numerous churches since many Poles are very religious. As one of the only national organizations allowed that is not controlled by the government, the Roman Catholic church plays an important symbolic political role, as well as a religious one.

The business area of the city looks like the downtown of any contemporary city in western Europe. There are many high-rise office buildings, hotels, and apartment buildings, with a good deal of traffic, many bus and streetcar lines, and a commuter rail system. Department stores and shops abound, although the offerings in them are sometimes quite limited and long lines of people waiting to make purchases are not an uncommon sight. Meat, gasoline, and chocolates are rationed, and the cost of many consumer items and rents are government-subsidized. Wages are also government-controlled.

Housing is scarce, and young people seeking their own homes must often wait several years before obtaining one. The chronic housing shortage is a reflection of both the widespread destruction that occurred during the war, and Poland's many economic problems in the postwar years. Private ownership of housing is permitted, but most people can only afford apartments, often in large apartment blocs in the suburbs.

In appearance, the Polish people tend to be sturdily built with generally fair skin, eyes, and hair. Business transactions are often very impersonal and even harsh, but friends and family members exhibit great affection for each other. There is no evidence of homelessness in the downtown business area, but there is evidence of drunkenness, especially at night. Gypsy women and children are sometimes seen begging around the major tourist hotels, and very poorly dressed elderly women sell flowers on the street. Gypsy men are sometimes seen selling their handmade kitchen knives and pots on the sidewalks of busy streets.

Modern Poland has been shaped by its subservient relationship with its dominant neighbor to the east, the Soviet Union. Communism has so far proven not to be as economically successful as had been hoped. There continues to be a chronic shortage of many consumer goods. Poland is a debtor nation, so that much of its income has to be used for debt payments rather than to purchase products that might make daily life more comfortable. Although some private enterprise is permitted, it is limited, and the range of consumer goods and social activities is much more limited than in Sweden or even Mexico. Although people seem to have secure lives with their basic needs met, there is considerable resentment of the Soviet Union and a widespread hope that Poland will one day soon regain its independence. As part of this dream, Poles revere their history and are proud of their independent spirit.

Sweden

Geographic Area Sweden is bordered by Norway and Finland on the north, Finland and the Gulf of Bothnia (part of the Baltic Sea) on the east, and Norway on the west. The country is relatively flat, with numerous lakes and streams, except for a mountain range in the northwest.

Major Cultural Groups Swedes are descendants of the Vikings and other indigenous groups. The population is relatively homogeneous. The two major

NORWEGIAN SEA

Kiruna

Lainioälv R.

Piteälv R.

Skellefteälv R.

Umeälv R.

Ångermanälven R.

Skelleftea

Indalsälven R.

Östersund

NORWAY

GULF
OF
BOTHNIA

FINLAND

Bollnäs

Sandviken ● Gävle

Lake Vänern

Örebo

Stockholm

Skövde

● Göteborg

Lake
Vättern

Visby

Kalmar

● Malmö

U.S.S.R

BALTIC SEA

The Land at a Glance—Sweden

minority groups are those of Finnish descent, and Lapps—a Mongolian people who inhabit a region in northern Sweden called Lapland. Sweden also has small groups of people from Chile and Vietnam who entered the country as political refugees, as well as Turks who immigrated in search of work. The Evangelical-Lutheran Church is the official state church, and all Swedes are automatically considered members unless they declare otherwise.

Economic Characteristics   Major industries in Sweden include metals and mining, transport equipment, and wood products. Industrial production makes up about 31 percent of the economy, and it is shared between private and government-controlled firms. Agriculture, forestry, and fishing comprise but 3 percent of the economy, with grains, livestock, and green crops of special importance. The remaining 66 percent of the economy is given over to the service sector. Unemployment is less than 2 percent.

Political Characteristics   Sweden is a constitutional monarchy with a parliamentary form of government. The current king, who exerts no political power and takes no part in politics, is Carl XVI Gustav. As in any parliamentary system, government policymaking is largely carried out by a cabinet

---

ON THE STREET IN GOTHENBURG

Gothenburg is Sweden's second-largest city after the capital, Stockholm. It is a major port city and is also the site of a good deal of industry. On the street in Gothenburg, an American feels right at home. At first glance, it seems very similar to a midsized American city, complete with a large indoor shopping mall at the edge of the downtown area.

Gradually, though, differences emerge. Like most of Sweden, the streets are generally clean and the buildings well-kept. Although there is a good deal of new construction, the older buildings are in excellent condition and continue in use. While there is a lot of activity in the downtown area, it is relatively quiet and calm. Park areas are plentiful and well cared for. Housing tends toward small apartment buildings rather than private homes, and public transportation—in the form of buses and street cars—is modern, plentiful, and clean.

Many Swedes, unlike the American stereotype, are dark-haired rather than blonde. However, they tend to be tall and robust, healthy in appearance, and generally well-dressed in contemporary styles. Some of the young people sport the latest international hairstyles, clothing, and jewelry. There is a sense of living in a calm, clean, orderly, and well-managed environment with little street begging and no evidence of homelessness.

Walking along the street in Gothenburg, one is impressed with the abundance in the stores. Products of all kinds are available, ranging from the most practical and basic to the most luxurious and stylish. Restaurants, too, are numerous, including small cafes, specialty restaurants, and popular eating places from fast-food chains to coffee shops. Even the port area seems clean and orderly. Gothenburg gives the impression of being part of a highly productive and affluent society.

headed by a prime minister. The leader of the party winning a majority of seats in the popularly elected Parliament becomes the prime minister. Once chosen, the prime minister selects the remaining cabinet members—invariably from among the ranks of his Parliamentary party colleagues. The Parliament is currently dominated by the Social Democratic Labor party, as it has been for most of the past 55 years, save for a 6-year interval from 1976 to 1982. However, there are several major political parties that compete vigorously during elections. The Social Democrats generally adopt moderate positions, and its members have been very supportive of social welfare legislation. Provincial and administrative levels of government are important in Sweden, and elections at these levels are also democratic (all data from Mayne, 1986:182–192, and The Swedish Institute, 1986:1).

The United States of America

Geographic Area   The United States is by far the largest of the four countries discussed in this book. With a surface area of just over 3,600,000 square miles, it is over thirty times larger in size than Poland, twenty times larger than Sweden, and nearly five times larger than Mexico. Its topography is varied, embracing all major climatic and geographic types including tropical rain forests in Hawaii and Puerto Rico, southwestern deserts, Alaskan glaciers, western mountain peaks, and lush midwestern farmlands. The mainland is bordered by Canada on the north, Mexico and the Gulf of Mexico on the south, the Atlantic Ocean on the east, and the Pacific Ocean on the west.

Major Cultural Groups   The U.S. population of approximately 240 million is also by far the largest of our four countries. Although Mexico City may be the world's largest city, the total U.S. population is over three times that of Mexico, six and one-half times that of Poland, and nearly thirty times that of Sweden. Indeed, the New York metropolitan area contains more than twice as many people as live in all of Sweden.

The U.S. population is also quite heterogeneous. Government figures indicate that Blacks, American Indians (including Eskimos and Aleuts), Chinese, Filipino, Japanese, Asian Indian, Korean, Vietnamese, and other minority groups comprise approximately 17 percent of the population. The remainder of the population has European roots, especially English, Irish, German, Italian, and Scandinavian. Close to 15 million people are of Hispanic origin, coming primarily from Central and South America, the Caribbean, and Spain. Among the 140 million people reporting church membership in 1983, the three largest groups were Protestants (77 million), Roman Catholics (52 million), and Jews (close to 6 million).

Economic Characteristics   Although suffering from a variety of ailments, the U.S. economy is the world's largest. Its gross national product is in excess of 3 trillion dollars, and the per capita income of over $14,000 is the highest of any of the four nations considered here and one of the highest in the world. The United States has a mixed economy with agriculture, manufacturing, and

CANADA

MAINE
Augusta

NEW HAMPSHIRE
Concord

VERMONT
Montpelier

MASSACHUSETTS
Boston

RHODE ISLAND
Providence

CONNECTICUT
Hartford

NEW JERSEY
Trenton

DELAWARE
Dover

MARYLAND
Annapolis

VIRGINIA
Richmond

NEW YORK
Albany

St. Lawrence R.

Lake Ontario

Lake Erie

Lake Huron

Lake Superior

Lake Michigan

PENNSYLVANIA
Harrisburg

WEST VIRGINIA
Charleston

OHIO
Columbus

INDIANA
Indianapolis

KENTUCKY
Frankfort

Ohio R.

TENNESSEE
Nashville

NORTH CAROLINA
Raleigh

SOUTH CAROLINA
Columbia

ATLANTIC OCEAN

Lake Okeechobee

FLORIDA
Tallahassee

GEORGIA
Atlanta

ALABAMA
Montgomery

MISSISSIPPI
Jackson

MICHIGAN
Lansing

ILLINOIS
Springfield

WISCONSIN
Madison

IOWA
Des Moines

MINNESOTA
St. Paul

Mississippi R.

MISSOURI
Kansas City

ARKANSAS
Little Rock

LOUISIANA
Baton Rouge

GULF OF MEXICO

NORTH DAKOTA
Bismarck

SOUTH DAKOTA
Pierre

NEBRASKA
Omaha

Missouri R.

KANSAS
Topeka

OKLAHOMA
Oklahoma City

TEXAS
Austin

MEXICO

MONTANA
Helena

WYOMING
Cheyenne

COLORADO
Denver

NEW MEXICO
Santa Fe

Rio Grande R.

IDAHO
Boise

Columbia R.

UTAH
Salt Lake City

Great Salt Lake

ARIZONA
Phoenix

WASHINGTON
Olympia

OREGON
Salem

NEVADA
Carson City

CALIFORNIA
Sacramento

PACIFIC OCEAN

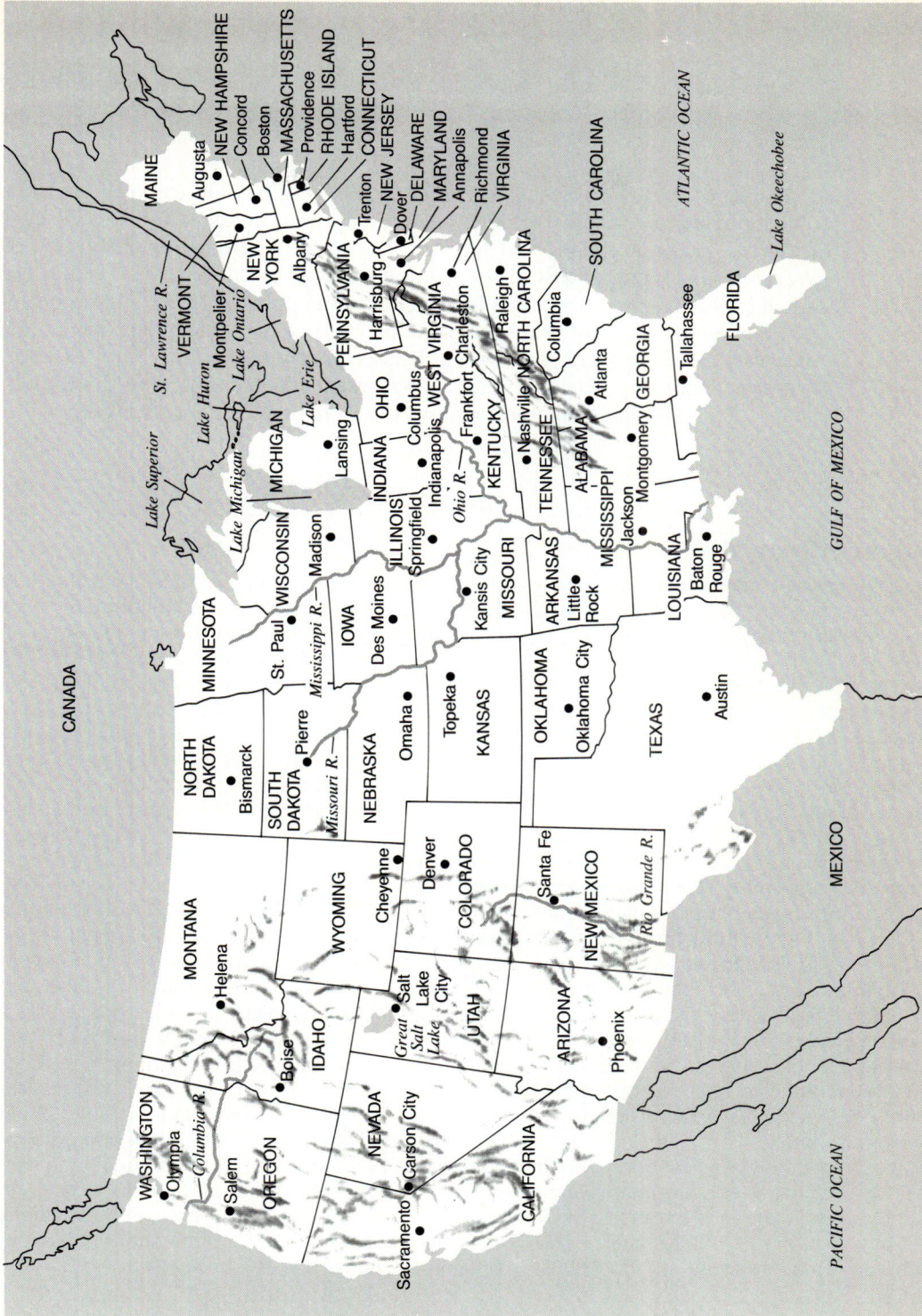

The Land at a Glance—The United States

service industries being of particular importance. The unemployment rate in 1984 was 7.5 percent. (All data are from the U.S. Department of Commerce, Bureau of the Census, 1986:30,50,390.)

Political Characteristics The United States is often said to be the world's oldest democracy, having recently celebrated the bicentennial of its 1787 constitution. It has a presidential form of government with a popularly elected President and Congress. It also has a federalist political system in which political power is shared by three levels of government—national, state, and local. The most important of the subnational levels of government are the states, of which there are fifty, each with a democratically elected governor and legislature. There are two major political parties, the Democratic and the Republican, which dominate electoral politics at the national and state levels.

ON THE STREET IN CINCINNATI, OHIO

Like many large American cities, downtown Cincinnati has experienced an economic rebirth. Sleek new high-rise office buildings and hotels have replaced decayed buildings, and many of the older buildings that remain have been restored or refurbished. A central square is surrounded by places to eat and to shop and by stores selling a wide variety of consumer goods. During the day, the downtown is congested with cars, buses, and pedestrians, but it becomes rather quiet after working hours.

During working hours, people on the street tend to wear business clothes and to be a mixture of black and white. In the evening, more adolescents are visible, as are more black people. This reflects residential patterns in the city. Downtown is ringed by an old residential area with decayed housing that is now inhabited by poor people, many of whom are black. The more affluent residents, most of whom are white, live in areas further from downtown. They can most easily enjoy the beautiful parks for which Cincinnati is famous, set among the scenic bluffs along the Ohio River that separates the city from Kentucky.

Cincinnati was settled by Germans, and their cultural influence is still evident. German restaurants continue to be popular, as is a massive brick architecture that epitomizes what successful German businesspeople preferred in the 1800s.

The city's German cultural roots are also evident in its love of music and the arts. Cincinnati has a world-class symphony orchestra, a fine art museum, and a professional ballet company. The fine old symphony hall testifies to the changes that have occurred in the city. Once located in a prosperous residential area adjacent to downtown, it now brings white residents of suburbia into an area of rundown housing inhabited by the poor.

The downtown area and the poverty-ridden residential area that surrounds it are home to beggars and homeless people. They are black and white, men and women, with some touched by alcoholism, drug use, or mental illness. Favorite haunts are the downtown central square, the bus terminal, and doorways. These residents of the city are not as numerous as in some other American cities, but they are easily noticed even so. Cincinnati seems a microcosm of the current scene in the United States. Economic vitality is evident in new construction, busy shops, and abundant traffic. But the limits of prosperity are also in view. Slum neighborhoods are riddled with crime and deteriorated housing. People damaged by social and personal problems and in need of help too seldom receive it. And the ongoing exclusion of many minority group members from the economic mainstream continues to take a heavy toll.

LET'S REVIEW

The purpose of this introduction has been to welcome you and offer you a sense of what you may learn from reading this book. You have seen that many dimensions of social welfare will be explored as you proceed through the book. These include the meaning of social welfare, the functions it serves, the way it is structured, the services it includes, and its relationships with other parts of society such as the family, the economy, and the political system.

This book's primary purpose is to help you understand the social welfare system in the United States. The approach taken is a cross-cultural one designed to help you better understand our welfare system. It does so in several ways by (1) highlighting the choices that shape social welfare; (2) linking those choices with specific decision-making structures; (3) expanding our thinking about social welfare by examining the experiences of other societies; and (4) illustrating how in any society social welfare develops in response to the knowledge, values, beliefs, and behaviors that characterize that society. Mexico, a developing nation, Poland, a socialist society, and Sweden, an advanced welfare state, will be used for comparative purposes. Basic information about the United States and these other three societies has been provided in this chapter to provide you with a background for better understanding the comparisons that are made later on in the book.

We are now ready to consider the first of our ten questions: What is social welfare? From time to time, you may find it useful to refer back to the material in this introduction. Reviewing the book's objectives and its structure can help you to focus your study efforts. Refreshing your memory about particular characteristics of the four societies covered in the book may also be useful when examining the effects of the social context on social welfare decision-making. For now, though, let's move ahead.

STUDY QUESTIONS

1 On a blank sheet of paper, write a paragraph describing your understanding of the goals of this book. Try to be as specific as you can. Then write a second paragraph discussing how these goals apply to you—why are you reading the book and what do you hope to get out of it? Insert this paper in your notebook, and reread these paragraphs every now and then as you proceed through the book. When you do, feel free to expand on them in light of your later impressions.

2 Take another blank sheet of paper. Select one of the four societies considered in this book, and write a brief description of your impressions of everyday life in that society. Then compare those impressions with information obtained from one or more reference sources to see which, if any, of those impressions seem to be incorrect.

3 Locate three articles in your local newspaper that are concerned with social welfare issues (for now, use your own sense of what social welfare is). Read each article carefully and identify the key choices made by each of the major participants. Consider, for example, decisions about whether people qualified for help, the kinds of services to be provided, budgetary decisions, the guilt or innocence of people accused of crimes, and so on. Then indicate your opinion as to the effect each of these

choices had on the outcome of the case involved and whether alternative outcomes might have been possible.

4 Take a few minutes to think about yourself and this book. Is the book organized so that it will be helpful to you? Which chapter tools do you particularly want to use? Do you have any learning needs that the book seems to overlook? If so, what can you do to obtain the resources that you need (perhaps with the assistance of your instructor or a classmate)?

REFERENCES

Eckstein, Susan. 1988. *The Poverty of Revolution,* rev. ed. Princeton, N.J.: Princeton University Press.

Mayne, Richard, ed. 1986. *Western Europe.* New York: Facts on File Publications.

Nelson, Harold D., ed. 1984. *Poland: A Country Study.* Washington, D.C.: U. S. Government Printing Office.

Rudolph, James D., ed. 1985. *Mexico: A Country Study.* Washington, D.C.: U. S. Government Printing Office.

Schopflin, George, ed. 1986. *The Soviet Union and Eastern Europe.* New York: Facts on File Publications.

Swedish Institute. 1986. *Fact Sheets on Sweden.* Stockholm: The Swedish Institute

Tagliabue, John. 1989. Poland sets free vote in June, first since '45; Solidarity reinstated. *New York Times,* April 6, pp. Alff.

U.S. Department of Commerce. Bureau of the Census. 1986. *Statistical Abstract of the United States 1986,* 106th ed. Washington, D.C.: U. S. Government Printing Office.

Ward, Peter. 1986. *Welfare Politics in Mexico.* London: Allen & Unwin, Ltd.

The World Bank. 1986. *The World Bank Atlas 1986.* Washington, D.C.: The World Bank.

CHAPTER 1

WHAT IS SOCIAL WELFARE?

WHAT TO EXPECT FROM THIS CHAPTER

Social welfare is concerned with helping people to live more satisfying lives. At first glance, this seems a readily understandable goal—we all believe we know what people need to live decently. In practice, however, there is often considerable disagreement over such questions as what constitutes a satisfying life, whether everyone is entitled to one, and who is responsible for making sure that people are satisfied.

An understanding of social welfare, then, must begin with the decisions made by people and societies as to what constitutes a desirable life and who will have access to the resources needed to live in socially desirable ways. The main focus of this chapter will be on how these decisions are made. It will begin with a general definition of social welfare and then explore four issues that influence the development of a society's social welfare objectives. They are:

1 *Responsibility.* Who is responsible for which social welfare efforts?

2 *Resources.* What resources are available for social welfare purposes?

3 *Services.* What social welfare services are provided, to what people, and in what way?

4 *Organization.* Why are social welfare services organized the way they are?

This chapter discusses each of these issues in some detail. We will see that a society's definition of responsibility is derived from its underlying values, which may be quite different in an industrialized than in an industrializing society. Decisions about the allocation of resources are closely tied to the society's economic condition, and to the priorities it has established for allocating resources. Decisions about services involve choices concerning the type of services provided, the people for whom these are intended, and factors that influence who is likely to use them. Finally, the way in which services are organized is influenced by a society's decision-making structures and processes.

This chapter will give you a sense of the whole of social welfare. You will see that it entails values (the willingness to meet people's needs), resources (making needed resources available), services (programs to make resources available to those who need them), and organization (the structures through which services are provided). Later chapters will explore each of these four areas in more detail, and will examine their links to other social structures such as the family and the political and economic systems. For now, though, we will focus on understanding the general purpose of social welfare, and the four issues listed above.

LEARNING OBJECTIVES

At the end of this chapter, you should be able to do the following:

1 Define social welfare accurately using your own words.

2 List the four issues that influence the development of each society's particular social welfare system.

3 Describe the role that values play in determining people's views of social welfare.

4 Discuss how decisions are made about who deserves to be helped, who ought to provide help, and what kinds of help should be provided.

5 Describe why the resources available in a society have an impact on social welfare.

6 List the needs that social welfare services usually try to meet.

7 Describe three factors that influence who has access to social welfare services.

8 List at least three levels of social welfare decision-making.
9 Discuss factors that influence the decision-making process in social welfare.

SOCIAL WELFARE AND HELPING

Fundamental to the idea of social welfare is the concept of helping. Robert Morris (1986:17) explains that social welfare is "...the sum of those efforts by governments and other organizations to relieve the poverty or distress of a people who are more or less helpless, that is, unable to meet their basic needs by their own labor or by their families." Naturally there is considerable variation among societies in the definition of who is helpless and what are basic needs. As a result, there are differences in the kind of help offered, the circumstances under which it is provided, and to whom and by whom it is provided. For example, in Poland, where work is believed to be a basic need and right, the government guarantees a job to all able-bodied citizens. Work is also highly valued in the United States, but our government does not assume a similar responsibility for providing a job for everyone who wishes to work.

You will see as you learn more about social welfare that there is a range of opinion about the nature and goals of social welfare. I take the position that *the goal of social welfare is to help people function effectively in their social environment. This means not only providing for people's basic survival needs (adequate nutritious food, clothing, shelter, medical care, clean air and water) but meeting all those needs necessary for them to be psychologically well and socially productive.* In addition to basic needs, this view of social welfare encompasses an education adequate for successful participation in the economic system, counseling to understand and address personal crises when they occur, and access to employment and other social activities.

Underlying this approach to social welfare is the notion of social cost. When people's needs are not met, they do not function well and social costs are incurred. Examples of these costs are those associated with the building and maintenance of prisons and mental health facilities, a poorly educated work force, babies born with birth defects as the result of inadequate prenatal care, and drug addiction.

Social welfare helping efforts must, however, focus not only on the individuals who are experiencing difficulty but also on the social conditions that contribute to the creation of these difficulties. It is appropriate, for example, to offer financial assistance or job retraining to the unemployed worker. However, if the worker's unemployment is the result of nationwide economic problems, unsuccessful business practices of individual firms, or changes in the way work is done—replacing assembly-line workers with automated tools, for example—broader action will also be appropriate.

By focusing simultaneously on individuals and their social environment, we can more clearly see the importance of the relationship between the two, and a need to incorporate it in our definition of social welfare. As a result, **social**

welfare *is defined as a society's governmental and nongovernmental efforts to help its members function more effectively as individuals and as participants in organized social structures.* This definition includes the informal and spontaneous things people do to help each other as well as organized efforts to help others. The most important point is that helping activities are an expected, approved, and organized part of society.

Like the family and other social institutions, social welfare has a distinct function to perform and structures that enable it to do so. *Social welfare is a social institution because it is socially approved and performs the social function of helping individual people as well as society itself to function more effectively. This occurs by distributing responsibility for helping, allocating resources for the purpose of helping, and organizing the activities of people who participate in helping efforts.* In other words, social welfare is a desired, planned, and organized part of social life. It is not something that arises by chance or solely from the charitable impulses of individuals.

Let's take a moment to explore the concept of **social welfare as a social institution** in a little more detail. *A **social institution** is a socially approved system of values, norms, and roles that exists to accomplish specific societal goals.* The major social institutions of any society are the family, education, religion, the political and economic systems, and social welfare. The family, for example, is the institution through which society provides for biological reproduction, the care and raising of children, and satisfying, intimate, relationships among adults. The family helps to accomplish these goals by organizing relationships among husbands and wives, parents and children, and other biologically related individuals.

What are the characteristics of a social institution and in what way does social welfare exhibit these characteristics?

First, social institutions are socially approved, meaning that society defines *what* they should do and *how* they should perform their functions. For example, social welfare's task is to help people function more effectively so that they become productive members of society and, as has also been noted and about which more will be said later, so that social unrest is minimized. The way in which this task is carried out in any given society, however, is determined by certain guidelines. These guidelines in turn arise from the society's values, values concerning how people should be treated, who deserves to be helped, and how resources should be used. In our society, for example, doctors may not refuse emergency treatment to someone who is ill or hurt. On the other hand, hospital care in the United States is readily available only to those who can prove they have proper insurance coverage or sufficient financial resources, because health care in our capitalistic society is primarily provided through the private sector.

A social institution needs people to perform its tasks. In the case of social welfare, these people include social workers, doctors, family members, friends, lawyers, the police, psychiatrists, marriage counselors, and many others who carry on the day-to-day tasks of helping. These individuals function within a larger social structure. For example, doctors and nurses are likely to work in hospitals, teachers in schools, and social workers in a range of community social welfare agencies. Family members are, of course, part of a social structure—the family—and friends are part of friendship groups in the workplace and in the community. Each of these structures has resources that are used by its members in the course of their helping activities.

What emerges, then, is a progression from social function to specific tasks. Social values guide the activities of social welfare practitioners and determine the societal resources allocated to social welfare. The resulting help is provided through social structures with which the helping people are associated, either because of membership (like the family) or through employment (such as a psychologist who works in a community health center). The characteristics common to social institutions and social welfare are summarized in Table 1.1.

Social welfare, then, is an instrument that society uses to achieve its larger goals. Much of the time this process occurs in planned and observable ways, as **manifest functions of social welfare.** Sweden's national labor policy, for example, is designed both to promote economic development and at the same time to meet the needs of individual workers by reducing unemployment (Forsberg, 1986:32–33). The visible and intended purpose of this policy is to create programs that help people get and keep decent jobs. It is believed that this will strengthen the national economy by creating a supply of well-trained, productive, and well-paid workers.

There may also be **latent functions of social welfare.** These are the less visible and, sometimes, unintended effects of social welfare programs that often benefit powerful groups in society rather than the needy. In many cases, most

TABLE 1.1 SOCIAL WELFARE AS A SOCIAL INSTITUTION

Characteristics of social institutions	Application to social welfare
1 Performs major social functions	Helps people function more effectively and promotes social stability
2 Approved by society	Yes, through legislation and the informal enforcement of helping values
3 Allocates societal resources	Allocates resources to support specific social welfare programs, as well as the informal sharing of resources
4 Organizes individual behavior	Examples: Social workers do case histories; patients cooperate with their physicians; teachers don't hit their students, and so on
5 Organizes social roles and resources	Examples: Social agencies supervise the work of their staff; professional associations enforce ethical standards; state legislatures pass laws that create and fund programs, and so on

citizens are not even aware of these effects. For example, the manifest function of unemployment insurance in the United States is to provide income for those who lose their jobs until they can find another. However, both to reduce the program's cost and to encourage workers to find a job as soon as possible, the level of benefits provided is low and the period of eligibility limited to a certain number of weeks. These limits work to the benefit of low-wage employers who are able to hire some workers simply because these workers lack sufficient time in which to find a better-paying job before their unemployment insurance benefits end. Thus, the program has both a manifest function, providing income for the unemployed, as well as a latent function, pushing workers into low-paid jobs. The unintended beneficiaries of the program are low-wage employers, some of whom may be quite wealthy and deliberately exploiting their workers.

The manifest and latent functions of social welfare can lead to controversy. Social welfare is intended by society to help those with problems, but its programs sometimes have unintended consequences. Some groups feel that programs that provide financial assistance for the poor have the latent function of promoting laziness and irresponsibility by making it unnecessary for them to work. Others assert that benefit levels for the poor are so inadequate that their latent function is to maintain a helpless underclass. Obviously these different perspectives are linked to different underlying beliefs and values.

Throughout this book you will have the opportunity to consider the manifest and latent functions of social welfare. For now, keep in mind that there are many dimensions to social welfare, and many ways to relate it to society as a whole. We will focus in this book on the formal structure of social welfare and its manifest functions. The latent functions are addressed from time to time, and understanding them is important. However, your own analytical and critical skills will gradually develop as you grapple with the definition and meaning of social welfare and its functions.

RESPONSIBILITY AS A BASIS FOR SOCIAL WELFARE

People help those for whom they feel some sense of responsibility because of their values. **Values** *are preferred ways of believing that prescribe appropriate behaviors called* **ethical behavior** (Suppes and Wells, 33–34). Values exist at many levels. Societies, religions, communities, families, and individuals all have values, and all of these values guide the behavior of those who accept them. Values vary among groups. This is called *value relativity*. **Relative values** *represent alternative ways of deciding what should be done based on a group's cultural traditions and the life experiences of its members*. Whether blue eyes are considered prettier than brown, whether children should be seen and not heard, and whether a gay or lesbian lifestyle is acceptable, are examples of values that may differ among groups and which can sometimes give rise to intergroup conflict.

THE HUMAN FACE OF SOCIAL WELFARE 2

Life in a Shelter for the Homeless (The Brand Family)

The homeless used to be mostly single men and women—many of them alcoholics, drug addicts or former mental patients. Now the National Coalition for the Homeless reports that families have become the fastest-growing group of people without permanent homes. A recent 25-city survey by the U.S. Conference of Mayors found that families accounted for 28 percent of the urban homeless; among the cities polled, there was an average increase in 1986 of 22 percent in the number of families seeking emergency shelter. In many parts of the country a shortage of low-income housing and cutbacks in social programs have made a bad situation worse.

The effects of living on the streets, or in temporary housing, can be devastating. In a recent Massachusetts study, Dr. Ellen Bassuk, a Harvard Medical School psychiatrist, found that 47 percent of homeless preschoolers were slow in language, physical or emotional development; at least half needed further psychiatric evaluation. "The road back is very, very hard," Bassuk says. "We're beginning to raise a generation of kids in the streets. That has dire consequences for the future." Behind the statistics are stories of families who have tried and failed—for the moment—to make an independent life for themselves. NEWSWEEK correspondent Patricia King reports on one family in Kansas City, Mo.:

It is 2 A.M. Quiet has finally settled on the Salvation Army Emergency Lodge. Three red exit lights glow in the dark. The day-time cacophony of running, screaming children has dwindled to one sick baby's cry. For 11 families, this place is a refuge of last resort. Their new "homes," small impersonal cubicles, ring the first floor of the four-story brick building. In the center of all this stands a glass-enclosed office. It has three security monitors and a refrigerator stocked with baby formula for early-morning feedings. Here the night staffer plays host to residents of the shelter who cannot sleep. Jim Brand, 37, is one of the wee-hour regulars. Brand's nervous wakefulness does not hide his fatigue. His usual blustery manner gives way to a moment of uncommon introspection: "To come here is one step ahead of blowing your damn head off," he says. "You don't want to admit you're a failure. You don't want anybody else to see how bad off you are.... We fought this for a long time."

For Brand, his wife, Peggy, 38, and their four children, age 5 to 11, the fight ended last fall; they were evicted for the second time in eight months. The Brands were both out of work and there were bills to pay. The emergency shelter was their only option. They loaded all their possessions into a storage locker and huddled together in the apartment where they were no longer wanted while they waited six days for an opening at the shelter. When the electricity was shut off, the children did their homework by candlelight. When the gas went off, a few blankets that doubled as makeshift beds were their only barrier against the bone-chilling autumn dampness. "If it was only me, I'd sleep in the car. I'm a survivor," says Brand, who was wounded three times in Vietnam. "But I wanted something better for my family."

A REAL HOME

Only a year earlier, the family did have something better. True, it was only a $296-a-month apartment in a low-income housing project in Shawnee, just across the Kansas border, but it felt like a real home. There were three bedrooms and a kitchen big enough for the kids to play in. There were lots of toys, a tabletop organ and even an encyclopedia set in the living room. Peggy Brand usually got home early from her part-time job as a Head Start teacher's aide so she could be with the kids after school. Jim's maintenance work around the apartment complex knocked $95 off the rent. In addition, there were food stamps and Jim's $267-a-month veteran's disability check for Vietnam injuries that include a hearing loss in one ear and nightmares that won't go away. No one could have mistaken them for rich people; but, says Jim, "we were making it."

At least they were making it as well as could be expected for a family headed by a man who hadn't had a steady job for a long time. Jim used to make as much as $14.75 an hour doing seasonal construction work. "And now it's come to this," he says. Six years ago he was a foreman at a factory that made rollers for printing presses. Then he hurt his back while carrying some heavy equipment. After surgery to shave one disc and remove three others, he returned to work. More bad luck; the company was sold. Although the new owners said there would be no changes, they soon started bringing in their own people from Chicago and Nashville. Jim knew he was in trouble when his bosses told him they wanted to cut him back to part time. Since then, Jim has learned, finding a job can be almost impossible for a guy who has had back surgery. He says his doctor thinks there are two more deteriorating discs above and below the ones that were removed; he takes pill after pill to mask the pain. But when Jim works too long or sits too long, the pain still stabs at him.

SERIES OF SNAFUS

Despite his injury, Jim had thought he could hold his family together in Shawnee doing odd jobs. But then things began to go wrong. Through a series of apparent misunderstandings, the Brands believe, they lost their apartment. Says eight-year-old Shauna: "I think what happened is that we paid the rent, but they didn't know it." That's why, she explains, the family left Shawnee even though it was "much funner" and the children could collect caterpillars that turned into butterflies. When the building's management changed, the Brands' rent went up and they got behind in their payments. Although they eventually scrounged up the money and were even able to pay some of the next month's rent in advance, they nonetheless got a notice in the mail to appear in court. When they called the landlord, they say, they were told that everything had been taken care of and that they didn't have to show up. Next thing they knew, the sheriff was knocking on their door with a deadline to get out. They had lost by default because they hadn't come to court. "It was three days to get out of Tucson," says Jim, falling back on the language of the Western novels he loves.

The eviction order forced the Brands into a three-month odyssey that was too depressing to be anything like the adventure stories Jim likes to read. Relatives tried to help, but they didn't have much money. First, the Brands stayed with Jim's brother in his 14-foot-by-80-foot mobile home in nearby Edwardsville, Kans. But it was impossible to cram nine people into a space that normally held three. The Brands left, Jim says, because "I wanted to keep my brother as my friend." Then they stayed with Jim's parents, where there was plenty of room. But the house was about to be sold. Jim's parents were moving because his father had emphysema and wanted to live in the South during the winter. Just as the last of Jim's parents' possessions were being auctioned off, Peggy and Jim found a two-bedroom, $295-a-month apartment in DeSoto, Kans. It was so tiny for six people that Jim dubbed it the "crackerbox."

Still, they had a roof over their heads. Peggy quit her part-time Head Start job and found higher-paying, full-time work in a factory. With that financial boost, the Brands seemed to be getting back on their feet. Then one day as Peggy got ready to go to work, the family's decaying 1968 Buick Electra refused to start. The nearest telephone was a mile away; when Peggy got to the phone, she couldn't get through to her boss at the temporary-employment agency that had placed her in the factory. She was fired. Once again the cycle of eviction began. This time the Brands lost even the crackerbox. The shelter was the end of the line.

It has not been an easy adjustment. When the shelter is packed, more than 60 people of all ages can jam the building. Each family is supposed to keep a constant eye on its own children. But Jim complains that some of the other parents "let the kids run wild." The families must share the combination television room and playroom near the office with a transient group of single men, who sleep downstairs, and with the single women, who sleep in a room on the first floor. It is not always the best place for children. When everyone does assigned chores, the rooms are clean. But there's always someone who doesn't do his share. Peggy, a meticulous housekeeper, gets annoyed when she has to clean up someone else's mess. The worst place, she says, is the women's shower and bathtub. Not only is there often a line to get in, but the drain has been clogged since the Brands arrived. There's no shower curtain; privacy is just a memory.

CLASSMATES' TAUNTS

Still, the family tries to keep up appearances. Every morning 10-year-old Jaime and her two sisters wait just inside the entrance for the school buses to stop at the shelter's front door. "I loved Shawnee," the gangly fifth grader says with a sigh. She is bored in the new school in Kansas City. "They just started division a few days ago," she says, wrinkling her nose. Despite her girlish bangs and giggles, Jaime plays the role of the wise elder, explaining to her younger sisters the ways of their new world. Rule number one: you can't let it bother you when the kids make fun of you and call you "Salvation Army Girl." Rule number two: you can't go visiting friends after school. The shelter is in a tough neighborhood, and it's dangerous to walk home after dark. "This is not like Shawnee," Jaime explains sternly.

Sometimes, Peggy says, she thinks that she must have done something very bad, and God is punishing her. How else can she explain her family's fate? Jim isn't the type to agonize about the reasons why his family has fallen on hard times. But he's determined to pass the work ethic on to his kids. "I've taught my kids work is a privilege," Jim says. He looks down on the "shirkers" at the shelter who don't do their chores. "They're professionals riding the system" he says. The Brands do more than the assigned tasks. "I don't believe in a free lunch," says Jim. Jim has become the resident handyman and nightly driver for the mobile kitchen that brings food to Kansas City's poor. He says that pouring steaming coffee for the street people, some of whom sleep in cardboard boxes under the Missouri River bridges, has made him realize that "there are people worse off than me."

That knowledge is small comfort to the Brands' oldest child, 11-year-old Dusty. The boy hates the shelter and its restrictions—especially the 8:30 P.M. curfew for children. "Baby hours," he calls it. Even on Friday night he is not supposed to be out of the Brands' 14-foot-by-16-foot shelter room after the curfew. There are worse indignities as well. Once Dusty borrowed a bike from one of the other kids at the shelter; on the way back, he was mugged and the bike was stolen. Jim worries that Dusty is "getting hardened" by such experiences. The boy is also going stir crazy in his shelter cubicle; even Jim says the room is too small to change your mind in. Dusty has always wanted a brother to hang out with; now he is cooped up in a shoe box with his parents and his three little sisters. It's even worse at night when the girls' cots are set up. The space is jammed full with three single beds and toys given to the kids by the doting Salvation Army staff. They also have their old television set, brought from the storage locker as an enticement to keep the kids in the room and out of trouble. Dusty has been helping his father fix cars for years; he wants to be a mechanic when he grows up. The only time he is happy is when he is outside working, helping with cars or loading Salvation Army trailers. Inside, he says, he can't shake his resentment; "I'm sick of living in this place."

The plight of the Brand family is a vivid illustration of the interaction of individual needs and the smooth functioning of society. The Brands are struggling for physical survival, psychological well-being, and a toe-hold in the larger society—the workplace and school for example. Their success or failure will have an impact on society. Their children will grow up to be either productive citizens or emotionally scarred and dependent adults. Their parents may stick it out together or separate. If the Brands make it, they will contribute to society. If they sink under the weight of their problems, society will continue to bear the costs of supporting them. This is the challenge of social welfare: how can we strengthen families like the Brands by providing services they need and by making the environment in which they live more supportive of their needs?

From A family down and out, *Newsweek,* January 12, 1987, pp. 44–46. (c) 1987, Newsweek, Inc. All rights reserved. Reprinted by permission.

A value consensus is more easily obtained in some societies than in others. The small size and cultural and religious homogeneity of the Swedish people make it relatively easy for Sweden to find common values. The strength of the Mexican social class system and the dominance of the political system by certain classes make it possible to impose certain values via the political and economic systems. In Poland, the values derived from a powerful political ideology are reflected in and imposed by the major social institutions, almost all of which are controlled by the government.

In the United States, by contrast, it is often difficult either to arrive at or impose a value consensus. The heterogeneous nature of the U.S. population means that there are many different cultural groups, each with its own values. In addition, the U.S. tradition of allowing freedom of thought makes it difficult for religious or political structures to impose any single set of values on the larger society. Instead, a working consensus on values sufficient to guide daily life is negotiated in the political arena, in community interaction, and through personal communication. The nation's cultural history and traditions provide guidelines within which negotiations take place. The process, however, is necessarily slow, complex, and virtually continuous.

A sense of responsibility for others is a value. All the societies discussed in this book accept some responsibility for their citizens. They vary, however, in the *degree* of responsibility they accept. In order to understand a particular society's social welfare system, we need first to comprehend the nature of its values, but this is quite different from imposing our own values about what a society *ought* to value and do. So, while we can safely say that social welfare can only exist where social values include a sense of responsibility toward others, the groups for whom responsibility is felt may vary greatly.

Societal values about social responsibility are interpreted and modified by organizations, groups, and individuals. Corporations may choose to provide social welfare services that are much more extensive than those required by law, or even by prevailing beliefs about corporate responsibility. Others may seek to evade prevailing legal and moral standards. Family members often make great sacrifices for each other, yet there are some families that are terribly abusive. Each of us also interprets values. We choose whether to help others in need, and how responsible we will be in carrying out commitments. It is clear, for example, that societal values support the equal treatment of members of minority groups, but most of us know people who do not agree. We can see, then, that societal values make a social welfare system possible, but its functioning will be affected by the interpretation and implementation of these values by organizations, groups, and individuals.

The nature of a particular society's values regarding responsibility for helping is shaped by its answers to three critical questions: (1) who deserves to be helped, (2) who should provide help, and (3) what kind of help should be provided? Each of these will be discussed below, but keep in mind that answering each is a part of the larger task of defining societal values about responsibility for helping others. Such decisions are constantly reexamined, and different groups within a society may modify societal values to make them consistent

SOCIAL WORK VALUES IN AMERICA

The National Association of Social Workers (NASW) is the major professional association of social workers in the United States. It provides an example of how an organization interprets societal social welfare values, and then seeks to instill them in its individual members. NASW has declared the following as values of the social work profession (Bartlett, 1958:6):

1 The individual is the primary concern of this society.
2 There is interdependence between individuals in this society.
3 They have social responsibility for one another.
4 There are human needs common to each person, yet each person is essentially unique.
5 An essential attribute of a democratic society is the realization of the full potential of each individual and the assumption of his [or her] social responsibility through active participation in society.

6 Society has a responsibility to provide ways in which obstacles to this self-realization can be overcome or prevented.

Each of these values is associated with certain ethical behaviors. For example, the first value, which emphasizes the importance of the individual, requires that all people be treated with dignity and respect. The last value, which concerns society's responsibility to eliminate obstacles to people's efforts to grow and develop, calls for concrete actions to reduce barriers like racism, ageism, homophobia, and sexism.

Values are important because people act on them—they serve as guides to behavior (ethical behavior). Speaking of this relationship between values and behavior, Bernice Madison notes, "There is no getting away from values because deliberate choices in decision-making are reflections of values" (Madison, 1980:34).

with their own beliefs or the life experiences of their members. Remember, too, that values change over time.

Who Deserves to be Helped?

Most people accept some responsibility to help others. For example, most parents expect to provide physical, emotional, and economic aid to their own children. Indeed, most societies have legal definitions of the responsibilities of parents toward their children. In addition, there are many informal expectations about responsibility, such as the widespread belief that adults should help a lost child even though they are not legally obligated to do so.

Being responsible for someone else is a commitment that usually involves scarce resources. Parents spend a lot of time, money, and physical energy caring for their children. It is not uncommon for them to forgo personal pleasures in order to provide for their children's needs. Accepting responsibility for helping others is a big step that is likely to generate considerable thought and discussion. People's willingness to accept responsibility is often influenced by three factors: (1) *the degree of need,* (2) *the identity of the party who has the need,* and (3) *the cause of the need.* Responsibility is more likely to be accepted when the reasons for being in need are obvious, when they seem beyond the control of those with the need, and when they are experienced by people who are valued.

Consider human infants and homeless adults. An infant is totally helpless through no fault of its own. As a result, adults usually accept responsibility for the care of infants. Homeless people, on the other hand, are often seen as at least partially responsible for their own plight and thus less deserving of help. Thus, while extreme conditions may prompt people to provide help that might otherwise be controversial—such as the provision of temporary shelter during periods of below-freezing temperatures—the ability of the homeless to get food, have access to a toilet, have proper clothing, or to get medical and psychiatric care, may be largely ignored. Many people believe that adults should provide such things for themselves, even if they are homeless. If this is the dominant view in a society, the needs most likely to be met by the larger society are those that are basic to survival. All other needs will be seen as the responsibility of the individuals involved, unless they have a condition that renders them helpless (illness, age, mental impairment, and so on).

It is not only society that defines need. Smaller social units have their own sense of responsibility, usually for their own members. Families, for example, are especially concerned about their own members, parishes about their parishioners, social agencies about their workers and clients, and communities about their residents. Each commonly seeks to identify its members' needs and, having done so, to accept responsibility for meeting those needs. For example, black churches have been concerned with stresses faced by black families, and some have developed programs to help their members in this area. The Church Connection Project, sponsored by six churches in Durham, North Carolina, is a health care project that includes providing birth control services to teenage women. Project SPIRIT in Oakland, California, Atlanta, and Indianapolis provides after-school tutorial and counseling, parenting skill programs, and improved pastoral counseling (*The New York Times,* 1988).

Some smaller social units even accept responsibility for meeting the needs of nonmembers. In such cases, we can see how one part of the social structure attempts to respond to a societal definition of need, or respond to a need not yet accepted by society as its responsibility.

Who Ought to Provide Help?

Public funds are used to provide programs that meet those needs for which society assumes responsibility. This is **public social welfare,** *helping efforts funded out of tax monies or through income obtained from government-mandated programs.* In an important sense, each citizen who pays taxes is helping society to operationalize its sense of responsibility for meeting people's needs.

Societal responsibilities can also be met through private voluntary giving. *Help provided to others by individuals (and private organizations) is called* **charity.** Charity is an important part of **private social welfare,** *helping efforts funded by the voluntary charitable contributions of individuals and organizations, by fees people pay for the services they receive, or by funds spent by corporations to provide social welfare services for their employees.* Private social welfare often addresses the same needs as those for which society has ac-

THE HUMAN FACE OF SOCIAL WELFARE 3

The Human Touch (Emma Blake's Soup Kitchen)

On this day, lunch was corned beef and hash and meatballs, baked beans, macaroni and cheese, two crackers and a cup of sugary iced tea, all that Emma Blake had managed to scrape together....

In the beginning, she paid for almost everything herself, spending as much as $70 a week. But now, there are often small contributions, and Mrs. Blake, a retired practical nurse who lives on Social Security benefits, has been able to cut back her share to about $30....

"You can alleviate some of the suffering," she said. "You're not going to solve it."

Mrs. Blake, 67 years old, spends most of her week preparing for Wednesday. She hunts for bargains, obtains food from the surplus food bank...and tries to use the donations to create a balanced meal....

Cooking often takes up all of Tuesday and keeps Mrs. Blake busy until 1 PM on Wednesday, when she pulls back the metal gates from in front of the kitchen door.

"I couldn't give them canned this and canned that all the time," Mrs. Blake said. "I wouldn't want it, so I'm not going to give it to them."

...Recently she directed three helpers, telling them where to stand and what to do as she spiced one dish, tasted another and rearranged pots.

The people who come to the soup kitchen, more than 200 lately, arrive early and might wait up to two hours for a meal....

A sense of responsibility for others manifests itself in many ways. For Emma Blake, it means running a food pantry one day a week in a church in a poor inner-city neighborhood. Emma Blake's food pantry is an unusual and touching example of one woman's effort to help people in a personal and direct way. Although based in a church, Mrs. Blake feeds all who come to her for help. By gathering resources via her community, she helps its members accept responsibility for helping the poor. In doing so, she supplements the larger society's more formal programs that are likewise the product of a sense of responsibility for others.

From Suzanne Daley, Keeping faith: Emma Blake feeds the hungry in Harlem, *The New York Times,* September 1, 1987, p. B1ff. Copyright (c) 1987 by The New York Times Company. Reprinted by permission.

cepted responsibility. For example, AIDS treatment is a priority of both the National Institutes of Health, a government agency, and the private Gay Men's Health Crisis program. Similarly, cancer research and treatment is a shared concern of both the national government and private groups such as the American Cancer Society.

As we have seen, smaller social units like families, churches, and communities often identify and accept responsibility for selected social needs. These may be needs shared with the larger society (as with Emma Blake's efforts to alleviate hunger) or they may be concerns of specific importance to the members of the social unit involved (the efforts on behalf of black families by black churches). And, whereas community efforts to meet needs typically involve the use of public funds, most such efforts by smaller social units rely on private funds. Here again we can see multiple levels of values—societal, family, community, organizational, and individual—and the way they affect definitions of responsibility and appropriate ways to operationalize them.

What Kind of Help Should be Provided?

Help can be provided either formally or informally. **Formal helping** *is an organized response to needs, while* **informal helping** *is help offered spontaneously to others*. Paying taxes to support government-run social welfare programs or making a donation to the American Cancer Society are both formal helping activities because the money provided goes to formally structured organizations that then provide the actual services. Putting money in a beggar's cup is informal help delivered from one person directly to another, as is the aid family members or friends may spontaneously offer to each other.

Both means of helping can be effective. Large industrial societies tend to emphasize formal helping because of the scale of their social and economic systems. In less affluent societies, many problems are dealt with informally.

In Mexico, for example, informal helping plays a vital role in dealing with many major social problems. The approach to social welfare in a town like Neza—see the boxed discussion—is basically informal. The problem of homelessness is solved by the homeless themselves who exploit Mexico's political and economic disorganization to establish a toehold for themselves at the fringe of urban areas. They then work together to gain access to the social welfare system, eventually building stable communities in which they have an economic stake and which are served by formal service delivery structures.

ON THE STREET IN NEZAHUALCOYOTL, MEXICO

In Mexico, as noted earlier, many people have been fleeing the depressed social and economic conditions in rural areas for Mexico City, in search of better working and living conditions. Already the largest city in the world, Mexico City cannot meet the housing needs of these immigrants, especially in the wake of the 1985 earthquake and current economic conditions. Nevertheless, the government has not stopped the flow of migration, partly to avoid social unrest and partly because politicians profit from it (Eckstein, 1988). The result is the creation of towns on the edge of Mexico City like Nezahualcoyotl, named after an Aztec prince and commonly called Neza. With 2.7 million people, it has over 100,000 inhabitants per square mile and a growth rate of 5 percent a year. Basic public services such as paved streets, adequate water, and trash disposal are at the breaking point (Rohter, 1988).

Towns like this have become part of Mexico's response to the need for housing. Typically, the first residents are squatters who build their homes of cardboard or wood, or erect tin shacks. Gradually the residents seek public services like roads, sewers, water, and electricity, and little by little they convert their shacks into more substantial homes. If they are successful in their quest for services—and sometimes they are not—the towns become permanent and are likely to resemble Neza. Those residents who are successful later move to other lower-middle-class suburbs (Eckstein, 1988).

The development of towns like Neza is encouraged by politicians who dispense resources and other favors in return for votes. Self-help is an important feature of life in such communities where residents are constantly organizing to fight for needed services and resist efforts to declare the community illegal. In addition, family members and neighbors help each other build their homes, find work, and obtain the basic resources needed to survive.

Homelessness is handled quite differently in the United States. The pervasiveness of property ownership has eliminated fringe areas in which the homeless can establish squatter's rights, and the political system is sufficiently powerful to prevent the takeover of property by the homeless. Instead, the available housing options—public shelters, welfare hotels, building low-cost housing, rent subsidies, and so on—are determined by the formal social welfare system. Another difference between the United States and Mexico is the composition of the homeless. In the United States, the homeless poor are mixed with others who have been discharged from treatment centers but are still mentally ill or are substance abusers. With such a mixed group, it is very difficult to develop the kind of self-help networks that are common in poor Mexican communities.

We can see, then, that formal helping provides the structure and continuity necessary for long-term solutions to problems. The residents of Neza know that, which is why they struggle to gain access to the formal system, relying in the interim on informal helping networks to meet their basic survival needs. Although the social problem involved is one most countries would no doubt wish to avoid, the Mexican solution to the problem of homelessness well illustrates the way in which the formal and informal helping systems can complement one another, a goal the United States still struggles with when trying to meet the needs of the homeless.

The Mexican case also reminds us of the importance and particular strengths of informal helping systems. Social welfare should not become so formalized that people have difficulty utilizing their own informal helping networks. Nor should programs become so formalized that those seeking help become nameless and faceless cases.

We have seen that taking responsibility for helping others can be a very direct personal activity, or it can be carried out more formally through organizations. Table 1.2 on page 38 illustrates the full range of possible ways to operationalize a sense of responsibility for others.

MEETING A VARIETY OF NEEDS

Most societies encourage people to be as self-sufficient as possible. Certain types of dependence, however, are defined as acceptable by virtually all societies. The very young and the very old are universally thought to deserve help, as are the ill and those with mental or physical limitations. Discrimination is gradually being better understood as a cause of dependency, especially for those who are hurt by racism, sexism, ageism, and homophobia. For example, racial minority groups whose members are denied access to quality schooling are at a disadvantage in the job market and thus less likely to attain economic independence (Washington Social Legislation Bulletin, 1987:80). Therefore, an important goal of social welfare is to remove social obstacles that prevent people from becoming independent.

**ON THE STREET IN THE UNITED STATES—
HOMELESSNESS**

The United States presents a striking duality in social welfare. On one hand it has an elaborate and
complicated network of social welfare services,
and on the other there are large gaps in the resources that are made available to people. No-
where is this duality more evident than in the treatment of the homeless.

Every large American city has a population of
people living on the street. Popular living areas include grates over exhaust vents where the escaping air provides life-giving warmth. Others find corners or doorways in which to set down cardboard
"beds" on which they sleep and live. Lacking sani-
tary facilities, it is not unusual to find street people
urinating or even defecating in a public place.

Other homeless people seek shelter within public places such as railroad terminals and bus stations. New York's Grand Central Terminal has a
large population of homeless who use its waiting
room as a dormitory and its corners as bathrooms.
Some live in the labyrinth of tracks and on at least
one occasion thousands of commuters were affected by fires started by homeless residents living
in unused train cars.

Lacking money and other resources, the homeless are not appealing to be near. They are often
dressed in rags that are torn and that may expose
skin, including genitals and open sores. Some are
shoeless, walking on gnarled and filthy feet that
are sometimes cut and bloody. Others are dressed
in many layers of clothing regardless of the season
and the temperature. Without basic hygiene facilities, many smell of sweat, dirt, and body wastes.

Estimates of how many homeless exist in the
United States vary widely. Dear and Wolch
(1987:175) cite figures ranging from the United

States Department of Housing and Urban Development's estimate of 350,000 per night to the figure
of 2.5 million offered by the National Coalition for
the Homeless. Included among these people are
individuals suffering from some form of mental disability, young unemployed drifters, alcoholics, substance abusers, people squeezed out of the job
market, and people too poor to afford escalating
rents, especially poor women and their children.

Does the United States have the resources to
eliminate homelessness? Yes. Poland, a far poorer
society, is close to doing so although housing
there is in short supply and far from luxurious.
Why, then, does homelessness in this country continue to exist and even to increase? There are
many reasons. Decent affordable housing is increasingly short supply. Many mental hospitals
have been closed, forcing their residents onto the
street in the absence of other facilities. An increasingly high-tech economic system has few jobs that
pay enough to live on to offer people with little
skill, education, and tolerance for stress. Stubborn
historical patterns of racism and sexism that continue to exclude members of minority groups from
access to adequate education, opportunities for
advancement, and economic security also contribute to the problem, and underlying all of these factors are values that deny the homeless the resources they need.

As a result, the homeless survive on their own
as best they can. Often they obtain help from a variety of sources, utilizing some parts of the formal
welfare system (such as temporary shelters and
hospitals), any available semiformal resources (like
Emma Blake's food pantry), and assistance from
informal helping structures (begging and seeking
help from other homeless people).

TABLE 1.2   THE RANGE OF RESPONSIBILITY TO HELP OTHERS

Most personal ◄---► Most general

Responsible for kin	Responsible for friends	Responsible for members of own community	Responsible for citizens only	Responsible for all in own society	Responsible for human-kind

The rhetoric of independence is sometimes different from the reality of social arrangements. Sweden, where equality and self-reliance for all is an explicit societal goal, uses many elements of the social welfare system to achieve this goal. Men and women are treated equally in the workplace, and family policy encourages equal participation in child-rearing by both parents (if there are two). Housing policy provides for the special needs of children, adolescents, the elderly, and those with physical limitations, so that all can develop fully and be as independent as their abilities permit. Even the subway system in Stockholm has ramps and elevators to ensure accessibility to all, from babies in carriages to the elderly and the physically limited. This kind of mobility strongly supports people's efforts to be independent. While the United States also values equality and personal independence, it has yet to find ways to translate this goal into day-to-day reality for many people.

However much self-reliance is stressed, there will always be people who cannot care for themselves. This may be a temporary or permanent condition, and may range from near-total incapacity to minimal levels of dependence. Social welfare services to promote the personal growth and development of infants seek to maximize their later self-reliance. Similarly, rehabilitation programs aim to move those who are dependent toward greater independence.

However, the goal of helping people to function more autonomously is likely to bump into the question of personal freedom. Deciding how to help people without depriving them of their freedom to live their own lives is a very sensitive task. The needs of individuals and societies sometimes conflict. Should the individual have the right to fail, even though society may then have to expend considerable effort to "rescue" him or her? How much control over individuals should society have in order to foster their self-reliance and thus enable social resources to be used most efficiently? The answers to these questions are in large part determined by the interactions of the society's political and economic structures, as we will see later in this book. For the time being, though, let's look in more depth at this question of resources.

RESOURCES AS A BASIS FOR SOCIAL WELFARE

The importance of resources for social welfare is cogently expressed by Heckscher (1984:105):

> ...welfare states more than others need an economic basis, which can be created only if the economy as a whole is prosperous; and in conditions of today it can remain prosperous only if it proves competitive in an international market where countries with other socioeconomic traditions and aims also attempt to achieve a growing share.

In other words, providing resources and services for people is costly. Those costs can take many forms: money for benefits, trained people to provide services, land and buildings to house programs, and the time spent by planners determining what services are needed. In advanced welfare societies like Sweden, these costs—among which are large government expenditures, the possibility of reducing people's motivation to work, and possible disincentives for people to save money as part of their planning for remaining self-reliant later in life—are increasingly the subject of debate (Heckscher, 1984:7). While research shows that most societies continue to believe the benefits of social welfare outweigh its costs, there is no doubt that these costs are being carefully watched (Alber, 1987).

The availability of resources is an important constraint on social welfare in many developing nations. Even though these nations may want to provide a high level of social welfare services, the lack of resources may make this impossible. Ward (1986:8) describes such a pattern in Mexico where total expenditures by the central government on social welfare declined 7.7 percent from 1972 to 1981 because of severe economic problems. Sokolowska (1987) describes a similar situation in Poland where the government's role in the health care delivery system has been declining due to what she describes as the country's "economic crisis."

These examples illustrate the range of resources that can be allocated to social welfare. The provision of money, services, and trained personnel characterizes highly developed formal social welfare systems. When these are in short supply, the human networks, caring, and expertise characteristic of informal helping systems become especially important. Formal and informal resources always coexist. What varies is the balance between them, a balance that reflects both the availability of resources and the values of the society. Without resources of some kind, either formal or informal, social welfare cannot exist, for the delivery of services requires tangible resources. Table 1.3 contains data on selected social welfare expenditures in our four societies.

SERVICES AS A BASIS FOR SOCIAL WELFARE

The development of **social welfare services**—*that is, the actual resources provided to help people function more effectively in their environment*—is tied to a society's definition of needs and the appropriate ways to meet them. In market-oriented industrial societies, the economic marketplace assumes major importance for meeting needs (Gilbert, 1983). We expect that most people will have the money to purchase essentials like food, clothing, and housing. Those who do not receive assistance from social welfare programs to help them meet these needs.

However, our definition of social welfare encompasses other types of services as well. These include helping people address the personal problems common to daily life, protection from abuse in interpersonal relationships and contacts with organizations, and providing opportunities to grow and develop in healthy and satisfying ways. So we can see social welfare as the product of a three-step progression: the commitment to social welfare values, the allocation of resources to operationalize these values, and the use of these resources to provide actual services for people. Now let us look more specifically at the types of services commonly provided.

TABLE 1.3   SELECTED INDICATORS OF COMPARATIVE SOCIAL WELFARE
SPENDING AND SERVICES

Public expenditures for education*	
Country	Percent of gross national product (GNP) spent on education
Mexico (for year 1983)	2.7
Poland (for year 1982)	4.1
Sweden (for year 1985)	11 †
United States (for year 1981)	6.8

Number of people per hospital bed (1981)‡	
Mexico	863
Poland	134
Sweden	67
United States	171

Public social welfare expenditures in the United States, 1960–1984§	
Year	Percent of gross national product (GNP)
1960	10.3
1970	14.7
1980	16.5
1983	19.3
1984	18.2

*Source: *Statistical Abstract of the United States 1987*, p. 823.
†Source: *Sweden in Brief, 1986*, p. 54. The figure provided here is for education as
a percentage of total government expenditures rather than GNP.
‡Source: *Statistical Abstract of the United States 1987*, p. 822.
§Source: *Statistical Abstract of the United States 1987*, p. 342.

Financial Services

Money is a basic resource needed to purchase life's necessities. Many social
welfare programs provide financial assistance so that people can purchase
what they need in the marketplace. *The services that attempt to ensure adequate financial resources are called* **income maintenance programs.** In the
United States some of the best known income maintenance programs are the
ones that issue social security payments to retired workers, "welfare" payments to single mothers, and pensions to disabled veterans. As a general rule,
income maintenance payments are relatively small. Their purpose is to enable
people to meet their basic needs while encouraging them to be as self-sufficient
as possible. The programs listed above are public, but there are private income
maintenance programs as well. These include corporate pension plans, medical and disability insurance, and grants from private agencies for food, clothing, or housing.

In-Kind Services

Income maintenance services need not necessarily involve giving people money. Some take the form of **in-kind services**, *services that provide a needed commodity itself rather than the funds to purchase it.* The food stamp program is a well-known public example. Food stamps can be used to purchase food items at grocery stores, thereby serving as a replacement for money. In-kind services are a vehicle for ensuring that the aid provided will be used for the intended purpose. Money given to someone for rent payments might instead be used to purchase other items, leaving the rent unpaid. Using a rent voucher instead of cash ensures that this will not occur.

Personal Social Services

Kahn and Kamerman (1977:3–11) popularized the term **personal social services** *to refer to nonfinancial social welfare programs that enhance people's personal development and functioning.* Education, protection from physical and emotional harm, and personal counseling to help people solve problems, manage interpersonal relationships, and participate more effectively in society are all examples of personal social services.

Kahn and Kamerman divide personal social services into two major categories: public social utilities and case services. **Public social utilities** *are services that are available to all members of society who have a need for them.* For example, public schools are available to all children and public police protection to anyone who is threatened with bodily harm. Other examples of public social utilities are public parks, public water and sewer systems, and the legal system. **Case services** *are meant to help those with personal maladjustments, problems, illness, or other difficulties.* Psychotherapy and marriage counseling are case services, as are job counseling, medical care, and nursing home care, all of which may be provided by either the public or private social welfare systems.

Another way that services are organized is around the specific needs of particular groups. Child welfare services, for example, help children whose parents cannot care for them, who suffer from physical or emotional abuse, or who are living in poverty. Services for the elderly focus on the elderly's special physical, health, housing, and income needs, as well as helping them to prepare for death. Families may need income assistance or counseling, while those in the workplace may be struggling with work-related stress or alcoholism. We will look in more detail later on at how specific services are organized.

While we usually think of social welfare services as being provided to individuals, it is important to remember that such services may also be provided to groups and communities. For example, the Bureau of Indian Affairs in the United States Department of Commerce seeks to meet the needs of the American Indian population in the United States. The Department of Housing and Urban Development ''...is the principal Federal agency responsible for programs concerned with...improving and developing the Nation's communities'' *(The United States Government Manual, 1986*:300). There are also private agencies that assist communities. These include major charitable foundations that seek to enhance community facilities for education or the arts, and disaster-relief agencies such as the Red Cross.

Social welfare addresses the full range of human needs, from those of individuals to those of the larger society, from infants to corporate executives. When people function better, communities and organizations benefit, and vice versa.

THE ORGANIZATION AND AVAILABILITY OF SERVICES

Now we are ready to add another and final piece to our sequence of steps that define the social welfare system: the organization by which services are made available. We have seen that while some services—the public social utilities—are intended to be available to all who need them, other services are provided on a more selective basis. Thus we distinguish between those services that are **entitlements,** *to which everyone has a right,* and those that have **eligibility requirements,** *requirements specified for receiving the service that applicants must prove they meet.* Everyone is entitled to walk in a public park or to seek assistance from a police officer. However, not everyone is eligible to receive social security. To qualify, a recipient must be a certain age, have been employed in a position covered by social security, and have contributed to the program. Social welfare organizations are responsible for administering programs in a way that ensures services are delivered to those for whom they are intended.

Most social services in the United States have eligibility requirements of some kind. Among the most common are: age (as with social security); level of income (many programs have an income ceiling); physical condition (usually some type of limitation); parental status (many programs are restricted to single parents with dependent children); place of residence (some programs differ from state to state or community to community); minority status (especially race, gender, and ethnicity); and employment status (unemployment is a requirement in some cases). By contrast, a society such as Sweden treats many more services as public social utilities, thus greatly reducing the emphasis on determining eligibility.

Societies debate how best to allocate scarce resources. As they do so, they must constantly balance commitments to improve the quality of life for all members of society against the needs of particular groups and must, therefore, also make sure that such needs actually exist before providing services. Inevitably, the tensions arising from the effort to meet the needs of everyone, respond to special needs, make efficient use of resources, respect individual rights, and promote self-sufficiency are a prominent feature of such debates.

The extent to which these multiple and sometimes conflicting objectives are met is further influenced by the characteristics of the organizations through which services are delivered (Landy, 1965).

Location

It is generally true that people in urban areas have better access to formal social welfare services than do those in rural areas. The population concentration in urban areas encourages the provision of services and makes delivery easier. Public transportation is more likely to be available in urban areas than in rural ones. Rural residents are often geographically isolated, making it easier to overlook their needs and more difficult to deliver services. However, the strains and anonymity of urban life mean that informal services are often less readily available in urban areas than in rural settings.

Structural Obstacles

Even when services are within geographical reach, there can be other structural obstacles. It may be too costly to travel to the service delivery location, or the fee may be beyond reach. Women with children often find it costly and difficult to bring their children along when traveling to social welfare agencies on public transportation, yet may have no alternative method of transportation nor anyone who can baby-sit for them. People with psychological or emotional problems may lack the organization and energy to utilize services. The blind, deaf, or otherwise physically limited face special problems in traveling to obtain services. Others fear the formal service delivery system, preferring to rely on the informal system even though it may not adequately meet their needs. This is especially true for undocumented aliens who, fearing the possibility of deportation, avoid social agencies.

Stigma and Values

Many people have been taught to reject formal social welfare services, seeing them as either a threat to their personal freedom or as an indication of personal failure. Rather than face the anticipated scorn of friends and neighbors, or the intrusion of "nosy" welfare workers, these people prefer to struggle on their own or rely on informal helping systems.

Lack of Information

The formal social welfare system is very complex. Application forms are sometimes long and confusing, especially for those whose reading and writing skills are limited. As a result, many people are either unaware of the services available to them or unable to master the required organizational procedures. Many people in need do not understand or speak English well, and agencies do not always have staff who speak their language. This further complicates efforts to learn about and use services.

For a variety of reasons, then, the mere existence of social welfare services does not ensure their use. It is a frustrating reality that some services remain unused because people do not know they exist, or because they are blocked in their efforts to obtain services. Organizational policies can be designed to remove as many barriers as possible through advertising, simplifying information and application procedures, and locating services where people can reach them. However, attitudes that link social welfare with failure and disgrace will continue to block some people from reaching the help they need.

SOCIAL WELFARE DECISION-MAKING

Before going further, it will be helpful to summarize where we are. We began with a definition of social welfare and noted its three basic components: a sense of responsibility to help others (values), the allocation of the resources necessary to provide specific social welfare services, and the organization of these services so that they are available to people. To round out our understanding of these points, we now turn to decision-making structures that affect values, resources, and services.

Social welfare is the result of decision-making at many levels. Private formal and informal services are the result of financial decisions by individuals and private organizations. People can choose to give money to a beggar, or choose not to. They can contribute to the United Way, or decide they will not. Relatives and friends decide whether they will loan money, provide babysitting, or furnish a ride to family members and personal acquaintances.

Formal welfare systems are likewise the product of decisions, often at multiple levels. In the private sector, agency policy and the implementation of that policy is debated by agency officials. The supervisors and service-delivery personnel who carry out the policies make certain decisions of their own on a daily basis—how much time to spend with a particular client, for example. Similar decision-making processes exist in public agencies to which must be added the influence of political decision-makers. In most societies, national social welfare policy is made at the national level. In the United States, national public social welfare policy and the specific programs through which it is implemented are established through legislation passed by Congress. For example, our existing public social welfare system is largely based on the Social Security Act of 1935 and its many subsequent amendments.

Part of national decision-making is specifying the role to be played by local governmental units. In all of the societies discussed in this book, responsibility for social welfare is shared by the national and local levels of government. In the United States, national social welfare programs are implemented and sometimes supplemented by state and local governments. There are, therefore, three levels—national, state, and local—of public decision-making involved in all public social welfare programs and policies. For even when policy is theoretically made at one level, the other levels or organizations involved in its implementation also make decisions about how services will be delivered, as we have seen.

Even private agencies are influenced by legislation. In part, this is because legislation mandates certain goals and procedures for the entire society—equal

SHARED GOVERNMENTAL RESPONSIBILITY IN SWEDEN

As in most societies, decisions about social welfare in Sweden are made at multiple levels. Responsibility for policymaking rests with the national level of government while implementation is carried out at the county and municipal levels. Each level is empowered to levy any taxes required to support its social welfare activities, making Swedes among the most heavily taxed people in the world. However, the resulting social welfare system is very comprehensive. Services are delivered to people in the neighborhoods in which they live, maximizing access to services and promoting contact and cooperation between those delivering services and those receiving them. Such closeness increases opportunities for early detection and intervention when problems arise.

National Level The current Swedish social welfare system is based on the Social Services Act of 1982 which was passed by Parliament in 1981. Its objectives, as described in that act, are as follows (Social Welfare Legislation in Sweden, 1986:1):

Public social services are to be established on the basis of democracy and solidarity, with a view toward promoting: economic and social security, equality of living conditions and active participation in community life. Social service activities are to be based on respect for the self-determination and privacy of the individual.

Primary responsibility for implementing social welfare services is assigned to The National Social Insurance Board whose responsibilities include ensuring that service delivery is based on a comprehensive view of social welfare:

The principle of maintaining a comprehensive view is characteristic of the social service system.... This implies taking into account the entire situation of the individual or family. A comprehensive view also means paying attention to the environmental factors that contribute to the social difficulties affecting an individual.

Taxes are levied at the national level to help support this system, and efforts are made to coordinate social welfare policy with other national policies (such as economic policy).

County Level At the county level, there are 23 county councils which have major responsibility for health care. Planning for medical care is carried out at this level in coordination with municipal primary care centers (see below). Counties also operate hospitals, provide health care training, and are responsible for mental retardation and preventive health care services.

These services are funded from county taxes, subsidies from the national government, and, in some cases, user fees (The Swedish Institute, 1985).

Municipal Level The 284 municipal governments in Sweden, each serving from 5,000 to 700,000 people, have primary responsibility for the delivery of social welfare services. These include education, child care, care of the elderly and those with mental or physical limitations, social services, recreation, and other services.

Municipal social service centers provide primary health care and most other social services. When necessary, patients are referred to county hospitals for specialized health care. As much as possible, services for the elderly and those with limitations, are delivered in their homes by interdisciplinary teams working out of the municipal social service center. Child care centers are scattered throughout each community so that they are accessible to parents and require minimal travel for children.

Municipal services are funded by municipal taxes, national government subsidies, and some fees for service.

In comparison with Sweden, the U.S. social welfare system has a similar overall structure but is financed and implemented in quite different ways. The United States has four levels of public policymaking: national, state, county, and municipal. Most taxes, however, are levied at the national and state levels, so counties and municipalities have much less autonomy and fewer resources than in Sweden. As a result, public social welfare policymaking is more centralized at the national and state levels in the United States than in Sweden.

As a consequence, there are more difficulties delivering services at the neighborhood level in the United States than in Sweden. In this country, there are too many levels above the neighborhood that set policy, and too few local resources for neighborhoods to control their own programs. These differences in structure reflect different social welfare values. Swedish levels of taxation, especially those at the municipal level, would not be acceptable in the United States. The two societies also differ in their beliefs about the types of social welfare services for which society is responsible. Finally, the United States has a much larger private social welfare network than does Sweden. In some ways, these services are a substitute for many of those provided by the more comprehensive public Swedish welfare system.

opportunity and nondiscrimination, for example. But there is also a good deal of **contracting** by public agencies with private ones. This means that *public agencies pay for private agencies to provide certain services in specified ways.* This happens on a large scale: "By 1980 federal programs provided over 50% of all the financial support that went to private nonprofit social service and community development organizations" (Gilbert, 1983:8).

Any given social welfare structure, then, exists in a particular society at any given time as a result of decision-making at three levels: governmental (at the national, state, and local levels), organizational, and personal. Here again we see how deeply enmeshed social welfare is with the entire structure of society. Obviously decision-makers at any of these levels are influenced by political and economic factors, as well as personal values and beliefs. In later chapters we will look in more detail at how these factors interact.

SOCIAL WELFARE REVISITED

Before we end this chapter, let's review the basics of social welfare. We have seen that *the goal of social welfare is to help people function effectively in their social environment. This means not only providing for people's basic survival needs (adequate nutritious food, clothing, shelter, medical care, clean air and water) but meeting all those needs necessary for them to be psychologically well and socially productive.* Accordingly, we have defined social welfare specifically as *a society's governmental and nongovernmental efforts to help its members function more effectively as individuals and as participants in organized social structures.* We also saw that social welfare is a social institution that addresses human needs and provides help in planned and organized ways.

By now, you should understand why values, the availability of resources, and the organization and actual structure of services are the major determinants of social welfare. In addition, the factors that influence social welfare decisions at the governmental, organizational, and personal levels are extremely important. Social welfare is an integral part of the fabric of society, so it influences and is influenced by all that goes on around it.

It is probably clear to you that the study of social welfare can be a mammoth undertaking. In addition to the services provided to people, many other areas of social life are relevant to such a study: the political system in which decisions are made, the economic system that affects resources and their allocation, social welfare organizations that employ and organize the people who deliver actual services, societal values and the ethical behaviors that flow from them, historical factors that have created patterns of inequality, and so on.

Social welfare is a social creation. What you learn about it will change as it changes in response to its dynamic environment. During your life you will see many changes, whether as a citizen, a user, or a practitioner. An understanding of where these changes come from will help you understand a changing and dynamic social welfare system.

LET'S REVIEW

This chapter began by focusing on the relationship between social welfare and helping. The goal of social welfare was discussed in terms of helping people to function more effectively in their social environment. So defined, social welfare encompasses a broad range of objectives including meeting basic physical needs, interacting more harmoniously with others, and participating more effectively in social life. This in turn leads to a definition of social welfare that focuses on efforts by governmental and other groups to help people function more effectively in society, both to improve the quality of life for individuals and to strengthen society itself.

We then turned to three basic dimensions of social welfare: responsibility, resources, and services. We saw that helping always involves a sense of responsibility, a sense that is shaped by the multiple values existing in any industrial society. Such value-based issues as who deserves to be helped, who ought to provide help, and what kind of help should be provided were discussed within the context of responsibility and values.

The relationship between resources and social welfare was explored, with an emphasis on resources as the basis for the creation of actual services. We saw that resources can be formal and informal, and that within any society there is always competition for how resources will be allocated. When resources are scarce, either in general or in the amount allocated to social welfare, it is difficult to create and maintain a comprehensive formal system of services.

The next section of the chapter discussed the various types of social welfare services. These included income maintenance services, in-kind services, and personal social services of two kinds—public social utilities and case services. Issues of eligibility and entitlement were discussed, along with the public and private delivery of services.

This was followed by consideration of reasons why social welfare systems take the form they do in particular societies at any given point in time. Levels of decision-making were discussed, including the governmental, organizational, and personal levels. This served to emphasize the close linkages between social welfare and other social institutions, especially the political and economic systems.

As you complete this chapter, you should have a reasonably clear idea of what social welfare is and some of the ways that it interacts with other parts of society. Now we are ready to move to the next chapter where we will explore some of the major reasons why people need social welfare services. We will see that the biological, psychological, cultural, and social structural dimensions of daily life often cause the problems that the social welfare system seeks to address. Other problems arise from the tensions and abuses flowing from the way societies organize interactions between people. Still others result from the choices people make for themselves. Regardless of people's needs, however, remember that the way in which societies choose to respond to these needs is the result of active choice.

As you leave this chapter, remember its main point—social welfare is society's ongoing effort to define a vision of what the quality of human life can and should be, and then to translate that vision into reality. Different societies approach this task in different ways because of their differing histories, cultural traditions, value systems, and resources.

CHAPTER OUTLINE

WHAT TO EXPECT FROM THIS CHAPTER

LEARNING OBJECTIVES

SOCIAL WELFARE AND HELPING
  The Human Face of Social Welfare 2: Life in a Shelter for the
    Homeless (The Brand Family)

RESPONSIBILITY AS A BASIS FOR SOCIAL WELFARE
  Social Work Values in America
  Who Deserves to be Helped?
  The Human Face of Social Welfare 3: The Human Touch (Emma
    Blake's Soup Kitchen)
  Who Ought to Provide Help?
  What Kind of Help Should be Provided?
  On the Street in Nezahualcoyotl, Mexico
  On the Street in the United States—Homelessness

MEETING A VARIETY OF NEEDS

RESOURCES AS A BASIS FOR SOCIAL WELFARE

SERVICES AS A BASIS FOR SOCIAL WELFARE
  Financial Services
  In-Kind Services
  Personal Social Services

THE ORGANIZATION AND AVAILABILITY OF SERVICES
  Location
  Structural Obstacles
  Stigma and Values
  Lack of Information

SOCIAL WELFARE DECISION-MAKING
  Shared Governmental Responsibility in Sweden

SOCIAL WELFARE REVISITED

LET'S REVIEW

STUDY QUESTIONS

1 Review the list of key terms and concepts that follows. Make sure you can define each in your own words and give an example based either on your own experience or on something you have read or seen.

2 Use the problem of homelessness to consider the issues of societal responsibility and the problem of dependency. Specifically, address the following issues: (a) who are the homeless (you should get some actual data to answer this question; pages 789–795 in the 18th edition of the *Encyclopedia of Social Work* is recommended); (b) who is responsible for helping the homeless (consider at least the following: the homeless themselves, their families, their communities, society as a whole); (c) what should the homeless do in return for being helped; (d) and what problems might result from helping the homeless? After doing this exercise, summarize what you have learned about issues of responsibility and dependency in social welfare.

3 What do you think the objectives of social welfare ought to be? Be sure to include manifest and latent functions. Then try to identify as many of your personal values as you can that seem to influence your view of what social welfare ought to be. Finally, think about where the values that you identify have come from (likely places to start are your family, your religion, school, friends, your own personal experiences, and so on).

4 Give an example of a situation in which you helped someone (remember that it does not have to have been a life-and-death situation). Now think of a situation in which you were helped. How did it feel to help someone? How did it feel to be helped? Why did you help the person you did? Did you feel that you had any choice? After you were helped, did you feel any sense of obligation? If so, to whom? How does this exercise help you to understand responsibility and self-sufficiency as a part of social welfare?

5 Write a one-page summary of what you learned in this chapter. Of what value do you think this material will be to you given your goals for yourself? Identify at least three questions that you have as a result of reading this chapter (either because the material itself was not clear, or because what you read stimulated your thinking about some other things). Make it your business to answer as many of your questions as you can.

KEY TERMS AND CONCEPTS

case services
charity
contracting
eligibility requirements
entitlements
ethical behavior
formal helping
in-kind services
income maintenance programs
informal helping
latent functions of social welfare

manifest functions of social welfare
personal social services
private social welfare
public social utilities
public social welfare
relative values
social institution
social welfare
social welfare services
social welfare as a social institution
values

SUGGESTED READINGS

Bellah, Robert, et al. 1985. *Habits of the Heart.* Berkeley, Cal.: University of California Press. This sociological study takes an in-depth look at people's perceptions of their connections with each other and with society as a whole. The authors focus on contemporary values that affect people's willingness to take responsibility for others in their communities and in society as a whole.

Heckscher, Gunnar. 1984. *The Welfare State and Beyond.* Minneapolis: University of Minnesota Press. The author uses the social welfare system of Sweden and other Scandinavian countries to explore the strengths and limitations of a comprehensive approach to social welfare. Includes a discussion of some of the major reasons why social welfare is controversial, including its cost, impact on tax rates, implications for economic growth, effect on informal helping efforts, and potential impact on self-sufficiency.

Morris, Robert. 1985. *Social Policy of the American Welfare State,* 2d ed. White Plains, New York: Longman, Inc. The author systematically examines United States social welfare policies in major service-delivery areas, focusing on the effects of policies implemented by the Reagan administration.

Murray, Charles. 1984. *Losing Ground.* New York: Basic Books. This book is generally considered the most forceful expression of the conservative perspective on social welfare. The author attempts to demonstrate that social welfare programs in the United States should be reduced because they hurt rather than help those they serve.

Olsson, Sven. 1986. *Growth to Limits: The Western European Welfare States Since World War II: The Case of Sweden.* Stockholm: Swedish Institute for Social Research. This monograph provides a thorough analysis of the costs and benefits of Sweden's approach to social welfare during the past decades. It also offers a thoughtful look ahead to the future of the welfare state.

REFERENCES

Alber, Jens. 1987. The crisis of the welfare state. Paper presented at the annual meeting of the American Sociological Association, Chicago, Ill., August 19.

Bartlett, Harriett. 1958. Toward clarification and improvement of social work practice. *Social Work* (April):3–90.

Black churches, endangered children. 1988. *The New York Times,* May 23, A18.

Burt, Martha, and Karen Pittman. 1985. *Testing the Social Safety Net.* Washington, D.C.: The Urban Institute.

Business panel recommends investment strategies for educationally disadvantaged. 1987. *Washington Social Legislation Bulletin* 30, issue 18, September 28.

Daley, Suzanne. 1987. Keeping faith: Emma Blake feeds the hungry in Harlem. *The New York Times,* September 1, B1ff.

Dear, Michael, and Jennifer Wolch. 1987. *Landscapes of Despair: From Deinstitutionalization to Homelessness.* Princeton, N.J.: Princeton University Press.

Eckstein, Susan. 1988. *The Poverty of Revolution,* rev. ed. Princeton, N.J.: Princeton University Press.

A family down and out. 1987. *Newsweek,* January 12, pp. 44–46.

Forsberg, Mats. 1986. *The Evolution of Social Welfare Policy in Sweden.* Lund, Sweden: The Swedish Institute.

Gilbert, Neil. 1983. *Capitalism and the Welfare State.* New Haven, Conn.: Yale University Press.

Heckscher, Gunnar. 1984. *The Welfare State and Beyond.* Minneapolis: The University of Minnesota Press.

Hopps, June. 1986. Compromise budget or compromised children. *Social Work,* 31, no. 3 (May–June):163–172.

Kahn, Alfred J., and Sheila Kamerman. 1977. *Social Services in International Perspective*. Washington, D.C.: U.S. Government Printing Office (SRS 76–05704).

Landy, David. 1965. Problems of the person seeking help in our culture. In *Social Welfare Institutions,* ed. Mayer Zald. New York: John Wiley & Sons.

Madison, Bernice. 1980. *The Meaning of Social Policy: The Comparative Dimension in Social Welfare*. Boulder, Colo.: Westview Press.

Morris, Robert. 1986. *Rethinking Social Welfare: Why Care for the Stranger?* White Plains, N.Y.: Longman, Inc.

———. 1985. *Social Policy of the American Welfare State,* 2d ed. White Plains, N.Y.: Longman, Inc.

Murray, Charles. 1984. *Losing Ground*. New York: Basic Books.

Quindlen, Anna. 1982. An old man who fears too much care. *The New York Times,* April 14.

Rohter, Larry. 1988. In plain of hungry coyote, millions dwell in hope. *The New York Times,* May 31, A4.

Sokolowska, Magdalena. 1987. The official health system and alternative solutions in Poland of the 80s. Paper delivered at the annual meetings of the American Sociological Association, Chicago, Ill., August 19.

Suppes, Mary Ann, and Carolyn Wells. Forthcoming. Manuscript of a textbook for the introductory social work course.

The Swedish Institute. 1985. *Local Government in Sweden*. Stockholm: The Swedish Institute.

———. 1986. *Social Welfare Legislation in Sweden*. Stockholm: The Swedish Institute.

The United States Government Manual. 1986. Washington, D.C.: The U.S. Government Printing Office.

Ward, Peter. 1986. *Welfare Politics in Mexico*. London: Allen & Unwin, Ltd.

Washington Social Welfare Legislation Bulletin. 1987. Vol. 30, No. 18 (September 28), p. 80.

Wojciechowski, Sophie. 1975. Poland's new priority: Human welfare. In *Meeting Human Needs 1*, eds. Daniel Thursz and Joseph Vigilante, Beverly Hills, Cal.: Sage Publications, Inc., pp. 169–195.

The World Bank. 1986. *The World Bank Atlas 1986*. Washington, D.C.: The World Bank.

CHAPTER 2

WHY IS SOCIAL WELFARE NEEDED?

WHAT TO EXPECT FROM THIS CHAPTER

This chapter addresses the question of why we, or any society for that matter, need a social welfare system. You will recall from the previous chapter that social welfare involves helping people and societies to function more effectively in their environment. In this chapter we will explore what it is about human beings and the way they live that makes helping a necessary part of their lives.

Social welfare raises issues that many people would rather avoid. Most of us like to think of ourselves as competent and self-sufficient. At some level, of course, we acknowledge that we have needed help at various times in our lives, especially when we were children. Furthermore, we see all around us people who encounter obstacles in their daily living—frail, elderly relatives, friends sick in the hospital, or physically limited people in their day-to-day activities. We are also aware of our own problems, whether they involve getting good grades in school, getting or keeping a job, or managing relationships with family members. So we know that aspects of living can be troublesome.

Still, many of us resist thinking about needing help. It seems as if admitting we need help compromises our sense of self-worth as adults. It is hard to ask for help without thinking we have failed in some way or are at fault. We worry that friends or colleagues may think less of us if we can't "make it on our own." Such thinking is reinforced by stories of self-made millionaires, heroes who have triumphed over incredible adversity, and poor hard-working folk who accept their lot quietly rather than ask for help. If they can do it, why can't we? Isn't it lazy or selfish to seek help rather than solving our own problems? Shouldn't we be content with what we have, even if it is very little?

This chapter will address these issues. It will begin with what are often called "common human needs," the needs all people have at some point in their lives. We will see that the timing of these needs and the way in which they are expressed vary for members of different groups. Then we will move on to explore four factors that make it difficult for people to meet their common human needs: (1) human biological characteristics; (2) changes associated with cognitive and emotional growth and development; (3) the impact of the environment; and (4) the fact that people make mistakes. The first part of this chapter, then, will discuss the reasons why people sometimes do not function effectively.

The focus of the chapter then switches to society's need for social welfare. Just as individuals sometimes need help to function more effectively, so does society. We will see that dysfunctional people are very costly to society. Social welfare enables society better to attain its goals by reducing the number of dysfunctional people. You might find it useful to review the concepts of manifest and latent functions in the previous chapter. This will help you understand how programs designed to help people meet their personal needs (their manifest function) can also strengthen society itself (their latent function).

Our discussion of the need for social welfare in this chapter draws upon evidence of two quite different types. One type is *empirical*, consisting of the findings of social scientists and human service professionals concerning the conditions that promote individual well-being and societal functioning. The other is *normative*, consisting of the values that affect people's perceptions of helping and being helped. Both types of evidence—the empirical and that which is value-based—shape our thinking about social welfare.

LEARNING OBJECTIVES

At the end of this chapter, you should be able to do the following:

1 Discuss the relationship between common human needs and the needs of diverse groups.

2 Define the major stages of the human life span.

3 List at least three biological factors that lead people to need help.

4 List at least three psychological, emotional, or cognitive factors that lead people to need help.

5 List at least three social or environmental factors that lead people to need help.

6 Discuss three types of mistakes or poor choices made by people that are likely to create the need for help.

7 Describe the relationship between individual needs and societal needs.

8 Use the concepts of manifest and latent functions to analyze the impact of social welfare programs on individuals and on society.

9 Distinguish between the "fixing" and developmental functions of social welfare.

10 Provide your own answer to the question of why social welfare is needed, based on the material in this chapter.

THE CONCEPT OF NEEDS

All human beings are born with an inherited biological potential into an environment that provides both resources and obstacles. The need for social welfare, then, springs in part from two sources.

The first is the *genetic capacity* with which people are born. Everyone requires help during the first few years of life because the human organism only gradually develops the physiological capacity to function autonomously. In addition, some people have physiological deficits that impose further limits on their potential for independence.

The *nature of people's interaction with their physical and social environments* is a second factor giving rise to the need for social welfare. Human life takes place in a physical context—air, water, vegetation, and other forms of life—that can facilitate or impede people's efforts to realize their genetic potential. Another powerful influence on human life is the social environment—the social arrangements created by people to structure their daily behavior, of which societies, social institutions, communities, and corporations are examples.

Successful living requires learning how to function in one's environment. However, there are a variety of social conditions that impede such learning, or that become obstacles to particular people. We will explore the physical and social environments in more detail later in this chapter after we examine the effect of the genetic capacity with which people are born on their need for social welfare.

UNDERSTANDING HUMAN NEEDS

Common Human Needs and Human Diversity

The concept of **common human needs** is a useful starting point for our exploration of the need for social welfare. As articulated by Towle (1965:6–11), *common human needs are those needs that are shared by all human beings because they are basic to their survival and development.* According to Towle, these include physical well-being, personality development, emotional growth, development of intellectual capacity, relationships with others, and spiritual needs.

The psychologist Abraham Maslow took Towle's list of common human needs one step further, ordering them according to importance (1970:35–46). As shown in Table 2.1, Maslow felt that some human needs were more basic than others, and that people sought to fulfill these needs in a particular order. First, he argued, come the physiological needs basic to physical survival, followed by other higher-level needs such as: safety needs, belongingness and love needs, esteem needs, and the need for self-actualization ("becoming everything that one is capable of becoming"). Nor, in Maslow's view, can any higher level of need be attained until and unless all preceding needs have been met. For example, someone struggling to find safe housing is unlikely to have time or energy to seek self-actualization. Common to both Towle and Maslow's views is the recognition that some or all of these common human needs might not be met for some people, giving rise to a need for help.

Helen Harris Perlman, a social worker like Towle, emphasized the holistic nature of common human needs. In her words (Perlman, 1957:6–7):

> Nevertheless, the person is a whole in any moment of his living. He operates as a physical, psychological, social entity, whether on the problem of his neurotic anxieties or of his inadequate income; he is product-in-process, so to speak, of his constitutional makeup, his physical and social environment, his past experience, his present perceptions and reactions, and even his future aspirations. It is this physical-psychological-social-past-present-future configuration that he brings to every life-situation he encounters [note that "he" should be read as he or she.]

This *unity of the biological, psychological, and social components of people* has come to be called the **biopsychosocial whole.** This way of thinking recognizes that, as biological and psychological beings, people seek to meet their

TABLE 2.1 THE HIERARCHY OF COMMON HUMAN NEEDS

Function	Need	Example
Self-fulfillment	Self-actualization	Graduating from college
Self-respect	Esteem needs	A promotion at work
Acceptance	Belongingness and love needs	Committed relationships
Security	Safety needs	System of law and order
Survival	Physiological needs	Food and shelter

needs through interpersonal relationships and the social patterns in their environment. These two concepts—common human needs and the biopsychosocial whole—are central to an understanding of people's interactions with their social and physical environment as they attempt to realize their full inherited potential.

While all people seek to meet their needs for growth, development, and survival, the way they do so varies. Common human needs are expressed and met in different ways by different groups of people (Berger and Federico, 1985:88), for diversity is a basic characteristic of our species. **Human diversity** refers to *the biological, psychological, social and cultural differences among people which in turn affect the way their needs are expressed and satisfied.* Some of the most significant types of diversity are gender, age, race, ethnicity, physical or mental ability, sexual orientation, and socioeconomic level.

There are many possible examples of the impact of human diversity on people's ability to realize their potential. Studies have shown that a child's physical welfare is affected by the socioeconomic status of its caretakers. Poor children are more likely to have birth defects, low birth weight, and illness at birth. They are also more likely to suffer from hunger and malnutrition and to be abused or neglected (National Association of Social Workers, 1987:3). Here in the United States, black and Hispanic people are more likely than whites to live below the poverty level (Herbers, 1987), so that their children are more likely to experience physical problems. Those with mental or physical limitations and gay and lesbian people may also encounter special problems in meeting their needs. Their families and neighbors often withhold the social acceptance and emotional support that they need to meet their love, esteem, and self-actualization needs (Dane, 1985:505–510; Slater and Wikler, 1986:385–390; Berger, 1987:798–805).

What we see, then, are two distinct sources of human needs. All people have certain common needs that range from physical survival through self-fulfillment. At the same time, the way in which people attempt to meet these needs is influenced by human diversity. Children and old people must both eat to survive, but they differ in what they eat, how they eat it, and how it is obtained. Similarly, both men and woman have a need for psychological security, but the precise form of these needs, and the way in which they can best be met, will vary.

NEEDS THROUGHOUT THE LIFE SPAN

Human needs are not static. They take on different forms over the course of human **life span.** *The life span is the period from conception to death. It is divided into chronological stages* (**life-span stages**) *each of which is associated with a distinctive set of social expectations about how needs will be met* (Berger and Federico, 1985:112–113). For example, it is generally expected that many of the psychological, emotional, and social needs of teenagers will be met at school. Adults entering the retirement stage of their lives are more

ON THE STREET IN SWEDEN

In Stockholm, subways are for people—all people. The design of the Stockholm subway system illustrates how obstacles in the social environment that could thwart people's efforts to meet their personal needs can be minimized.

Subways in Stockholm, as in most large cities, are a valuable tool in helping people carry out their daily activities. Adults travel to work and students to school. Parents take their children shopping and elderly citizens go visiting. Although many Swedes have cars, public transportation (buses, suburban trains, and the subway) is a popular way to move around the city.

Many subway systems around the world have characteristics that discourage the frail and disabled from using them. Stairs (and even escalators) create obstacles for the physically limited, parents with youngsters, and the elderly. Crime also makes many people reluctant to use subways. Dirty and isolated corridors and subway platforms further limit the appeal of underground travel to many potential users.

Stockholm has taken these problems seriously and created a subway that is accessible to everyone. Elevators are provided at all stations, as are ramps, so that the stations are readily accessible to those in wheelchairs or who are accompanied by grocery carts or baby carriages. Many corridors in the system feature shops that make it possible to combine shopping activities with traveling to one's destination. Crime is minimal, and the subway system is kept clean. Some of the stations have art-

work or interesting architectural features that enhance their esthetic appeal.

The result is a public social utility that is accessible to virtually everyone. Neither people's physical safety nor their psychological sense of well-being is threatened when they use the system. Their sense of participation in their urban environment is enhanced. They are able to go where they need when they want to go there. The Stockholm subway provides a good example of how the physical and social environment can be designed to minimize potential obstacles to the realization of human potential.

Of course, the Stockholm subway system did not just happen. It is the product of active choice by those responsible for designing and operating the system. Most of all, it is a result of a view in which a physical limitation is seen not as the individual's problem but as a problem in the interaction of the individual and society. In this view, those with physical limitations can meet their common human needs and participate effectively in community life if their environment simply provides the resources they need.

Other communities, viewing matters differently, often resist making their public transportation systems accessible to those with limitations, perceiving the added costs involved as "too expensive" in relation to other purposes preferred by the community. Whatever the reasoning, the net effect of such decisions is a public transportation system that represents an obstacle blocking those with limitations from utilizing their abilities to the fullest.

likely to meet these same needs in the workplace, via intimate relationships, and through recreational activities.

The social expectations concerning the expression and fulfillment of needs at each stage of the life span usually reflect the biological capacities associated with, and the resources commonly available to, people at that stage. For example, young children in our society are not expected to earn a living because they are not yet physically or mentally capable of doing so. It is expected that they will be nurtured and protected by their families until they are able to be financially independent. These general expectations prevail even though we know that not all families are able or willing to care for and protect their children, and that poor children—who are disproportionately likely to be members of racial and ethnic minority groups—must often find a way to earn a living much earlier than those who are better off.

We can see, then, that each stage of the life span is associated with certain general biological, psychological, and social characteristics. Let's look at these in more detail.

Biological Processes

Human physical, psychological, and social development is a lengthy process, and it is many years after birth before people become independent. Genetic programming heavily influences the rate and extent of human biological and physical development, but so too do disruptive illnesses, accidents, and natural disasters, which may occur at any time. In addition, few people in industrialized societies can grow all their own food, construct their own housing, or make their own clothing. Thus, meeting basic physical needs requires collaboration with others. Most people must work to earn an income that enables them to purchase necessities from others. Meeting one's physical needs in today's world involves interaction with a complex social environment.

Periods of biological helplessness can also influence other needs. Children are especially dependent on others for meeting their emotional, intellectual, personality, and social needs in addition to ensuring their basic physical survival. The elderly may find that their social relationships and their sense of psychological well-being are jeopardized if they become dependent on others. Adults at any age can also experience difficulty in their social relationships, social participation, and sense of well-being if their independence is lessened through illness or accident.

Table 2.2 on page 60 illustrates the different ways in which basic physical needs are met throughout the life span. Notice that the same needs persist throughout life—physical survival and well-being. However, the resources available to meet these needs change, as do the obstacles encountered. Keep in mind that the pattern shown here is typical of people in general but not necessarily of any single individual, whose life history will, of course, be shaped in part by human diversity. Note too that a similar chart could be made for other types of needs.

Emotional and Cognitive Growth

As people move through the life span, they meet their basic needs in different ways. Emotional tasks such as managing stress, expressing affection for others, perceiving the environment accurately, and controlling one's feelings are managed more effectively as people mature emotionally. Intellectual development also brings changes. The ability to reason cognitively grows, and the storehouse of knowledge increases. Thus, new opportunities and new decisions emerge. The integration of cognitive capacity with spiritual and moral

TABLE 2.2 MEETING PHYSICAL NEEDS THROUGHOUT THE LIFE SPAN

Stage	Strategies for meeting physical needs
Prenatal	Dependent on the mother's health
Birth	Influenced by birthing events and the birth environment
Infancy	Dependent on caretakers, usually family members and medical personnel
Childhood	Heavily responsive to caretakers, especially at home and in school; growing importance of friends and own activities
Adolescence	Limited dependence on caretakers; growing importance of own activities and decisions, especially regarding smoking, drinking, nutrition, sexual activity, friends, and so on
Young Adulthood	Much less dependent on family; assumption of economic and nurturing roles for self; significant relationships with spouse/lover/friends that include mutual care
Middle Adulthood	Maximum autonomy and self-care; continuation of mutual care relationships
Retirement	Continue self-care and mutual care patterns as much as possible; increasing dependence on spouse or lover, family, friends, health care professionals
Death	Final loss of control over physical self

standards takes place. Personal goals are usually better understood, and strategies for meeting them can be purposefully chosen.

As an illustration of the importance of emotional and cognitive development to need-meeting behavior, consider the changing role of women in American society. In comparison with the past, women today have greater access to education and employment opportunities. The increased opportunities for cognitive development and functioning that accompany being educated and gainfully employed have in turn affected the emotional growth of many women, enhancing their sense of autonomy and well-being. Among the beneficial results of this development is a reduced likelihood that women will be victimized by abusive personal relationships (Finkelhor, 1983:18). Since studies suggest that children who are abused are themselves likely to become adult abusers, a reduction in the incidence of abuse of adult women is likely to spare their children from abuse as well (Straus, 1983:219). Thus, enhancing women's opportunities to grow and develop cognitively and emotionally may help break the generational cycle of child and spouse abuse (Herrenkohl et al., 1983). In this case, as in many others, as individuals become better able to meet their needs effectively, a significant social problem is reduced.

Need meeting, then, is never static. As people move through the life span they grow and change, using new resources to meet their basic needs and encountering new obstacles at each stage. We can see in this process the holistic nature of human life, particularly the interaction of biological, psychological, and social factors. As one change spawns others, people engage in a process of ongoing adjustments to their perceptions and behaviors.

The Impact of the Environment

Just as people themselves change throughout the life span, so does the environment in which they live. This is especially true of the physical and social environments.

The physical environment is subject to short- and long-term changes. Droughts and floods, earthquakes and volcanic eruptions can quickly change the conditions under which people live. Long-term changes, such as the gradual destruction of arable land and forests through agricultural mismanagement, overpopulation, or urbanization has created major problems in many nations including Mexico and the United States. Technology is having an increasing effect on the physical environment as well. The nuclear accident at Russia's Chernobyl power plant and the deadly oil spill in Prince William Sound in Alaska are two recent examples. Events of this magnitude that have immediate life-and-death significance for people are relatively rare, but less-dramatic developments that create obstacles or imperil the availability of resources are all too common.

Changes are even more frequent and important in the social environment. As developing nations industrialize, corporate takeovers occur in capitalist societies, and socialist nations experiment with free enterprise, the conditions of economic survival are significantly altered. Inflation, balance of trade problems, and the growth of multinational corporations all affect the availability of jobs and the economic well-being of millions of people. The October 1987 stock market crisis in the United States had an immediate effect on stock market prices around the world. And, by depressing consumer spending, it also affected such things as the volume of U.S. imports and the number of jobs available in those nations with industries dependent on exports to this country.

Economic factors have an impact on many other aspects of social life. Communities have to respond to issues of poverty, homelessness, and crime. Families are affected when both parents work in order to maintain the family's economic base. Rural residents of economically depressed areas move to locations where they hope job opportunities will be better. This reduces the tax base of the communities they leave and may at the same time strain the roads, housing stock, and schools of the communities to which they move. Citizens of societies experiencing economic or political problems emigrate—sometimes illegally—to new societies where they may experience—and their presence may aggravate—cultural conflicts, housing shortages, or unemployment.

In an increasingly interdependent world, national responses to such changes may lead to further change. In 1986, the United States enacted legislation designed to limit the number of immigrants and control the influx of illegal aliens. Mexico renegotiated trade agreements with the United States in 1987 and 1989 to bolster its economy, while many developing nations constantly re-negotiate loans with major banks (one, Citibank in New York, posted a sub-stantial loss as a result).

Immigrants are especially vulnerable to dislocation as a result of changes in their social environment. In response to economic stress, the most employable members of a family may emigrate to other societies in the hope of eventually earning enough money to reunite the family. Often, however, immigrants are refused permission to become citizens of the new society, and are instead al-lowed to stay only temporarily to meet short-term employment needs. Turkish and Finnish workers who have emigrated to Sweden have experienced pre-cisely this type of difficulty as have Mexicans in the United States. People who try to immigrate illegally risk their lives. Recently, a group of Mexicans at-tempting to enter the United States died when they were locked in a railroad car without adequate food, water, and ventilation by people they had paid to smuggle them across the border.

Immigration, one of the most common responses to changes in the social environment, itself creates both problems and opportunities. Members of im-migrant groups are encouraged to become educated and to work in the schools, social agencies, and businesses that serve their compatriots. Women from these populations are usually able to enter the workforce, although often in part-time and low-paid positions. Some communities have become econom-ically stronger as a result of immigration, while others have become more eth-nically diverse. Multinational corporations have brought jobs to nations strug-gling to meet the needs of their workforce, although sometimes under exploitative conditions. As always, change and the responses it generates cre-ate both problems and opportunities for people and societies.

Making Choices

So far in this chapter we have examined two sources of social welfare: needs based on genetic inheritance, and needs created by changes in the physical and social environments. Now we are ready to turn to the third and final source of social welfare, which is the choices people make.

Everyone begins with access to certain resources in the form of their in-herited abilities and the opportunities afforded by their environment. Some-times these resources are used very skillfully to meet needs. Sometimes they are not. There are, of course, many reasons for this including the limiting effects of genetic characteristics and environmental constraints. People's choices, therefore, are not made independently of the other factors we have discussed, but rather are closely related. Thus we can see once again how the biological, psychological, and social components of human behavior inter-act. Now let's look in more detail at three types of choices that people must make.

THE HUMAN FACE OF SOCIAL WELFARE 4

Social Change Through the Eyes of Immigrants

Due largely to immigration since 1965, 1,675,000 foreign-born residents in New York City were counted in the 1980 census; adding an estimated 450,000 to 550,000 illegal aliens, the city's foreign-born population approaches the 1930 record of 2,359,000. Nearly one in three New Yorkers, counting the illegal aliens, is an immigrant. Put another way, there are now more foreign-born residents in New York than total residents in Warsaw, Manila, Budapest or Philadelphia.

The greatest number of new immigrants come from the Caribbean, Latin America, and Southeast Asia....

[The] appeal of New York to its newcomers [is] economic opportunity and the chance to educate their children for a better life. Such attractions draw the middle class as much as the impoverished; the city's post-1965 immigrants are arriving with more skills and more education than did their predecessors in the 1880–1924 period....

New York means backbreaking and demeaning work for many newcomers. In the garment factories of Chinatown, where the average annual wage is $6,000, women hunch over sewing machines in the glare of fluorescent lamps. Some of the women's husbands work in restaurants hours outside New York, seeing their families only one day a week. Many immigrants who held professional jobs in their homeland must settle for menial labor here because they do not speak English or because their foreign credentials are not accepted....

Yet most of the immigrants sacrifice willingly, hoping someday to regain a position of stature or to give New York's opportunities to their children. It is almost impossible for a native-born American to appreciate the appeal of this country, this city, to foreigners....

Emigrating to a new society entails many changes. Old cultural patterns are replaced or supplemented with new ones. Personal and family goals are rethought and expanded to take advantage of new opportunities, but are sometimes prematurely dashed by unanticipated problems and failures.

The impact of the changes associated with immigration on the immigrants themselves and their families varies greatly. Some people thrive, others retreat into despair. Unaccustomed stresses may drive families apart or weld them together. Communities that provide homes to immigrants of many different cultural backgrounds may experience intergroup conflict and economic problems. The workplace is affected by the influx of new employees who may displace existing workers or alter working conditions or wage scales.

Such wide-ranging issues must be addressed by the social welfare system. The impact of immigration on individuals, their families, and the affected communities and workplaces is an excellent example of a complex set of related problems that not only require the attention of the social welfare system but a holistic approach to the delivery of services.

From Samuel Freedman, The new New Yorkers, *The New York Times Magazine,* November 3, 1985, p. 24ff. Copyright © 1985 by The New York Times Company. Reprinted by permission.

Using Available Resources   People do not always use the resources available to them. All of us know youngsters who are bright and capable but seem not to be able to mobilize their talents. Similarly, when we examine the social welfare system, we find many people who do not know what programs exist nor how to gain access to them. Were they able to do so, they might be far more successful in meeting their needs.

However, it is important to note that one reason people often do not use resources is because they are blocked from doing so. Lack of an adequate education, for example, makes it far more difficult for those affected to learn about resources or to carry out successfully the daily activities needed to obtain them. Battered women have frequently noted that they become so psychologically depressed and insecure that they do not believe in the existence of any options to their present plight (Fedders and Elliott, 1987). Fear is also a factor in many cases. Illegal aliens often avoid seeking assistance via social welfare programs because they are afraid of being deported.

Avoiding Destructive Behavior People sometimes engage in behavior that is self-destructive or that injures others. Reckless driving, smoking, abusing alcohol and other drugs, unsafe sex, poor eating habits, using violence to try and solve problems, and similar behavior are all likely to create more needs than they solve. Once destructive patterns are learned they become self-reinforcing and are difficult to change. Breaking destructive behavior patterns is itself a need for some people. Finding ways to successfully avoid destructive behavior not only helps the individual. By eliminating a source of problems for others, it also helps those affected by the individual's destructive behavior and thus society.

Planning Most people try to meet their needs. However, planning to meet needs has both a long- and a short-range component. Education is a good example. It not only meets immediate needs for knowledge and personal growth, but it also lays the foundation for more advanced studies and provides access to desirable jobs. Many students attend school on a daily basis, yet fail to perceive the connections between this behavior and the larger context of educational, career, and lifestyle planning.

Long-range planning is often difficult to do. The impact of what one does today on one's future ability to meet needs is not always clear. Moreover, meeting one's daily needs today may require so much energy that there is little time or inclination to think about the future. Many people never have enough stability and security in their lives to believe that long-range planning is even possible, let alone to carry it out. Young people, especially members of minority groups, who face bleak employment prospects may find it difficult to plan for the future. Advanced education, a family, a rewarding career, and preretirement planning are likely to seem like only vaguely attainable goals. Yet without planning, need meeting may remain episodic and frequently ineffective.

Although most people are successful in meeting the majority of their needs, many are unable to do so at one time or another. As we have seen, there are several reasons why this is so. Biological factors can limit people's ability to meet their needs, or may create special needs that are especially difficult to fulfill. The environment can create physical or social obstacles that make need attainment problematic, or that generate additional needs. As people grow and develop emotionally and cognitively their perception of needs and acceptable need meeting strategies changes. And, finally, people don't always use resources effectively, sometimes making choices that create additional needs instead of moving toward need fulfillment.

All of this is to explain why people need help. To be sure, the need for help is sometimes the result of poor choices. However, we have seen that the complex interplay of biological, psychological, and environmental forces puts many people in positions where their ability to meet their own needs is very limited. Neither people nor the conditions under which they live are perfect.

With this as background, we are ready to focus on society's responses to people's needs. We will see first that society has its own needs for structure and order. As a result, society's task becomes one of enabling people to meet their *individual* needs while at the same time working toward the attainment of *societal* needs. This reminds us yet again of the holistic nature of human life. We will also see how social welfare must fit into a larger network of societal efforts to organize people's behaviors so that the needs of everyone are more or less met simultaneously. We will return to this topic later in this book.

HUMAN NEEDS AND SOCIETAL RESPONSES

The organization of social life for the most part facilitates people's efforts to meet their personal needs. Social institutions such as the family, schools, organized religions, and the economic and political systems function together to provide the resources that people need. Social welfare, as we will see in this section, attempts to support and supplement the efforts of these other social structures.

Our expectations concerning differences in human needs at different life span stages influence the type of resources society attempts to provide. Public schools, and a curriculum that focuses on their developmental needs, are provided for children. Young adults who have children can usually expect to receive child care and some financial assistance from their parents and other relatives. The elderly often have resources to help them remain active and socially involved, such as senior citizen centers, church programs, reduced admissions fees at museums and theaters, and the availability of college courses at little or no cost. These are examples of how social structures are organized so as to simultaneously promote orderly patterns of behavior and meet the needs of individuals and of society itself.

The Usefulness of Social Order

Social order, *the maintenance of predictable patterns of behavior,* makes it possible for people to live together. Society is essentially an agreement among its members to follow certain rules (Cuzzort and King, 1976:31–36). If that agreement breaks down, organized behavior becomes impossible and society disintegrates into a series of unplanned interactions among individuals and groups.

This type of disorganization makes it far more difficult for most people to meet their needs.

The agreements that support society are pervasive. Even social competition and conflict involve agreement upon a basic set of rules. Airlines compete with each other for passengers, but all are subject to a variety of governmentally imposed safety regulations. Similarly, in the political arena, there are certain rules of fair play that govern conflicts between political parties.

Society employs two major techniques to maintain the social order. We will look briefly at each.

Consensus

Ideally, societies would operate by consensus. If everyone shared the same goals, beliefs, and values, patterns of interaction would be stable. This is often the case in preindustrial societies where there is little differentiation among people so that they tend to act and think alike (Federico and Schwartz, 1983:12). Consensus also can occur in large industrial societies, but it is far less likely in such settings because of the social fragmentation and specialization—in terms of vocation, lifestyle, ethnic and cultural background, and education, to name a few examples—that characterize such societies.

A recent study of American society illustrates the difficulty of attaining consensus in a society such as our own. In *Habits of the Heart,* the authors examined why many Americans find it increasingly difficult to feel close to other family members, their neighbors, and their fellow citizens (Bellah et al., 1985). They conclude that such diverse factors as the growing number of two-wage-earner families—itself the result of economic pressures—geographic mobility, the weakening of traditional family patterns, and an increasing desire for personal gratification all contribute to a sense of estrangement or isolation from others. In such a society, consensus cannot be relied on as the only basis for social order.

Social Control

Of the various strategies used by societies to discourage people from disrupting established behavior patterns, the most common and effective is **socialization,** *teaching people appropriate behavior.* Most socialization occurs during infancy and childhood when behavior patterns and social expectations are learned at home and in school. Much learning occurs through observation as children copy the behavior of their parents and peers. Socialization continues throughout the life span, however, although less intensively than during early childhood.

Socialization is effective in most situations for most people. It is an efficient means of controlling behavior because it is built into the operation of many social institutions, especially the family, the school system, and organized religion. Naturally, the diverse cultures in American society socialize their members according to their own distinctive beliefs and behavior patterns. Nevertheless, the values and behaviors imparted are sufficiently similar to contribute to social cohesion.

Other social control mechanisms come into play when established norms of behavior are violated. These range from informal expressions of disapproval (such as a frown), to legal penalties (such as parking tickets), and on to actual physical restraint (such as arrest and imprisonment).

Maintaining order usually contributes to helping people meet their needs. It makes it more likely that they will share reasonably common perspectives on needs and appropriate strategies to attain them. Any form of social control inevitably raises the issue of potential conflicts between the needs of society and the rights of individuals. Socialization limits choice by teaching people that certain forms of behavior are unacceptable and, if pursued, may lead to arrest, imprisonment, or other restraints upon one's physical behavior.

There is always the risk that the dominant groups in society will use their power to oppress other groups, denying them the right to pursue their needs in accordance with their own beliefs. The historical treatment of American Indians and blacks in the United States illustrates this phenomenon only too well, while Jews in Poland and Indians in Mexico have experienced similar treatment. While the maintenance of social order is generally necessary if people are to be able to meet their needs, it can also become a tool of oppression and thus, for at least some members of the society, an obstacle to meeting human needs.

SOCIAL WELFARE'S CONTRIBUTION

As we saw in the last chapter, helping people meet their needs is the primary goal of social welfare. In that sense, society's efforts to promote social functioning and the social welfare system complement one another. Both help people meet their needs.

The social welfare system does this via three methods: (1) reducing obstacles, (2) strengthening people's ability to overcome obstacles, and (3) providing needed resources. We will look at each in more detail below.

Like all the social institutions, social welfare focuses on preserving the existing social order by strengthening the linkages between people and the society in which they live. In most instances, these efforts are beneficial, helping provide most people with access to resources they need to survive and develop—money, education, housing, counseling, and so on. This in turn is usually beneficial for society, for the overall quality of life is enhanced when people function better. In other words, the manifest function—helping individuals—has a latent function—strengthening society.

Difficulties arise when the existing social order hurts people, thus requiring change. For example, black and Hispanic youngsters drop out of school much more often than their white counterparts because of the disadvantaging social and economic conditions under which they live. The reduction or elimination of these conditions requires change at the societal level. In other words, changing society in some way is sometimes one of social welfare's manifest functions. Such efforts will, of course, have the effect (latent function) of helping some individuals.

As you read the rest of this chapter, it is important to remember, therefore, that social welfare may both strengthen the existing social structure *and* work to change it. The immediate needs of people must be met, and doing so often does not necessitate change at the societal level—although it often does require change in smaller social units, such as the family or the workplace. But in other cases individual needs are not being met primarily because of structures or patterns such as discrimination or economic policies that can only be addressed at the societal level. These must be changed if the individuals who are disadvantaged by existing arrangements are to have a better chance to meet their own needs.

Reducing Obstacles

One way that social welfare attempts to help people meet their needs is by reducing the obstacles they face in doing so. Children with physical limitations, for example, are like other children in that they need education to help them develop their intellectual capacity, social skills, and physical abilities. In addition, they need physical therapy, medical care, and environmental modifications to help them overcome the obstacle of their sometimes obvious physical limitations. One of the social welfare system's functions is to provide precisely such assistance.

However, physically limited children may face many other obstacles as well. Their families sometimes have little understanding of their needs or are ashamed of their condition (Konle, 1983:87–95). The family may also be unable to respond to the child's special needs as a result of poverty or discrimination (Wells and Masch, 1986:13–18). In such cases, parental knowledge and values, the structure of the family, and the social conditions that perpetuate the family's poverty are all further obstacles to meeting the child's needs. Efforts to overcome these obstacles are as important as the provision of physical care, education, and modifications to the child's physical environment.

Almost always, reducing obstacles involves change at the individual, environmental, and social levels. A troubled spouse can learn how to modify disruptive behavior, but others who are directly involved—the spouse, children, in-laws, and friends—may also need to learn new behavior patterns in response to the changed behavior. In some cases, marital tension is in part a result of larger societal factors, as when the merger of two companies results in large-scale layoffs and financial anxiety on the part of those directly affected. Unemployment causes problems for individuals, their families, and their communities, and the resulting needs must be addressed at all these levels. And when unemployment results from discrimination or structural factors in the economy, these obstacles too require attention.

THE HUMAN FACE OF SOCIAL WELFARE 5

Going Home to Die

AIDS strikes most often in big cities, but many of...[those who have become ill] have come from small towns like Waseca, a quiet place of 8,000 people in the farm country of southern Minnesota.

Often just out of college, many young people had left for New York or Chicago or San Francisco, ambitious and bursting with notions about life in a glamorous metropolis. For gay men, there loomed all this and more: the promise of tolerance in the city, a chance to live out loud a way of life that had been unspeakable back home....

[Those gay men who have moved to big cities and who become ill with AIDS] most often return to Mom, because her arms are usually open, even as so many doors are slamming shut...[because of their illness in the cities where they have been living].

But [Dean Lechner] did not know how Waseca would greet its native son, back from a life in San Francisco.

In other small towns around the country, he knew, [persons with] AIDS...had been excluded from schools, restaurants, swimming pools. In one case, a house was burned....

[Mr. Lechner knew that he might face hostility when he returned to his hometown. He had when young and it was one of the reasons he had moved away]. The yearbook gave no clue that classmates called him "queer" behind his back or that his car was scrawled with venomous graffiti.

At a school dance, he was hit over the head with a beer bottle. He picked himself off the floor to leave, only to be followed by his tormentors in a car and a pickup truck that tried to run him off the road. At home that night, he closed the garage door and left the car motor running for a time. And he pondered taking his 17-year-old life....

[Fortunately Dean Lechner's family was more tolerant and understanding]...this was a family that knew something about sickness, and about

stigma. In 1948, five years before Mr. Lechner was born, the state Health Department nailed a black and white sign to the family's front door, warning the public to stay away. His brother was stricken with polio.

For six weeks, the family was quarantined. Their groceries were left on the back steps.

His sister, who was then 12 years old, had squared off with the boys who would knock her younger brother down and throw his crutches in the snowdrifts....

[Even so, the family has had to adjust to Mr. Lechner's homosexuality. His mother said] "I have trouble talking about it, even with my minister....But Dean has my support all the way."

He has known that for a long time. Not long after he moved to San Francisco, she had gone to visit him. At the time, he did not know quite how he would explain his way of life.

When she arrived, she saw that he was living with a man in an apartment with one bedroom.

Not a woman at ease with words, she had stammered a bit in trying to explain her feelings. Her son does not remember precisely what she said that day, but the meaning was clear: "You are my son, and I love you"....

[After he had moved back to his hometown, Dean Lechner attended his high school reunion.] At the reunion, Mr. Lechner saw the faces of those who had tormented him in high school. One by one, they came to him and apologized.

Mr. Lechner accepted each apology with a handshake. And later, he turned to...[a] woman who had [earlier] warned him not to come [to the reunion]. He raised a glass of champagne and said, "I understand."

She turned and walked away.

———

This account of the experiences of a gay man with AIDS illustrates how helping individuals may entail social action. Among Dean Lechner's needs are medical care, financial assistance (since he can no longer work), and counseling for himself and his family, all of which are customarily available through the social welfare system.

People like Dean Lechner have other needs, however, needs that can only be addressed by social change. The social discrimination against gays that drives gay men like Dean Lechner to leave their families and their hometowns often leaves them socially isolated, financially vulnerable, and exposed to drugs and unsafe sex practices. Enduring the pain and humiliation of harassment by peers increases their risk of mental illness, low self-esteem, and suicide. It also subjects them to other forms of physical harm (as when Dean Lechner's car was forced off the road or when he was attacked with a beer bottle). It is social welfare's unique role to help people meet their needs by focusing directly on those immediate needs and the social conditions that have created them.

From Dirk Johnson, Coming home, with AIDS, to a small town, *The New York Times,* November 2, 1987, pp. A1ff. Copyright © 1987 by The New York Times Company. Reprinted by permission.

You are probably thinking that there is a big difference between trying to change an individual's behavior and trying to change structural factors in the economy—and you are correct. We will see in later chapters that social welfare agencies and providers tend to specialize, with some focusing on the needs of individuals and others addressing larger issues. However, even given this specialization it is important for all social welfare workers to understand the relationship between individual needs and larger social processes. Only then can they hope to identify and bring to bear on a particular problem the entire range of appropriate services, thus dealing with the problem in a holistic way.

Strengthening People

Another strategy for helping people is to improve their ability to meet their own needs and overcome obstacles. Again, this is part of a two-pronged effort: helping the individual while at the same time reducing obstacles.

Often people lack either information or confidence in their own abilities. They may not know that potentially useful services exist, nor how to obtain them. They may doubt their ability to solve problems, or feel that no one cares whether they do. Thus, some social welfare services are specifically designed to deal with such problems by providing information and strengthening people's ability to act on their own behalf, assuming, of course, that the person involved is psychologically healthy. If not, then the psychological dysfunction becomes an obstacle to be reduced, as discussed above.

It may seem odd that people need help in order to mobilize their own resources, but this is surprisingly common. The society in which we live is very complex, and at times even overwhelming. This is especially so for people with little education, limited intellectual capacity, who have been deprived or abused, who are members of immigrant or minority groups, and who lack experience dealing with large-scale social structures. Such everyday activities as voting, enrolling a child in school, using the emergency room of a hospital, taking public transportation, and knowing how to deal with physical or emotional crises confuse and intimidate many people.

In order to be able to obtain and use information, and to make use of available resources, people need a sense of entitlement and a willingness to advocate for themselves. One objective of many social welfare programs, therefore, is to empower people to develop the skills needed to manage their own lives. This involves education, learning how to use organizations, and knowing one's rights. Developing better interpersonal skills is also important. As these abilities grow, people feel less helpless when confronted by an obstacle or problem. They become more effective advocates of their own needs, and more effective participants within their own family, their community, their place of work, or their society. Once again the importance of the interaction between individual and social functioning is clear.

Providing Resources

The most common conception of how social welfare helps people meet their needs is by providing needed resources, and this is indeed an important function. Social welfare provides money, food, housing, clothing, medical care, counseling, emotional support, legal aid, physical protection, and many other resources for people who need them. In later chapters we will look at some of the specific programs that provide such services.

Here too, though, there is a need for action at both the individual and social levels. Social welfare agencies provide unemployment insurance to individuals out of work. But they also attempt to increase the number of jobs available by influencing the economic decisions of communities, corporations, and the government. Agencies seek simultaneously to make more nursing home beds available while lobbying on behalf of a more coherent policy of care for the elderly that will enable more of them to remain in the community. Premature infants of teenage mothers receive the special medical care they need while community programs are developed to reduce teen pregnancy.

For whom, then, does social welfare provide resources? As you would expect, resources are provided for individuals (a social security check) but also for families (housing), corporations (alcoholism counseling for employees), communities (senior citizen centers), and society (a healthy and educated population). Everyone benefits from social welfare because everyone has needs that social welfare helps meet. These needs exist at many levels, and resources must, therefore, be provided at each level as appropriate, beginning with the individual and extending upward to the society as a whole.

THE "GLUE" OF SOCIAL WELFARE

By now you should be able to understand social welfare as a type of social glue. It helps to make whole broken people, broken relationships between people, and broken bonds between people and the social organizations in which they live. It does so by a combination of strengthening people and organizations, reducing obstacles, and providing resources.

This effort gives rise to some interesting manifest and latent functions. At the most obvious level, social welfare performs the manifest function of helping people observe prevailing standards of what is right and decent. This meets society's need for social order and, ideally, the person's need for a satisfying life.

At the same time, there are inequities built into the social order. Thus, as Piven and Cloward and others have pointed out, by helping to maintain the existing order, social welfare actually functions to perpetuate inequality (Piven and Cloward, 1971; Ryan, 1976). For example, in 1988 the average monthly social security payment to disabled workers was $508, (Disability, 1988:13) while in 1984 the average monthly payment to a single-parent family receiving AFDC in Oklahoma was $259 (Statistical Abstracts, 1987:365). Such payments are insufficient for survival, let alone to help those who depend on them out of poverty. Essentially, these social welfare programs function to "glue" recipients into their existing places in society.

On the other hand, some social welfare services generate change. Legal Aid allows people to fight for their rights, and to challenge laws and behaviors that perpetuate inequality. Education makes it possible for people to grow and use their abilities to take advantage of opportunities. Teaching people how to be advocates for their own interests allows them to improve their lives. Providing shelter and protection for abused and exploited people gives them an option so that they don't have to be victimized. This is a different kind of "glue." It bonds people together through common purpose—seeking a decent life and equal opportunity for all.

In an important way, then, social welfare becomes a crucible for change. By confronting the questions of who should be helped, how, and by whom—the fundamental questions of social welfare—society is pushed into more clearly identifying its goals and the means to attain them. Different groups in society compete to have their needs and preferred strategies for meeting those needs included in the dialogue. As long as this competition is conducted within the society's generally accepted rules, social order is likely to be maintained.

The importance of this dual focus on meeting people's immediate needs and enabling them to participate in planned change efforts is highlighted by an unusual event that occurred recently in West Germany. On November 12, 1987 an unemployed and homeless East German refugee set fire to the Frankfurt Opera House (*The New York Times,* 1987). The damage was estimated at $2.1 million, and officials estimated that it would take 2 or 3 years to repair. The 26-year-old man who set the fire said he had entered the building through an open window during the night looking for food. When he did not find any, he started the fire. People who are as desperate and alienated as this man are a threat to the social order.

On the other hand, efforts to more adequately meet the needs of refugees often require basic social change in societies that have large refugee populations, including the United States. Social welfare helps *people* survive on a day-to-day basis while also trying to help *society* make the changes needed so that all people can not only survive but thrive on their own. It is not too much to say that, in the long run, the survival of society depends in large part on the success of social welfare's efforts.

LET'S REVIEW

This chapter has sought to explain why social welfare is needed. People have common human needs because they require certain basic resources for their biological, psychological, and social development. These needs are linked to life span stages, and are expressed and fulfilled differently by members of different groups.

The social institutions of society seek to enable people to function effectively. However, it is the unique role of the social welfare institution to focus exclusively on this task. It does so in three ways: by reducing obstacles to effective functioning and need meeting, by strengthening people so that they can better meet their own needs, and by providing resources that are otherwise lacking. In carrying out these tasks, social welfare works both to preserve the social order and facilitate planned change.

Now that you understand why social welfare is needed, it should come as no surprise that the roots of social welfare go back into antiquity. However, the help provided and the manner in which it has been provided have changed considerably over the years. In the next two chapters we will look at some of these changes, showing how they have had an impact on our current thinking about social welfare.

CHAPTER OUTLINE

STUDY QUESTIONS

1 Think about your own needs for a moment. At this time in your life, what do you think are your more important physical, emotional, and social needs? List each need and describe its importance in your life in a sentence or two.

2 Research Mexican-Americans in your library, seeking the help of the reference librarian if necessary. Find out as much as you can about their lifestyles, income levels, special health problems, and the types of discrimination, if any, they have encountered in the United States. On the basis of your research, list the biological, psychological, and social needs that you would expect most Mexican-Americans to have. Then attempt to identify the available resources for dealing with each of these needs, including at least one available from within the group, and one available from within the larger United States society.

3 Review Dean Lechner's story (The Human Face of Social Welfare 5) in this chapter. List his physical, psychological, and social needs as an adult gay man with AIDS. If necessary, do supplemental reading on homosexuality and AIDS. (A good place to start is the section on homosexuality in *The Encyclopedia of Social Work,* 18th edition.)

4 Social welfare is controversial both because it helps to maintain the social order and because it encourages planned change. Some people think that disadvantaged groups should be encouraged to rebel rather than to accept their current lives. Others believe that change is unnecessary and that people should be grateful for what they get. What do you think? In your opinion, what should be the role of social welfare in helping people meet their needs?

5 Select a story from a newspaper or a news magazine (like *Newsweek,* for example) that discusses a situation in which people are in need. Identify the needs, remembering that these can be experienced by individuals, groups, organizations, or society as a whole. Then identify the kinds of social welfare services that you think would be needed to solve these problems. Try to identify services that would do one or more of the following: eliminate obstacles to need meeting, strengthen people's ability to meet their needs, or provide needed resources.

6 In this chapter we have talked a lot about needs. You now have a *cognitive framework* to use in identifying types of needs and responses to them. However, people also usually have *feelings* about needs. What are yours? To what degree do you think

people should be responsible for meeting their own needs? How many people, in your opinion, are freeloading off of society rather than helping themselves? How strict should the social welfare system be when providing help to people? In this exercise don't worry too much about justifying your ideas. Just try to honestly think about these issues in ways that make sense to you. Share your ideas with your classmates and discuss any differences that emerge.

KEY TERMS AND CONCEPTS

biopsychosocial whole
common human needs
human diversity
life span

life-span stages
socialization
social order

SUGGESTED READINGS

Clausen, John. 1986. *The Life Course.* Englewood Cliffs, N.J.: Prentice-Hall. An excellent and concise overview of the life span and life-span stages. Systematically looks at the biological, psychological, and social needs of people at each point in the life span.

Devore, Wynetta, and Elfriede G. Schlesinger. 1987. *Ethnic-Sensitive Social Work Practice,* 2d ed. Columbus, Ohio: Merrill Publishing Company. This book provides a clear analysis of the impact of human diversity on people's needs and discusses the implications of diversity for the delivery of social welfare services.

Hellman, Judith Adler. 1983. *Mexico in Crisis,* 2d ed. New York: Holmes and Meier Publishers. The interaction between individual, family, and community needs and society's efforts to maintain a social order is well portrayed in this study, as is the impact of political and economic variables on efforts to provide social welfare services.

Moon, J. Donald, ed. 1988. *Responsibility, Rights, and Welfare.* Boulder, Colo.: Westview Press. This book examines three aspects of social welfare: the reasons for its existence, its origins, and the right to be helped. It provides a thoughtful and in-depth analysis of why social welfare is needed by individuals and society.

Towle, Charlotte. 1965. *Common Human Needs,* rev. ed. Silver Spring, Md.: National Association of Social Workers. This classic work examines people's needs and the responsibility of society and the social welfare professions to meet them. A caring and powerful book that argues on behalf of fundamental human values.

REFERENCES

Arson at the Frankfurt opera. 1987. *The New York Times,* November 13, A9.

Bellah, Robert, et al. 1985. *Habits of the Heart.* Berkeley, Calif.: University of California Press.

Berger, Raymond. 1987. Homosexuality: Gay men. In *Encyclopedia of Social Work,* 18th ed., vol. 1. Silver Spring, Md.: National Association of Social Workers, pp. 795–804.

Berger, Robert, and Ronald Federico. 1985. *Human Behavior,* 2d ed. White Plains, N. Y.: Longman, Inc.

Clausen, John. 1986. *The Life Course.* Englewood Cliffs, N.J.: Prentice-Hall.

Cuzzort, R. P., and E. W. King. 1976. *Humanity and Modern Sociological Thought.* Hinsdale, Ill.: Dryden Press.

Dane, Elizabeth. 1985. Professional and lay advocacy in the education of handicapped children. *Social Work,* 30, no. 6 (November/December).

Devore, Wynetta, and Elfriede G. Schlesinger. 1987. *Ethnic-Sensitive Social Work Practice,* 2d ed. Columbus, Ohio: Merrill Publishing Company.

Disability (1988). Brochure published by the Social Security Administration, Publication No. 05-10029 (January).

Fedders, Charlotte, with Laura Elliott. 1987. *Shattered Dreams.* New York: Harper & Row.

Federico, Ronald, and Janet Schwartz. 1983. *Sociology,* 3d ed. New York: Random House.

Finkelhor, David. 1983. Common features of family abuse. In *The Dark Side of Families,* eds. David Finkelhor et al. Beverly Hills, Calif.: Sage Publications Inc., pp. 17–28.

Hellman, Judith Adler. 1983. *Mexico in Crisis,* 2d ed. New York: Holmes and Meier Publishers.

Herbers, John. 1987. Black poverty spreads in 50 biggest U.S. cities. *The New York Times,* January 26, A27.

Herrenkohl, Ellen, with Roy Herrenkohl and Lori Toedter. 1983. Perspectives on the intergenerational transmission of abuse. In *The Dark Side of Families,* eds. David Finkelhor et al. Beverly Hills, Calif.: Sage Publications Inc., pp. 305–316.

Johnson, Dirk. 1987. Coming home, with AIDS, to a small town. *The New York Times,* November 2, A1ff.

Konle, Carolyn. 1983. *Social Work Day-to-Day.* White Plains, New York: Longman, Inc.

Maslow, Abraham. 1970. *Motivation and Personality.* New York: Harper & Row.

Moon, J. Donald, ed. 1988. *Responsibility, Rights, and Welfare.* Boulder, Colo.: Westview Press.

National Association of Social Workers. 1987. Public service drive to hit child poverty. *NASW News,* January.

Perlman, Helen Harris. 1957. *Social Casework.* Chicago: University of Chicago Press.

Piven, Francis, and Richard Cloward. 1971. *Regulating the Poor.* New York: Vintage Books.

Rosen, Sumner, et al., eds. 1987. *Face of the Nation 1987.* Silver Spring, Md.: National Association of Social Workers.

Ryan, William. 1976. *Blaming the Victim.* New York: Vintage Books.

Slater, Mary, and Lynn Wikler. 1986. ''Normalized'' family resources for families with a developmentally disabled child. *Social Work,* 31, no. 5 (September/October).

Straus, Murray. 1983. Ordinary violence, child abuse, and wife-beating: What do they have in common? In *The Dark Side of Families,* eds. David Finkelhor et al. Beverly Hills, Calif.: Sage Publications Inc., pp. 213–234.

Towle, Charlotte. 1965. *Common Human Needs,* rev. ed. Silver Spring, Maryland: National Association of Social Workers.

U.S. Department of Commerce. Bureau of the Census. 1986. *Statistical Abstract of the United States 1986.* Washington, D.C.: U.S. Government Printing Office.

Wells, Carolyn C., and M. Kathleen Masch. 1986. *Social Work Ethics Day to Day.* White Plains, N. Y.: Longman, Inc.

CHAPTER 3

WHAT ARE THE HISTORICAL FOUNDATIONS OF SOCIAL WELFARE?

WHAT TO EXPECT FROM THIS CHAPTER

This chapter examines the historical development of social welfare. The approach is thematic in that the chapter focuses on four major historical themes that have shaped our thinking about social welfare and its structure. These are: (1) developing a sense of responsibility for others; (2) the evolution of helping roles; (3) the intellectual traditions that have shaped ideas about social welfare; and (4) categorizing the needy and appropriate responses to the needs of each group. A section of the chapter is devoted to each of these four themes, and the discussion within each section is organized chronologically. In each case, the objective is to examine the influence of the theme involved on the development of social welfare.

Chapter 4 will continue our historical view by focusing on some of the major events that have had an enduring impact on social welfare. Taken together, Chapters 3 and 4 will give you a sense of the thinking, the people, and the events that have helped to shape contemporary views of social welfare.

The primary goal of this chapter is to expose you to the major ideas that have shaped the western world's thinking about social welfare. This is an important task because those same ideas continue to influence contemporary social welfare. At the end of the chapter you should have a better understanding of the intellectual origins of our current social welfare system. This, combined with Chapter 4's discussion of specific events that have shaped social welfare, will give you an appreciation for the interplay of ideas and events as a shaping force in human life.

LEARNING OBJECTIVES

At the end of this chapter you should be able to do the following:

1 Describe how the genetic structure of human beings provides a basis for social welfare.

2 List at least three social units that promote the development of a sense of responsibility for helping others.

3 Distinguish between formal and informal helpers, describing how they function independently and cooperatively.

4 List and describe at least three intellectual approaches that have had a major impact on social welfare.

5 Identify one example of how each of the three intellectual approaches listed in the previous objective has influenced social welfare.

6 List and define three categories used to differentiate among the needy in the Elizabethan Poor Law of 1601.

7 List and describe the types of services provided under the Elizabethan Poor Law for the needy in each of the three categories listed above.

8 List at least two more recent methods of allocating social welfare resources to people.

9 Describe in your own words how social welfare in the United States has changed from 1700 to today.

10 Briefly summarize the relationship between the themes identified in the chapter and the historical development of social welfare.

ENDURING THEMES IN THE ORGANIZATION OF SOCIAL WELFARE

The four themes discussed in this chapter have had an enduring influence on the organization of social welfare. Our concern here is with the historical development of that influence up to the present day. As we examine the first of our major themes, the development of a sense of responsibility for helping others, we will trace its origins to four sources: family and kin, relationships between the wealthy and their dependents, religion, and the community.

DEVELOPING A SENSE OF RESPONSIBILITY FOR HELPING OTHERS

Family and Kin

Our first sense of responsibility for others often derives from our family experience. The development and persistence of the human family is deeply rooted in a sense of responsibility toward biologically related others who require our assistance. As we have already noted, infants and children require the assistance of others. Before they can function independently, they must learn many things and perfect the skills necessary to survival. Without physical care, human infants will die, and without nurturing and social stimulation, their psychological and social potential will not be realized.

At birth, the human infant has traditionally been linked most directly to its biological parents, receiving food—in the form of milk—from its mother, and warmth, nurturing, and protection from its two parents, mother and father. In the structure of the traditional family unit, then—mother, father, and children—and all of its more contemporary variations, lies one of the fundamental sources for the development of a sense of responsibility for others.

Thinking about the family as we do today, it may seem a limited base for developing a sense of responsibility for helping others. However, during most of human history the family was a much larger unit. In a society in which birth control methods are unknown or considered undesirable, large families are far more common than in the contemporary United States. Such a family is economically desirable in a predominantly agricultural society because it provides the labor necessary to the survival of the family unit. In such a society, family members of almost all age groups can do something productive—gather roots and berries, plant and harvest, hunt, make clothes, cook, or care for children.

Moreover, the structure of the family in traditional societies was often different than that of the nuclear family—consisting of parents and their children—with which we are most familiar. Families in such societies were extended families, consisting of grandparents, parents, children, and other kin, all of whom often lived together or nearby. These extended family units provided large numbers of people who felt some degree of responsibility for each other, and who cooperated in meeting daily needs.

When kin-based groups have inhabited a geographical region for a long time, they take on the characteristics of a community. They feel bonds toward each other and often share common beliefs, behavior patterns, and even a distinctive language. American Indian tribes in the United States are examples, but so are ethnic neighborhoods in urban communities. These can be seen as larger units of shared responsibility that extend the notion of kin to those who share ethnic and cultural characteristics. Thus, through the biologically based bond of the parent-child relationship as extended through larger family, kin,

and ethnic networks, we find an important basis for a shared sense of responsibility for helping others.

Relationships Between the Wealthy and Their Dependents

As Robert Morris has shown, reciprocity and exchange as a basis for helping
strangers can be traced back at least as far as ancient Greece (Morris, 1986:86–
99). When travel was hazardous and life in general was uncertain, aid was extended in part because the giver could imagine being in a similar situation,
knowing that life itself might easily depend on being helped by a stranger.

So too reciprocity and exchange also came to provide a basis for help extended by the wealthy to those on whom they depended and who were dependent in return, especially servants and workers. Landowners and others who
depended on the efforts of their workers and slaves came to recognize that
meeting the basic needs of these individuals was a basic responsibility, albeit
one often rooted in self-interest, including the pursuit of political support.

The Influence of Religion and the Church

The intellectual roots of charity in the western world can be traced back to the
writings of early humanists such as Cicero and Seneca in ancient Rome. However, prescriptions about helping others were also formalized in early western
religious writings. For example, Keith-Lucas (1972:140–141) notes that certain
basic ideas derived from the Judeo-Christian tradition expanded the responsibility for helping to include all humanity. These include a belief in: (1) the fal-
libility (weakness) of humans; (2) a responsibility to serve God by serving people; (3) the inadequacy of people's ability to judge their fellow humans; and (4)
the supremacy of love over force.

Religious beliefs about responsibility for others were important in two
ways. First, they greatly expanded the group for whom responsibility was felt.
In many faiths, this group theoretically included all humankind, although reality often limited the effective scope to members of the same religious group.
Nevertheless, the sense of responsibility went far beyond family and kin
(Klein, 1968). Second, these beliefs led many religious groups to provide social
welfare services. Churches and monasteries dispensed food, clothing, shelter,
and even money to those in need. Convents and monasteries protected the
poor and the orphaned, and provided a vehicle for wealthy people who sought
opportunities to serve others. We will see later in this chapter that organized
religion continues to provide a wide range of helping services.

The Community

The community emerged as the focus for an expanded sense of responsibility
to help others because it contained many of the groups discussed above—kin,
wealthy people and their dependents, and organized religious groups. The

THE CHARITABLE IMPULSE

Some insight into how religious beliefs have motivated people to perform charitable acts is seen in the following excerpt.

[The] origins [of the obligation to be charitable] may be found in the Old Testament. Toward the poor God demanded both justice—they should be given what they had been deprived of—and compassion—they should be given relief with sympathy. In the subsequent teachings of Christ and his disciples, acts of charity became expressions of the selflessness that was to characterize the brotherhood of humanity under God. The virtues of charity were joined with the necessities of survival. The first Jews and the first Christians were members of weak, impoverished, persecuted sects. Mutual assistance was a vital part of their struggle for existence. Although the Judeo-Christian concept of charity was universalistic and transcendental in character, to be applied to all human relations as evidence of devotion to God, the charitable efforts of Judeo-Christian sects have often reflected the

historical function of providing help to those of the faith. Whether the good works were confined to particular sects or offered to the world at large, the values of charity became cornerstones of the Jewish and Christian religions.*

A full-page ad entitled "Jews Don't Only Help Jews" by the American Jewish World Service gives contemporary expression to the religious basis of efforts to help others (*The New York Times,* December 14, 1987, C24). The ad, which featured a large picture of a starving African, said in part:

As Jews, we have known suffering too deeply, too personally, to turn away from the pain of others.
We do not see a child with eyes wide with need, with limbs shrunk by starvation, and ask the child's faith. We only ask, "How can we help?"

*From Reid, William, and Peter Stimpson. 1987. Sectarian agencies. In *The Encyclopedia of Social Work,* 18th ed. Silver Spring, Md.: National Association of Social Workers, p. 546.

community was especially important in agricultural societies where most people did not move very often. Thus, when England reorganized its helping services in the 1500s, it gave local government (called parishes) a prominent role. Government officials sought to coordinate helping efforts by religious groups and the wealthy so that the needy would be served effectively (Steinberg, 1963:280).

The community's sense of responsibility was enhanced by the effects of the **Industrial Revolution.** *The Industrial Revolution was that period during which machine power replaced human and animal power in the production process.* It began in England in the late 1500s and rapidly grew in importance (Schenk and Schenk, 1981:44). The first large-scale application of industrial technology occurred in England in the wool processing industry. As a result, the wool trade quickly became more profitable than farming. The Industrial Revolution had a dramatic effect on the sources and distribution of wealth in society. Whereas wealth had previously resulted from land ownership, it now became associated with the control and ownership of the means of production, such as machines, factories, and the capital necessary to build them.

The big losers in this shift were wealthy landowners and the church, both of whom had derived much of their power from their land holdings. As their wealth decreased, so did their ability to provide social welfare services. At the same time, the need for social welfare increased as workers were displaced from the land where they had lived and worked, often moving to urban slums where crime and disease were major problems. Despite the difficulties the Industrial Revolution created for individuals, its effects were advantageous for the new industrialists. They needed a mobile workforce which, when clustered in the densely populated areas that sprang up around factories, also provided a large and readily accessible market for the new mass-produced goods.

The newly powerful industrialists in England wanted to destroy regional boundaries built around the large landholdings of powerful aristocrats. Their interests were better served by a more centralized government that made it less difficult to obtain the resources needed for the production process, and easier to market their goods. This ultimately led to the concept of a national government that we take for granted today.

However, another role for the national government also emerged as a result of the Industrial Revolution. Workers had little control over their new living and working conditions, while those to whom they could earlier have turned for help—landowners and the church—were increasingly powerless (Mencher, 1967:27). Thus, it became apparent that the community and later the national government had to assume more responsibility for social welfare (Coll, 1969).

All of these changes resulted in the passage of the **Elizabethan Poor Law of 1601.** *This law created a system of national standards of social welfare that was administered at the parish (local government) level.* The law provided for a land tax to generate funds for social welfare services when private charity was insufficient for this purpose. This was the first such use of public funds. Thus, the Poor Law was the first formal acknowledgement of governmental responsibility for the well-being of citizens.

Today many nations are undergoing their own industrial revolutions. Mexico is an example. Prior to the 1910 Revolution, Mexico was an agricultural society in which the church wielded a great deal of power through its landholdings and its spiritual teachings. Following the Revolution, which was in part a response to the beginnings of industrialization, the government assumed ownership of all land (Hellman, 1983). This effectively weakened the power of previous landowners, including the church. Shortly thereafter, the Constitution of 1917 transferred responsibility for many social welfare functions to the government—including the power to set a minimum wage, to regulate working conditions, and the responsibility to provide compensation for work-related injuries. Subsequent legislation in 1931, 1943, and 1973 further expanded the Mexican public social welfare system (Social Security Programs Throughout the World, 1986:170).

The rise of industrialization has been a stimulus for the passage of social welfare legislation. Two factors help to account for this. One is the economic capacity of industrialized nations to support extensive social welfare programs. The second is the increased vulnerability of the workers, a majority of whom are dependent on wages and live in small family units, often in urban areas. Most western industrial societies passed significant social welfare legislation in the early part of the twentieth century when economic capacity, ev-

TABLE 3.1   SOCIAL WELFARE LEGISLATION IN COMPARATIVE PERSPECTIVE

	Year legislation enacted			
Type of Benefit	Mexico	Poland	Sweden	United States
Retirement insurance				
First offered	1943	1927	1913	1935
Current plan	1973	1982	1962,1976	1984§
Sickness benefit				
First offered	1943	1920‡	1891‡	1965,1972
Current plan	1973	1974	1962	Same¶
Work injury benefit				
First offered	1917	1884	1901	1908,1911
Current plan	1973	1975	1962,1976	by 1920
Unemployment compensation				
First offered	NA*	NA†	1934	1935
Current plan	NA*	NA†	1956,1973	1935

*Mexico has a lump sum compensation for those losing their jobs.
†There is no officially acknowledged unemployment in Poland.
‡Medical care is essentially free in these societies; sickness benefit refers to salary payments while ill.
§Date of the most recent amendment; the 1935 law is still in effect.
¶Sickness benefits are primarily determined by employers.
Source: Social Security Programs Throughout the World-1985. 1986. Washington, D.C.: United States Government Printing Office.

idence of human need, and progressive political ideas converged. Later legislation tended to extend earlier benefits. The dates of the major pieces of social welfare legislation in the four countries discussed in this book are listed in Table 3.1.

We have seen in this section how a sense of responsibility for the well-being of others has developed and expanded over time. Starting with the family, it grew into a gradually widening web of social networks responsible for the needs of their members. These included the family, larger kin-based groups, wealthy people and their dependents, communities, and finally the government. Of these, the family continues to be important, while the charity of the wealthy toward their dependents has been largely replaced by employer benefits. Most important, the government has now become a major source of social welfare services. We will see later why the government's role has become so important.

THE EVOLUTION OF HELPING ROLES

Informal Helping

Evolving as it did out of first the biological and then the social relationships between family and kin members, *helping* has been first and foremost a function performed by people in the course of their everyday activities. Rarely have those involved, be they family members, neighbors, or friends, had spe-

THE HUMAN FACE OF SOCIAL WELFARE 6

The Government and the Workplace

From outside, the building...looked as if it had been abandoned years ago. A layer of grime coated the windows and a rusting metal grate stretched across the store-front. But [the inspector] knew better. He found a battered door on the side and pushed it open.

Inside a small factory buzzed with activity. Along cluttered aisles, dozens of women hovered over sewing machines, chatting in Spanish as they furiously assembled dresses that would later be sold for $80 apiece. Near the entrance, a punch clock read 9:00 AM even though it was only 8:10....

For three months, [the inspector] and seven other members of a new state task force have visited dozens of factories, looking for safety hazards and violations of the labor laws....

Definitions of sweatshops vary....The task force considers them to be factories that "take liberties with every law: safety, minimum wages, child labor, compensation" to "get a competitive edge"....

Unlike legitimate garment businesses, many of which are unionized, sweatshops frequently do not pay their workers the legal minimum wage of $3.35 an hour or overtime after 40 hours of work. The sweatshop owners also do not provide worker's compensation, health insurance or other benefits....

More than 90 percent of the workers [in sweatshops] are women from Asia, the Caribbean, or Latin America....

Potential fire hazards [in one shop] included an inadequate ceiling and blocked exit in the basement, poor ventilation and exposed wires touching fabric....

———

Laws governing the conditions under which people work are an example of government intervention to protect people from some of the dangerous effects of industrialization. Such efforts have expanded over the years to include regulations concerning the number of hours worked, minimum pay scales, and occupational safety. These laws exist because some employers cannot be trusted to assume responsibility for the welfare of their employees, even though, as we have seen, a modern employer's responsibility toward his or her employees is thought by many to be similar to that of the wealthy toward their workers or servants in ancient times.

From Michael Freitag, New York is fighting the spread of sweatshops, *The New York Times,* November 16, 1987, p. A1. Copyright (c) 1987 by The New York Times Company. Reprinted by permission.

---

cial training in helping others. They have simply done what seemed to be needed as best they could.

Within the family, responsibilities for helping have tended to be divided along gender lines. Broadly speaking, and with some notable exceptions, responsibility for child care and other nurturing activities have been assigned to women (Bernard, 1981:38–94). Men have generally been responsible for providing the basic resources needed by family members—food, clothing, shelter—through hunting, fishing, farming, or paid employment in wage-based economies.

Much help has also been provided through religious groups whose representatives—priests, ministers, rabbis, and others—were trained to meet people's spiritual needs. This was a source of great comfort to many who sought solace for life's problems. However, their training was generally limited to the use of prayer as a solution. When concrete services such as food, housing, and schooling were dispensed by the church, those who provided help often had little to guide them beyond their own sense of responsibility and personal experience.

The fact that early helping efforts were carried out by people with no special social welfare training does not mean that it was ineffective. Indeed, help provided by nonprofessional helpers who are motivated by caring about others is still the most common form of assistance. Parents care for children, friends and relatives provide emotional and financial support, priests and ministers offer advice and counsel, and neighbors watch out for one another. Many of people's daily needs are met more effectively by informal helpers than by trained workers.

Formal Helping

The emergence of formally organized social welfare services with trained workers was the result of two developments. The first was the ever-present struggle to translate limited public and private resources into the most help possible. The second development was the rise of modern science. The 1700s and 1800s saw dramatic developments in the physical sciences. The work of Isaac Newton (1642–1727) in physics, Charles Darwin (1809–1882) in biology, and G. J. Mendel (1822–1884) in genetics led to optimism about science's ability to solve social as well as physical problems. This optimism was reinforced by the successful application of scientific knowledge to industrial techniques that made the Industrial Revolution possible.

At the heart of science lies the scientific method, a method advocated by Francis Bacon (1561–1626) and Newton, among others, as the most effective source of accurate knowledge about the world. *The scientific method is the use of empirical data to test hypotheses derived from theory* (Federico and Schwartz, 1983:30–31). The scientific method's logical and systematic approach to problem solving contrasted substantially with earlier views which were derived from humanist theorizing and religious theology. As Lieby expresses it, reformers in the late 1800s "carried forward old ideals of humanitarian reform and social justice, of social progress, but increasingly they aspired to be scientific. By this they meant secular, rational, and empirical as opposed to sectarian, sentimental, and dogmatic" (Lieby, 1978:91).

"Scientific Charity"

The result of this kind of thinking was "scientific charity" or "scientific philanthropy" (Lieby, 1978:114). **Scientific philanthropy** *involved the collection of empirical data concerning each person or family to be helped coupled with efforts to coordinate the help provided by different social agencies within the community.* (Based on Lieby, 1978:114–115.) The goals of scientific philanthropy were to avoid fostering dependency, to reduce cheating, and to prevent the wasteful duplication of services. This new approach was embodied in the work of the **Charity Organization Societies** that originated in London and which were introduced into the United States beginning in 1877.

These societies introduced a number of innovations. People seeking aid were investigated to assess the type and extent of their need. Individualized helping plans were developed based on these assessments. Directories were compiled of all the helping agencies in a community along with a registry of families receiving aid. These last two actions were intended to reduce duplication of helping efforts (Brieland, 1987:740; Lieby, 1978:115–116). Suddenly charity was no longer based simply on the desire to do good. The Charity Organization Societies sought to attain the scientific philanthropy goal of rational, systematic helping.

At first, the people who did investigations for the Charity Organization Societies, called **friendly visitors,** were not given any special training. However, it gradually became clear that serious efforts to understand need and develop useful helping plans required specialized knowledge and skills. This led Mary Richmond (1861–1928), first a worker and later a leader in the Charity Organization Society network, to provide formal training for workers in these agencies (Lieby, 1978:120–122). A summer training program inaugurated in New York in 1898 was converted into a 1-year program in 1904, and to a 2-year program in 1910. Eventually this program became what is now the Columbia University School of Social Work (Columbia University School of Social Work Bulletin, 1987:23). In the process a new profession was born: social work. Growing out of the scientific philanthropy movement, its mission was to develop trained professionals to provide social welfare services to those in need.

Efforts to apply the scientific method to human behavior resulted in the emergence of what we now call the social and behavioral sciences. Two of these, psychology and sociology, have been particularly important to the development of formal helping roles. Community and group approaches to treatment were stimulated by sociology and social psychology, while clinical practice was heavily influenced by the work of Sigmund Freud in the early 1900s. Ongoing developments in these fields continue to be incorporated into the education and training of social welfare professionals in social work and other fields.

The Interaction of Informal and Formal Helping

While the trend toward greater reliance of formal helping is a worldwide phenomenon, there is considerable variation in the proportion of formal to informal assistance. Poland represents an interesting intermediary position in the use of formal and informal helpers (Rosner, 1976:28–31). In Poland, medical and social work personnel often work together in community health centers. While the doctors and community nurses are full-time professionals, the social workers are a combination of trained professionals and volunteers. The volunteer social workers are responsible for assessing needs in their neighborhood and bringing these to the attention of professional workers, who draw up the plans for delivering services. Even the volunteer workers, however, receive some training and have access to the specialized skills of professional social workers, lawyers, psychologists, teachers, and sociologists who also supervise their work.

This system seeks to make maximum use of the informal networks that exist in the workplace and the community. Volunteer social workers carry out their assessments where they work and live. They are familiar with people's needs, and in many instances have the trust of those they help. Training programs provide them with a certain amount of expertise in assessing needs and the resources available. The actual services are then provided by those who do have specialized expertise. We can see in such a system a continuum of assistance ranging from informal help provided by family and friends, to assessments carried out by partially trained volunteers, to service delivery by formally trained professionals.

Poland's system makes maximum use of limited resources and is consistent with the collective approach to social life common to socialist societies (Madison, 1968:107–108). Other societies, especially developing nations whose resources are even more limited, also tend to rely more heavily on informal helping than do the more highly developed western welfare states. These wealthier nations have substantial resources and are willing to devote a goodly share of them to social welfare.

All societies rely on informal helping provided by the family, friendship networks, and the community. In addition, the industrialized societies have developed extensive formal helping networks staffed by social workers, educators, medical personnel, and others. In between are the societies whose resource limitations and values have led them to make maximum use of informal helping as a supplement to their limited formal social welfare goals.

INTELLECTUAL CURRENTS

As we have already seen, social welfare is very much affected by prevailing ideas. An emphasis on helping others has been common to many major religions, for example. Similarly, the rise of science not only led to the Industrial Revolution that altered social life and human needs, but to a scientific approach to solving human problems. Social welfare is influenced by intellectual currents because it is so closely tied to the other institutions of society. Ideas and values that arise in society's other institutional areas inevitably have an impact on thinking about helping. This section will briefly summarize some of the other important intellectual developments in western society that have had a lasting impact on social welfare.

Protestantism

The rise of organized religion and the charitable activities it supported provided a foundation for helping efforts. However, the Roman Catholic Church,

THE HUMAN FACE OF SOCIAL WELFARE 7

The Professional View

Deciding just how far one's responsibility to clients goes and how to coordinate that responsibility with the work of other professionals is often a problem for conscientious [professional] social workers....

Last fall, a young Hispanic worker came to the [out-patient medical] clinic complaining of nausea, stomach pain, and headaches.... [D]octors...at the clinic began to suspect chemicals at...the fabric-coating factory where he worked pouring solvents.

Doctors finally determined that the worker had a noninfectious form of hepatitis. In subsequent weeks, other...workers...complaining of similar symptoms sought treatment at the clinic... [and] tests showed that ten...had the same noninfectious hepatitis, and another 20 of the factory's approximately 50 employees showed liver damage.

[The social worker's] part in the early stages of the response to the outbreak was to provide traditional, direct services to workers and their families, helping them apply for benefits and find other employment....

But she grew concerned with the direction of the follow-up with the stricken workers.

[At the factory] empty chemical drums littered the overgrown, trash-strewn yard. The basement was crowded, poorly ventilated, hot from the ovens, with chemical odors everywhere, making some workers vomit. Workers dipped chemicals from open vats with ladles and did not have protective clothing, gloves, respirators, or training in handling dangerous substances. Some even heated their lunches in the drying ovens.

[Suggestions for improving conditions were made and accepted by the factory. The social worker felt, however] that simply working privately with [the factory] owners was not enough. She told her co-workers that the...workers should be informed of their right to contact federal investigators from the Occupational Safety and Health Administration (OSHA)....

[The social worker also contacted the union representative who] involved OSHA officials, state Department of Environment officials, the state attorney general, the...mayor, the [city] Health Department, the media, and an organization of neighbors who wanted the factory shut down....

Eventually, investigators found [the factory] had violated air-quality standards and hazardous waste laws, allowed improper food storage and consumption, failed to provide adequate protective equipment for workers, and failed to adequately train workers in safety procedures. [The union became active in negotiations with the firm that resulted in substantially improved working conditions.]

[The social worker] feels strongly that the social work skill of advocacy—especially in occupational social work, but in any field where people are at risk—is vital. "Social workers need to understand that without this skill, their efforts may not lead to where they want to go," she said.

In Chapter 1 we saw an example of informal helping: Emma Blake's soup kitchen. Emma is motivated by her own sense of caring, and she does the best she can with the skills she has and the resources she can obtain. Her results are impressive, and testify to the power of informal helping.

The above account demonstrates how professional training prepares people to tackle complex problems that involve multiple systems. First comes direct work with people—counseling, helping clients to obtain financial and medical benefits, and so on. But the professional social worker goes further, identifying environmental problems, making use of the legal system, empowering clients, and working with professional colleagues in other fields. This social worker shares Emma Blake's human concern and desire to help. Both do so effectively. However, the social worker described above has more training and access to more resources than Mrs. Blake, and thus is able to tackle more complex and difficult problems.

From Social worker champions plant workers. Copyright © 1987, National Association of Social Workers, Inc. Reprinted with permission from *NASW News*, October 1987, p. 3.

the dominant western church prior to the Protestant Reformation, also had noncharitable aspects. It gradually developed a powerful and hierarchical structure that was sometimes rigid, authoritarian, corrupt, and intolerant. This led to two intellectual responses.

The first was Martin Luther's (1483–1546) successful theological challenge to the Roman Catholic Church that led to the establishment of Protestantism. Protestants objected to the Catholic doctrine that placed the clergy in the role of intermediary between God and man, arguing instead for a direct relationship between the individual and God, thus eliminating the need for much of the ritual and structure of the Roman Catholic Church. Although Protestants favored charity, they also placed great emphasis on the value of work and, in at least some instances, tended to view economic success as an indication of salvation (Morris, 1986:123).

This association of economic success with personal salvation was especially important to two Protestant groups, Calvinists and Puritans. Often persecuted in Europe because of their unorthodox religious and political views, and their outspoken rejection of many popular forms of pleasure and relaxation, many members of these and other Protestant groups fled to America and established their religious faith here (Macarov, 1978:201–202). Their beliefs helped to create what came to be called the **Protestant ethic,** *the belief, based in Protestant religious values, that work fulfills God's will and that those who do not work are sinners.*

The Protestant ethic was well-suited to a developing nation like the United States. Much hard work was needed to settle and develop the land. Living conditions were not easy and resources were scare. A doctrine that urged people to work, and that provided a rationale for denying aid to those unwilling to do so, was well-suited to the environment. These ideas, combined with the English roots of many of the original settlers, led to the widespread adoption in the colonies of social welfare legislation derived from the Elizabethan Poor Law. The principles embodied in the Poor Law—the emphasis on work and the establishment of categories to determine who should be helped—became the policy of the new nation. In addition, the Protestant work ethic became part of a societal tradition that soon took on a life of its own until it was no longer linked to a particular set of religious beliefs.

The equating of work with salvation was a restraining influence on social welfare. As we will see in the next section, the Elizabethan Poor Law was designed to provide aid only to those whose reason for needing assistance was obviously beyond their control—because they were old and sick, for example. In general, the heavy emphasis on the value and necessity of work that became ingrained in American culture during the early years of the new nation has tended to limit interest in examining the reasons why some people who were obviously in need could not work. Only in relatively recent decades have we begun to amass empirical knowledge about the relationship between parenting responsibilities, single parenthood, emotional health, educational background, and the functioning of the economy and people's ability to seek and maintain employment. The proper balance between work and social welfare remains a major issue in the United States today—an issue we shall explore further in later chapters.

Humanism

The second intellectual reaction against Roman Catholicism was humanism. Humanist philosophers disputed the literal interpretation of the Bible and advocated a more just and equal world based on reason rather than church teachings. Two of the more influential of these were the English philosopher, John Locke (1632–1704), and Jean Jacques Rousseau (1712–1778) of France. Locke, Rousseau, and others argued that society was based on a "social contract," an implicit agreement to establish a form of government and a social structure designed to serve the common needs of all members of society. Such an argument challenged the unbridled power of the aristocracy and the church by asserting the equality of all human beings and the obligation of the leaders of society to protect and enhance the lives of the common people (Locke, 1690; Rousseau, 1762). The views of the "contract philosophers" played an important role in the great democratic revolutions in France and the United States in the 18th century, and reinforced the belief that government has an obligation to help its citizens.

The humanists had a dual impact on social welfare. First, their thinking was inherently supportive of the idea of helping. The concept that government had an obligation to provide help laid the foundation for what we now call welfare states. The humanist analysis of the social causes of human need provided a basis for aid that to some extent countered the Protestant ethic's emphasis on work and self-reliance. Both humanism and the Protestant ethic have become part of the intellectual tradition of modern western society. Much of the controversy over social welfare that is discussed in later chapters, especially Chapter 8, reflects these dual and inconsistent parts of our culture.

The second way in which humanism influenced social welfare was by laying the groundwork for what we now call *scientific thinking*. As long as church doctrine could not be questioned, it was impossible for people to promote ideas, even those based on empirical analysis, that contradicted the teachings of the church. Galileo's views concerning the nature of the solar system, which directly challenged church-approved doctrine, were condemned by church officials, and he was prevented from continuing his research (Redondi, 1987). Through their advocacy of empirical study, humanists made possible the scientific study of human and social life. As we will see shortly, this had a powerful impact on social welfare.

Applications of the Scientific Method

With the new scientific approach to the study of social life came several developments that proved to be especially significant for social welfare. The first of these came in the new field of economics, where the Scottish social philosopher, Adam Smith (1723–1790), advanced the idea that the most efficient and productive system was one based on the principles of **laissez faire,** *the least possible intervention of the government into economic activities* (Smith, 1776). Smith's views, which in due course became the cornerstone of classical economics, were highly compatible with the Protestant ethic. Both placed a great emphasis on the value of work and economic success.

The work of Robert Malthus (1766–1834), another early economist, also called the usefulness of social welfare into question. Using mathematical techniques to estimate world population trends and food production capacity, Malthus concluded that population growth would inevitably outstrip the earth's ability to produce food. Given this, the most important problem facing society was finding ways to limit world population, since the alternative was global starvation.

Malthus's ideas were reinforced by the work of Charles Darwin (1809–1882). Darwin, a biologist, popularized evolutionary theory which held that life, rather than having originated with the creation of Adam and Eve by God, had instead evolved through natural processes. The driving mechanism of evolution was the **survival of the fittest,** *Darwin's label for the mechanism whereby the strongest members of a species are the ones most likely to survive and thus to breed and thereby pass their genetic traits on to future generations.* In this manner, the weaker members of the species are gradually replaced by the stronger, those most suited to their environment, thereby strengthening the species as a whole.

Darwin's ideas were based on research with plants and animals, but they were applied to human society by Herbert Spencer (1820–1903), who first popularized what came to be known as **social Darwinism.** *Advocates of social Darwinism believed that Darwin's principle of the survival of the fittest applied to humans as well as other species* (Schenk and Schenk, 1981:11–12). Thus, they argued, it was right and natural that the weak should perish while the strong survived.

The combination of laissez faire economics, the Malthusian view of population, and social Darwinism argued against help for the needy. Those in need were seen as weak. Helping them would only drain society's resources and weaken the human species. Furthermore, governmental intervention on behalf of the poor could only result in a less efficient economic system. While there had always been controversy about the role of social welfare, the coming together of the Protestant ethic, laissez faire economics, Malthusian ideas about population growth, and social Darwinism provided a serious intellectual obstacle to social welfare. Although later modified or rejected as inaccurate, these ideas heavily influenced the thinking of their time.

Intellectual support for social welfare, on the other hand, came from a variety of sources. These included religious teachings and the developing social sciences.

The first successful application of scientific methodology to the study of individual and social life came in medicine. Illness, it became clear, was much influenced by the environment. Next, the work of sociologists such as Charles Horton Cooley (1864–1929) and George Herbert Mead (1863–1931) showed how much individuals are affected by their interactions with others. Their findings were supported and extended by the work of other sociologists during the first half of the 1900s who demonstrated how much social life is influenced by community structures. Subsequent sociological research provided hard evidence of the magnitude of income differentials within society and the linkage between the living conditions of the poor and such problems as illness, family breakdown, and crime (Zimbalist, 1977:73–175).

An intellectual development that had a striking effect on social welfare was the work of Sigmund Freud (1856–1939). His theory of psychoanalysis greatly increased people's awareness of the complex factors that influence individual growth and development (Brenner, 1957). He went further to explore the nature of organized social life. Although he recognized social organization as essential to the well-being of individuals, he also suggested that the interaction between social organizations and people results in stresses and limitations on individual behavior that can be harmful to people's psychological health (Freud–Strachey, 1962). The work of Freud and his successors helped to expand the domain of social welfare to include many levels and areas of psychological functioning that had previously been poorly understood and for which few services were available.

The use of scientific methods to research fundamental issues about who should be helped and how has not resolved the debate between those who believe society should provide more services for people in need and those who believe society's role should be minimal. The major reason is because this dialogue grows out of differing value bases. Thus, those who believe social welfare helps people do research to prove their point, and those who believe the opposite do the same, while the results are rarely conclusive enough to provide a definitive answer. In addition, the social and behavioral sciences most relevant to social welfare—particularly sociology, psychology, and economics—are still young. Their theories and research findings are often incomplete and subject to multiple interpretations.

Whatever their limitations and ambiguities, history shows us that the currents of intellectual discourse in a society affect its social welfare system. Values are particularly important and have often had a far greater impact on social decision-making than research findings or data. A working knowledge of the effectiveness of birth control devices, for example, becomes useful only if one believes that practicing birth control is acceptable behavior. Further, values often influence the type of data collected and their interpretation. The struggle between values and data will no doubt continue to influence social welfare in the years to come. No matter how good the quality and scope of our data, the uses to which these data are put and the interpretations we reach will always be influenced by our values.

CATEGORIZING NEED AND APPROPRIATE RESPONSES

Deciding Who Should be Helped

In attempting to determine who should be helped, most societies have developed categories to sort people into groups to whom help should or should not be offered. Often, even those considered worthy of help have been further subdivided into groups eligible for different kinds of help. There are two major reasons why categorizing the needy has been popular. The first is the widely held belief that it is healthier for people to be self-sufficient if at all possible. This is thought to promote individual well-being as well as social prosperity. The second is the cost of helping.

The cost of helping has long been a matter of concern. During the early stages of the Industrial Revolution, for example, many people were displaced from their homes, worked in unsafe or unhealthy factories, or found themselves unemployed—and thus in need—while the resources available for social welfare were limited. In addition, there were no rules requiring those who could afford to pay for social welfare services to contribute anything above and beyond that which they might choose to donate voluntarily. In such circumstances, limiting social welfare to the truly needy was seen to be morally responsible and economically prudent.

Because we continue to categorize the needy today, it is useful to see how this process has developed historically. Over time our knowledge of human behavior and how it is affected by environmental factors has changed the types of categories employed. At first, only the most obvious misfortunes were considered to be grounds for unqualified help—illness and extreme age, for example. Gradually other sources of need have been accepted as qualifications for help, such as mental illness and illiteracy, being a single parent, an abused spouse, or a political refugee. In general, there has been an increasing willingness to categorize the needy according to predictable life span transitions and crises.

Early Categorizing Efforts and the Elizabethan Poor Law of 1601

Morris (1986:88–98) traces the origins of categorizing the needy to ancient Greece and Rome. He notes that people who fell into need through no fault of their own were considered most worthy of assistance. The connection between a failure to achieve independence despite having attempted to do so and eligibility for help developed into a theme that has endured through the ages. Those who suffer misfortune in spite of their best efforts to succeed have always been viewed more favorably than those who are seen as improvident or otherwise the cause of their own problems.

The Elizabethan Poor Law of 1601 is often regarded as a major milestone in social welfare legislation. It divided the needy into three categories: the helpless, the involuntarily unemployed, and vagrants (Federico, 1983:95).

The **helpless** *were those with a disabling condition over which they had no control.* This has always been the easiest group to accept as needing help and includes the ill, those with severe mental or physical limitations, the disabled, the orphaned, and the frail elderly. The **involuntarily unemployed** *were those who had suffered some kind of misfortune.* These people were thought to bear some responsibility for their problems and thus were considered less worthy than the helpless. They included people who had been robbed, single mothers, families with many children, victims of fires, and those who lost their jobs. **Vagrants** *were those who had no roots in the community.* They were not considered to be the responsibility of the community and were usually not eligible for assistance but were instead forced to return to their point of origin. What we see, then, is a progression from those considered to have no responsibility for their condition to those thought to be able to care for themselves if they wished to do so.

The type of assistance provided under the Elizabethan Poor Law varied by category of need. Four major types of services were provided (Leonard, 1965:137). The helpless were cared for in two ways. Those who could not remain in their own homes lived in **almshouses,** *residences in which the most helpless could live and be cared for.* Almshouse life was spartan but decent. People had a bed, food, and whatever physical care they needed, but little was provided beyond the basics.

The helpless who could continue to live at home received **outdoor relief,** *aid provided in the homes of those needing assistance but who were capable of managing on their own given help.* The types of assistance provided included financial aid, medical care, or other kinds of personal care services. Most people preferred outdoor relief because it was less disruptive to their lives and less stigmatizing than being in an almshouse.

The involuntarily unemployed were sent to **workhouses,** *residences for the involuntarily unemployed where basic needs were provided in return for work.* Although considered worthy of aid, the involuntarily unemployed were expected to earn their assistance. They lived and worked in communal quarters that offered little privacy and few comforts, but where food, clothing, and other necessities were provided. Since they were considered partially responsible for their condition, they were expected to work toward becoming independent. Additional incentive to do so was provided by the stigma associated with living in a workhouse.

However, the worst stigma was reserved for those who were put in **houses of correction,** *facilities which housed criminals, vagrants, and workhouse residents who violated the rules.* Here living conditions were primitive and abuse was common. Houses of correction represented society's most punitive response to need, and were designed for those considered unworthy of humanitarian aid.

The Elizabethan Poor Law also formalized a system of child welfare. *Called* **indenture,** *it placed orphans and children that had been removed from needy families in the homes of people who agreed to provide care in return for the* *child's work.* In 1601, when the law was passed, child labor was widely practiced. Axinn and Levin (1982:19–20) note that "the family that could not maintain financial independence was not simply unsuccessful but actually dangerous, both economically and morally. Such families could not by example, precept, or education be expected to prepare the young for adult, independent living." Therefore, in the thinking of the time, it made sense to place the child with a family that could provide what was considered a wholesome family environment.

The categorization of the needy and the services provided for each group as established by the Elizabethan Poor Law in 1601 have been a significant influence on later efforts to separate those most in need from others seeking help. The approach embodied in the Elizabethan Poor Law was readily adopted in the American Colonies because it was part of their English heritage and because it served their needs (Axinn and Levin, 1982:16–24). The early colonists struggled to survive, American churches were not wealthy, and there was a scarcity of labor. Distinguishing between the truly helpless and those able to help themselves was functional for society. Further, providing help primarily at the community level made sense in a society without a strong national government.

The Use of Indoor and Outdoor Relief Today

The debate over the relative merits of outdoor and indoor relief emerged at a very early point (Axinn and Levin, 1982:103,111). Those who believed outdoor relief was too expensive favored the use of **indoor relief,** *services provided in a residential setting.* The underlying assumption is that it is less expensive to serve people in one location (like an almshouse) than to provide services in their own homes.

Those favoring outdoor relief, on the other hand, pointed out that indoor relief isolated the needy from the community and created communal living conditions that could weaken families, promote illness, and foster violence and abuse. Outdoor relief was more "natural" in the sense of being less disruptive to established life patterns, but even it did not necessarily avoid such problems as unhealthy living conditions and abuse. This debate has never really been resolved, and services continue to be delivered on an outdoor (at home) and an indoor (in a residential facility) basis.

Although current thinking tends to view outdoor relief as more effective, more humane, and less costly (Dear and Wolch, 1987:61–68), many services continue to be provided in residential (indoor) settings. Mental hospitals, treatment centers for delinquent or disabled youths, and prisons are currently important elements in social welfare systems throughout the world. The appropriate balance between these two approaches remains an open question.

At least two current attempts to blend the indoor and outdoor approaches are worthy of note. These are halfway houses and deinstitutionalization. **Half-**

way houses *are small residential facilities that provide treatment and supervision while at the same time allowing clients to be at least partially integrated into community life.* Halfway houses have two principal uses. One is for those who are able to function in the community but cannot, for whatever reason, live with their own families. Clients of this type include youths with relatively minor behavior problems, those with mild physical or mental limitations, abused or neglected people, and those struggling with substance abuse or other addictions that are not so severe as to be life-threatening. The halfway house provides them with help and support while allowing them to participate in community life.

Halfway houses are also used as an intermediary step between residential facilities, such as a prison or mental hospital, and independent life in the community. Halfway houses have been most widely used in this fashion in conjunction with deinstitutionalization. **Deinstitutionalization** *is removing the needy from residential facilities and placing them in the community where help can be provided in less restrictive ways through the use of community support systems.* The halfway house is one such community support system, providing supervision and counseling to help the individual as he or she encounters difficulties readjusting to independent life. This approach has been widely applied to the mentally ill and prisoners.

Deinstitutionalization has been controversial when it has not been effectively linked to halfway houses or other community support systems. For example, it has been considered a significant cause of homelessness because "...a steamroller policy of deinstitutionalization occurred without prior development of community-based service systems or proper preparation of communities that were expected to receive and support the flood of clients...[as a result, clients] were left to fend for themselves in the community" (Dear and Wolch, 1987:65). We can see, then, how, nearly 300 years after the Poor Law created them, indoor and outdoor relief remain with us as helping strategies. As with any such strategy, however, their effectiveness depends on how they are used.

Decisions about the most effective helping strategies inevitably return us to the issue of resources. How should we calculate the cost-effectiveness of services? It may be cheaper to treat the mentally ill in the community rather than in mental hospitals. However, the stress of independent living may generate additional problems for the mentally ill and thus create community problems as well. The monies saved by providing treatment in the community, therefore, must be balanced against the added costs of potential associated problems such as homelessness or violence. In addition, helping approaches that address immediate needs without proper regard for long-term consequences may be less costly in the short run but more costly over the long haul. It is easy to see that a homeless person needs shelter and to provide it. But unless the forces that make that person homeless are addressed, the problem is likely to recur and even worsen.

Alternative Strategies for Allocating Help

Categorizing the needy is only one of several possible approaches to social welfare, albeit a very common one. With the development of the modern welfare state, alternative approaches have emerged. These include viewing help as a social utility, linking help to life-span needs, and approaches based on the marketplace.

Help as a Social Utility We noted in Chapter 2 that some services are viewed as social utilities to be provided to all. The police and public parks are resources available to everyone. No attempt is made to categorize users in terms of whether or not they qualify. The only limitations relate to the appropriateness of the help sought. The police are not expected to arrange for adoptions, and the public parks are not supposed to be the locale for counseling centers. But anyone who is in danger can seek police protection, and the parks are available to everyone who wishes to use them for recreation. The idea that social welfare is a social utility is seldom voiced in the United States but enjoys considerable support in the more advanced welfare states of western Europe and in the socialist bloc.

Linking Help to Life-Span Needs Certain needs, it is clear, are predictably associated with certain life-span stages, and there has been a growing recognition of this fact in recent years. Even the categories established by the Elizabethan Poor Law recognized this by acknowledging that the very old and the very young were likely to have special needs. Gradually programs were developed for these and an ever-expanding range of groups facing special developmental conditions. Free public education and free medical care for the poor were provided at an early point, and were followed by care for the mentally ill, income support programs for the retired and the unemployed, compensation for workers injured on the job, and many others. These programs categorize people according to the life tasks they face, and provide services specifically needed at particular stages in the life span.

Using the Marketplace A third approach, and one that is heavily utilized in the United States, is to use economic resources as a way of determining who shall receive certain services. These services are then provided to those who can afford to pay for them. This often allocates services by price. Those who can afford to pay have access to a greater range of services, and to more elaborate services, than those who cannot.

Medical care is a good example. Health care in the United States is generally provided on a ''fee for service'' basis, and patients utilize those doctors and health care facilities whom they can afford. Those who rely on the Medicaid program must obtain treatment from physicians and other health care providers who will accept Medicaid's relatively low payments. Many of the most prestigious doctors and medical facilities will not accept such payments and are, therefore, unavailable to the poor and those with low incomes.

Among our four societies, there is no single pattern for the use of these various approaches common to all. All four societies treat some services as social utilities, to be provided to all, although the services involved vary. Poland and Sweden provide free education at all levels, for example, while only elementary and secondary education is so provided in the United States. Some services are linked to life-span needs in all four societies, but here too there are variations. Poland emphasizes work as a highly significant life-span activity and builds many services around preparing for employment, the work experience, and retirement. Sweden adopts a much broader view of life-span needs, emphasizing prenatal care, early childhood development, family relationships, health care, housing, and retirement needs. Public services geared to all of these predictable life-span needs are provided to all Swedes.

In the United States, there are often two or more levels of service provided—a bare-bones public level of service provided on a life-span basis, and a more elaborate level of service allocated by market principles. This is true of such services as prenatal and early childhood care, services that are sometimes available through the public system but are more commonly purchased from private sources. When available on a free basis, many of these services carry with them a social stigma, an unpleasant helping environment, and sometimes questionable program quality. Further, they are generally provided only for those who are judged eligible, a holdover from the Elizabethan Poor Law's approach of categorizing on the basis of personal responsibility.

The United States is not the only society in which public services may be of poorer quality than private ones. This is also true in Mexico, Poland, and to a lesser degree even Sweden. However, this dual system is far more widespread in the United States because its public sector is much less extensive than those of our other three societies.

To summarize, categorizing the needy to determine who should receive help has a long history. Many of our current programs and policies have their intellectual origins in the Elizabethan Poor Law of 1601, and feature eligibility requirements based on a continuing belief that those who are responsible for their need should receive less help. Other, and less punitive, alternatives to categorizing the needy as a basis for allocating helping services have emerged over the years. Among these, the social utilities and life-span-based approaches have generally expanded the help provided and reduced restrictions on who can obtain it. Providing services through the marketplace has increased the kinds of services available but limited the number who have access to the full range of possibilities. Rationing services in this fashion has also tended to create two levels of service quality.

The quality of service care is more uniform in societies with comprehensive social welfare systems such as Sweden. Sweden, however, is obviously an unusual case. Most societies have a much less comprehensive welfare system and categorize the needy in a more restrictive way. Today, social values and available resources continue to influence our definition of needs and the way in which we meet them—just as they have for thousands of years. Neverthe-

MEDICAL CARE IN SWEDEN

People get sick in Sweden just like everywhere else. However, all Swedes are covered by the National Health Insurance that makes illness less problematic than it is in many other countries.

Outpatient services are provided in community health centers, and there is a set charge of about $8 per visit. Included are x-rays, laboratory tests, radiation treatments, and free referrals to specialists. Inpatient care in hospitals is free. Treatment by paramedical personnel carries a set fee of about $4 and includes such services as physiotherapy, speech therapy, occupational therapy, and psychotherapy.

There is a limit of about $8 on the cost of prescription drugs per visit. Life-saving drugs are free. People needing frequent outpatient visits and prescription drugs have to pay only for the first fifteen visits or prescriptions. Travel costs to receive medical care are reimbursed if they exceed about $4.50 per visit. A similar reimbursement is provided to parents visiting a child under age 10 who is in a hospital. Birth control is included in medical visit and prescription policies.

For dental care, patients pay 60 percent of the first $350 (approximately) and 25 percent of the remainder. Children receive free dental care until the age of 16.

Workers receive 90 percent of their annual earned income (up to a maximum earned income of about $15,500) that is lost due to illness. Stay-at-home spouses receive a daily sickness benefit of about $1.25. The benefit begins on the second day of the illness, and the worker must have reported sick to the social insurance office.

Expectant working mothers are entitled to a 12-month leave from work with pay. This leave may be taken at any time during the child's first four years, and may be used by the father and mother in whatever proportion they wish. During the first nine months, the remuneration rate is 90 percent of gross income, and during the final three months about $7 per day. In addition, fathers are entitled to 10 days of leave with pay when a child is born. Adoptive and foster parents are also eligible for a maximum leave of 6 months for adopting a child under age 10. Parents who must take time off from work to care for a child under age 12 due to illness are entitled to up to 60 days' leave with pay per year per child for this purpose. Parents who wish to visit the day care center or school that their child is attending are also eligible for an additional 2 days' leave with pay per child.

The Swedish approach to health care does not categorize people, but it does respond to different needs. Everyone needs basic health care, so it is available on an equal basis to all. However, children and parents receive special benefits which reflect their special needs. In addition, there is a ceiling on the amount of earned income taken into account when computing sickness benefits, thus ensuring that those with exceptionally high incomes do not receive a sickness benefit above the level guaranteed to all.

As might be expected, the Swedish health care system is generally regarded as one of the best in the world. Life expectancy in Sweden is 78 years compared with 75 in the United States, 71 in Poland, and 66 in Mexico. The Swedish infant mortality rate is 8 per 1,000 births in contrast to 11 for the United States, 19 for Poland, and 52 for Mexico (these data are for 1983 and are from the World Bank, 1986:8–9).

Such a comprehensive system is necessarily expensive, yet in 1986 Sweden spent less of its gross national product on health care than did the United States—9.0 percent versus 11.1 percent. Total health spending per person in Sweden in 1986 was $1,195 compared to $926 in the United States, of which the government share was 90.9 percent as compared to 40.8 percent in the United States (Health in Sweden, 1982:3; *The New York Times,* 1988). These figures demonstrate the continued importance of the private sector to the provision of health care in the United States.

Adapted from *Social Insurance in Sweden.* 1986. Stockholm: the Swedish Institute, pp. 1–2.

less, we can see in many societies a general movement toward outdoor relief coupled with less restrictive and punitive definitions of who is needy. In part, this reflects the greater affluence of industrialized nations, an affluence which enables them to afford more services. Even so, there is little reason to believe that the widespread practice of categorizing the needy will disappear in the near future.

LET'S REVIEW

This chapter has examined four important, recurring themes that have shaped the historical development of social welfare. These are: (1) developing a sense of responsibility for others; (2) the evolution of helping roles; (3) intellectual currents; and (4) categorizing the needy. Although our views about helping have ancient roots in the biological nature of human beings and the traditional religious injunction to be charitable, we have seen that the Industrial Revolution had a major impact on social welfare. It affected people's need for help, the ability of existing social structures to provide help, and the application of scientific thinking to the helping process.

The allocation of helping services has often been determined by categorizing the needy. The way in which these categories are drawn often reflects dominant social values about the individual's personal responsibility for being in need, although these schemes have tended to become less punitive over time as other views of the causes of human need have come into play. Our increasing knowledge of the helping process has led to the development of persons specially trained as helpers, although they supplement rather than replace informal helping networks.

This chapter has focused on ideas that have shaped social welfare through the centuries. The next chapter also examines the historical development of social welfare, but from a complementary perspective. It focuses on the events that have had an enduring impact on social welfare. In many instances these events have also altered the dominant intellectual ideas of the time, so that the interplay between events and ideas is a never-ending one.

CHAPTER OUTLINE

STUDY QUESTIONS

1 What, in your view, are the likely consequences for social welfare of the current administration's policies? What, in particular, do you believe the current President's views are toward each of the four major themes discussed in this chapter? (Before attempting to answer this question, you may wish to research the President's speeches and interviews during the 1988 campaign, along with editorial commentary on his views, to learn more about his position on social welfare issues.)

2 Do you think that highly industrial nations like the United States can coexist peacefully with the much poorer and less industrially developed nations of the Third World? In answering this question, try focusing on the kinds of needs that people have in each type of society, and the society's ability to meet them. To shed light on the differences between industrial and preindustrial societies, you might want to use Mexico as an interesting case of a society in the midst of industrialization.

3 As far as you can see, does the United States still categorize the needy in a fashion similar to the Elizabethan Poor Law? Try to focus on the thinking underlying these categories rather than the actual form each took. For example, we don't have workhouses but do have sheltered workshops for those with physical and mental limitations, and "workfare" for welfare mothers. Feel free to discuss this question with your classmates to get ideas and to share information about existing social welfare programs.

4 Interview three social welfare professionals and ask them what contemporary ideas or theories they believe are having the greatest impact on social welfare. Ask them to explain their views. Then go to the library and read at least one book or article about each idea or theory mentioned. Conclude by writing a one-paragraph summary of the essential content of each idea or theory.

5 Read the chronological history of social welfare found in pages 755–788 of the 18th edition of the *Encyclopedia of Social Work* published by the National Association of Social Workers, which should be in the reference section of your library. You will find this a useful supplement to the material in this chapter and the one that follows.

2

KEY TERMS AND CONCEPTS

almshouses
Charity Organization Societies
deinstitutionalization
Elizabethan Poor Law of 1601
friendly visitors
halfway houses
the helpless
houses of correction
indenture
indoor relief
Industrial Revolution

the involuntarily unemployed
laissez-faire economics
outdoor relief
Protestant ethic
scientific method
scientific philanthropy
social Darwinism
survival of the fittest
vagrants
workhouses

SUGGESTED READINGS

Axinn, June, and Herman Levin. 1982. *Social Welfare: A History of the American Response to Need,* 2d ed. White Plains, N. Y.: Longman, Inc. This is an excellent history of social welfare, focusing on the United States. It uses a chronological approach, and includes excerpts from actual historical documents.

Forsberg, Mats. 1986. *The Evolution of Social Welfare Policy in Sweden.* Stockholm: The Swedish Institute; and Brzozowski, Ryszard, et al., n.d. *Social Welfare and the Lines of Its Development in the Polish People's Republic.* Translated by Przemyslaw Slomski. Warsaw: Polish Medical Publishers. These two small books describe the historical development of social welfare in Sweden and Poland, respectively. They provide interesting insights into the ideas and events that influence social welfare.

Morris, Robert. 1986. *Rethinking Social Welfare: Why Care for the Stranger?* White Plains, N. Y.: Longman, Inc. An analysis of social welfare that combines a historical approach with an examination of the philosophical underpinnings. It is particularly strong on social welfare in ancient societies. There is also a stimulating discussion of current social welfare issues and their significance.

Sheahan, John. 1987. *Patterns of Development in Latin America.* Princeton, N. J.: Princeton University Press. Although technical at several points, this is a helpful work for understanding the impact of the industrialization process on developing nations. The relationships between population growth and distribution, economic productivity, and political decision-making are clearly drawn, along with their implications for social welfare. The writing is clear, and the major social welfare points can be grasped by reading selectively and skimming.

Wilensky, Harold, and Charles Lebeaux. 1965. *Industrial Society and Social Welfare.* New York: The Free Press. A classic work. Parts One and Two are especially recommended for their thorough analysis of the impact of industrialization on social life and human need. Discusses with insight and passion the social welfare needs of societies struggling with the demands of industrialization.

REFERENCES

Axinn, June, and Herman Levin. 1982. *Social Welfare: A History of the American Response to Need,* 2d ed. White Plains, N. Y.: Longman, Inc.

Bernard, Jessie. 1981. *The Female World.* New York: Free Press.

Brenner, Charles. 1957. *An Elementary Textbook of Psychoanalysis.* New York: Anchor Books.

Brieland, Donald. 1987. History and evolution of social work practice. In *The Encyclopedia of Social Work,* 18th ed. Silver Spring, Md.: National Association of Social Workers, pp. 739–754.

Brzozowski, Ryszard, et al., n.d. *Social Welfare and the Lines of Its Development in the Polish People's Republic.* Translated by Przemyslaw Slomski. Warsaw: Polish Medical Publishers.

Coll, Blanche. 1969. *Perspectives in Public Welfare.* Washington, D.C.: U. S. Government Printing Office.

Columbia University. 1987. *Columbia University Bulletin.* New York: Columbia University School of Social Work.

Dear, Michael, and Jennifer Wolch. 1987. *Landscapes of Despair: From Deinstitutionalization to Homelessness.* Princeton, N. J.: Princeton University Press.

Federico, Ronald, with Janet Schwartz. 1983. *Sociology,* 3d ed. New York: Random House.

Forsberg, Mats. 1986. *The Evolution of Social Welfare Policy in Sweden.* Stockholm: The Swedish Institute.

Freitag, Michael. 1987. New York is fighting the spread of sweatshops. *The New York Times,* November 16, A1.

Freud, Sigmund. 1962. *Civilization and Its Discontents.* Translated by James Strachey. New York: W. W. Norton & Co.

Health in Sweden. 1982. Stockholm: The Swedish Ministry of Health and Social Affairs.

Hellman, Judith. 1983. *Mexico in Crisis,* 2d ed. New York: Holmes and Meier Publishers.

Keith-Lucas, Alan. 1972. *Giving and Taking Help.* Chapel Hill, N.C.: University of North Carolina Press.

Klein, Philip. 1968. *From Philanthropy to Social Welfare.* San Francisco: Jossey-Bass Publishers.

Leonard, E. M. 1965. *The Early History of the English Poor Relief.* New York: Barnes and Noble.

Lieby, James. 1978. *A History of Social Welfare and Social Work in the United States.* New York: Columbia University Press.

Locke, John. 1960. Two Treatises on Government. London. In *Theories of Society,* vol. I. Eds. Talcott Parsons, Edward Shils, Kaspar Naegele, and Jesse Pitts. Glencoe, Ill.: 1961, pp. 101–103.

Macarov, David. 1978. *The Design of Social Welfare.* New York: Holt, Rinehart and Winston.

Madison, Bernice. 1968. *Social Welfare in the Soviet Union.* Stanford, Calif.: Stanford University Press.

Mencher, Samuel. 1967. *Poor Law to Poverty Program.* Pittsburgh, Pa.: University of Pittsburgh Press.

Morris, Robert. 1986. *Rethinking Social Welfare: Why Care for the Stranger?* White Plains, N. Y.: Longman, Inc.

Redondi, Pietro. 1987. *Gailileo: Heretic.* Translated by Raymond Rosenthal. Princeton, N. J.: Princeton University Press.

Reid, William, and Peter Stimpson. 1987. Sectarian agencies. In *The Encyclopedia of Social Work,* 18th ed. Silver Spring, Md.: National Association of Social Workers, pp. 545–556.

Rosner, Jan. 1976. *Cross-National Studies of Social Service Systems: Polish Reports.* Ann Arbor, Mich.: Xerox University Microfilms.

Rousseau, Jean Jacques. 1762. A Treatise on the Social Compact. Paris. In *Theories of Society,* vol. I. Eds. Talcott Parsons, Edward Shils, Kaspar Naegele, and Jesse Pitts. Glencoe, Ill.: 1961, pp. 119–125.

Schenk, Quentin, with Emmy Lou Schenk. 1981. *Welfare, Society, and the Helping Professions.* New York: Macmillan.

Sheahan, John. 1987. *Patterns of Development in Latin America.* Princeton, N. J.: Princeton University Press.

Smith, Adam. 1776. Inquiry Into the Causes of the Wealth of Nations. London. In *Theories of Society,* vol. I. Eds. Talcott Parsons, Edward Shils, Kaspar Naegele, and Jesse Pitts. Glencoe, Ill.: pp. 104–106. 1961.

Social Security Programs Throughout the World—1985. 1986. Washington, D.C.: U. S. Government Printing Office.

Spending on health care: a look at 8 countries. 1988. *The New York Times,* August 7, 12.

Steinberg, S. H., ed. 1963. *A Dictionary of British History.* New York: St. Martin's Press.

U.S. Department of Commerce. Bureau of the Census. *Statistical Abstract of the United States.* 1987. Washington, D.C.: United States Government Printing Office.

Wilensky, Harold, and Charles Lebeaux. 1965. *Industrial Society and Social Welfare.* New York: The Free Press.

World Bank. 1986. *The World Bank Atlas 1986.* Washington, D.C.: The World Bank.

Zimbalist, Sidney. 1977. *Historic Themes and Landmarks in Social Welfare Research.* New York: Harper & Row.

WHAT HAS BEEN THE HISTORICAL DEVELOPMENT OF SOCIAL WELFARE?

WHAT TO EXPECT FROM THIS CHAPTER

You will recall that the previous chapter focused on the historical roots of social welfare. We examined the ideas that had an impact on people's views of social welfare and its role in society. These included such issues as the responsibility for helping others, the proper role of government in helping, and the influence of religious and scientific ideas concerning the causes of and appropriate response to human need. We saw that our concept of social welfare has gradually expanded, as have the quantity and quality of social welfare services.

This chapter will continue our historical analysis. However, instead of concentrating on the power of ideas to shape social welfare, it will emphasize the impact of events. We will see that economic changes, war and natural disasters, and demographic changes have significantly shaped the development of social welfare as have changes in the prominence of particular groups at different times in history. Finally, social welfare has been influenced by the growth of modern government and its ability to centralize societal planning and economic activity. All of these forces will be examined in this chapter.

Like its predecessor, this chapter will use a thematic rather than a chronological approach. This chapter will help you to see the linkages between the ideas discussed earlier and the events presented in this chapter. When you have concluded this chapter you should have a clear understanding of the major ideas and events that have shaped social welfare through the centuries. You will also know how they continue to influence our thinking about social welfare and our efforts to help people meet their needs.

LEARNING OBJECTIVES

At the end of this chapter you should be able to do the following:

1 List at least three types of historical events that have had an impact on the development of social welfare.
2 Identify at least three demographic factors that can influence the need for social welfare services.
3 Identify at least five special populations whose needs have received special attention from the social welfare institution.
4 Describe why special populations should have services targeted to their particular needs.
5 Explain the relationship between the needs of special populations, civil rights, and advocacy.
6 Discuss how the relationship between public and private services has evolved over time, and explain why.
7 Describe the role of the judicial system in social welfare.
8 Briefly summarize how your understanding of social welfare has been enhanced by a knowledge of the major events that have affected its development through history.
9 Describe the impact of at least three historical events and their related ideas on social welfare.

SOCIAL WELFARE AND HISTORICAL EVENTS

This discussion of the relationship between social welfare and history will be organized around three types of historical events: changes in the economic system, war and natural disasters, and demographic changes. Let's begin with economic changes.

Economic Changes

The Industrial Revolution We have already seen that the Industrial Revolution marked a turning point in human history and in social welfare. Land ownership as a source of power was supplemented by ownership of the means of industrial production such as factories, machines, technology, and the raw materials used in the production process. National governments gradually emerged and dominated local governing units. The power of the church was reduced as its landholdings became less valuable and because of competition with newly emerging national governments. In addition, the rise of science challenged the dominance of religious ideas, as we saw in the previous chapter. One consequence of all these developments was a gradually increasing role for the government in the provision of social welfare.

The Industrial Revolution had other effects as well. Industrialization created a number of new social problems. Families were uprooted and became dependent on a wage economy. As jobs changed and moved, so did families. Smaller families could best adapt to a changed workplace that provided a set wage and encouraged geographic mobility. As families became smaller, however, their helping capacity was reduced, making it more difficult for the family to care for children and the elderly. Also, most people found themselves now unable to grow their own food and thus supplement their income (Axinn and Levin, 1982:144).

Urban areas developed rapidly around factories, outstripping the ability of technology to create safe, hygienic, and humane living conditions. In addition, working conditions in factories were often noisy, dangerous, and exhausting. For many years men, women, and children worked long hours under brutal conditions for little pay.

In response, new forms of social services emerged. In the United States, existing churches and new religiously affiliated groups such as the Salvation Army, established in 1880, provided assistance to the destitute, especially those in urban areas. In addition, a variety of charitable groups that provided social welfare services emerged. Many of these, like the Young Men's Christian Association (YMCA) which was established in 1851 and offered lodging, social, and educational programs to those otherwise unable to afford them, had a religious orientation.

The problems of urban industrial life led to many other developments as well. The American Medical Association was founded in 1847 to improve standards of medical care. Following the Civil War, the first unions appeared and eventually became powerful enough to protect workers from some of the worst problems in the workplace. Unions were among these groups supporting the first worker's compensation laws passed in 1911 (Axinn and Levin, 1982:145). The Charity Organization Societies, discussed in the previous chapter, focused on helping families adapt to urban industrial life. In addition, several major laws designed to limit the power of big business and protect workers and consumers were passed at this time. These included the Interstate Commerce Act (1887) and the Sherman Antitrust Act (1890) (Axinn and Levin, 1982:95).

The Great Depression   In wage-based industrial societies, periods of economic depression took on greater importance. Without a job and a wage, people had no means of survival. It is not surprising, therefore, that economic depressions were a catalyst for the development of new social welfare programs. By far the most important of these, the Great Depression, began in the United States with the stock market crash in 1929 (Axinn and Levin, 1982:175):

The rudeness of the stock market crash of October 24, 1929, the near collapse of the whole credit structure of the American economy, and the spiral of falling sales, rising unemployment, declining income, further production cuts, and more unemployment touched all....

With the Great Depression came the realization that the well-being of individuals was in many ways a function of the health of society itself. Hardworking people were unemployed because there were no jobs. Those who had never been poor became so. In due course it became clear even to many who had previously opposed the expansion of government activities that only the government had the power and the resources to help a nation mired in such an economic crisis.

Early responses to the Great Depression were partial and fragmented. They were directed at specific parts of the problem, especially unemployment. In spite of their partial success it soon became apparent that a more fundamental change in the nation's economic and social welfare structures was necessary. One result was the proposal by President Franklin D. Roosevelt and the passage by Congress of the Social Security Act of 1935.

The Social Security Act created several new programs. One of these was Old Age and Survivors Insurance (OASI), a program designed to provide retirement income for workers and benefits payable to their widows and minor children in the event of the worker's death; it was later expanded to include disabled workers. The act also created unemployment insurance to provide income during periods of temporary, involuntary unemployment and several other aid programs. The latter included programs targeted to the financial needs of blind persons, dependent children, and the elderly (later expanded to include the disabled). We will look at these programs in more detail in the next two chapters.

The major point here, however, is the link between economic conditions and social welfare services, a link that continues to the present day. The Vietnam war in the 1960s and 1970s drained resources from the economy with the result that social programs established during the preceding era of "The Great Society" were reduced or terminated. The slump in oil prices of the 1980s so reduced Mexico's income that expenditures on social programs actually declined (Ward, 1986:8). Plans to greatly increase consumer prices were announced in Poland in 1987 in response to economic problems. They included a new system of family grants designed to reduce the impact of the price increases on people's standard of living (*The New York Times,* 1987a:A11).

Wars and Natural Disasters

Wars and natural disasters are similar in that both create human need by generating widespread death, the loss of homes and belongings, illness, disability, and broken families. These needs have a double impact. Not only are individuals, families, and communities affected, but society as a whole is likely to suffer. Poland, for example, took many years to recover from World War II, having suffered widespread destruction of its factories, farmlands, and housing, and the loss of large numbers of working-age men. In the United States, which has never suffered destruction of this magnitude from war, communities, counties, or states struck by natural disasters such as tornados or floods are often declared disaster areas so that they qualify for federal funds with which to rebuild.

War especially has had an enduring impact on social welfare. Former soldiers and their dependents have been seen for centuries as entitled to special help with needs incurred as a result of their service to society. As early as 1624 the Virginia colony passed legislation to assist disabled veterans and their families (Axinn and Levin, 1982:31). Based on earlier legislation passed in England in 1593, this approach was gradually adopted by most of the other colonies. The new nation—the United States of America—passed similar federal legislation in 1862 during the Civil War. In addition, the Grand Army of the Republic, a veterans' organization, was formed in 1866 to advocate programs for the needs of its members (Axinn and Levin, 1982:92).

The Civil War also had an unanticipated effect on the condition of black Americans. By the end of the war, the south in general was badly damaged, but freed blacks were especially vulnerable. Lacking educational or economic preparation for independent living, their task was made even more difficult because the economy was in ruins. In recognition of the general problems of the region, but especially those of blacks, the Freedmen's Bureau was created by Congress in 1865. This became the first federal welfare agency (Axinn and Levin, 1982:94). It provided food, shelter, help in reuniting families, medical care, and child welfare services to both blacks and whites. In addition, it created a network of public schools and colleges for black youths, and helped black adults find employment where they were treated and paid fairly.

United States involvement in the two world wars led to further changes in social welfare. The Veterans Bureau was created in 1921 to coordinate and oversee benefits for veterans, including medical care, pensions, and vocational rehabilitation services (Axinn and Levin, 1982:156). World War II, which involved over 16 million United States military personnel, resulted in the Servicemen's Readjustment Act of 1944, commonly called the G.I. bill. As its name implies, its primary purpose was to help veterans readjust to civilian life. It did so by providing benefits to pay for education and job training, loans to purchase homes or businesses, employment services, and pensions (Axinn and Levin, 1982:243). The G.I. bill greatly expanded the services available to those who had served their country during wartime, and it solidified their position as a very special group in the social welfare structure.

The Korean war (1950–1953) did not have a major impact on social welfare, but the Vietnam war (1963–1973) did. For the first time, Americans could actually see on television what war was like, and the view was horrifying. It was hard to think of the war in Vietnam as a noble fight for freedom when the daily reality was blood and shattered bodies. The widespread use of drugs by U.S. military personnel in Vietnam destroyed some of the earlier clean-cut,

American-youth image of the military. Both the Korean and the Vietnam wars also brought to the surface the nation's deep suspicion of nonwestern cultures. Saving Italy, France, Germany, or England—the countries from which many American families first came to the United States—was an idea that linked the average American with his or her ancestral roots. It was much harder for Americans to have this same sense of connectedness to Korea and Vietnam, two unfamiliar Oriental cultures.

One result was a distinct retrenchment in services provided for Vietnam veterans. In contrast to earlier wars when benefits had been provided to anyone who had served, only Vietnam veterans who were actually wounded were considered eligible for full benefits. Funds for education and training were reduced, and medical services cut back. Worse still, many Vietnam veterans felt their sacrifices were unappreciated or even scorned by the larger society, which made it more difficult for them and their families to put their war-related problems behind them.

American ambivalence toward war and the military was evident in the continuing political conflict over military issues between President Reagan and the Congress during the 1980s. The two major points of contention were the President's proposals for funding the Contra rebels' effort to overthrow the Nicaraguan government and for developing a space-based defense against ballistic missiles (the ''Star Wars'' program). Even so, the Veterans Administration was elevated to cabinet status in 1987, partially in response to the voting power of the nearly 80 million Americans who receive benefits from veterans' programs (*The New York Times,* 1987b).

The best known of the nongovernmental agencies created to deal with the needs of military personnel and their families is the Red Cross, which today responds both to wars and natural disasters. Created during World War I, the Red Cross originally provided medical care and helped families maintain communication with members serving in the Armed Forces. Over time, its mission gradually broadened to encompass general humanitarian services, including the provision of help to military families during peace as well as war and disaster relief services. The history of the Red Cross, then, exemplifies the similarity in the problems created by war and natural disasters, as well as the way in which both have prompted joint public and private responses. (You will learn more about the Red Cross and its relationship with the government in the next chapter.)

Demographic Changes

Variations in the size, composition, and distribution of a population are called **demographic changes.** These include changes in birth and death rates, immigration and emigration, regional movement within a society, and changes in the size of groups within a society. Population variables are important because they affect the human resources available, the relations among major groups in the society, and the kinds of needs that exist.

THE ROLE OF THE RED CROSS IN POLAND

The Red Cross in Poland has carved out a unique role for itself in response to that society's experiences in World War II and its form of government. As in the United States, the Polish Red Cross runs blood drives, provides health education, and cooperates with activities of the International Red Cross. However, two additional functions are unique to Poland.

Poland suffered substantial losses of people and property in World War II. An estimated 6 million Polish citizens were killed during World War II, half of whom were Jews. In addition, the Nazis located several major concentration camps in Poland, with the result that several million additional people were sent to Poland from all over Europe, and many of these were also killed. The massive destruction caused by the 1939 joint German-Soviet invasion, the 1941 German attack on the Soviet Union, and the successful 1944–1945 Soviet campaign turned many Poles into refugees. The changes in Poland's boundaries at the end of the war only worsened the refugee problem while creating other administrative nightmares. All of these factors created a large number of missing people, especially concentration camp victims and refugees, along with the usual problem of accounting for missing soldiers. As a result, locating missing people quickly became one of the most important functions of the Red Cross in Poland. This is a task that remains unfinished even today, and to which has been added in recent years the task of locating current victims of political oppression.

A second special role for the Red Cross in Poland is as a provider of social services under contract to the Polish Ministry of Health and Social Welfare. It specializes in providing homemaker and home care services for the elderly and other homebound people. It pays and trains its own personnel who work in collaboration with professional social workers and medical personnel. It is currently expanding its services by developing nursing homes in cooperation with Poland's public health centers.

This type of cooperation between public and private organizations is common in Poland. In part, it reflects a political emphasis on self-help common to Soviet-style regimes. However, it, like the Polish Red Cross's efforts to locate missing persons, is also an outgrowth of World War II. The massive destruction of resources in the war resulted in effects that are still felt, especially given Poland's ongoing economic problems. Cooperation between public and private agencies, and the creative use of volunteers and professionals help to stretch resources that continue to be quite scarce.

Population Movement   Population movements have been common from the early years of human history. Nomadic groups moved in response to climate, hunting needs, and agricultural conditions. Global exploration led to colonization and the movement of conquered peoples to serve as slaves or servants. The resulting contact between people from different cultures led to exchanges of knowledge, beliefs, and technology along with the spread of disease. For example, diseases introduced by European explorers and settlers led to high death rates among American Indians, greatly reducing their number.

We have already seen that the Industrial Revolution led to radical shifts of population in England and created many new social problems. The movement from agricultural to urban areas continues throughout the world, but it is especially vigorous in industrializing nations. When economic opportunity is stagnant and schooling and other resources are limited, poor rural residents often migrate to urban areas in search of better opportunities and more services (Sheahan, 1987). When planned, such population movements can be beneficial to economic development. When not, widespread poverty, social unrest, and political oppression may result, as it has in many parts of Africa and Central and South America.

Internal population movements also occur in industrial nations. During the past few decades, the United States has experienced significant shifts of population from the northeast and midwest to the south, west, and southwest. These have occurred in response to job opportunities, differences in living costs, and the desire of older workers to retire to a milder climate. The generally lower costs of doing business in the south and southwest combined with the oil boom of the 1970s to attract people from outside the region. The mild climate of these areas has also been a magnet, giving rise to the phrase "the Sun Belt."

Whatever their reason for moving, those who relocate often experience need. The fall in world oil prices in the 1980s left many Sun Belt states short of funds and jobs at the same time they were experiencing a population increase. Just when social welfare services were most needed to deal with unemployment and related problems, reduced tax revenues caused by the business slowdown made them least available (*NASW News*, 1986). As a result, poverty, unemployment, and homelessness increased. The elderly, too, may need help when they retire and relocate. Many find it difficult to establish new social networks and to maintain links with family members, especially adult children from whom they have separated.

The United States has also been significantly affected by external immigration and emigration, that is, population movement between societies. Priding itself as "a land of opportunity," the United States encouraged such immigration for many years. Between 1820 and 1880, some 10 million people emigrated to the United States, 95 percent from northern and western Europe. In addition, approximately 6 million slaves were imported by 1860 (Jenkins, 1987:873). Although the first significant legislation to restrict immigration was passed in 1882, the arrival of newcomers continued at high rates. From 1881 to 1910 it is estimated that about 17.7 million people entered the United States (Jenkins, 1987:873). They tended to come from southern and eastern Europe. Over time, continuing sentiment to restrict immigration led to a series of legislative restrictions, the most recent being enacted in 1986. In general, current legislation features quotas on the number of immigrants to be admitted from each nation, makes special provisions for political refugees, encourages people with certain job skills, and seeks to help families remain together (Jenkins, 1987:874–875).

The settlement house movement was an early response of social welfare to the special needs of immigrants. **Settlement houses** *were community social welfare agencies established in the late 1800s, primarily to serve immigrants, and that used community-oriented approaches to serving people.* Generally located in cities, settlement houses assisted immigrants with their personal, family, health, housing, language, and employment needs by providing education programs, social services, counseling, and recreational services. Settlement houses also fought for reform and encouraged political action on behalf of immigrants and their communities (Loavenbruck and Keys, 1987:556–557). Among the best known were Jane Addams' Hull House in Chicago, founded in 1889, and the Henry Street Settlement in New York, established in 1893. Unlike the family approach used by the Charity Organization Societies, settle-

ment houses favored group activities, efforts to mobilize communities to identify and meet their own needs, and political action. These strategies became
significant parts of the emerging profession of social work, and they supplemented the case approach advocated by Mary Richmond described in the previous chapter.

Traditional strategies for helping immigrants have been sorely tested by rad-
ically different immigration patterns of the 1980s. Figure 4.1 shows the dramatic shift in groups entering the United States. The earlier dominance by
European groups has given way to large numbers of people coming from Asia,
the Caribbean, and Central and South America.

As immigrants with increasingly different language and cultural backgrounds enter the United States, they face greater problems fitting into
American society. American society has also become more complex and requires higher levels of job skills. Immigrants have always tended to cluster in

FIGURE 4.1   Changing immigration patterns. (Sumner Rosen et al., eds. 1987. *Face of the Nation 1987,*
Silver Spring, MD: National Association of Social Workers, p. 11. Based on unpublished data
from the United States Immigration and Naturalization Service.)

U.S. immigration patterns, by region of origin, 1945–1985 (percentage)

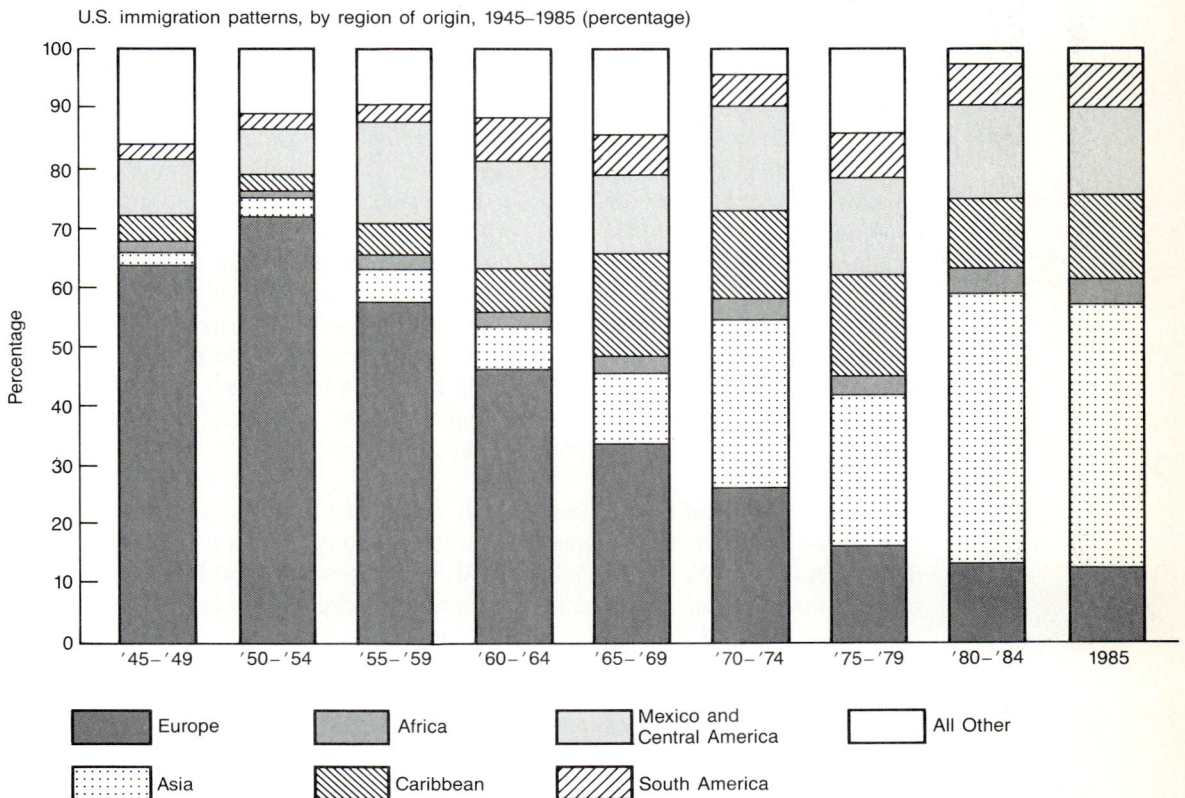

neighborhoods where they can help each other, but today's stricter immigration laws make many fear deportation as undocumented aliens. As a consequence, many immigrants use their communal ties to avoid contact with authority, including helping professionals who find it more difficult to locate and work with those in need.

Immigration patterns often reflect a symbiotic relationship between industrialized and less-developed nations. Industrial societies such as Sweden and the United States have high standards of living that are attractive to citizens of poorer societies. At the same time, workers from these nations are more willing to accept relatively low-paying and unappealing jobs that are unattractive to the more highly educated workers of industrial societies. Thus, many Mexicans—an estimated 8 million of them by 1980—have come to the United States in search of jobs (Rendon, 1985:3). Sweden's largest immigrant populations are from Finland, Yugoslavia, Turkey, Poland, and Greece, the last four of which are all either relatively unindustrialized or experiencing serious economic problems (The Swedish Institute, *Fact Sheets on Sweden,* 1984:1). Poland is an interesting example of a nation that neither encourages immigration nor is seen as an appealing destination by potential immigrants. Hence, its population is approximately 98 percent ethnic Polish (Nelson, 1983:106).

Those who emigrate from less-developed to highly industrialized nations are confronted with many changes that can be stressful. Societies differ in their efforts to help immigrants. Swedish national policy is to provide education to immigrants in their native language and also to provide social welfare services via workers who speak the recipients' native language. The United States has yet to make a similar commitment, although many social welfare agencies attempt to provide services in the recipient's native language insofar as possible.

The problem of delivering services in the recipient's own language is complicated in the United States by the tremendous diversity of groups that have emigrated to this country in large numbers. Even so, we know that when social welfare and education are not provided to immigrants in an effective way, they are likely to live in poverty and work in dead-end jobs where exploitation is a daily occurrence. Thus, the continuing influx of immigrants poses ongoing challenges for the social welfare system.

The Birthrate and Population Growth   Let's shift now to another important population effect: natural population growth through an excess of births over deaths. As societies have industrialized, birthrates have tended to decline for reasons noted earlier: Smaller family units are more mobile and better adapted to urban industrial life. Between 1973 and 1983, for example, the population growth rate for Sweden was 0.2 percent and 1.0 percent for the United States, but it was 2.9 percent for Mexico (World Bank, 1986:8–9). These figures raise several important social welfare issues.

Population growth has become a global concern. The earth's natural resources are increasingly exploited to sustain growing numbers of people. This exploitation includes the destruction of forests to provide fuel and building material, the slaughter of wildlife to provide food and clothing, the pollution of water supplies, and overgrazing of farmlands so that they become barren. Many developing nations are especially pressed by rapidly growing populations and primitive technology or political corruption that allow the waste of valuable natural resources. Widespread poverty and starvation result. Yet efforts to control population growth encounter numerous obstacles. Cultural norms, low levels of education, and controversies over birth control strategies are some of the factors influencing the success of birth control efforts.

Even though industrial societies have low birthrates, they too have an impact on the global population problem. Their industries create pollution that contributes to the destruction of the natural environment. This includes the "greenhouse effect," the potentially destructive warming of the earth's atmosphere. High standards of living often result in the copious use of items like food and fuel that, if more evenly distributed around the world, would go far to solving problems of starvation in developing nations.

Wealthy industrial societies are the object of conflicting attitudes among citizens of poorer nations. Many of these citizens seek to emigrate to wealthier societies so that they and their families may lead more comfortable lives. Others resent the economic disparities and find them objectionable. At the broadest global level, then, high population growth rates and differences in these rates between industrialized and developing nations raise serious concerns and are a source of potential conflict.

A high rate of growth strains a nation's resources, an especially significant problem in developing nations where resources are already limited and are needed for economic growth. Population growth increases the number of children who need care and education if they are to grow into healthy and productive adults, while the resources to provide these services may not be available. Nations with low birthrates are likely to face a problem at the other end of the population span. With relatively few younger people entering the population, who will be the workers of tomorrow and who will care for the elderly? Under such circumstances, simultaneously meeting the needs of the young and the old becomes a serious challenge for the social welfare system, as is illustrated by Poland's recent baby boom.

Population Growth in a Multicultural Society   A complicating factor in assessing the implications of population growth for social welfare in a multicultural society is that growth may occur unevenly across subgroups within the population. This is the case in the United States. Between 1970 and 1980, the U.S. population as a whole increased by 11.5 percent. However, the Spanish-origin population increased by 61 percent and the black population by 17.3 percent (Estrada, 1987:733). Tables 4.1 and 4.2 provide more detail about these two population groups.

As the data in Tables 4.1 and 4.2 indicate, the median family income of whites in the United States is considerably higher than that of Hispanics or

THE HUMAN FACE OF SOCIAL WELFAFE 8

Poland's Baby Boom

Poles are having more children than Government demographers thought they would, and more children in relation to population than any country in Europe.

Schools in cities are often in triple session. Nurseries and day-care centers have long waiting lists.... In a country that lost one out of every six citizens in World War II, and that reached its prewar population of 35 million only five years ago, such fecundity is often a matter of pride and joy....

[A Polish demographer] said it was not the growth of the population itself that was troublesome as much as the dislocations and imbalances caused by the unanticipated demographic trends. For example, he said that with the prolonged baby boom, the ratio of productive to nonproductive citizens was growing. He added that needs for schools, clinics, nurseries, textbooks, notepads and crayons were confounding planners who already had to deal with a longstanding housing crisis.

Another study...[said substantial population growth] would necessitate a 40 percent growth in agricultural production. But farm productivity has risen only slightly in the last decade, and meat is still rationed....

Adding to the complexity of Poland's demographic picture are the sensitive and ambivalent attitudes toward birth control and abortion in what is both an overwhelmingly Roman Catholic society [the church prohibits artificial methods of birth control and abortion] and a Communist nation [Communist ideology allows birth control and abortion].

———

For reasons demographers don't understand, Poland is currently experiencing a baby boom. Until recently, Poland's birth rate was low, like that of other European and Eastern Bloc nations, and was expected to stay that way. Starting in 1981, however, it began to increase and has continued to do so.

As the excerpt above indicates, the Polish baby boom is creating a variety of dislocations. Social welfare is affected because there is the need for more day care, schools, and housing, as well as for basic educational materials like books, pens, and paper. The population increase itself is not considered a problem—indeed, it is welcomed. Nevertheless, it creates difficulties for a society whose economic resources are very limited.

From Michael Kaufman, Poland's mixed blessing: Its many, many babies. *The New York Times,* October 16, 1986, p. A4. Copyright (c) 1986 by The New York Times Company. Reprinted by permission.

blacks. These economic disparities have the results we would anticipate; more Hispanics and blacks live in poverty than do whites. In 1986, 31.1 percent of blacks, 27.3 percent of Hispanics, but only 11 percent of whites lived below the poverty level (Welniak and Littman, 1987:24–25).

Several factors contribute to these differences. The mean family size for the total population is 2.98, but 3.41 for blacks and 3.49 for Hispanics (Welniak and Littman, 1987:33), both of whom tend to have more children than whites. Thus, as the tables indicate, the black and Hispanic populations in the United States contain a disproportionately large number of dependent children. At the same time, many blacks and Hispanics have relatively low educational levels, and thus higher levels of unemployment and lower average incomes.

TABLE 4.1   SPANISH-ORIGIN POPULATIONS IN THE UNITED STATES

Composition and Size

Ethnic Origin*	Number	Percent
Mexican	9.5 million	59.8
Puerto Rican	2.2 million	13.8
Cuban	0.9 million	5.5
Other (Dominican Republic, Panama, Colombia, etc.)	3.3 million	20.9
Total Spanish Population†	15.9 million‡	100.0

Selected Characteristics

Age	Spanish origin	Non-Spanish origin
0–9 years	21.9 percent	14.1 percent
10–19 years	21.1 percent	17.1 percent
30–39 years	13.6 percent	13.9 percent
40–49 years	33.4 percent	36.7 percent
50–59 years	7.0 percent	10.5 percent
70+ years	3.0 percent	7.7 percent
Percent high school graduates in 1983	58.0 percent	88.0 percent
Median family income 1982†	$16,227	$23,907

*From Rendon, Armando B. 1985. *We....* Washington, D.C.: U.S. Government Printing Office, pp. 2–3.
†From Kincannon, C. Louis. 1983. *Conditions of Hispanics in America Today*. Washington, D.C.: U.S. Government Printing Office, pp. 3, 6, 7, and 13.
‡Equals approximately 6.5% of total U.S. population.

TABLE 4.2   THE BLACK POPULATION IN THE UNITED STATES

Age (1980)*	Black	Nonblack
Under 15 years	28.1 percent	21.1 percent
15–64	64.0 percent	66.7 percent
65+ years	7.9 percent	12.2 percent
Percent high school graduates in 1983	79.0 percent	87.0 percent
Median family income 1984	$15,430	$27,690
Total population	28.2 million†	211.8 million

*From U.S. Department of Commerce. Bureau of the Census. 1987. *Statistical Abstract of the United States 1987*. Washington, D.C.: U. S. Government Printing Office, p. 35. All other data from Johnson, Dwight L. 1986. *We, the Black Americans*. Washington, D.C.: U.S. Government Printing Office, pp. 2, 6, and 12.
†Approximately 11.8% of total U.S. population.

Relatively rapid growth in these two segments of the U.S. population, therefore, has implications for social welfare. If current population growth trends continue, we can anticipate a need for economic, educational, and employment-related services among black and Hispanic families. Furthermore, there is an increasing need for community and political action to remedy the structural problems that affect black and Hispanic citizens.

Another rapidly growing segment of the U.S. population is the elderly. The U.S. population is aging. Between 1980 and 1985, the number of people over age 65 increased by 11 percent compared with an increase of 4 percent for those under 65 (AARP, *A Profile of Older Americans,* 1986:1). In addition, the older population is itself getting older. That is, the number of people living beyond age 85 as a proportion of those 65 and over is increasing. Also, women over 65 greatly outnumber men: 147 women for every 100 men in 1985. These trends too have implications for the social welfare system.

Demography and Populations with Special Needs

Demographic trends often include growth in population subgroups that have special needs, as with blacks, Hispanics, and the elderly in the United States. The reasons for such trends are often historical and cultural. The U.S. Hispanic population continues to grow, for example, because of continuing immigration from Spanish-speaking countries, because many Hispanics are Roman Catholics, and because many are young. The elderly segment of the U.S. population is increasing because of social values that encourage people to have fewer children and modern medicine's ability to keep people alive longer.

The social welfare system has traditionally responded to the needs of these special groups. Sometimes this response has been prompted by a social consensus concerning the legitimacy of the particular groups or needs involved. In other cases, the response originated with social welfare professionals who first identified a set of needs and worked for societal recognition and action. Through the years many groups have been targeted for special social welfare attention. Among these are children, the elderly, and blacks. The historical development of services for these special groups, as well as for women, those with physical or mental limitations, and gay and lesbian people, is examined below.

Children   When the United States was an agricultural society it was common for families to have large numbers of children, just as it is today in developing nations around the world. In this country's early years, it was assumed that most children would work, and most did, often on the family farm. Later, as industrialization proceeded, many children were employed in factories where they worked long hours, often under dangerous conditions and for little pay. Their education was sacrificed to the demands of their jobs, and many could look forward to little other than a life of hard, low-paying work.

These conditions notwithstanding, children were considered a special population from the earliest years of the modern social welfare system. As indicated in the preceding chapter, the Elizabethan Poor Law of 1601 paid special attention to the needs of children, providing for the care of those without adequate family support via the indenture system. By the late 1800s, attempts were made to remove them from almshouses and the adult correctional system where they were sometimes housed with their destitute parents or as a result of their own misbehavior (Axinn and Levin, 1982:108).

In the United States, child labor legislation appeared at the beginning of the 1900s, and the Children's Bureau was created by the federal government to monitor conditions affecting children in 1912. The obvious link between the well-being of children and the integrity of the family ultimately led to legislation providing economic support for families, especially mothers. The passage of the Social Security Act in 1935 was an important expression of this support since it established a pension plan and a variety of other income support programs for dependent women and children.

These family-oriented provisions were later extended in the 1962 and 1967 amendments to the Social Security Act, both aimed at strengthening family life and child care. The Economic Opportunity Act of 1964 established, among others, the Head Start Program offering early education for disadvantaged children, and the Job Corps to provide educational, training, and job opportunities for needy youths (Axinn and Levin, 1982:256–257). The Supreme Court affirmed the right of children to due process in 1967, an important foundation for more recent efforts to protect children from abuse and neglect.

Modern technology and contemporary lifestyles have given rise to many new concerns about children's needs. Parents can now know before birth the gender of the fetus, and whether it has congenital mental or physical limitations. Children can be conceived through artificial insemination or even in test tubes. Those parents who can afford the costly medical procedures involved can now choose not only whether to have a child but increasingly can make choices concerning the type of child they wish to have. This raises a host of ethical issues that are just beginning to be addressed. Some of them relate to the rights of fetuses and children, issues that will no doubt generate future child welfare legislation.

Cultural values concerning children have also changed. With both parents working there is less time for child rearing. In addition, the high cost of raising a child, and the particularly high costs of caring for a child with physical or mental limitations, lead many parents to want children who are "perfect." Such preferences are only reinforced by continuing discrimination against those with physical or mental limitations, and, even now, against women. As medical science increases our ability to identify certain types of congenital problems before birth, the vexing question of parental versus fetal rights becomes increasingly significant. The issues involved are doubly significant for poor people. Lacking the money to pay for sophisticated medical tests or even adequate prenatal care, poor families are far more likely to include children with physical or mental limitations. Because their families are often unable to bear the economic costs involved, these children are unlikely to receive the care they need.

Future social welfare legislation and programs will have to address these issues. All children deserve the chance to grow and prosper. Yet many of the programs and services that were once appropriate to meet children's needs are insufficient in the face of today's changed circumstances. Today, we need new perspectives on social welfare's role in meeting the needs of children.

The Elderly   Before the Industrial Revolution, the elderly usually remained with their families where they were responsible for child care and other chores. As families grew smaller in response to the economic and social changes associated with industrialization, many elderly were no longer able to remain with their families. For this reason, the Elizabethan Poor Law of 1601 provided almshouses (indoor relief) for elderly adults who either had no family or whose family was unable to care for them. This enabled older adults to live out their lives quietly and with some sense of security. As improved living conditions and better medical care enabled more people to live longer, the need increased for programs designed to help the elderly remain independent. Once again, the landmark piece of legislation in the United States was the Social Security Act of 1935. It established a retirement and survivors pension plan, and provided for income maintenance grants that allowed the destitute elderly to remain in their own homes (outdoor relief).

The basic programs established in 1935 have been continued and expanded over the years through a series of amendments. To these have been added the programs established by the Older Americans Act in 1965, the next major effort on behalf of the elderly. It created a network of agencies at all levels of government to plan, coordinate, and deliver a range of special services for the elderly. These include housing, recreation, transportation, nutrition, and counseling (Maldonado, 1987:102). Medicaid and Medicare were added to the Social Security Act in 1965 for the purpose of better meeting the health care needs of the elderly. The Supplemental Security Income Program of 1974 further refined the types of financial help available to poor or disabled elderly people. These programs have substantially improved the economic situation of the average elderly person. Current efforts on their behalf focus on the prevention of abuse, housing, and long-term custodial and health care.

American Indians   The indigenous population in what is now the United States was quickly dominated by the new European settlers. Outnumbered almost from the outset, the American Indian population was further reduced by the spread of diseases introduced from Europe. Further, the new settlers possessed a clearly superior military technology. The result was widespread killing of American Indians and displacement of whole tribes from their original homelands to reservations established by the government. The federal government took on a custodial role toward American Indians, primarily through the activities of the Bureau of Indian Affairs (BIA). Created in 1824, the BIA promoted assimilation into the majority culture through the tribal educational system—which it controlled—and by removing many children from their homes, placing them instead in white families. In recent years, it has relocated adults from reservations to urban areas to receive job training. All of these activities weakened tribal cohesion and disrupted what had been a strong and effective informal social welfare network.

It was not until the Economic Opportunity Act of 1964 that the government made a substantial effort to promote self-determination among American Indians. This effort was continued and expanded under the Indian Child Welfare Act of 1978 which was designed to strengthen the ability of tribes and communities to raise their own children and determine the type of education they receive (Blanchard, 1987:147). The role of the government in the affairs of American Indians is currently ambiguous, and periodic conflicts still erupt over ownership of land and self-determination. Like other minority groups, American Indians are increasingly turning to the courts for help with these issues.

Like other minority populations, American Indians have been faced with a series of choices between preservation of their own culture and assimilation. In general, they have sought to preserve their own culture, something many outsiders have found it difficult to understand for at least two reasons. The first is that each American Indian tribe is a distinct cultural group with ties to its particular land and history. Outsiders are often unaware of these distinctions and propose to treat all American Indians as alike. The second issue is that most American Indians do not share the larger society's commitment to controlling the social and physical environment via the use of technology. Theirs is a culture that places its highest values on consensus, group self-determination, and a respect for the environment, the elderly, and tribal history.

It has proven difficult to accommodate American Indian culture within the larger society's quite different set of values. Today, American Indians have somewhat more legal protection than in the past and are not so often forced to live in ways and places that violate their cultural beliefs. In addition, their numbers are growing rapidly. From 1970 to 1980 the American Indian population increased 72 percent from 574,000 to over 1,300,000 (Blanchard, 1987:142). For these reasons, American Indians may be able to act on their own behalf more effectively in the future.

Blacks   Most African blacks were originally brought to the United States as slaves. As noted in the last chapter, the Freedmen's Bureau was created after the Civil War to help blacks with the problems they faced when suddenly freed. It proved useful but was subsequently terminated during Reconstruction. The period that followed was one of little federal action in spite of the passage of a rash of discriminatory "Jim Crow" laws at the state level, and especially in the south.

During this time, blacks organized to help themselves through the formation of such groups as the National Association for the Advancement of Colored People (NAACP) in 1909 and the National Urban League in 1910 (Axinn and Levin, 1982:151). The Brotherhood of Sleeping Car Porters, an all-black union, was formed in the early 1900s by A. Philip Randolph and became an advocate for equal rights for black people. The great need for labor generated by U.S. participation in World War II (1941–1945) resulted in openings for blacks in many areas previously closed to them, including the military and many government agencies (Axinn and Levin, 1982:239). Even this much progress, however, was not accomplished without race riots in the early 1940s.

The Supreme Court's 1954 decision in *Brown v. Board of Education* that the existence of separate educational facilities for racial groups was inherently unequal ushered in an era of major legal challenges to racism. Galvanized by the courageous action of Rosa Parks in 1955 who refused to move to the back of a Birmingham, Alabama, bus, blacks organized to seek their rights, sometimes in the face of violence. Nevertheless, they were ultimately successful in eliminating segregation of public facilities. Much of this progress occurred under the leadership of people such as the Reverend Dr. Martin Luther King, Jr., and Whitney M. Young, Jr.

Major progress was made in obtaining civil rights for black Americans in the late 1950s and early 1960s. The Civil Rights Act of 1957 created the Commission on Civil Rights to strengthen federal enforcement abilities. Black civil rights activists organized a massive march on Washington in 1963 to press for needed civil rights legislation and were rewarded with passage of the Civil Rights Act of 1964. This landmark legislation further expanded procedures for enforcing civil rights laws, particularly those pertaining to voting rights (Schroeder, 1987:280–287). It further mandated desegregation of public education and the workplace, and established the Equal Employment Opportunity Commission to help in this effort.

Following the social activism of the 1960s, much of the progress toward equality for blacks has taken the form of Supreme Court decisions, a development that highlights the importance of the relationship between legislation and the judiciary. Legislation may establish policies, but their effectiveness often depends on the way they are implemented. For blacks and other minority groups, the courts have become the arena within which they have sought to ensure that policies once established via legislation are, in fact, carried out.

Blacks, as we have already seen, are a significant part of the total U.S. population—12 percent in 1985. As a group, they are also poorer and receive less education than whites. In addition, an increasing number of black families are headed by a single parent, usually female—41.9 percent in 1983 compared to 28.3 percent in 1970 (McAdoo, 1987:196). There are many reasons for this, including the lower wages earned by blacks, high death rates among black men that reduce the number of potential husbands among blacks, and the pressures of poverty that drive families apart.

Unfortunately, female-headed families are likely to be poor, and this is especially true among blacks. Some 64 percent of black single mothers are poor, compared to 40 percent of their nonblack counterparts (McAdoo, 1987:198). Since 50.6 percent of black children lived in female-headed families in 1984, it is little surprise that 46.5 percent of all black children were living in poverty in that year (McAdoo, 1987:197–198). With so many black children growing up poor, it is no wonder that so many of them become progressively more disadvantaged as they grow older.

United States society has yet to undo the patterns that have contributed to discrimination against blacks through the years. Progress has been made in some areas, but serious problems remain. Until systemic change is accomplished, many blacks will continue to be prevented from realizing their full potential and contributing to society to the full extent of their abilities. This loss of talent is enormously costly, as is the ongoing use of social welfare programs to meet needs among a disadvantaged population. In the short run, social welfare must seek to meet these needs more effectively. In the long run, substantial social change is needed.

Other Special Populations   Over the years, there have been other groups whose needs have prompted special attention. As we have already seen, military veterans and their families are one such group. Mental patients have been another. Dorothea Dix is famous for her advocacy of more humane treatment for the mentally ill in the 1840s. A more recent effort to provide mental health care in the community—deinstitutionalization—was intended to improve the quality of treatment and reduce the likelihood of abuse and neglect often associated with institutionalization, although it has not always had that effect.

The needs of those with mental or physical limitations are also receiving more attention. Modern medicine has made great strides in treating many physical limitations, and there are today many more programs for the physically limited than in the past. These programs are designed to provide training and employment opportunities, access to public transportation and facilities, community-based housing, and protection from abuse and neglect.

The needs of women have recently begun to receive special attention. The changing role of women in industrial societies has led to new thinking about their needs. Once viewed as tied to a family unit—to children, a man, and a household—women are today granted greater social acceptance as autonomous people who control their own lives. As a result, women have improved educational opportunities, the right to vote, expanded employment opportunities, better treatment in the workplace, increased financial support for single mothers, improvements in medical care, and better protection from abuse and neglect in comparison to the past. Nonetheless, much progress remains to be made.

Refugees have been another special population whose plight has received attention in recent years. Often separated from their families, subjected to threatened (or actual) bodily harm, and from different linguistic and cultural backgrounds, refugees have suffered from high levels of unemployment and have often been the target of intergroup hostility. In response, new social welfare programs have been created to meet their basic needs and to provide legal assistance and help in reuniting families.

Finally, gay and lesbian people have also been making progress in their fight for equal protection under the law. Struggling against unequal treatment in the workplace, they have also sought—and in recent years begun to receive—increased opportunities to meet and socialize, improved housing, opportunities to parent, protection from physical violence, and needed medical care. Discrimination in many of these areas, however, has become a far more serious issue with the advent of the AIDS crisis.

All of these four groups—women, those with physical or mental limitations, refugees, and lesbian and gay people—continue to fight societal stereotypes that are inaccurate and that perpetuate discrimination.

TABLE 4.3 RECENT LEGISLATIVE AND JUDICIAL PROGRESS TOWARD SOCIAL JUSTICE

Event	Importance	Year	Group affected
Brown v. Board of Education	Supreme Court decision prohibiting racially segregated educational facilities	1954	Black people
Civil Rights Act	Established the U.S. Commission on Civil Rights	1957	All minority group members
Equal Pay Act	Established equal pay for men and women who do equal work	1963	Women
Civil Rights Act	Prohibited discrimination based on race, color, religion, or national origin in public places, government facilities, federally assisted programs, and employment practices. Gender was included in the mandated employment equality	1964	Black and ethnic people, women
Voting Rights Act	Prohibited use of voting procedures to deny the vote to eligible minorities of race, color, age, or language group	1965	Black, ethnic, and elderly people
South Carolina v. Katzenbach	Supreme Court decision upholding the Voting Rights Act	1966	Black, ethnic, and elderly people
Age Discrimination Act	Prohibited use of age to discriminate in employment practices	1967	Elderly people
Indian Civil Rights Act	Guaranteed rights of individual American Indians in tribal actions and in society at large	1968	American Indian people
Graham v. Richardson	Supreme Court decision protecting the rights of aliens	1971	Members of ethnic groups
Griggs v. Duke Power Company	Supreme Court decision prohibiting employment practices that disadvantaged women or other minorities	1971	Women and other minority groups
Swann v. Charlotte-Mecklenburg Board of Education	Supreme Court decision that approved busing as a school desegregation strategy	1971	Black people
Education amendments	Prohibited discrimination based on sex or impaired vision in federally assisted education programs	1972	Women and visually limited

TABLE 4.3   RECENT LEGISLATIVE AND JUDICIAL PROGRESS TOWARD SOCIAL JUSTICE   (*continued*)

Event	Importance	Year	Group affected
Rehabilitation Act	Prohibited discrimination against those with mental or physical limitations in government and federally assisted employment	1973	People with limitations
Frontiero v. Richardson	Supreme Court decision upholding spousal rights of women in the military	1973	Women
Equal Education Opportunity Act	Prohibited discrimination in public education based on race, color, sex, or national origin	1974	Women, black, and ethnic people
Lau v. Nichols	Supreme Court decision protecting the rights of non-English speaking students to public school education	1974	Members of ethic groups
Equal Credit Opportunity Act	Protected credit rights of people regardless of race, color, sex, religion, national origin, marital status, or age	1974	Women and black, ethnic, elderly, single people
Morton v. Mancini	Supreme Court decision gave American Indians preference in hiring at the Bureau of Indian Affairs	1974	American Indians
Age Discrimination Act	Protected the elderly in federally assisted programs	1975	The elderly
Education of All Handicapped Children Act	Provided for free public education for all those with mental or physical limitations	1975	People with limitations
American Indian Religious Freedom Act	Protected American Indian religious beliefs and practices	1975	American Indians
Plyer v. Doe	Supreme Court decision that protects public education rights of children of aliens	1980	Ethnic groups
Youngberg v. Romeo	Supreme Court decision that protects rights of involuntarily committed retarded people	1982	People with mental limitations

Sources: Alexander, Chauncey. 1987. History of social work and social welfare: Significant dates. In the *Encyclopedia of Social Work,* 18th ed. Silver Spring, Md.: National Association of Social Workers, pp. 777–788; and Blassingame, John W. 1982. The revolution that never was: The civil rights movement 1950–1980. In *Perspectives: The Civil Rights Quarterly,* vol. 14, no. 2 (Summer): 3–15.

THE DEVELOPMENT OF SOCIAL WELFARE SERVICES

The Private Sector

The development of social welfare has been accompanied by a general movement from private (nongovernmental) to public (governmental) sources of help. As we saw in the previous chapter, helping was originally carried out primarily within families, tribes, and communities. The sense of mutual obligation engendered by family and kin bonds was a powerful motivating source. In addition, the wealthy often cared for their workers in exchange for work and political support. Finally, the Judeo-Christian tradition encouraged people to help others, broadening the responsibility for helping to extend to those beyond one's immediate kin network. In addition, the church and other organized religious groups often provided direct help in the form of money, shelter, food, and education.

The network described above is nongovernmental, but it has both formal and informal aspects. Most people in family and kin networks did not think of themselves as helpers. Daily life patterns simply included activities in which people assisted each other. The relationship between the wealthy and their workers was more structured. Basic needs were met in return for expected levels of work and other kinds of support. However, even in these relationships spontaneous helping might occur.

The church's helping efforts tended to be more formal. One of the declared purposes of most churches was, and is, to help others. While some churches established strict rules governing the provision of help, there was often some degree of flexibility in the formality of their helping activities. Nonetheless, the church's response to need generally represented more than a simple charitable impulse. It was an enduring commitment implemented through structured activities.

The extent of the contemporary church's role in social welfare in the United States is illustrated by the data in Table 4.4. The data here are for 1984 and pertain to the Catholic Church. Other major denominations provide similar services.

As Table 4.4 indicates, member agencies and institutions of the National Conference of Catholic Charities spent over $514 million on program services in 1984, and served over 4,600,000 people. Although a substantial sum, the $514 million spent by Catholic agencies in 1984 represented but a small fraction of public expenditures in that same year. In that year, total government social welfare expenditures in the United States were $672 billion, of which $419.3 billion were spent by the federal government and $252.7 billion by state and local governments (U.S. Department of Commerce, Statistical Abstract, 1987:342).

By comparison, total private sector expenditures on social welfare in 1980 were estimated to be less than one-third of this amount. Total private spending on social welfare in 1980 is estimated to have been between $116.4 billion and $181 billion, depending on the definition of private agency used (Tropman and

TABLE 4.4   THE HELPING ROLE OF THE CATHOLIC CHURCH IN THE UNITED STATES TODAY

Service	People served
Counseling	803,496
Residential care	105,698
Nonresidential care	91,060
Homemaker services	236,758
Health and medical services	114,371
Education	102,707
Legal services	69,333
Employment services	40,785
Recreational services	284,761
Transportation	122,429
Food	1,242,586
Adoption	49,004
Socialization services	283,317
Access services	530,421
Emergency shelter	166,496
Emergency assistance	683,915

Source: 1984 data for member agencies and institutions of the National Conference of Catholic Charities published by the Conference in Washington, D.C.

Tropman, 1987:829). Approximately 60 percent of this money—using the $116.4 billion figure—went for health care, 22 percent for education and research, and 11 percent for social services.

The Public Sector: Trends and Developments

As the social welfare system has evolved over the years, a number of trends have become evident. One of these has been the gradual shift toward reliance upon public expenditures and resources, the reasons for which we discussed in the previous chapter. In addition, the public social welfare system has itself evolved slowly over time. Today's public social welfare system is itself the product of many trends and historical developments that account for its present form and structure. Among these, several trends stand out. These include the involvement of multiple levels of government, the increasing involvement of the courts, and, in recent years, a variety of attempts to call into question the government's role in social welfare.

The Involvement of Multiple Levels of Government   Under the Elizabethan Poor Law of 1601, primary responsibility for social welfare rested with local governments whose officials were granted the right to tax citizens for this purpose, if necessary. In the United States, a similar pattern was followed until 1865 when the Freedmen's Bureau was established. Created in response to the dislocations of the Civil War, the Freedmen's Bureau was the first federal wel-

---

THE HUMAN FACE OF SOCIAL WELFARE 9

A Poor Church Attempts to Help Others

Most of the people who worship at St. Luke's Church...have very little money to spare. But yesterday, as they filed out after the service, they were asked to give to a group that is even poorer than they are—the homeless....

Its parishioners are mostly Hispanic people and mostly poor, and church officials say it is difficult to ask them to give even a little. But many of the people who dropped coins and slipped dollar bills into a collection box at the church doors yesterday said they had an obligation to help, despite their own difficulties.

"I feel it is my duty to help the needy person" said...a parishioner. "If they are out on the streets, who is going to help them?"

The church's appeal for money was part of a weekend-long effort by the Partnership for the Homeless, a multi-denominational group....

The group's effort has particular resonance for churches such as St. Luke's, in neighborhoods where residents are poor and homelessness is visible.

At midmorning in a vacant lot down the street from the church...an unkempt man rifled side-by-side with a stray dog through the garbage, looking for something to eat. Residents said the sight was not uncommon....

[A parishioner] gave each of her two children a coin to drop in. "Now I have a little bit, but tomorrow—who knows, I may have nothing at all," she said, speaking in Spanish as her daughter translated. "I want to help people who have nothing today."

As this account indicates, some churches not only attempt to provide services to others but also emphasize the need to act charitably toward others and encourage their members to do so.

From Sarah Lyall, A poor parish strains to help the homeless. *The New York Times,* November 30, 1987, p. B1ff. Copyright (c) 1987 by the New York Times Company. Reprinted by permission.

---

fare agency. Intermediary levels of government began to get involved in 1910 when Kansas City created a system of local overseers in city and county departments of social welfare (Axinn and Levin, 1982:136). Illinois extended this concept to the state level in 1917, thereby laying the foundation for our current system of shared federal, state, and local responsibility for public assistance programs.

The states shortly moved into social welfare in other ways as well. In 1911, several states established systems to compensate workers for job-related injuries, while legislation creating pensions for the elderly was passed by several states in 1923 (Axinn and Levin, 1982:145).

The Great Depression that began with the stock market collapse of 1929 precipitated a greatly increased social welfare role for the federal government as people's inability to cope independently with larger economic forces became apparent. In particular, the passage of the Social Security Act of 1935 reflected societal recognition that people's well-being was often dependent on forces beyond their control. These included not only the economic forces that determined the availability of work, but dangerous working conditions and life-span related factors such as old age and childhood.

The Social Security Act also addressed some other important issues. It re-affirmed society's commitment to have a public social welfare system that involved all three major levels of government. This approach was consistent with the basic principles of the U.S. political system, itself a federal system in which responsibility is shared between the states and the federal government. Thus, while some programs (such as retirement benefits) were entirely federal in scope and operation, others (such as unemployment benefits) were federally mandated but implemented by the states. States were also free to decide how they wished to share responsibility with local communities, the level at which many services are actually delivered.

The role of the government in social welfare was accepted and acknowledged, but care was also taken to minimize governmental intrusion into the marketplace and the private helping system. For example, retirement benefits were intended to supplement people's savings rather than replace them. Furthermore, the programs created primarily addressed people's financial needs. Services intended to enhance the individual's social development or provide counseling were not a major feature of the original Social Security Act. Perhaps the one major exception to this rule was public schooling, an extremely important social development program that had been widely accepted as an appropriate function for government by the mid-1800s.

The various programs created by the Social Security Act were gradually refined and expanded through subsequent amendments. Financial benefits have been increased, and medical services and programs for those with mental and physical limitations have been expanded substantially. The creation of the Supplemental Security Income (SSI) Program in 1974 was of particular importance. Under SSI, responsibility for grant programs for the destitute blind, disabled, and aged was transferred to the federal government rather than being shared by federal and state agencies as had been the case. Finally, the establishment of the Medicare and Medicaid programs in 1965 ushered in a new era in public social welfare in the United States since it represented an acknowledgement of the public sector's responsibility for meeting people's medical care needs. Both programs, furthermore, are mandated and (primarily) funded at the federal level but implemented at the state level. As such, they are prime examples of the continuing pattern of shared federal and state responsibility for social welfare in this country.

The Increasing Role of the Courts   A sometimes overlooked consequence of the Social Security Act was greater involvement of the courts in social welfare. When benefits are a matter of public law, citizens have recourse to the courts to challenge treatment they believe to be inequitable or inadequate. This sense of entitlement and empowerment has been a significant benefit of moving social welfare into the public arena. Indeed, cultivating a sense of empowerment among clients was one of the objectives of the Economic Opportunity Act of 1964. One of the operating principles of this landmark act was the notion that the **participation of the poor** was needed in planning for social welfare programs. In order to do this, the act created programs to improve educational and employment opportunities for the poor, and to promote volunteer efforts among the nonpoor. The purpose was to empower people to take control of their own lives and even to challenge major social institutions when necessary.

Although the effectiveness of the Economic Opportunity Act was limited because of political and economic problems caused by the Vietnam war, it had a lasting impact. Its enactment coincided with the civil rights movement of the 1960s that challenged structural obstacles faced by minority groups and the poor. The empowerment made possible by the Economic Opportunity Act and the civil rights movement resulted in significant civil rights legislation and Supreme Court decisions that profoundly affected social welfare.

Questioning Society's Commitment to Social Welfare The election of Richard Nixon as President in 1968 ushered in an era of attacks on public social welfare programs and, more importantly, the values and principles on which they were based. The Nixon administration's opposition to school busing as an effective civil rights tool stimulated antibusing legislation in 1972 that has seriously weakened school busing in concept and practice. Nixon also supported what has been called **workfare,** *the practice of making recipients of public assistance participate in work or training programs.*

The workfare approach, although politically palatable, tends to create serious difficulties for single mothers with young children, those with physical and mental limitations, and the elderly. Further, its implementation raises serious issues whenever the available jobs require skills unlikely to be possessed by welfare recipients, when low-paying jobs pay less than welfare and poverty levels, and when welfare recipients are used as cheap replacements for regular workers. Nevertheless, several states passed such legislation followed by national legislation mandating workfare as part of the Family Support Act passed in 1988.

Nixon was also a proponent of what has come to be known as the **new federalism.** Under the new federalism, *the federal government continues to provide grants for a variety of purposes, including welfare, to the states but has eliminated many of the regulations governing how the money must be used.* These grants have taken two forms: revenue sharing and block grants. **Revenue-sharing grants** *are unrestricted; that is, the federal government imposes no restrictions on how monies may be used by the states.* **Block grants** *are earmarked for a specific social welfare purpose but are accompanied by relatively few guidelines regarding program design and implementation.*

The new federalism represented an effort to transfer as much decision-making as possible from the federal level back to state and local governments. However, it also involved a reduction in the amount of federal funds provided for social welfare programs. Thus, state governments were given more freedom to decide how to spend fewer social welfare dollars. The result was to force existing programs to compete with one another for scarce funds—highway repairs versus library services, for example—and an overall reduction in social welfare services. Equally important, the new federalism ran counter to the underlying philosophy of existing federal programs, control over which had deliberately been assigned to the federal government in an effort to reduce the inequities associated with earlier programs administered at the state and local level.

In 1974, Nixon left office in disgrace as a result of the Watergate scandal. He was succeeded by Gerald Ford (1973–1976) and Jimmy Carter (1976–1980), neither of whom attempted any major changes in social welfare. The election of Ronald Reagan in 1980, however, ushered in an era during which the objectives, principles, and programs of federal social welfare policy were subjected to relentless attacks.

Picking up where Nixon had left off, President Reagan continued to use revenue-sharing and block grants to reduce the federal role in social welfare. He also sought to reduce the size and role of the federal government, which he thought was too expensive and too intrusive. Ironically, while cutting social programs and reducing government revenues through substantial tax cuts, he simultaneously increased military spending to such an extent that the overall cost of government actually increased. The final result was a record federal budget deficit, a greatly expanded military establishment, and severe cutbacks in helping services (Burt and Pittman, 1985).

The Reagan administration relied heavily on an economic philosophy known as *supply-side economics*. This proved to be controversial. *Supply-side economists argued that increasing incentives for business investment and expansion would create jobs and increase incomes*. In this fashion, it was argued, new jobs would be created and personal and corporate income would rise while inflation would be held in check. Inevitably, said the policymakers involved, some of these jobs and a significant proportion of this income would go to the poor—the "trickle-down" theory. Thus, social welfare programs were cut to reduce government costs and because they would presumably no longer be needed. In addition, taxes were cut as a stimulus to investment.

To a degree, these policies worked. That is to say, inflation during the Reagan years (1980–1988) was held in check, many new jobs were created (although there is considerable controversy about the quality of the jobs involved), and the administration was able to claim, as it left office, that it had accomplished many of its economic objectives.

There were, however, disquieting signs on the economic horizon. There was, for one thing, a series of record federal deficits which cumulatively had increased the national debt at a rate greater than any previous time in history. There was also the great stock market crash of October 19, 1987, a crash exceeded in severity only by the one in 1929.

One result of these developments was the Gramm-Rudman-Hollings Act passed in 1985 in an effort to create a means of forcing Congress—rather than the President—to reduce federal spending and thus prevent further increases in the national debt. While the Gramm-Rudman-Hollings Act was designed to cut federal spending across the board, it necessarily implied further reductions in federal spending on social welfare, this in the wake of the series of earlier cutbacks. In the absence of a clear-cut plan for dealing with the various budgetary and economic problems confronting the United States at the close of the 1980s, it was clear only that the decade had been a difficult one for social welfare.

It had also been a difficult one for civil rights. The Reagan administration, like the Nixon administration, opposed busing to achieve school desegregation and did little to enforce existing civil rights laws (Federico, 1984:124). Indeed, it took a number of actions that seemed to undermine existing laws and precedents. These included changing the composition of the Civil Rights Commission by appointing a highly conservative majority, reinterpreting laws without amending any statute or regulation so that neither the Congress nor the public could respond, and attempting to appoint justices to the Supreme Court whose records showed little support for civil rights. In addition, President Reagan indicated his willingness to support racist schools, prayer in the schools, and antiabortion measures, all issues that have implications for social justice and equality. In spite of his personal popularity, the President experienced increased resistance toward his policies during the last half of his second term. This indicated what opinion polls confirmed—that social welfare and civil rights continue to be important to most Americans.

The public system's dominant role in social welfare is the product of a long and difficult evolution. The growth of public social welfare has been a response to the multiple needs of the large number of people who make up a heterogeneous mass society. In addition, the government's role in social and economic planning ensures its importance to social welfare. In spite of philosophical differences in the attitudes of individual leaders, it is unlikely that there will be a large-scale retreat by the government from the social welfare arena. Were that to happen, it would signal a fundamental shift in the nation's commitment to helping and that is not evident at this time.

It is important to note, however, that the debate over the future of public social welfare is not confined to the United States. Today, in almost every industrialized society, one hears talk of a "welfare crisis." Can the western industrialized world maintain or expand its current level of social welfare services? Table 4.5 lists some of the major variables involved.

To conclude this chapter, we can see that social welfare has developed into a helping system that goes far beyond day-to-day survival needs, although these continue to be very important for the millions who still live in poverty. The biological, social, and psychological aspects of human existence are being addressed in new and expanded ways. We will see in the next two chapters, however, that the programs comprising the U.S. social welfare system are often quite fragmented. Despite the existence of many individual programs, the "whole person" may be untouched and his or her basic plight left unresolved. Nevertheless, social welfare has over the centuries proven to be an adaptable and effective element in helping people to improve their lives.

LET'S REVIEW

This chapter has focused on the historical events that have shaped social welfare's development in western industrial societies. The economic and social ef-

TABLE 4.5 THE STATE OF SOCIAL WELFARE IN TODAY'S WORLD

Variable	Mexico	Poland	Sweden	United States
Total expenditures on social welfare	Down	Down	Up	Up
Economic situation	Weak	Weak	Strong	Uncertain
Political situation	Changing	Changing	Stable	Uncertain
Consensus about the value of social welfare	Moderate	Strong	Strong	Moderate
Potential for growth of social welfare in near future	Limited*	Limited*	Limited†	Moderate‡

*Mexico and Poland both face uncertain economic futures. Recent movement toward more political openness and economic reforms may help to revive their troubled economies which would then make more resources available for social welfare purposes.

†Sweden may have reached a plateau of services where people feel basic needs are met and that higher taxes for additional services are not desirable. Its immediate goal may be to preserve its existing structure of services.

‡The United States has many programs that could, and—from the standpoint of meeting human needs—should, be expanded. However, troubling economic factors—especially a large foreign debt—may reinforce conservative arguments to the effect that the nation cannot afford a major expansion of its social welfare system.

fects of the Industrial Revolution, and the impact of wars, natural disasters, and of demographic changes were analyzed because of their special importance. The most important demographic factors include immigration, population size, and population composition. Certain groups within a population are especially important because of their special needs.

The chapter also pulled together information about the movement from private to public social welfare. While both continue to be important, the dominance of the public sector reflects changing economic conditions and values about the role of government in the life of its citizens.

Taken together, this chapter and the previous one have attempted to give you a firm foundation for understanding the current social welfare system in the United States. You will see in the next two chapters that our current social welfare system is comprised of many programs, but that each tends to focus on specific needs. An overall framework to coordinate service delivery is lacking, leading to gaps in coverage and administrative inefficiencies. Knowing how social welfare developed will help you to understand why the existing system is so fragmented and incomplete. Later in the book, when we look toward the future, your knowledge of history will again be especially useful.

For now, though, we leave the past and return to the present. The next two chapters will introduce you to the current social welfare system in the United States, with provocative glimpses at social welfare in our other three societies. First, you will see how the whole structure is conceptualized, and then how it is translated into specific programs. These coming chapters, then, will show you the actual structure of social welfare in day-to-day operation.

CHAPTER OUTLINE

STUDY QUESTIONS

1 What historical event in your own lifetime has, in your opinion, had the greatest effect on social welfare? Is this event an example of a war, natural disaster, demographic change, or an intellectual advance? In what way did this event reinforce or counteract the effects of earlier similar events?

2 Do you think that highly industrial nations like the United States can coexist peacefully with the much poorer and less industrially developed nations of the Third World? In answering this question, focus on the kinds of needs people have in each type of society, and the extent to which these needs are met. You might want to use Mexico as an interesting case of a society that is in the midst of industrialization.

3 Select a historical event in the United States and research its impact on social welfare in terms of either the needs it created or the social welfare responses it produced.

4 Obtain census data about the racial and ethnic composition of your community. (If you need help doing this, consult your library's reference librarian.) Prepare a chart showing the numerical size and the percentage of each population group. When pre-

paring the chart, use the most specific categories possible, e.g., Chinese, Japanese, Korean, Vietnamese, East Indian, and so on rather than simply "Asian."
5 Identify the group whose needs you think are currently being met least well by the social welfare system and list this group's needs as specifically as you can. Why do you think society has not yet paid attention to these needs?

KEY TERMS AND CONCEPTS

block grants
demographic changes
new federalism
participation of the poor

revenue-sharing grants
settlement houses
workfare

SUGGESTED READINGS

Esping-Andersen, Gøsta, and Walter Korpi. 1984. *From Poor Relief Towards Institutional Welfare States*. Stockholm: Institute for Social Research. A monograph that analyzes the development of Sweden's advanced welfare state and the factors that shape the growth of social welfare.

Flora, Peter, ed. 1986. *Growth to Limits: The Western European Welfare States Since World War II,* vol. I. New York: Walter de Gruyter Publishers. This volume examines the factors that have limited the growth of social welfare in the four Scandinavian societies. Future volumes will do the same for other European societies.

Green, James W. 1986. *Cultural Awareness in the Human Services,* 2d ed. Englewood Cliffs, N.J.: Prentice-Hall. This book provides valuable information about the effects of culture on need, the perceptions of need, and appropriate responses. Includes useful information about the historical, demographic, and immigration experiences of various cultural groups.

Sheahan, John. 1987. *Patterns of Development in Latin America*. Princeton, N.J.: Princeton University Press. Although it draws heavily upon economic theory, this work is nonetheless very helpful for understanding the impact of industrialization on developing nations. The relationships between population growth and distribution, economic productivity, and political decision-making are clearly described, along with their implications for social welfare.

The United Nations. 1979. *Patterns of Government Expenditure on Social Services*. New York: The United Nations. This monograph examines the pattern of government expenditures on social services, and the factors underlying those patterns, in developing countries, western industrial societies, and industrial societies with centrally planned economies.

REFERENCES

American Association of Retired Persons. 1986. *A Profile of Older Americans.* Washington, D.C.: American Association of Retired Persons. Pamphlet.

Axinn, June, and Herman Levin. 1982. *Social Welfare: A History of the American Response to Need,* 2d ed. White Plains, N.Y.: Longman, Inc.

Blanchard, Evelyn Lance. 1987. American Indians and Alaska Natives. In the *Encyclopedia of Social Work,* 18th ed. Silver Spring, Md.: National Association of Social Workers, pp. 142–150.

Burt, Martha, and Karen Pittman. 1985. *Testing the Social Safety Net.* Washington, D.C.: The Urban Institute.

Esping-Andersen, Gøsta, and Walter Korpi. 1984. *From Poor Relief Towards Institutional Welfare States.* Stockholm: Institute for Social Research.

Estrada, Leobardo. 1987. Hispanics. In the *Encyclopedia of Social Work,* 18th ed. Silver Spring, Md.: National Association of Social Workers, pp. 732–739.

Federico, Ronald. 1984. *The Social Welfare Institution,* 4th ed. Lexington, Mass.: D.C. Heath and Company.

Flora, Peter, ed. 1986. *Growth to Limits: The Western European Welfare States Since World War II,* vol. I. New York: Walter de Gruyter Publishers.

Green, James W. 1986. *Cultural Awareness in the Human Services,* 2d ed. Englewood Cliffs, N.J.: Prentice-Hall.

Jenkins, Shirley. 1987. Immigrants and undocumented aliens. In the *Encyclopedia of Social Work,* 18th ed. Silver Spring, Md.: National Association of Social Workers, pp. 872–880.

Loavenbruck, Grant, and Paul Keys. 1987. Settlements and neighborhood centers. In the *Encyclopedia of Social Work,* 18th ed. Silver Spring, Md.: National Association of Social Workers, pp. 556–561.

Maldonado, David. 1987. Aged. In the *Encyclopedia of Social Work,* 18th ed. Silver Spring, Md.: National Association of Social Workers, pp. 95–106.

McAdoo, Harriett. 1987. Blacks. In the *Encyclopedia of Social Work,* 18th ed. Silver Spring, Md.: National Association of Social Workers, pp. 194–206.

Nelson, Harold, ed. 1983. *Poland: A Country Study.* Washington, D.C.: U.S. Government Printing Office.

Oil price plunge forces cuts in services. 1986. *NASW News,* 3. Silver Spring, Md.: National Association of Social Workers.

Poland announces big economic shift. 1987a. *The New York Times,* October 11, A1ff.

Rendon, Armando. 1985. *We...* Washington, D.C.: U.S. Government Printing Office. Brochure.

Schroeder, Oliver, Jr. 1987. Civil rights. In the *Encyclopedia of Social Work,* 18th ed. Silver Spring, Md.: National Association of Social Workers, pp. 280–287.

Sheahan, John. 1987. *Patterns of Development in Latin America.* Princeton, N.J.: Princeton University Press.

The Swedish Institute. 1984. *Immigrants in Sweden.* Stockholm: The Swedish Institute, Fact Sheet on Sweden. Pamphlet.

Tropman, Elmer, and John E. Tropman. 1987. Voluntary agencies. In the *Encyclopedia of Social Work,* 18th ed. Silver Spring, Md.: National Association of Social Workers, pp. 825–842.

The United Nations. 1979. *Patterns of Government Expenditure on Social Services.* New York: The United Nations.

U.S. Department of Commerce. Bureau of the Census. 1987. *Statistical Abstract of the United States 1987.* Washington, D.C.: U.S. Government Printing Office.

Veterans stampede Congress. 1987b. *The New York Times,* December 14, A22.

Ward, Peter. 1986. *Welfare Politics in Mexico.* London: Allen & Unwin, Ltd.

Welniak, Edward, and Mark Littman. 1987. *Money Income and Poverty Status of Families and Persons in the United States: 1986.* Washington, D.C.: U.S. Government Printing Office.

World Bank. 1986. *The World Bank Atlas 1986.* Washington, D.C.: The World Bank.

CHAPTER 5

WHAT IS THE STRUCTURE OF SOCIAL WELFARE TODAY?

WHAT TO EXPECT FROM THIS CHAPTER

In the previous chapter, we discussed some of the factors that have influenced the development of social welfare. This chapter will focus on the present: How are social welfare services organized in today's world? You will see that this chapter and the one that follows are closely related. This one examines the various ways in which service delivery may be *structured* while the next chapter describes specific *programs*. We have seen in earlier chapters that people have needs of several general types: biological, psychological, and social. Broken down into their component parts, human needs serve as a useful and logical way to structure social welfare programs. Thus, social welfare programs are often designed to meet specific needs such as medical care, adequate nutrition, housing, or education.

Knowing that we wish to devise a program to meet a specific human need does not tell us much about how to structure the program to ensure its effectiveness. How the program will be financed, who will be eligible, and how the program will be administered are among the questions that must first be answered.

You can begin to understand, then, that the design of specific programs is often determined by the overall structure of the social welfare system. It is this structure, or design, that you will be studying in this chapter. Once grasped, it will make it much easier for you to understand specific programs like Medicare, social security, and unemployment insurance. These will be the subject of the following chapter.

LEARNING OBJECTIVES

By the end of this chapter you should be able to do the following:

1 Describe the difference between the structure of social welfare and a specific social welfare program.

2 Explain why both formal and informal social welfare services are needed.

3 List at least three differences between public and private social welfare programs.

4 Discuss the advantages and disadvantages of having both public and private programs, rather than just one type.

5 Define income maintenance as a type of program.

6 Define services for personal development and enrichment.

7 Differentiate between family integrity, income maintenance, and empowerment as types of programs.

8 Define social insurance.

9 Explain why grant programs are often controversial.

10 Give an example of an in-kind program.

11 Describe the social welfare purpose of a tax benefit.

12 Define a public social utility.

13 Explain what is meant by a "cradle-to-grave" approach to social welfare.

FORMAL AND INFORMAL HELPING REVISITED

Let's begin by returning to familiar territory—formal and informal helping. As you know, this book is primarily concerned with formal helping, the services provided in a purposeful way by society for its members. Nevertheless, the design of social welfare includes both types of helping and they are mutually interdependent. Sometimes that interdependence is planned. Sometimes it is not.

Let's look at Poland to illustrate how these relationships can develop. By law, the Polish family is responsible for meeting the needs of its members, both young and old (Brzozowski et al., n.d.:18). Given this mandate, the family becomes an important source of informally provided social welfare services. It is also people's primary link with the formal social welfare structure because services to individuals are generally provided through their families. The Polish family, then, represents an important link between informal and formal helping structures.

However, Poland suffers from a severe housing shortage. It often takes 10 or more years of waiting before an apartment is available to families needing them (Les, 1985:2–3). As a result, three or even four generations may live together in small apartments. In this sense, the Polish family functions as an informal social welfare system, providing housing for its members when the formal structure is unable to do so. On the other hand, data show that such crowded living conditions create problems for family members (Les, 1985:4). The inability of the formal social welfare system to provide adequate housing strains the informal resources of the family, thereby generating additional needs for counseling and other kinds of help.

Unlike Poland, families in the United States are not legally responsible for caring for their adult members. Nevertheless, the current shortage of affordable housing has created a relationship between the informal and formal social welfare networks that is similar to the one in Poland. When people in the United States cannot find affordable housing, their first recourse is often to stay with friends or family while looking for a place to live. This was what happened to the Brand family (discussed in Chapter 1) after they were evicted from their home. This is usually a temporary solution, and eventually either housing is found or the family becomes homeless. If homelessness occurs, other problems generally follow—marital instability, difficulty getting the children to school, exposure to violence, and so on. (You will recall that the Brand family experienced many of these problems.)

We can see in the above examples how the informal helping network can be a valuable supplement to the formal system. However, informal resources are usually limited, and they can be easily overwhelmed by serious problems. Ideally, the informal system would provide as much help as it could and then the formal system would take over. In Sweden, for example, the government is experimenting with an innovative housing policy designed to deal with the problems that arise when several generations live together. The proposed solution involves building apartments that contain separate miniapartments for elderly family members or teenagers. This allows the family members involved to have some independence while still participating in family life. It improves the family's chances of meeting more needs of its members and avoiding the need for formal social welfare services.

As we have already seen, the informal and formal systems do not always work well together. Both systems may become overburdened, resulting in new problems. Nevertheless, it is important to remember that the two systems are linked, often by design (the role of the family in Poland) and sometimes by necessity (the homeless in the United States). How well they work together is a function of the overall design and basic structure of the social welfare system.

PUBLIC AND PRIVATE HELPING

Another subject mentioned in earlier chapters that can now be explored further is the relationship between public and private helping. In societies with free-market economic systems, such as the United States, the public sector is intended to be "...neither a handmaiden to capitalist exploitation nor a usurper of freedom in the market economy. Rather...the welfare state is considered a counterforce to balance against the excesses and hazards of capitalism without inhibiting the free market's productive energies" (Gilbert, 1983:164). In other words, social welfare's role is to protect those who are hurt by free-market competition without altering the fundamental nature of the economic system.

Notice that in other societies the objectives of the economic and social welfare systems may be more closely related to one another. Wojciechowski (1975:191), for example, notes that "Poland is a country strongly committed to the concept of governmental intervention through planning." In a socialist society such as Poland's, one of the purposes of the economic system is to achieve certain social welfare goals. Similarly, Sweden also believes in the use of centralized planning as a way of managing market forces to achieve agreed-upon social goals. In both countries, the public sector is by far the largest component of the social welfare system. Private services are either very limited, as in Sweden, or closely tied to the government, as in Poland.

In the United States, on the other hand, private agencies are an important part of the social welfare system. There are two primary reasons for this. The first is that social welfare can itself be provided on a free-market capitalistic basis. For example, there are social welfare agencies that are operated for profit and have stockholders, just like any other business. The second is a prevailing belief in the United States that government activity should be limited to those areas where it is absolutely necessary—levying taxes and providing for the national defense, for example. While some human needs—such as providing a minimum income for the elderly—are acknowledged to be a governmental responsibility, others are left to be provided by the private sector—most medical care, for example.

In the United States, public and private agencies can be differentiated in four major ways. Later we will see how, in spite of their differences, they work closely together.

Accountability

By law, public agencies are accountable to the public whereas private agencies are accountable only to their governing body, usually a board of directors. As a result, the public has the legal right to obtain information about the operation of public agencies. Access to similar data about private agencies is likely to be limited to those who are part of the organization that runs the agency.

Responsibility

Public agencies form the backbone of the social welfare system because they have been created to meet the basic needs of all citizens. Private agencies can be much more specialized, providing certain kinds of services to targeted user groups.

Resources

Public programs have access to government funds, whereas private agencies depend on contributions, fees, and contracts. Therefore, most public agencies have a much larger resource base than do private ones. This usually enables them to assist many more people and provide a wider range of services than private agencies can.

Flexibility and Participation

Public agencies are open to input from citizens through the political process. However, this is usually time consuming and cumbersome, so these agencies often find it difficult to respond quickly to new situations or problems. Private agencies receive input from their members, and decisions are made by their governing body. As a result, they often respond fairly quickly to new ideas, needs, or situations.

The differences between public and private agencies are illustrated by the New York City foster care example (see The Human Face of Social Welfare 10 in this chapter), which also makes another point: public and private agencies work together. Indeed, the boundaries between them are increasingly difficult to identify in some cases. Gilbert (1983:6) talks about the current phase of **welfare capitalism** as one in which it is believed that *capitalist profit-making strategies can and should be used by the welfare state*. This has encouraged the development of what is commonly called **privatization,** *delivering social welfare services through the private sector.*

Privatization is not new. However, what *is* new is the belief that private services can be profit-making, and the extent to which public funds are used to support private services. For example, Abramovitz (1986:261) notes that in 1977 nearly 80 percent of nursing homes operated for profit, and that public funds accounted for about two-thirds of their revenues (primarily through the Medicare and Medicaid programs). Abramovitz points out that for-profit hospital chains are especially lucrative. One, the Hospital Corporation of America, had after-tax profits in 1983 of over $243 million.

Contracting between public and private agencies is becoming increasingly common. **Contracting** *occurs when one agency pays another to provide certain services.* This is routinely done, especially by public agencies who often contract with private agencies, either because the private agency is better able to provide the service, or because it is less expensive to use an existing private service than for the public agency to itself develop a similar program. The New York City foster care account is an example. The need for additional foster care was met faster and at less expense by contracting with several already-existing private foster care agencies than it would have been by creating a

THE HUMAN FACE OF SOCIAL WELFARE 10

Public Resources, Private Services (Foster Care in New York City)

Though New York City is legally responsible for children in foster care, the city actually provides little of the services the youngsters receive. Only about 1,700 youngsters are housed in city-operated foster homes. The remaining children are distributed—literally allocated in a process that often resembles a human bazaar—among the 57 [private] agencies that care for the children, under contracts [between the city and the private agencies] worth $300 million a year....

The public and private agencies that run New York City's...foster care system are deeply split over who should control the system....

Even government officials who are nominally in charge are saying that a major part of the problem is that the system is complex, unwieldy and not really under anyone's control....

A 15-year-old Protestant girl who had given birth a year earlier was sent to the Mission of the Immaculate Virgin, a foster care center...run by the [Catholic] archdiocese. She told administrators there that she was sexually active, but they refused to provide her with birth control services. When she obtained birth control pills on her own, administrators took them away. A few months later, she became pregnant again.

A Protestant teenager was at the top of a list for placement in a group home run by a Jewish agency, but the spot was taken by a Jewish youngster lower on the list. The teenager had to go instead to a group home run by the city that did not have the supervision or the care for which the Jewish agency was known. The teenager dropped out of the program and ended up in prison on a weapons charge....

"I just can't say, 'Do it,' and it gets done," [a city official] said. "There is a diffusion of responsibility and control that makes it difficult to manage. When you want to change something to make the system more efficient or more effective there are an awful lot of steps."

The preceding excerpt illustrates some of the differences between private and public agencies. Major responsibility for foster care in New York City rests with the public sector, which is far larger and has far greater resources than the private agencies involved, in part because of the much greater scope of its responsibilities. Unfortunately, as the example also suggests, accountability is sometimes difficult to maintain in such large systems.

The case also illustrates the ability of private agencies to establish their own policies about service delivery. While public agencies must serve all who qualify, private agencies often provide services only to special groups.

Finally, the example also illustrates the greater flexibility of private agencies to utilize treatment methods that are responsive to problems and needs. In this case, the public agency was apparently struggling with less effective treatment strategies. This helps to explain why the teenager in the public group home received inadequate help. Here we can see the inflexibility that is often inherent in large public agencies that are subject to input from many competing groups via the political process. Private agencies are usually more responsive to the needs and wishes of those they serve.

From Goldman, Ari, and Michael Oreskes. New York foster care: A public–private battleground. *The New York Times,* April 9, 1987, p.B1. Copyright (c) 1987 by The New York Times Company. Reprinted by permission.

comparable public program. In addition, the quality of care was improved by using private agencies known for their fine foster care programs.

Abramovitz also mentions another common type of relationship between public and private agencies. This is a relationship in which services provided by the private sector (nursing home care and hospital care, for example) are paid for from benefits provided by public programs (Medicare or Medicaid, for example). Indeed, a recent study indicated that approximately one-third of the budget of an average private agency comes from public money (Sosin, 1986:44).

Such relationships raise at least two types of questions. One is the ethical question of whether public monies intended to help people should become a source of financial profit. There is a basic distinction between **nonprofit private agencies,** *ones that use all of their resources to provide services,* and **for-profit agencies,** *ones that seek to maximize income and reduce expenditures so that they make a profit.* In a market-oriented society such as our own, the profit incentive is thought to increase efficiency, which, in the case of social welfare, would reduce the cost of services, a desirable goal. Whether this actually happens, the question still remains whether public money should go to support agencies operated on a for-profit basis.

A related ethical issue is whether the urge to make a profit leads agencies to reduce the quality of services available and exclude the most needy, who are usually the most expensive to help. This is a complex question that is still hotly debated, and the data are not clear. Abramovitz (1986:261) presents data and arguments to suggest that the level of care and its availability to those who are especially disadvantaged do suffer in profit-making agencies.

The second type of issue has to do with effectiveness. Do existing relationships between public and private agencies result in better care? The New York City example illustrates how private agencies are sometimes more effective (the Jewish agency for the people it agrees to serve) and sometimes less so (the Catholic agency's reluctance to accept birth control). When private agencies are able to provide services superior in quality to those likely to be available from the public system, contracting seems to make sense. This arrangement enables the public agencies to specify the type and quality of services to be provided while at the same time taking advantage of the flexibility and specialization characteristic of the private sector.

In evaluating the proper relationship between public and private agencies, one question to be addressed is whether the operating assumptions of capitalistic economic systems fit social welfare. When businesses compete, three assumptions are made: (1) that consumers will be able to make informed choices; (2) that they will be able to make choices freely; and (3) that the competition is "free," meaning that anyone can choose to compete and that the market will weed out the most inefficient and undesirable services.

It is questionable whether these conditions prevail in the social welfare market. People needing help may lack the education or the psychological ability to make informed choices. Their freedom of choice may be limited due to a lack of resources, the nature of their problem, lack of geographical mobility, lack of information, or inability to meet specified standards. Whether competition is really "free" is also questionable. For example, the shortage of nursing home beds and the fact that government payments are only loosely tied to the quality of nursing home care makes it questionable whether the market can weed out the most inefficient and ineffective providers of residential care for the elderly.

In spite of these problems, the collaboration of public and private agencies is growing. Not only is it increasingly popular in the United States, but it is also being studied in Sweden, where the private social welfare sector is minimally developed at the present time, and in Poland, where efforts are being made to reduce the government's control over the formation of self-help organizations. Mexico has for some time had a system that encourages the use of private funds to build agencies, with operating funds then coming from the public sector.

To summarize, public and private agencies are fundamentally different in their structure and functioning. Each developed in response to different needs—the public sector to meet the basic needs of all citizens; the private sector in response to the particular needs of special groups. The recent past has seen an upsurge in contracting between public and private agencies, and in the use of benefits from public programs to pay for services delivered by private agencies. The most extreme example of this is privatization and the growth of for-profit private agencies, developments that raise a number of ethical and practical issues. However, there is little indication that relationships between public and private agencies in the United States will weaken in the near future.

ORGANIZING PROGRAMS TO MEET NEEDS

Now we are ready to move into the main subject of this chapter: how social welfare programs are organized. There are, as we'll see, at least two different ways in which to approach the subject. The first is by classifying social welfare programs in terms of the basic human needs to which they are designed to respond. As we'll see, these needs have organizational implications. The second is to examine the structural effects of decisions such as who will be served and where the resources will come from.

We begin with four basic types of human needs for which many social welfare programs are designed to provide help. These are income maintenance, family integrity, personal development, and empowerment.

Income Maintenance

Income maintenance programs *are programs designed to increase the economic resources available to people.* These programs are especially important for poor people because they make it possible for them to satisfy their basic biological needs—food, clothing, and shelter. However, income support programs also exist for the nonpoor. Temporarily unemployed workers and retirees whose income is insufficient for their long-term needs are examples of groups of people who are not poor but who are eligible for and benefit from income maintenance programs. Some income maintenance programs are also designed specifically to increase the **disposable income** (*that is, the amount of their income that they actually have available to spend*) of certain groups of people. Such programs have a dual purpose. They are designed first to benefit directly those receiving assistance, and second to stimulate spending because it is good for the economy.

Income maintenance programs employ several service delivery strategies. One is direct financial assistance. For example, most retired workers get a social security check from the federal government each month. In a similar manner, many poor families receive a monthly "welfare" check from their state's Aid to Families With Dependent Children (AFDC) program. These and several other programs provide direct cash payments to people who qualify. This money can be used to meet whatever needs the recipients consider important.

In addition to direct payments, there are several other ways of increasing people's disposable income. One is to give people coupons or vouchers that can be exchanged for specific items such as food or housing. Coupons or vouchers "stretch" people's incomes, assisting them with the purchase of selected necessities. The food stamp program is a well-known example of such a program. Jointly run by the federal Department of Agriculture and Department of Health and Human Services along with state and local departments of social welfare, food stamps are coupons that recipients can exchange for food at retail grocery stores. Only those with incomes below a certain level are eligible for this program.

You might wonder why coupons are used rather than simply giving people money. The reasoning here is that this is one way of ensuring that the aid is used for the designated purpose. For example, a drug addict might use a "welfare" check to support his or her habit rather than to buy food. Food stamps are much more likely to actually be used for food. Nevertheless, many people feel that the use of coupons and vouchers is demeaning to the recipients. Not only does it question their ability to manage their own affairs, it also publicly identifies them as welfare recipients when they use their coupons or vouchers.

Other programs use the tax system for income maintenance purposes. Many people are familiar with tax exemptions such as interest on home mortgage payments or charitable contributions. Allowing people to deduct certain expenses from their taxable income decreases the amount of tax they have to pay. This has the effect of increasing their disposable income. Tax exemptions may be viewed as incentives to spend money for certain purposes. Giving tax exemptions for interest on home mortgage payments encourages people to buy homes by making it less expensive for them to do so. Exempting contributions to charitable groups encourages people to donate money to such organizations.

There is a major difference between tax incentives and other forms of financial assistance. Tax-related programs are only usable by people who pay taxes.

The more taxes they pay, the more valuable the exemptions. Therefore, tax incentives are of greatest value to those who are not poor. The poor after all pay little or no taxes anyway (they don't earn enough). In contrast, the other types of income maintenance programs mentioned here are of greatest value to those with low incomes.

We have thus far discussed public income maintenance programs, but there are private ones as well. Given their limited resources, private social welfare agencies favor programs that offer people things they need rather than money (Sosin, 1986). For example, the Salvation Army provides meals and overnight shelter for needy people. Nevertheless, some private agencies do furnish limited cash grants to clients. The Red Cross does so in cases of natural disasters, and Traveler's Aid sometimes gives small grants to stranded travelers.

Remember, too, that in the United States many types of income maintenance services are available for purchase from the private sector. Health insurance is one example. Such policies pay benefits in the event of illness that offset the cost of medical care. Other widely available policies include disability insurance that pays benefits to workers who become disabled and are unable to work, and life insurance to ensure the economic welfare of one's survivors. In addition, many workers in the United States are covered by private retirement pension plans paid for either in whole or in part by their employer.

In a wage-based economy protecting the source of one's income is extremely important. All of the societies discussed in this book have public and workplace-related income maintenance programs. The United States is un-

---

APPROACHES TO TAXATION IN SWEDEN AND THE UNITED STATES

There are interesting similarities and differences in the way Sweden and the United States make use of taxation for social welfare purposes. Both have a progressive income tax,* but tax rates in Sweden are much higher than in the United States because of Sweden's much more extensive network of social welfare services. Social welfare services in Sweden are in part funded by an income tax levied by local governments. In contrast, counties and municipalities in the United States seldom have the power to tax incomes and must rely heavily on property taxes. (Sweden also has property taxes.)

Both Sweden and the United States offer tax exemptions for interest on home mortgages, but these are more generous in the United States. Other types of tax exemptions in America, such as for child care expenses incurred by working parents and for charitable contributions, are not widely used in Sweden. This is because child care is provided as a social welfare benefit and because private charitable organizations are uncommon in a country with so extensive a public social welfare system. Finally, many social welfare income benefits are taxed in Sweden. Pensions and benefits paid to workers when they are ill, for example, are considered taxable income in Sweden. In contrast, social welfare benefits are rarely taxed in the United States. Social security benefits paid to individuals whose total income exceeds a specified amount is one notable exception.

The Swedish approach to social welfare differs in many ways from that used in the United States. The use of taxes as part of social welfare policy provides one striking example, and it illustrates the many forms that social welfare can take. It also shows how social welfare fits into the larger web of societal values and behavior patterns.

A progressive tax is one in which those people with higher incomes pay more tax than those who have lower incomes.

usual, however, in its use of vouchers, the extensive use of tax exemptions, and in having such a widely developed network of private income maintenance services, especially those provided on a for-profit basis.

We have also seen that income maintenance programs may be designed for people at a variety of economic levels. Grant programs are of special importance to the poor, but some such programs serve the nonpoor as well (unemployment insurance and social security are examples). Voucher programs and others that provide goods rather than money are primarily intended for the poor, but tax-based programs are of greatest value to the nonpoor. The many private income maintenance programs available for purchase are utilized by many people but are most easily afforded by the nonpoor.

Obviously, the social welfare system has not been designed to serve just the poor. Its many programs serve the needs of the total population, although certain programs tend to focus on the needs of particular groups such as the very poor, retired people, those who are sick, and others. Although different groups of people are served by different programs and sometimes by different types of programs (cash grants versus tax exemptions, for example), the social welfare system provides assistance to everyone in society.

Finally, a word about informal income maintenance services. Do they exist? Of course! Some parents provide their adult children with money for down payments on homes, siblings may lend each other money, relatives house each other in cases of emergency, and so on. These are all informal strategies whose purpose is to increase the financial resources available to people. As we would expect, informal help often supplements the formal system, such as when friends or relatives lend money to a family whose "welfare" check is late or lost.

Strengthening Family Integrity

Programs designed to strengthen family life represent another type of social welfare program. To be sure, income maintenance programs also help families by making it possible for them to meet the basic life needs of their members. *Programs to strengthen family integrity may also be nonfinancial in nature, however, and these are the programs of concern here.*

Efforts to strengthen the family have two major purposes: to improve parenting and child care, and to improve the marital relationship. There are a number of programs that fall under the general heading of **child welfare** *because they seek to improve the parenting that children receive.* Three of these are of particular importance: foster care, adoption, and day care.

Foster care *is care for children whose parents cannot provide it themselves.* Foster care is intended to be temporary. It is used in situations where there is reason to believe that the child's family can eventually resume its parenting functions. Ideally, foster care is provided in a foster home by caring adults who are themselves successful parents and are able to provide the care needed by a foster child. When a foster home placement is not available or if the child

TABLE 5.1   INCOME MAINTENANCE PROGRAMS IN THE UNITED STATES: AN OVERVIEW

In the United States both the public and private social welfare sectors include a number of income maintenance programs. The goal of all such programs is to improve the financial well-being of the recipients. Some provide direct money payments, others provide needed goods or other resources that allow recipients to conserve their limited finances. You should note the wide range of groups who are served by these programs. This list includes most of the major income maintenance programs but it is provided for illustrative purposes only. It is not a complete list of all such programs.

PUBLIC PROGRAMS

Program	Who it serves	Benefits provided
Old age insurance	Retired workers age 62 or older, and their families	Monthly pension check
Survivors insurance	Widows and widowers and their families	Monthly pension check
Disability insurance	Partially or totally disabled workers and their families	Monthly pension check
Medicare	Persons age 65 or older	Payment for medical expenses
Medicaid	Poor people	Free medical care
Unemployment insurance	Involuntarily unemployed workers	Temporary weekly check
Worker's compensation	Workers injured on the job	Payment for medical expenses and lost wages
Supplemental Security Income Program (SSI)	Poor people who are old, blind, and disabled	Monthly check
Aid to Families with Dependent Children (AFDC)	Poor families	Monthly check
Public housing	Poor people	Free or subsidized housing
School lunch programs	Low-income school children	Free meals
Food stamps	Poor people	Free or subsidized food
Tax deductions for dependents	Families	Reduced tax payments
Tax deductions for home mortgages	Homeowners	Reduced tax payments
Pell grants	College students	Tuition subsidies
Home Energy Assistance Program	Low-income people	Reduced utility payments
Housing shelters	Homeless or abused people	Free (temporary) housing

PRIVATE PROGRAMS

Program	Who it serves	Benefits provided
Life insurance	Those who buy it	Cash payments to survivors and retirement benefits
Health insurance	Those who buy it	Assistance with medical payments
Pension programs	Workers who buy it or who receive it as a benefit from their employer	Monthly pension check
Disaster relief	Disaster victims	Temporary medical care, food, housing
Soup kitchens	Poor people	Food
Housing shelters	Homeless or abused people	Free (temporary) housing
Disability insurance	Those who buy it	Monthly check
Auto insurance	Those who buy it	Money to repair or replace stolen or damaged auto, payment for medical expenses to treat injuries and for legal costs
Home insurance	Those who buy it	Money to repair damage or replace property

needs a more structured environment, he or she may be placed in a group or institutional setting such as those described in connection with the New York City foster care program earlier in this chapter.

There are many reasons why parents may not be able to care for their children. Economic pressures, the strains of single parenthood, psychological or physical problems, and immaturity may all be factors. Children removed from their families have often suffered physical or emotional abuse and neglect. Foster care programs, therefore, always involve efforts to address whatever problems exist in the child's natural family so that he or she can be returned to the parental home as soon as possible. Unfortunately, this does not always happen, and some children remain in foster care settings for years.

Adoption is a second type of child welfare program. **Adoption** *is the permanent removal of a child from the natural parents accompanied by a legal transfer of custody to the adopting parents.* Adoption gives the child a new family identity, and adopting parents assume all legal responsibilities for their adopted child. Adoption generally requires that the natural parents agree to give their child up for adoption. Many do so at birth because they believe that they cannot give the child adequate care. In other cases, families experience long-term difficulties and parents decide that their child would have a better life in another family.

Foster care and adoption services are primarily provided by public agencies, usually state and local Departments of Social Services (or their equivalent). These agencies are responsible for identifying families and children that need help, and for locating suitable foster families and adoptive parents. They also monitor placements and adoptions to ensure the child's well-being. Furthermore, they are expected to provide services to strengthen troubled families, especially when a child is in foster care and is expected to return to the natural family. Problem families are usually identified as a result of referrals from the public schools, law enforcement agencies, and medical professionals. Their personnel are often the first to spot evidence of child abuse, neglect, or troubled behavior.

There is also a well-developed private adoption network that includes physicians, lawyers, and private social agencies that specialize in providing such services. Some physicians who deliver children whose parents wish to release them for adoption will work jointly with lawyers to place these children with parents seeking to adopt a child. Such arrangements sometimes involve international adoptions, in which children born in one country are adopted by parents in another. The fees involved can be very substantial. Also, when done outside the existing social welfare agency structure, the selection of adopting families and the monitoring of subsequent child care is sometimes problematic. The private agencies that arrange adoptions generally have procedures to carefully manage each step in the process. They, too, charge fees and sometimes arrange international adoptions.

Day care is a third common type of child welfare service. **Day care** *is the supervision of children during hours when working parents cannot care for* *their children or want them to be in a supervised program with other children.* Much of the need for day care results from the increasing necessity of both parents to work outside the home. In addition, some parents place their children in day care because they believe it is socially and intellectually advantageous for their children to be with other children in a structured environment. The prevalence of this belief has increased in recent years with the general trend toward small families with only one or two children. In a good day care program, the children are placed in settings where they receive physical care, emotional support, and social and intellectual stimulation.

Today, there are both public and private day care facilities. These include care provided by homemakers in the child's own home, child-minders who use their own homes for child care, day care centers, and school-like settings. Public day care facilities are primarily intended for children from low-income families (Kamerman and Kahn, 1976:58–60). Private services charge fees, although some of these expenses are tax-deductible. Such deductions, of course, are most useful to those with substantial incomes.

The provision of child care through the workplace is of increasing interest. Such arrangements can include policies designed to give parents released time for child care activities, flexible work hours that accommodate family responsibilities, job sharing that enables parents to share both work and family duties, and the provision of day care centers at the workplace (Fernandez, 1986:137–172). Such programs can be the product of public or private policies. In Sweden, for example, social welfare policy provides for leaves that allow parents to care for their children. In the United States, such policies are established by individual employers.

The various types of child welfare services described above are all designed to strengthen families. They are not the only type of program designed to meet this need, however. A variety of other services whose objective is to improve the ability of the family to function are also available, notably programs designed to improve parenting skills and relationships between spouses. The public school system is one vehicle by which basic information about human

---

ALTERNATIVE APPROACHES TO DAY CARE: POLAND AND SWEDEN

Both Poland and Sweden provide free or very-low-cost day care for working parents. However, the two societies have taken different approaches to the problem. Poland provides much of its day care through facilities located in the workplace where parents can bring their children as they come to work each day. Sweden has instead created a community-based system with small child care centers scattered throughout residential neighborhoods.

These two approaches have had rather different effects on children. The Polish model requires that children travel from their homes to a distant location. Since most factory workers use public transportation to commute to work, the children must often make lengthy trips that begin early in the morning via crowded buses, trains, and streetcars. The Swedish system keeps the child close to home in familiar surroundings. Often, the children can walk to their day care center, avoiding lengthy and tiring travel.

Poland is now moving toward a community-based system similar to Sweden's. It is doing so to ease the strains on parents and children imposed by the current system.

biology, sexual reproduction, mental hygiene, and homemaking is commonly provided. Courses dealing with these subjects are also available through public and private continuing education systems.

Information and assistance in this area is also available through a variety of other sources. These include the community mental health system, which not only provides information but also counseling services. Although not commonly thought of as a helping agency, the police are often called upon in cases involving family violence, especially incidents of spouse abuse and child disobedience, and are increasingly given special training to deal with such situations.

Other sources of assistance with family-related problems include "welfare" offices that may provide programs designed to deal with domestic problems and increase basic skills in areas such as budgeting. Maternal and child health programs are also available through the public sector. In addition to attempting to improve the health of pregnant women and infants, these programs often involve some training in parenting skills and basic nutrition. Finally, there are public work training programs that prepare people to become more economically self-sufficient and competitive in the job market. Many of these programs are primarily for poor people.

In the private sector, there is a wide range of programs to address child-rearing and relationship issues. The church has long been a source of counsel for families experiencing problems. Agencies such as Planned Parenthood and the Red Cross offer classes and counseling about sexuality and family life. Agencies such as Family Services, Catholic Charities, and others offer recreational programs, counseling, and support for self-help groups. Community-oriented agencies such as the YMCA/YWCA and settlement houses run classes in homemaking skills, basic education, and parenting, as well as recreational programs. Many such private-sector programs are offered on a fee basis, but in such cases the fees charged are often based on a "sliding scale" related to the client's ability to pay.

Efforts to strengthen the family, then, are the objective of many public and private social welfare programs. The services offered tend to emphasize parenting, the well-being of children, and help with interpersonal relationships, especially between spouses. The public sector programs primarily serve low-income people and often supplement income maintenance services. Collectively, these programs reflect the importance of the family as a basic social institution for meeting human needs. When the family malfunctions, the resulting problems often affect both current and future generations. The social welfare system's efforts to strengthen the family are designed to resolve and prevent such problems.

Services for personal development and enrichment

Some social welfare services are designed not so much to strengthen family life as to help people address their personal developmental needs. Primarily psychological or social in nature, the programs involved include education,

On the Street in Cuernavaca, Mexico

Mexico's social welfare system is divided into three major parts: one for government employees, one for employees of large corporations, and one for the remainder of the population. Each of these systems operates parallel services for its own members. Day care is no exception. In Cuernavaca, a rapidly growing city with 700,000 residents, there are three day care systems.

The system for government employees, ISSSTE (Instituto de Seguridad y Servicios Sociales de los Trabajadores del Estado) operates a charming center tucked behind a wall away from the noise and congestion of the city. A beautiful old home and its spacious yard have been transformed into a delightful day care center for children of government employees. There is no charge for this service; it is supported with funds withheld from employees' wages for this and other types of social services. The buildings (the main building and an outbuilding) have been brightly painted and decorated with murals. Given the mild climate in Cuernavaca, they are open to the outdoors and the inviting yard.

In Mexico, children are accepted in day care centers from age 45 days to 6 years, when they start school. The children are divided into age groups, and their programs are structured so as to meet their age-related needs for food, rest, play, and learning.

The center has a substantial staff: a pediatrician, nurse, psychologist, social worker, dietician, cook, lactarian (to manage milk), teachers, a director, and a support staff. The program is designed to address children's total needs including their physical health, their social and psychological development, their education, and their need for wholesome play and food. Observed at play in the yard, the children seem outgoing and healthy, affectionate with each other and comfortable with adults.

The center tries to involve mothers in its program. For example, a sample of the lunch to be served that day is on view at the entrance when children are brought in the morning. This is to encourage the mothers to serve an evening meal that will complement the nutritional value of the child's lunch, and also to educate mothers about good nutrition. A pediatrician or nurse examines each child when it arrives, and any child who is sick cannot stay. This reduces the risk of illness to the other children. The mother then has to decide how the sick child will be cared for (she might have to stay home from work, her husband could do so, the child could be brought to a relative, and so on).

It is clear that the center provides a stimulating, enjoyable, and healthful environment for children whose mothers work and cannot care for them during the day. Unfortunately, few Mexican children have access to such facilities. The capacity of the ISSSTE center, for example, is only about 100 children, and there are long waiting lists for places in Cuernavaca's other child care centers. Also, regulations are such that only children whose *mother* is employed by the government qualify. In this requirement, we have an example of how societal values influence the structure of social welfare programs. In Mexico, mothers are assumed to be responsible for child care.

counseling, recreation, artistic opportunities, self-help groups, and activities designed to promote personal insight. These services are often targeted toward particular groups. The public school system makes many of them available to youngsters. Adult day care centers provide them for the elderly. They are even sometimes available in residential facilities like hospitals. Community mental health centers are also important providers of personal counseling services. Public agencies that are primarily concerned with income maintenance or family integrity may also provide some of these kinds of services.

A wide range of individual development services are also available through the private sector. The providers include art schools, exercise studios, summer camps, Big Brother/Big Sister programs, private therapy, private psychiatric hospitals, cosmetic surgery, self-help groups, and others. Here, too, the agencies involved often target special groups such as children, housewives, alcoholics, or the elderly.

Empowerment

Last, but not least, are social welfare programs whose purpose is empowering people to take control over their own lives. In some cases, empowerment occurs as a by-product of the delivery of individual developmental services. A woman who takes a course to increase her assertiveness skills, for example, may find that she then can make use of these in her marriage or in her job. On the other hand, empowerment often involves group as opposed to individual action if it is to be effective. "Black power," for example, refers to the black community's ability as a group to identify, express, and work to achieve goals on behalf of its members.

Helping people to organize on their own behalf is basic to the effective representation of their interests, and the right to do so is a basic principle of American politics. In any case, the collective expression of needs and goals is a far more powerful political tool in any society than scattered demands from individuals. It is also an important economic strategy. Whether it involves organizing a boycott of grapes (as done by the migrant farm workers union) or a particular brand of beer (undertaken by the homosexual community) in the United States, or calling a general strike in Poland in support of the Solidarity movement, organized action can have a tremendous economic impact on businesses and governments. Such tactics are often effective in bringing about improvements in the quality of people's lives.

Having said that, it must be noted that there are relatively few agencies and programs, especially in the public sector, that attempt to help people empower themselves via group action. Public housing agencies have sometimes helped groups of tenants organize a rent strike to force a landlord to improve housing conditions and treatment of tenants. In many communities, there are public legal aid offices whose purpose includes helping people to challenge unfair treatment through class action suits (that is, instituting a lawsuit on behalf of the whole class of people who are represented by the person actually bringing the suit). In addition, some agencies and branches of government have established ombudsman programs to assist people in their dealings with the agency or organization involved.

Typically, the private sector has been a more likely source of programs designed to help people empower themselves as a group. Settlement houses have traditionally played a role in helping communities to organize on their own behalf. Advocacy organizations serve this same function for people who share characteristics such as race (the Urban League, for example), sexual orientation (the National Gay Rights Organization), gender (the National Organization of Women), or age (the National Association of Retired Persons). It is through the activities of organizations like these that many people first learn about the resources available to help them with their empowerment-related problems as well as how to advocate effectively for their own rights and needs.

Empowerment is an important but sensitive part of the social welfare system. On the one hand, a democratic society supposes that citizens will be able to clearly and effectively express their views. On the other hand, when organizations and groups compete over scarce public resources, the resulting conflict may make consensus difficult. Nevertheless, it is difficult for purposeful and productive change to occur unless people have the ability to identify and advocate for their own needs in an effective way.

STRUCTURING HELPING PROGRAMS

One way to categorize social welfare programs is in terms of the needs they are designed to meet, as we have just done. Another, to which we now turn, is to examine the way in which they are structured. As we do so, you will see that there is some overlap between the two approaches. This is especially true of income maintenance programs. One of the purposes in this discussion will be to clarify how the two approaches relate to one another.

In the discussion that follows, we will examine five types of structural arrangements. These are social insurance programs, grants, in-kind programs, tax benefits, and public utilities. As usual, we will look at each in turn, providing examples as we go.

Social Insurance Programs

Social insurance operates much like any other type of insurance. *Purchasers make regular payments (much like insurance premiums) which go into a fund from which payments are made if the risk covered by the insurance occurs.* Car insurance covers the risk of an accident or an injury. Social insurance programs cover other kinds of risk such as unemployment, illness, disability, retirement, and so on. Regardless of the risk covered, however, the principle is the same. People pay into a fund from which they are paid benefits if and when they qualify (just as you collect on your auto insurance only if and when you have an accident or are injured).

Certain characteristics of social insurance programs are especially important. First, people are getting their own money back. In other words, benefits from social insurance are not a handout paid for by someone else. This is why people are not ashamed to receive such a benefit—they feel that they have earned it. A second point is that social insurance, like any insurance, involves probabilities. Someone may pay for insurance but never collect any benefits. (If you never have an accident, you are unlikely to collect from your car insurance.) Others will receive benefits far in excess of their contributions (you might wreck your car after paying only a few months of premiums). Medicare, for example, is a mandatory health insurance program for which money is deducted each month from nearly all workers' paychecks. However, only those who are at least 65 are eligible for benefits. Those workers who die before reaching the age of 65 never receive benefits. Someone who lives to be 95, on the other hand, may collect benefits worth far more than the amount they contributed.

To collect insurance benefits you must prove that you qualify. This usually includes proof that you are covered (that is, that you have paid your premiums), and that the risk covered by the insurance has in fact occurred (that you have been hospitalized for illness, for example). In addition, benefit payments may be subject to other conditions. Medicare, for example, requires payment of a deductible before any benefits can be paid, it will only pay for a certain number of days of treatment, and it pays a percentage of the bill rather than the whole bill (usually 80 percent of the "customary and usual charges" as defined by Medicare). Most insurance programs have conditions that determine how, when, and for how long benefits will be paid.

Social insurance may be public or private. Medicare, for example, is public. It is collected by the Social Security Administration and contributions are deposited in a special government fund from which benefits are paid. There are also many private health insurance programs, Blue Cross–Blue Shield, for example. Private health insurance operates just like with Medicare. Contributions are placed in a fund from which benefits are paid. However, this whole process is managed by a private corporation which competes with many other companies that also sell health insurance. Government insurance programs are usually not optional, while private ones generally are.

Social insurance programs are popular for a number of reasons. They lack the stigma of grant programs (described below) because people feel they have earned the benefits. They preserve a sense of self-responsibility because participants are acting prudently to protect themselves against the possibility of future problems. They are thought to preserve the incentive to provide for oneself by providing benefit levels that cover only a portion of anticipated costs, thus encouraging people to establish a savings program to supplement insurance benefits. Finally, social insurance programs are far less costly than many other kinds of programs. Benefits are paid from a fund created for this purpose rather than coming from other sources, such as tax revenues. Many public insurance programs are self-supporting, while private insurance programs may even be profit-making.

There are many types of social insurance. The chart which follows summarizes some of the major ones. In the next chapter we will study a few of the most important public social insurance programs in more detail.

Grant Programs

*A **grant** is a monetary payment to someone who has not previously contributed to the source of funds from which payments are made.* A grant is quite different from social insurance. In the latter, as we have seen, people receive ben-

TABLE 5.2   SOCIAL INSURANCE PROGRAMS IN THE UNITED STATES: AN OVERVIEW

PROGRAM	COVERAGE	ADMINISTRATION	ILLUSTRATIVE BENEFITS	FUNDING
Old age insurance	Retired workers and their families (workers in about 95% of all jobs are covered).	Social Security Administration (federal agency)	In 1989, a retired person received an average monthly payment of $546	A tax of 15.02% is paid on the worker's annual taxable income up to $48,000 (no tax is paid on income above this
Survivors insurance	Families of insured workers who have died (same coverage as above).	Same	In 1985, a widower or widow received an average monthly payment of $433. Children of deceased workers received $330.	amount). This tax is shared equally by the employer and the worker (data are for 1989). This tax pays for old age, survivors, and disability insurance coverage, as well as for medicare.
Disability insurance	Workers who have become disabled and their families (same coverage as above).	Same	In 1988, a disabled worker received average monthly payments of $508.	
Medicare (Part A)	Persons 65 or over who qualify for the above programs. Others who are 65 or over may buy coverage.	Health Care Financing Administration (federal agency)	Pays all of approved and customary charges for hospital care. Also pays up to 150 days of skilled nursing home care for each benefit period, and a lifetime maximum of 190 days of inpatient psychiatric care.	Funded from the above tax collected while the insured is employed. When insured retires, pays $564 yearly deductible; (data are for 1989). Also, an income tax surcharge is payable by those who pay at least $150 in federal income taxes.
Medicare (Part B)	Persons 65 or over who qualify for the above programs and who have elected this coverage.	Same	Pays 80% of approved charges and reasonable cost of doctors' charges. There is a maximum $250 payment for mental disorders.	Funded from a monthly fee of $31.90. There is a yearly deductible of $75.00. The insured must pay any fees over what the program considers approved and reasonable (data are for 1989).

efits from a fund to which they have contributed. This gives them the sense that they are getting their own money back. This relationship between giving and receiving does not exist with grants. The grant distributes money collected from one group of people to another group of people. This is why grants often

TABLE 5.2   SOCIAL INSURANCE PROGRAMS IN THE UNITED STATES: AN OVERVIEW (*continued*)

PROGRAM	COVERAGE	ADMINISTRATION	ILLUSTRATIVE BENEFITS	FUNDING
Unemployment insurance	Involuntarily unemployed workers whose employers have contributed (97% of workers covered in 1986).	State administered, most commonly in its Department of Labor	$127 average weekly payment in 1985. 26 weeks is the maximum time that benefits are paid in most states.	In 1985, employers paid an average of 3.1% of taxable wages.
Worker's compensation	Workers injured on the job (about 87% of workers were covered in 1986).	Same	Wage replacement and medical benefits which vary greatly from state to state.	In 1982, employers paid an average of 1.7% of their payroll (actual amount varies by how hazardous the work is).
Private health insurance	Workers whose employers offer it; others who purchase it themselves.	The company selling it	80% of covered hospital and physicians' services is typical; health maintenance organizations may provide additional coverage.	Using myself as an example, I paid $46.55 each month in 1989 to cover myself and my family.
Private life insurance	Anyone who buys it; sometimes offered as a benefit to workers by employers.	The company selling it	The insured person decides how much of a death benefit and/or annuity is desired.	Depends on the size of the benefit desired, the age of the insured, and company policy. The insured pays a yearly premium.
Automobile insurance	Anyone who buys it; required in many states.	The company selling it; sometimes there are state-run programs	The insured person decides how much of a benefit is desired (there may be a state minimum); usually includes payments to fix or replace damaged or stolen cars, and to pay for medical expenses and legal judgments.	Depends on the value of the car, the driver's age, gender, and driving record, and where the car is registered and driven. The insured pays a yearly or 6-month premium.

Source: Social Security Programs in the United States—1986, Social Security Handbook 1986, Statistical Abstract of the United States 1987, and various Social Security Administration announcements, all Washington, D.C.: U.S. Government Printing Office.

have the stigma of being handouts, with the consequence that recipients are labeled freeloaders.

Public grant programs are generally funded from tax revenues. The federal, state, and local taxes that we all pay are used in part to pay grants to people who qualify for them. The best-known grant programs are for the poor. The Aid to Families With Dependent Children (AFDC) program, for example, provides monthly cash grants to poor families. The Supplemental Security Income (SSI) program does the same for the disabled or elderly poor (in 1987 the basic federal monthly payment per recipient was $354). There are also private grant programs for the poor which are primarily supported by contributions. Agencies such as the Red Cross, the Salvation Army, and Traveler's Aid make small grants from the funds they receive from contributors and from grants received from foundations or from the government.

The issue of who pays for and who receives grants is actually a complex one. Under a social insurance program, as we saw, some people receive far more in the way of benefits than they pay in contributions while others collect far less or nothing at all. Does this mean that those who receive more than they contribute are "freeloaders?" In a similar fashion, those who receive funds from public grant programs may well have paid taxes for many years before becoming poor and in need of help. Indeed, recent data indicate that lower-income groups are actually paying an increasingly larger share of federal taxes (*The New York Times,* 1987). Are they, therefore, in some sense getting their own money back when they receive public grants?

Such questions must be considered within the context of social life seen as a shared risk. Social insurance programs do this very directly—we are all at risk of becoming disabled, for example, but only some of us actually will. We have no way of knowing who will become disabled or when, so we collectively contribute to a fund (part of the social security program) to help those who are actually affected. In so doing, we are effectively taking steps to protect ourselves—it *could* happen to us. If it does not, we consider ourselves fortunate and consider our contributions well spent even though we never collect benefits from them. In this way, we as a society share risks and resources.

Taxes, like insurance premiums, may be viewed as a means of sharing risk. Some of the services we "buy" with our taxes we may never use. If, for example, our parents send us to private school and we either do the same for our children or simply have no children, we may never use the public school system. We may never become poor, and thus never collect public income maintenance grants. But we *could* need these services, and our paying taxes helps ensure that they will be available. Then, too, we usually hope that those who do use the services for which we have paid will ultimately pay us back. Educated people generally go on to become productive citizens who then pay taxes. If our grant programs are successful, the families helped will in due course become productive citizens who will pay taxes just like us. As with social insurance, then, when we pay taxes that fund grant programs we are sharing a risk and may feel that we have gotten our money's worth even if we never ourselves collect benefits from the programs involved.

The example of education illustrates another feature of public tax-supported programs like grants. Although many well-known ones (mentioned above) do so, such programs do not only serve the poor but rather all classes of society. Education and the police are useful examples, as are tax-supported grant programs for college students, even though those with lower incomes are usually eligible for larger grants.

Thus we can see that it is overly simplistic to assume that only those who receive assistance directly from grant programs benefit from such services, or that recipients do not contribute to such programs. Rather, all of us receive benefits—in the form of protection against social risk—from the share of our tax monies which goes to grant programs, even though we may not receive any actual cash payments. Further, grants do not only go to the poor who don't pay taxes; some go to members of the middle and higher classes. Even those who are poor may have contributed in the past, and hopefully many will do so again in the future.

Even though grants should not be viewed as the rich giving handouts to the undeserving poor, these programs are nevertheless very controversial. We will return to this issue in more detail in a later chapter, but for now we can note several commonly raised objections. One is that such programs represent a costly drain on general tax revenues that could be used more productively for other purposes. A second is that they destroy people's incentive to take control over their own lives and to better themselves. This assumes that people would prefer to sit home collecting free money rather than working for it. A third, usually mustered when arguing on behalf of stricter eligibility requirements, is that too many people who don't deserve or need them are receiving grants. This last objection is closely related to the myth that people on welfare drive around in Cadillacs.

In the next chapter, we will look at several grant programs in detail. You will see that they are very complex, in part because they try to address the objections about cost, incentive, and fraud listed above. For now, let's end this section with a peek into the daily lives of poor people who live on public grant programs.

In-kind Programs

You have already had some exposure to **in-kind programs.** *These are programs that provide people with needed resources rather than the money with which to purchase them.* Free or subsidized meals and housing are examples. So are programs that collect and distribute clothing and toys for needy families. The boundary between in-kind benefits and money payments is sometimes fuzzy. Are food stamps equivalent to money because they can be exchanged for food, or are they an in-kind benefit because they cannot be used for anything other than food? Is Medicare's reimbursement of medical costs more like a money payment or the in-kind provision of medical care? How you answer these questions is less important than your ability to grasp the under-

THE HUMAN FACE OF SOCIAL WELFARE 11

The Cost of Living Free (Barbara Jiggett)

There are no curtains on the windows of Barbara Jiggett's 20th floor apartment.... There are no lights in the bedroom shared by her 7 and 8 year old daughters and only one in the living room where Ms. Jiggett sleeps (her 4-year-old son has the other bedroom). She has a television set and a terrace but no phone and only three kitchen chairs, which makes it difficult to join her three children at the table for meals....

Every month, Ms. Jiggett's apartment costs her $381, or $111 more than the rent allowance she receives from welfare. Which means one of three things: she has a hidden source of income, which she says she does not; she is an extraordinary money manager, which the city says she is not; or she routinely has to dip into the $266 in welfare payments, plus $172 in food stamps and $50 in child support, she receives to feed, clothe, and otherwise care for herself and three children.

That would leave her, on the average, less than $13 a day to provide for a family of four....

Until 1975, welfare workers had wide latitude in reimbursing the poor for their rent. Then the state imposed a ceiling of $218 for a family of four. The ceiling was raised only once, in 1984, by 25 percent, to $270. In the same period, by one measure, rents in the city rose 95 percent or more; the number of apartments renting for under $300 fell by 44 percent.

Tenants who fall behind in their rent can get emergency grants. But the grant system favors those whose rents are below the ceiling—a policy that, in effect, encourages those welfare recipients to dip into rent allowances for other expenses...

If Ms. Jiggett is evicted, she says she has no place else to go, which means the city would be obligated to house her family either in a hotel, at an annual cost of about $23,000, or in a long-term group shelter, at more than $26,000. Her [current] annual rent...is $4,573.80, of which welfare already pays all but $1,332....

The Legal Aid Society, representing Ms. Jiggett and two other welfare mothers...is seeking a...change. Suing in State Supreme Court last month, Legal Aid lawyers argued that the existing shelter allowance violates the government's obligation to provide a level of rental assistance that enables parents to raise children in their own home.

Barbara Jiggett's expenses are paid by others—she receives child support and a grant from the city in which she lives through the Aid to Families with Dependent Children (AFDC) program. However, living free turns out to be very costly for Ms. Jiggett in terms of the quality of life for her family. Think about the issues that are associated with grant programs: cost, incentive, and fraud. How would you evaluate them in the case of Ms. Jiggett? Do you think the AFDC program is helping her in a cost-effective way? Does she have an incentive to become independent? Is she being cheated, or are we, the taxpayers?

lying issues. In fact, there are no definitive answers; there are plausible arguments on both sides.

In-kind programs may be either public or private. There are, for example, public and private housing shelters, subsidized housing, free food programs, and collections of clothing and toys for the poor. You will recall that one argument for in-kind programs is that they guarantee that the resources provided will be used only for a designated purpose, but that this sometimes generates accusations that such programs demean people's self-respect. The highly public manner in which many in-kind services are distributed, via soup kitchens and housing shelters for example, is also considered very unpleasant and humiliating by many people.

In-kind services attempt to minimize the cost of helping others. It is common for these programs to distribute surplus or unwanted items, such as used clothing and surplus food. Because of their narrow focus—on providing meals, for example—in-kind programs are unlikely to have much of an impact on the long-term and multifaceted problems that have created the need for the assistance involved. Nevertheless, in-kind programs are an efficient way of meeting immediate needs and can likewise be a useful part of a comprehensive helping plan.

Tax Benefits

You are already familiar with the use of tax benefits as a social welfare service delivery strategy. We have seen that tax benefits can be used to increase people's disposable income, and that they are of greatest value to those in higher tax brackets. Their value in stimulating the economy has also been mentioned—when people have more money to spend they usually do so, thereby stimulating the production of goods and services.

At this point a couple of other characteristics of tax benefits deserve mention. One is the relationship between increasing disposable income and reduced tax revenues. When individuals pay lower taxes, the government's tax revenue is reduced. This diversion of money may increase some people's ability to be self-sufficient but it also reduces the funds available to help those who remain in need. A second point about tax benefits is their relationship to free-market mechanisms. Any increase in disposable income yielded by tax benefits is likely to be used to purchase what people want from the marketplace. Those with sufficient income to do so, for example, are likely to use their increased income to shop for food or eat in a restaurant rather than obtain a free meal from a social welfare agency.

We can see, then, how the use of tax benefits illustrates the impact of social policy on social welfare. The use of tax benefits tends either to increase or decrease the tax revenues available for social welfare purposes. In a free-market economy, the extent to which money provided in the form of tax benefits will be used to meet people's needs is determined by the behavior of the recipients in the marketplace. Similarly, the amount of assistance provided in the form of tax benefits affects the amount of aid provided through nonmarket social welfare programs. Finally, tax benefits primarily provide social welfare services to the nonpoor.

Public Social Utilities

Some years ago, Wilensky and Lebeaux (1966:138–140) explained that there were two ways in which to view social welfare—the residual view and the institutional view. The **residual view of social welfare** *sees social welfare as a response to a breakdown in the normal functioning of the market and the family.* The **institutional view** *emphasizes the preventive role that social welfare should play in modern industrial societies.* In other words, social welfare can either be designed to help people when they have problems, or it can be designed to prevent the occurrence of problems that would otherwise result.

The difference in the two approaches can be seen in the way different societies deal with the need for child care. In Sweden, all parents have the right to leave from work to care for very young or ill children. In the United States, working parents have to solve this problem for themselves, depending on where they work and what their family situation may be. Social welfare services to help with this type of problem are available, but only once it occurs. U.S. policy does not seek to prevent the problem, as Swedish policy does. In this instance, Sweden has taken a more *institutional* view while the U.S. approach has been more *residual.*

The difference between the institutional and residual approaches is reflected in the way services are structured. Kahn and Kamerman (1977:7–8) distinguish between *case services* and *public utilities.*

Case services *are services provided to people who have a problem of some kind.* **Public social utilities,** *on the other hand, are services built into the social structure.* Case services are residual in nature; public social utilities are based on an institutional view of social welfare.

Consider the difference between two approaches to drug abuse: drug counseling and free public drug education. Drug counseling is provided to those with drug problems via clinics and counseling centers. Such services are case services. They reflect a residual approach to the problem of drug abuse. Drug education included as part of the public school curriculum, on the other hand, represents a public social utility, and its inclusion in the curriculum reflects an institutional approach to the problem of drug abuse.

Public social utilities are usually available to everyone, at least everyone for whom they are intended. For example, free public education is *automatically* available to *all* children between the ages of 5 or 6 and 16 or 17 in the United States. Police protection, public parks, and public sewage systems are other examples of services provided on a public utility basis.

Case services are provided more selectively. Not only must you have the specific need the service is designed to meet (drug addiction, for example), but you must usually also meet certain additional criteria before qualifying. Thus, you might have to pay a fee, be able to certify that you are poor, or prove that you are a first-time drug abuser.

The public utilities approach to social welfare is more popular in societies like Sweden and Poland than in the United States. At least in part, this reflects differences in the various societies' acceptance of centralized economic and social planning. Societies that make greater use of centralized planning tend to approach social welfare from an institutional perspective. Those that make little use of centralized planning, the United States for example, often take a more residual approach.

THE STRUCTURE OF SOCIAL WELFARE REVISITED

In this chapter, we have examined the structure of social welfare by employing two different approaches. First, we discussed social welfare programs in terms of the different types of human needs to which they are designed to respond. Second, we reexamined social welfare programs in terms of their basic structure and the types of benefits provided.

As we conclude this chapter, it is important to see that our two approaches are not mutually exclusive. A program whose purpose is meeting peoples' need for income maintenance, for example, may provide that assistance in the form of social insurance, grants, in-kind services, or tax benefits. Similarly, a program whose primary purpose is income maintenance may also contribute, either directly or indirectly, to strengthening the family, personal development, or empowerment. All of which is to say that (1) there is more than one way to structure programs designed to meet a particular need, and (2) that programs may be designed in such a way as to meet more than one need.

It is likewise true that one can employ a particular type of structure for a range of purposes. It is possible, for example, to design a social insurance program to promote income maintenance, family integrity, or personal development. Retirement programs that provide a regular monthly income to families (income maintenance) also help them to maintain their previous life patterns (strengthen family integrity) while simultaneously enabling recipients to take more time for leisure and self-improvement activities (personal development). The same is true of grants, in-kind programs, and tax benefits.

The two types of programs whose relationship to the others is least obvious are empowerment (a category of human need) and public social utility programs (a structural category). Interestingly, the two are often related to one another. Teaching people to advocate for their own interests is a component of the public education and legal systems, both public social utilities. In school, people learn about their rights and the existing mechanisms to protect those rights, thus enhancing their ability to become effective advocates for themselves. Retaining custody of a child or appealing the denial of a request for benefits from a grant program both require knowledge of one's rights and how to fight for them. Empowerment programs and some public social utilities impart the attitudes, skills, and information that make such actions possible. In addition, advocacy skills enable people to lobby for improvements in the system so that it will meet their biological, psychological, and social needs more effectively.

Perhaps the fact that empowerment programs and public social utilities often enable people to challenge conditions they perceive to be unjust explains why these two types of programs receive the least attention in the design of the social welfare system. They make social change possible, and change is not always welcome. It is less unsettling to focus on specific objectives—such as reducing the cost of medical care or ensuring a decent retirement income—than it is to question the effectiveness of the social welfare system. When people begin asking questions about whether social welfare programs treat all people equally, or whether the needs of some groups are ignored, the whole social welfare structure may be called into question. Perhaps in a country like Sweden, where there is a strong social consensus concerning the importance of social welfare, this is less likely to be the case than in the United States, Mexico, or even in Poland.

LET'S REVIEW

The purpose of this chapter has been to give you some sense of the larger design of the social welfare system. Social welfare is not just a collection of programs. It is instead a system that seeks to address certain needs by distributing and redistributing resources in a way that helps to meet the human needs of the total population. It does so through structural arrangements that reflect concerns with cost, effectiveness, and maintaining people's sense of personal responsibility. In general, the structure of the system will reflect the linkage between these concerns and societal values.

We began by reviewing formal, informal, and public and private helping. We then discussed the purposes and structure of social welfare programs. In particular, we analyzed social welfare programs from two perspectives; first, from the perspective of the human needs they are designed to address, and second, from the perspective of the way in which they distribute resources (their structure). Under the first heading, we discussed income maintenance, family integrity, personal development, and empowerment programs. Under the second, we examined social insurance, grants, in-kind services, tax benefits, and public social utilities.

The purpose of this chapter has been to help you better understand the overall design of the social welfare system. In the next chapter, we will examine the specific programs that make up the system and through which resources are distributed to people. As you learn about these programs, you will want to keep in mind their role in the larger system.

CHAPTER OUTLINE

WHAT TO EXPECT FROM THIS CHAPTER
LEARNING OBJECTIVES
FORMAL AND INFORMAL HELPING REVISITED

STUDY QUESTIONS

1 Consider your own family. Make a list of the ways in which it helps you meet your income maintenance, family integrity, and personal development needs. Does it also help you to meet your empowerment needs? If this last question seems difficult to answer, consider your family's attitudes toward women's career choices, what you have been taught about your family's ethnic (or racial) group, and similar matters relating to your ability to advocate effectively on your own behalf.

2 Research the distribution of income in the United States according to gender, race, age, and ethnicity. Summarize your findings in a short report that focuses on those groups most likely to be poor and the impact of their poverty on their needs.

3 Make a list of your current income maintenance, family integrity, personal development, and empowerment needs. Make a list of the social structures, institutions, and programs from which you are receiving assistance in meeting these needs and classify them in terms of public and private, formal and informal. Then summarize, in a brief report, the extent of your current involvement with the elements of the social welfare system discussed in this chapter.

4 What are your feelings about social insurance programs, grants, in-kind programs, and tax benefits? Do you think that some of these types of programs are better than others? If you had your way, would you eliminate some and increase the use of oth-

ers? Which ones and why? If you believe they all have a place in the design of social welfare, do you think they are currently being used most effectively? If not, what changes would you make?

5 Do you think that social welfare should just be for the poor? Explain the reasons for your thinking. Then compare your analysis with that of a friend who is not taking this course. Are there any differences in your thinking? Why or why not?

KEY TERMS AND CONCEPTS

adoption	income maintenance programs
case services	in-kind programs
child welfare	institutional view of social welfare
contracting	nonprofit private agencies
day care	privatization
disposable income	public social utilities
for-profit private agencies	residual view of social welfare
foster care	social insurance
grant	welfare capitalism

SUGGESTED READINGS

Fernandez, John. 1986. *Child Care and Corporate Productivity*. Lexington, Mass.: Lexington Books. This book uses the issue of child care for working parents to illustrate the relationship between public policy and adequate social welfare services. It focuses on how workers and the corporations which employ them attempt to find solutions to the need for adequate child day care in the absence of adequate public services.

Kahn, Alfred, and Sheila Kamerman. 1975. *Not for the Poor Alone*. Philadelphia, Pa.: Temple University Press. The authors use examples from several European societies to illustrate how the public sector can meet several different kinds of needs. They focus on nonfinancial services, which, they argue, should be made available to the entire population, not just the poor.

Ruggie, Mary. 1984. *The State and Working Women*. Princeton, N.J.: Princeton University Press. An examination of the impact of institutional and residual approaches to social welfare on the work opportunities for women. The author concludes that an effort to incorporate a range of financial and nonfinancial resources into social policy is more effective at providing opportunities than a strategy that addresses employment-related problems as they occur.

Sheehan, Susan. 1975. *A Welfare Mother*. New York: New American Library. A well-known case study of a poor family and the way in which it survives by making use of available public and private services. The book illustrates the interaction of physical, personal, and social needs and describes the web of formal and informal services that the family attempts to locate and use.

Sosin, Michael. 1986. *Private Benefits: Material Assistance in the Private Sector*. Orlando, Fla.: Academic Press. A study of private agencies and their use of income maintenance, grant, and in-kind services. Clearly illustrates the interdependence of private and public agencies, as well as the different functions and characteristics of each.

REFERENCES

Abramovitz, Mimi. 1986. The privatization of the welfare state: A review. *Social Work,* 31, no. 4 (July–August):257–264.

Brzozowski, Ryszard, et al. n.d. *Social Welfare and the Lines of Its Development in the Polish People's Republic.* Warsaw: Polish Medical Publishers.

Fernandez, John. 1986. *Child Care and Corporate Productivity.* Lexington, Mass.: Lexington Books.

Gilbert, Neil. 1983. *Capitalism and the Welfare State.* New Haven, Conn.: Yale University Press.

Goldman, Ari, and Michael Oreskes. 1987. New York foster care: A public–private battleground. *The New York Times,* April 9, B1–B2.

Kahn, Alfred, and Sheila Kamerman. 1975. *Not for the Poor Alone.* Philadelphia, Pa.: Temple University Press.

———. 1977. *Social Services in International Perspective.* Washington, D.C.: U.S. Government Printing Office.

Kamerman, Sheila, and Alfred Kahn. 1976. *Social Services in the United States.* Philadelphia, Pa.: Temple University Press.

Les, Ewa. 1985. Some social threats in Poland in relation to procedures and models of social policy. Paper presented at the 13th Regional Symposium on Social Welfare of the International Committee on Social Welfare, June, Turku, Finland.

Roberts, Sam. 1987. New York City on $13 a day: A welfare tale. *The New York Times,* April 2, B1.

Ruggie, Mary. 1984. *The State and Working Women.* Princeton, N.J.: Princeton University Press.

Sheehan, Susan. 1975. *A Welfare Mother.* New York: New American Library.

Sosin, Michael. 1986. *Private Benefits: Material Assistance in the Private Sector.* Orlando, Fla.: Academic Press.

Tax burden is found to rise for poor in U.S. 1987. *The New York Times,* November 12, A26.

Wilensky, Harold, and Charles Lebeaux. 1966. *Industrial Society and Social Welfare.* New York: The Free Press.

Wojciechowski, Sophie. 1975. Poland's new priority: Human welfare. In Daniel Thursz and Joseph Vigilante, eds., *Meeting Human Needs,* vol. I. Beverly Hills, Calif.: Sage Publications Inc., pp. 169–195.

A SOCIETY IN PICTURES — MEXICO

Paseo de la Reforma, Mexico City

Mexico City is the largest city in the world. In overall appearance, it resembles many other large modern cities. It has beautiful boulevards and narrow side streets, modern high-rise buildings and elegant older structures, and a wide range of restaurants and shops. (See "On the Street in Mexico City," Introduction.) (Russell Dian/Monkmeyer)

Mexico City—Venus de Milo after the 1985 Earthquake

Mexico City suffered a devastating earthquake in September 1985. Even now, the visitor will find evidence of that event in the form of partially or completely destroyed buildings, especially in the old downtown section near the Zona Rosa and Alameda Park. (Abbas/Magnum)

A Shantytown in Juarez

Shantytowns are found throughout Mexico, particularly surrounding the major cities where they often provide housing for large numbers of people. Some 38 percent of the residents of Mexico City live in such towns, of which the largest, Nezahualcoyotl— commonly called Neza, houses some 2.7 million people. (See "On the Street in Nezahualcoyotl, Mexico," Chapter 1.) (Abbas/Magnum)

168

Street Vendor in Taxco, Mexico

Street vendors are a common sight in many Mexican cities. Once a predominantly agricultural society, Mexico has in recent years experienced a great increase in its urban population as rural families move to the cities in search of better living conditions. One of the ways in which many of these families support themselves upon moving to the city is by selling goods on the street. (F. B. Grunzweig/Photo Researchers)

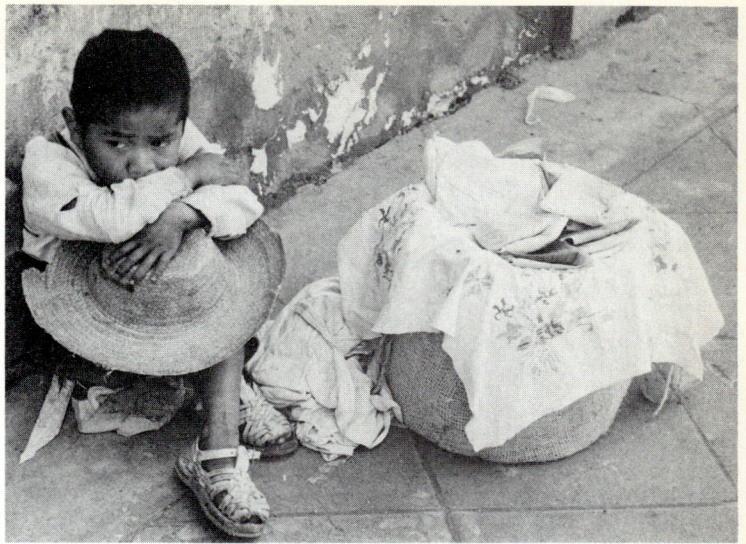

A Classroom Scene in a Suburban School Outside Mexico City

In a developing society like Mexico's, money for capital intensive public facilities is limited. These children from a poor suburb attend school in a building where their desks consist of concrete building blocks. (Abbas/Magnum)

A Kindergarten in Cuernavaca

Children in Mexico enter school at the age of six. Given the relatively mild climate, the school buildings where they attend class are sometimes open to the outdoors or, as here, to an inviting yard. (Georgia Engelhard/Monkmeyer)

169

A SOCIETY IN PICTURES—POLAND
A View of Warsaw Today

The business area of Warsaw looks like the downtown of any contemporary city in western Europe. There are many high-rise office buildings, hotels, and apartment buildings. The view here is of the city center looking north from the Palace of Culture over office and apartment buildings. (See "On the Street in Warsaw," Introduction.) (Porterfield-Chickering/ Photo Researchers)

Warsaw 1964

Much of Warsaw was destroyed during World War II so that virtually all existing buildings are either new or rebuilt. Housing is particularly scarce, and most new housing consists of high-rse apartment buildings. Here, in a picture taken almost 20 years after the close of World War II, the ruins of Warsaw contrast with the new apartment building in the background. (Elliott Erwitt/Magnum)

Small Village in Poland near the Russian Border

While nearly 60 percent of the Polish people live in cities, the remainder live in rural settings where traditional extended families are still common. Poland is a homogeneous society in which 98 percent of the population, like this grandmother and her two grandsons, are of pure Polish extraction. (Jill Hartley/Photo Researchers)

170

Street Scene in Downtown Warsaw

Poland experienced a baby boomlet in 1982, the year of martial law. Sunny weather brought out evidence of the surge in births almost everywhere, including downtown where these shoppers stroll in an area reserved for pedestrian traffic. (See "Poland's Baby Boom," The Human Face of Social Welfare 8, Chapter 4.) (Hubertus Kanus/ Photo Researchers)

Shoppers Waiting in Line in Warsaw

Department stores and shops abound in downtown Warsaw but the goods available for purchase are often limited. Meat, gasoline, and chocolate are rationed, and the price of many consumer items is regulated by the government. Long lines of people waiting to make purchases are not an uncommon sight. (Jill Hartley/Photo Researchers)

A Political Lesson in a Warsaw School

Poland's economic difficulties in recent years have led to social discontent and the imposition of martial law for extended periods of time. Here an unidentified Polish army officer instructs a class of girls at a Warsaw school on the implications of martial law. (AP/Wide World Photos)

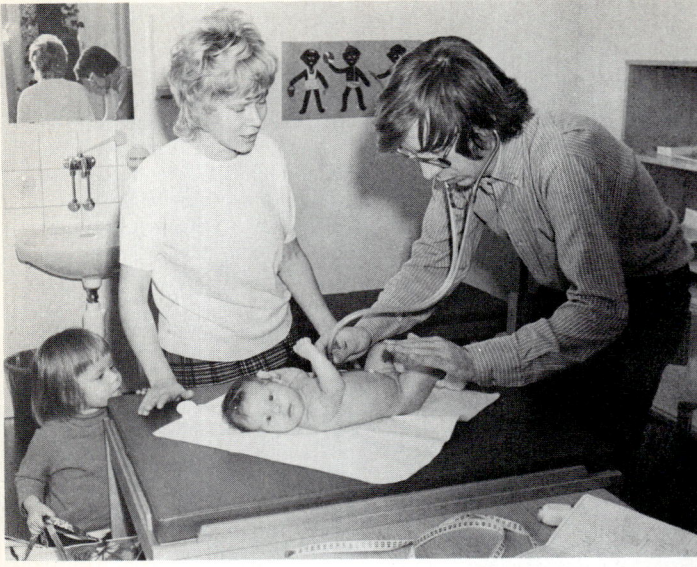

A Swedish Child Welfare Clinic

The first child welfare clinics appeared in Sweden in the early 1940s. Emphasizing preventive medicine, the 1,260 clinics located throughout the country provide checkups for 99 percent of all one year olds and two-thirds of all other preschool children. Infants are brought to the clinics an average of ten times per year, 1-year-olds three times, and older children two times per year. In addition, clinic nurses make house calls, mainly to families with infants. (See ''Medical Care in Sweden,'' Chapter 3.) (Courtesy of Swedish Information Service)

Nursery School in Gideonsberg, Sweden

Nursery schools in Sweden are primarily run and financed by county government. Kindergartens receive two classes a day, one in the morning and one in the afternoon, each for 3 hours. In addition, there are many day nurseries designed to provide day care for children whose parents are employed outside the home. Day nurseries are open from 6:30 A.M. until 6:30 P.M. and provide an instructional program similar to that offered in kindergarten. (Courtesy of Swedish Information Service)

Interior of a Swedish Nursery School

In Sweden, it is considered desirable for children to attend either a kindergarten or nursery school beginning at the age of 4 or 5 at the latest. Both kindergartens and day nurseries provide free health care and, as here, meals when appropriate. (Courtesy of Swedish Information Service)

Physically Limited Students in a Swedish School

One of the goals of Swedish social welfare policy is to enable people who encounter major difficulties in their daily lives for physical, mental, or other reasons to participate in social activities and live like other people. This philosophy extends to education where the physically limited are integrated into the regular classroom and attend school with other children. (Courtesy of Swedish Information Service)

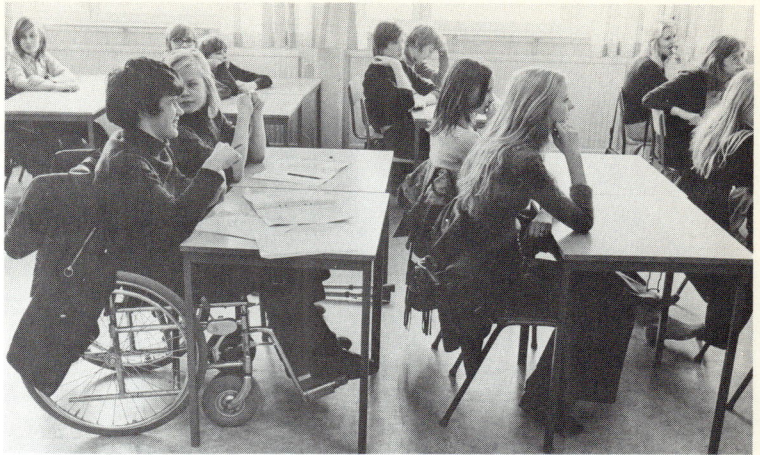

Ramp for the Physically Limited in a Swedish Store

Among the steps taken in Sweden to provide access to public places for those with physical limitations are audible signals added to traffic lights and access ramps in buildings. In addition, the municipal transport system enables the physically limited, as well as the elderly, to ride taxis or specially equipped vehicles while paying about the same fares as on the regular public transportation network, which is itself designed to be accessible to those with limitations. (See "On the Street in Sweden," Chapter 2.) (Courtesy of Swedish Information Service)

Special Furniture in a Swedish Apartment

The effort to provide the physically limited with a normal life in Sweden extends to the home where special equipment and furniture is provided as necessary, as in the case of this young woman's apartment where the furniture has been adapted to wheelchair height. In addition, artificial limbs, hearing aids, and other technical aids are provided at no charge. (Courtesy of Swedish Information Service)

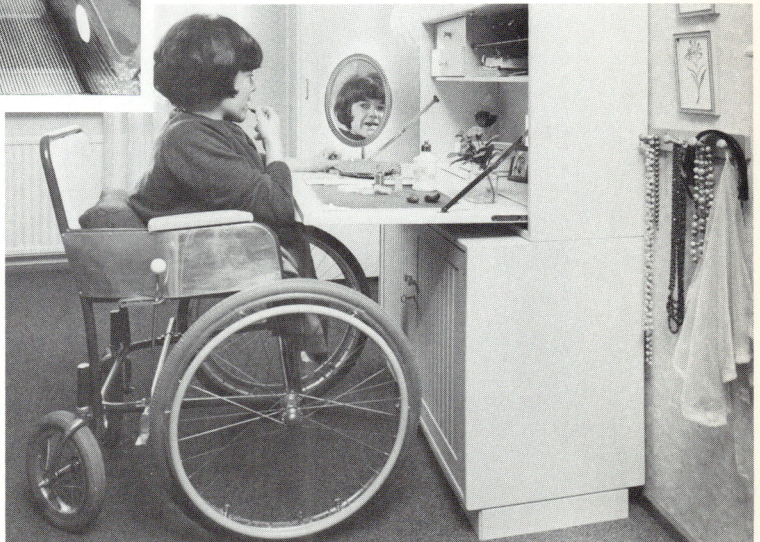

173

A SOCIETY IN PICTURES— THE UNITED STATES

Cincinnati, Ohio

As with many large American cities, downtown Cincinnati has experienced an economic rebirth. Sleek new high-rise office buildings and hotels have replaced decayed buildings, and many of the older buildings that remain have been restored or refurbished. In this view of the downtown Cincinnati skyline, Riverfront Stadium is on the left, Riverfront Coliseum on the right. (Tom McHugh/ Photo Researchers)

A Sweatshop in Chinatown

Throughout American history, immigrants have provided a continuing source of vitality, new cultural ideas, and, in many instances, low-cost labor. In the garment factories of Chinatown, where the average worker's annual income is less than $6,000, women hunch over sewing machines in the glare of overhead lamps. (See "Social Change Through the Eyes of Immigrants," The Human Face of Social Welfare 4, Chapter 2.) (Eugene Gordon/Photo Researchers)

Illegal Aliens Filling out Legalization Forms, New York, 1987

Illegal immigrants, most from Latin America, have entered the United States in great numbers since the mid-sixties, attracted by opportunities that, however unpromising to most Americans, appeared far more attractive than those available in their native lands. In an attempt to grapple with this problem, the United States instituted an amnesty program in 1987 that induced many "illegals" to register with the Department of Immigration and Naturalization Services. (Barbara Rios/ Photo Researchers)

A Teen Mother and Her Child

Teenage pregnancy is a major social problem in the United States. For too many teen mothers, pregnancy means dropping out of school, and becoming a single parent with little hope of economic self-sufficiency. Programs like the New Futures School in Albuquerque, New Mexico are intended to help young mothers break out of the poverty cycle. (See ''A New Approach to Sex Education,'' The Human Face of Social Welfare 12, Chapter 7.) (Bruce Davidson/Magnum)

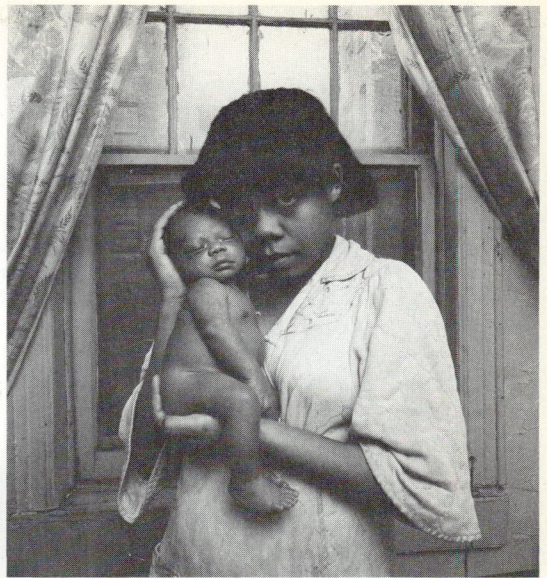

Homelessness in Greenwich Village, New York City

Every large American city has a population of homeless people living on the street. Popular living areas include grates over exhaust vents where the escaping air provides life-giving warmth. Others find corners or doorways in which to set down cardboard ''beds'' on which they sleep and live. (See ''On the Street in the United States—Homelessness,'' Chapter 1.) (Ralph Guillumetti/Photo Researchers)

Sparse Life Under the Palms

Homelessness in the United States is not confined to the older cities of the northeast and midwest. Here a resident of a Phoenix homeless shelter cooks breakfast inside the facility. The homeless population in Sun Belt cities like Phoenix often expands during the winter months as those without living accommodations in more northern areas migrate to a warmer climate, thus exacerbating the housing problem in the south and southwest. (AP/Wide World Photos)

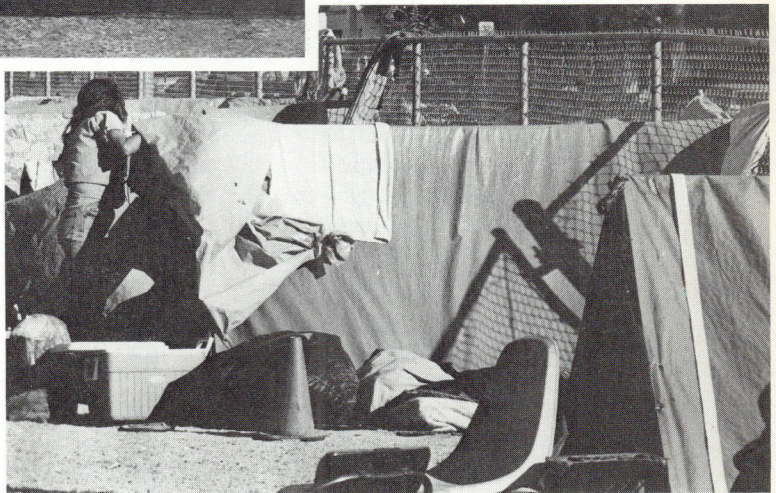

CHAPTER **6**

WHAT DOES SOCIAL
WELFARE LOOK LIKE
IN DAILY LIFE?

WHAT TO EXPECT FROM THIS CHAPTER
LEARNING OBJECTIVES
SERVICE AREAS
RESOURCES, PROGRAMS, AND AGENCIES
DEALING WITH THE ORGANIZATIONAL COMPLEXITY OF THE
SYSTEM
UNDERSTANDING SPECIFIC SOCIAL WELFARE PROGRAMS
LET'S REVIEW

WHAT TO EXPECT FROM THIS CHAPTER

This chapter focuses on the actual delivery of social welfare services. It begins with a brief look at the major categories or types of social welfare services and the public and private agencies that deliver them. This overview of service areas and agencies will enable you to link needs with the services intended to address them. We will then move on to see how *resources* (or services) are organized into *programs* delivered by *agencies*. As you already know, this occurs through public and private social welfare structures. Knowing what services and programs are provided by which agencies is basic to participation in the social welfare system, either as a worker or a user.

The third part of the chapter looks in some detail at several particularly important public programs. You will learn how these programs are structured, what services they provide, and how people gain access to them. This is important information for professionals and users alike. However, in addition to learning about the programs themselves, you will learn how to analyze *any* social welfare program. This skill will be useful whenever you need to learn about the resources available to address a particular need.

This chapter concludes what is, in effect, the first part of the book. Starting with Chapter 1, you learned about the concept of social welfare and the way it has been implemented in the United States, Mexico, Poland, and Sweden. You saw in Chapter 2 how it grows out of predictable life-cycle needs, while Chapters 3 and 4 traced its historical development in response to economic, political, demographic, and environmental conditions. Chapter 5 examined the overall structure or design of social welfare systems. This chapter goes a step further by looking at the actual programs through which services are delivered. At the conclusion of this chapter, then, you will have moved from understanding what social welfare is to knowing the actual programs and resources that are available to people.

In the second part of the book, you will use what you have learned to relate social welfare to the rest of society. We will explore its relationships with other social institutions (the family, for example), and then examine why these relationships are sometimes controversial and problematic. The book's final section will focus on social welfare careers—what is it like to actually ''do'' social welfare? But that is getting ahead of ourselves. Let's now turn to social welfare in daily life.

LEARNING OBJECTIVES

At the end of this chapter, you should be able to:

1 List at least ten categories or types of social welfare services.

2 Discuss the relationship between resources, programs, and the services provided to people.

3 List at least five federal agencies that provide social welfare services.

4 Describe how social welfare services are organized at the state level.

5 Discuss the principle of local delivery of services within the context of local, state, and federal cooperation.

6 List at least ten private organizations that provide social welfare services.

7 Describe the relationship between local and national service delivery in the private sector.

8 List at least three sources of information about the social welfare services available in a particular community.

9 List five elements of a framework useful for analyzing any social welfare program.

10 Use the framework to analyze at least three social welfare programs of your choice, public or private.

SERVICE AREAS

We have seen in earlier chapters that people often have more than one type of need simultaneously, and that these needs are often interrelated. Job-related stress, for example, may lead to alcohol or drug abuse, which in turn will have an adverse effect on the marital relationship and parenting. From the user's point of view, then, it would be desirable to be able to obtain all the various types of help needed to address one's needs from a single source. Unfortunately, services are seldom organized in this way. Instead they tend to be organized by problem area, with one program (or set of programs) dealing with one problem, another with another, and so on.

This sort of specialization occurs because formal organizations (social welfare agencies, for example) find it easier to organize their activities around specific goals. Having done so, they almost inevitably find it easiest to hire professionals whose expertise matches those goals and to obtain funds for directly related services.

As a result, problems tend to be addressed in a sequential way. People seek help for one problem—perhaps alcohol abuse—and in the course of solving that problem a need for additional services may be identified. The result is a referral to another agency or agencies that can provide the needed assistance. Such specialization is not necessarily the most effective way to meet people's needs, but it is typical of the social welfare system in the United States. Other societies, especially Sweden and to a lesser degree Poland, adopt a more integrated approach.

Now let's look at the major types of social welfare services provided in the United States.

Child Welfare

As we saw in the last chapter, programs designed to help children and to strengthen family life are considered very important in the United States. Such services include income support programs for families with children, foster care, and adoption. They also include programs designed to prevent child abuse and neglect, as well as school meal programs, day care, recreation programs such as the Boy Scouts and Girl Scouts and YM/YWCA and YM/YWHA, planned parenthood programs, prenatal and infant care programs, and many others.

Counseling

Many programs are available to help people with personal problems. These include job, personal, marital, and financial counseling; behavior modification; and support groups for those who must deal with specific problems such as divorce, single parenthood, or the illness or death of a loved one. In addition, there are programs to help people improve their ability to relate to others, to

ON THE STREET IN SOLLENTUNA, SWEDEN

A Comprehensive Approach to Care

Sollentuna is a suburban community on the outskirts of Stockholm. It has a population of 49,000, 8 percent of whom are immigrants representing some 70 nations. As is typical of Swedish communities, its system of municipal governance is carefully planned.

All aspects of social welfare are centrally planned and then administered locally through four decentralized municipal offices. All housing, for example, must be approved by the municipal government which owns most of the land in the community. The purpose of this policy is to ensure that the housing needs of all residents will be met in a fair and satisfactory manner. Approximately 450 apartments are built in Sollentuna each year, some by private developers and others by the government. Regardless of who builds them, their construction and their design must be approved by the municipality. This applies even to single-family homes.

In addition, housing prices are regulated and rents are controlled by the municipal government. An apartment containing two rooms (plus a kitchen) rents for an average of 2,500 krona per month—as against an average monthly wage of 10,300 krona for workers in the public sector. Special housing assistance is provided for the elderly and the handicapped.

Health and social services in Sollentuna are provided in conformity with national Swedish policy, but services are actually delivered via four decentralized municipal offices. The professional staff is comprised of specialists, primarily doctors, social workers, and those with psychological training. Their offices, however, are clustered together, and they often collaborate in delivering services. Primary health care for local residents is delivered by a local team of physicians and nurses. When more specialized health care is needed, the patient is referred to a nearby hospital. (The service area of the average Swedish hospital contains about 100,000 residents.) When discharged, the patient again becomes the responsibility of the local health care team.

Teams of nurses and social workers provide care to the elderly and the disabled in their place of residence, as well as to others who may require home care. Medical personnel refer any non-medical problems they identify to social workers, who handle medical problems they identify in a similar fashion. Because the local health staff becomes involved before a newborn leaves the hospital, it has a close relationship with families and can identify problems in their early stages. Infants are monitored especially closely—weekly until they are 6 months of age, monthly until the age of 1 year, and as needed thereafter. The services provided to the families of infants include instruction in child care and parenting skills. Any family problems identified as a result of this contact are referred to social workers. These services, it is important to note, are provided to everyone, not just low-income, minority, or problem families.

Since Sweden has a well-developed system of financial aid to needy individuals and families, social workers can offer their clients a range of financial and personal development services. When this is combined with Sweden's comprehensive health care, the result is a nearly comprehensive system. Teams of nurses and social workers visit the homebound regularly, make sure that they have proper meals each day, are bathed as needed, and adequately housed. Further, the simple act of visitation provides welcome human contact and stimulation.

As impressive as the social welfare delivery system is in Sollentuna, local professionals note that there are some problems. There is limited contact between hospital staffs and local medical personnel, making post-hospitalization care less efficient than it might otherwise be. Psychological problems tend to be referred to hospitals where they are treated medically rather than being referred for psychological and social treatment within the community. This makes for problems in the continuity of care.

In spite of these problems, Sollentuna provides an interesting example of how people's needs can be met in a holistic manner via an integrated system of social welfare services.

deal with discrimination or abuse, and to cope effectively with a range of other problems.

Community Development

Community development programs are designed to help communities and neighborhoods function more effectively. Such programs help people organize to obtain a variety of objectives including neighborhood improvements, increased voter registration, legal aid to address discrimination or injustice, and fund raising for needed community resources. Other programs are designed to assist with the formation of community self-help groups to address problems such as crime, racial and ethnic tensions, inadequate social welfare services, pollution, dangerous traffic patterns, and to increase the community's political effectiveness.

Criminal Justice

The criminal justice system provides law enforcement and related services. The apprehension of criminals is basic to orderly social life and especially to the protection of particularly vulnerable groups, such as children and women. Further, poor families often rely on the criminal justice system for help with interpersonal difficulties. The police are called upon to break up fights and stop spouse or child abuse among people who are too poor, too frightened, or too isolated to make use of other social welfare services.

The criminal justice system is responsible for controlling and rehabilitating those who are jailed, as well as preserving their personal relationships with friends and family. The two main approaches used to minimize the problems resulting from the isolation of prison inmates from their communities are *probation* and *parole*. **Probation** *is the device of allowing convicted offenders to serve their sentence under supervision in the community instead of in prison.* **Parole** *is the practice of allowing prisoners to complete their sentence under supervision in the community after a period of imprisonment.* Probation and parole programs are implemented by workers—parole and probation officers—whose responsibility includes linking their clients with whatever social welfare resources they may need.

Finally, civil rights activists and organizations often seek the protection and assistance of the criminal justice system in their struggle for civil rights. When successful, this effort has resulted in the system's providing protection against discrimination and abuse to vulnerable groups by punishing those who seek to deny others their rights.

Education

Because it is so pervasive in industrialized societies, education is easily overlooked as a social welfare resource. Education's major function is to help people develop the cognitive, emotional, and social skills that will help them grow

into mature, productive, competent adults. Free universal education also contributes to equality of opportunity, especially for women and poor people
(Ruggie, 1984:151–153; Sheahan, 1987:32–48). Education contributes, therefore, to personal growth and development, as well as to social stability.

Many other social welfare resources are linked to education. These include
child health services—such as free or subsidized school meal programs, personal counseling, family planning, job counseling, child abuse and neglect services, day care, job training, recreation, and community development. In addition, some programs connected to education, such as scholarships and
governmental tuition assistance programs, provide income maintenance services.

Employment and Unemployment

Work-related services are an important part of social welfare. Work is the major source of income for most people, and useful and rewarding work promotes
personal growth and social development. Education may be thought of as a
social welfare service related to work since one of the major purposes of education is to provide basic preparation for employment. Other social welfare
services more directly concerned with work include job training programs, job
placement services, unemployment insurance and assistance programs, unions
(which advocate for the rights and needs of workers), and mediation of job disputes. Other programs monitor occupational safety or provide tax incentives
to stimulate investment and job creation, child care for working parents, and
targeted employment programs for special need groups such as the disabled
and the elderly.

Family Services

As we saw in the last chapter, the family is the focus of many kinds of social
welfare services including counseling. Family-related social welfare services
include adoption services, foster care programs, day care, family planning,
and marital and personal counseling. Other family service programs are designed to provide recreational opportunities or education and training in homemaking skills, money management, parenting skills, and the management of
children or elderly family members with special needs.

Health

Health is a major social welfare concern. Among the social welfare services
concerned with health are a variety of educational services and programs in
such areas as nutrition, exercise, the use of alcohol, safe sex, and smoking.
The social welfare system also encompasses hospital care, community-based
care by physicians and other licensed medical personnel, home health care for
the homebound, programs to ensure the availability of prescription and over-

the-counter drugs, and efforts to prevent or reduce pollution that damages human health.

Income Maintenance and Meeting Basic Needs

Income maintenance is a basic social welfare function. As we saw in the previous chapter, income maintenance programs include social insurance, grants, in-kind, and tax benefit programs. These programs help people to obtain basic needs such as food, housing, clothing, transportation, schooling, vocational training, health care, and others. Income maintenance services are often provided in conjunction with nonfinancial services such as those related to child welfare, care for those with mental or physical limitations, and so on.

Mental and Physical Limitations

The provision of mental health care and assistance to those with mental or physical limitations is an important social welfare service. Mental limitations include **mental retardation,** *which results from abnormal or insufficient development of the brain.* Such limitations are distinct from **mental illness,** *in which cognitive and personality functioning is disturbed by biological or emotional factors.* Both mental retardation and mental illness are often associated with **physical limitations,** such as the limited mobility of those with muscular dystrophy or the impaired speech of autistic people. However, physical limitations—the loss or restricted use of bodily organs or limbs, for example—also occur independently as the result of illness, accidents, or genetic causes.

There are widely varying degrees of mental or physical limitation. The primary objective of most efforts to provide assistance to those with such limitations is to "normalize" the environment as much as possible, thus permitting them to participate in regular social life as fully as their limitation permits. The types of services provided directly to the affected individuals may include housing in a protected or enriched environment, physical therapy, personal counseling, financial assistance, medical and psychiatric care, diagnostic and rehabilitation services, and—when needed—prostheses. (*A* **prosthesis** *is an artificial replacement for a limb or other bodily part,* such as an artificial leg.) Other social welfare programs attempt to educate the general population about the abilities of those with limitations and to modify the physical environment in ways that make it more accessible to people with limitations.

Recreation

Recreation programs may have both manifest and latent purposes. Their manifest purpose is to provide opportunities for people to enjoy themselves in healthful, productive, and enriching ways. A second, and usually latent, purpose is to occupy people in productive rather than destructive activities. After-school recreation programs provide children with opportunities to play, com-

POLISH COOPERATIVES FOR THE DISABLED

As a socialist society, Poland emphasizes the right and responsibility of people to work if they are able. There is no official unemployment. Everyone who wants a job is guaranteed one, although not necessarily in the occupation or location of their choice. This emphasis on work carries over to those with mental or physical limitations.

At the close of World War II, Poland was devastated. Approximately 6 million Poles had been killed and large numbers of others injured during the war (Nelson, 1983:105). At a time when its economic capacity for doing so was severely limited, Poland was faced with the need to assist its many citizens injured during the war. In order to provide this assistance, Poland established cooperatives for the disabled.

Cooperatives for the disabled are independent organizations, governed by their own members and economically self-sufficient. They are supported by membership fees and from income earned through the production and sale of consumer goods. They receive no government grants but are given tax benefits and the exclusive right to produce certain products. At least 70 percent of the membership of the cooperatives must be disabled; other members assist the disabled in their rehabilitation, work, and training.

In 1984 there were 452 Polish Cooperatives of Disabled People whose efforts were coordinated through the Central Union of Invalids' Cooperatives (Mikulski, 1987:22,16). The Union coordinates its activities with the Ministry of Health and Social Welfare and the Ministry of Labor, Wages, and Social Affairs, the government bodies responsible for most social welfare services. Of the 1.9 million people with mental or physical limitations in Poland in 1984, 395,000 were vocationally active, 174,000 of them through cooperatives for the disabled (Mikulski, 1987:9).

The cooperatives provide work and a setting for that work that reflects the needs and abilities of their members. Such work constitutes a regular form of employment, and the disabled are paid salaries whose average level is about two-thirds of the national average (Mikulski, 1987:39). It is up to the management of the cooperatives to make sure that they remain economically competitive.

In addition to jobs, the cooperatives provide many other services for their members. These include rehabilitation, vocational training, counseling, protheses, medical care, social and recreational opportunities, and vacation resorts. These services are provided free. In addition, members of cooperatives are eligible for services provided through the regular Polish social welfare system.

Cooperatives for the disabled employ psychologists, physical education instructors, physiotherapists, social workers, nurses, and physicians to provide services for their members. They also run their own in-patient and out-patient facilities for work, training, rehabilitation, and recreation. The residential facility at Konstancin, outside of Warsaw, where disabled young adults are prepared for productive personal and professional lives is one example of such a facility (The Educational and Rehabilitation Center for Disabled People, 1986).

Poland's cooperatives for the disabled are an interesting demonstration of the way in which social welfare services are shaped by a society's prevailing values and practices. The centrality of work as an organizing force in Polish life has helped Poland create an innovative service delivery structure for those with mental or physical limitations. It integrates them into the economic system while at the same time reducing the need for other social welfare services. A cooperative approach also makes efficient use of the available resources in a society whose resources are severely limited. Finally, the cooperative model provides a holistic approach to meeting the needs of those with limitations. It is an approach that could profitably be studied by the United States and other societies.

pete, or learn hobbies under supervision. Recreational facilities such as public parks and campgrounds, playgrounds, and gymnasiums are an important element of recreation services which also include private volunteer programs like those offered by the Boy Scouts and Girl Scouts. Other common recreational services and programs include social groups, exercise programs, team sports, amateur music and dance groups, museums, continuing education programs, and many others.

Retirement

The increase in the elderly as a proportion of the population in most industrialized societies has focused more attention on their needs. In the United States many communities have developed housing, recreation, and transportation oriented toward the needs of the elderly. Other services include pre-retirement planning, geriatric medicine, special meal programs, day centers, homemaker and home health services, counseling concerning the special needs of elderly family members, improved income maintenance benefits, the formation of groups to advocate for the needs of older people, and special efforts by the business community to serve elderly consumers.

Substance Abuse

Substance abuse *refers to the excessive, uncontrolled, and injurious use of alcohol or drugs, including prescription or over-the-counter drugs.* The factors that lead to substance abuse are varied and complex. They probably include genetic factors, social learning, and environmental stresses, as well as the unintended physiological dependence on alcohol or drugs resulting from prolonged use (Anderson, 1987:135–136; Roffman, 1987:480–481).

The services provided to substance abusers are diverse. Some are primarily medical, designed to treat the physical effects of alcohol or drug poisoning and the physical injuries resulting from substance abuse (accidents, suicide attempts, injuries incurred in fights, and so on). Other services attempt to end the abuser's dependence on alcohol or drugs through medical and psychological treatment. The self-help approach, such as that exemplified by Alcoholics Anonymous, is popular in this field. Self-help groups attempt to confront substance abusers with the reality of their addiction and provide peer support while the abuser learns to accept responsibility for changing his or her behavior.

The criminal justice, health care, and educational systems are also involved in combating substance abuse. The criminal justice system attempts to control the availability of illegal drugs and to apprehend users. The health care system is increasingly called upon to deal with particularly serious health problems associated with substance abuse. Currently, the greatest concern in this area is focused on the large number of intravenous drug abusers who are at great risk of contracting AIDS, and on the increasing number of infants born with the AIDS virus or drug addictions. In response to these problems, the educational system is making an increased effort to alert people to the dangers of substance abuse. Relatively little attention, however, has thus far been paid to the needs of those who abuse prescription or over-the-counter drugs.

The Workplace

The delivery of social welfare services has for many years been linked to the workplace in the sense that benefit levels have been determined by past or present earnings. This has been particularly true for basic income maintenance programs for the retired, the physically or mentally limited, the unemployed, and survivors of deceased workers. In addition, many workers receive benefits that are directly linked to their job. Such is the case with many union benefit programs as well as "fringe benefits" provided by employers like health insurance and paid vacations.

In recent years, a number of new services have appeared that are linked to the workplace. An important one is **pre-retirement planning,** *helping people to plan ahead so that they will be emotionally and financially prepared for retirement.* Some employers now offer personal counseling to their employees, particularly for problems such as alcoholism or family dysfunction that interfere with job performance. Finally, the need for child care is a workplace-related concern of increasing importance. A variety of strategies to meet this need are currently emerging (Fernandez, 1986; Quinn, 1988; *The New York Times,* 1988).

The total number of agencies involved in providing social welfare services in the United States is vast. There is also substantial variation in the number and types of agencies found in each of the fifty states. Nevertheless, there is some general consistency in the *types* of agencies.

Table 6.1 contains a sample of the public and private agencies that deliver social welfare services in Westchester County, New York—where I live. Although incomplete, this list will give you some sense of the complexity and scope of the social welfare system, and the many types of agencies involved. Remember, however, that New York State is a relatively wealthy state whose social welfare system is more extensive than that of many other states. Also, Westchester County, which borders New York City on the north, is not typical of counties across the country. Even though it has pockets of severe poverty, it is a generally wealthy county with a household income well above the national average.

RESOURCES, PROGRAMS, AND AGENCIES

Now that you have a sense of the major types of social welfare services, let's look at how they are organized. We will begin by exploring the relationship between resources, programs, and agencies.

You already know that social welfare provides resources that people need. We have seen that these resources can be financial or nonfinancial, and that they can help people deal with problems ranging from basic needs to personal growth. Thus, we can say that **social welfare resources** *are the services that people receive from the social welfare system which are intended to help them function more effectively.* Money is a resource, as is counseling. A meal is a resource, and so is treatment for an illness. Access to a playground is a resource, as are child care, education, vocational rehabilitation, ramps to facilitate movement by those in wheelchairs, and the court system.

Social welfare resources are distributed to people in a planned way. You have already seen that they may be categorized in terms of specific types of

TABLE 6.1 THE ABCS OF SOCIAL WELFARE AGENCIES

Service Area	Public	Private
Child Welfare	Municipal Youth Boards (prevention of juvenile delinquency); Westchester County Department of Health (preventive health services, maternal health care); Westchester County Department of Social Services (adoption, foster care)	Children's Village (special education and clinical treatment for emotionally disturbed youngsters); Blythdale Children's Hospital (care for emotionally and physically limited children); Exchange Club/Child Abuse Prevention Center of Westchester (counseling for families with child abuse problems); Parents Place, Inc. (services to improve parenting skills); Grace Church Community Center (day care center, day camp)
Counseling	Westchester County Department of Community Mental Health and municipal departments of community mental health services (a wide range of personal and family counseling and psychological therapy services); Legal Services Corporation (legal counseling)	Jewish Board of Family and Child Services; Family Service Association (both agencies provide personal and family counseling); Women in Self-Help; Legal Aid Society (legal counseling)
Community Development	Municipal councils of community services (facilitates cooperation between the many social welfare agencies in the community); New York State Ombudsman Program (works on improving communication between citizens and the government); Town of Greenburgh Department of Community Development and Conservation; New York State Division of Housing and Community Renewal (improvements in housing)	Council for the Arts (promotes cultural development in communities); Housing Action Council for Community Development and Preservation (improved housing); Latin American Community Enterprises (helps form tenants' organizations and develop neighborhood conservation programs in areas with many Hispanic residents)
Criminal Justice	New York State Division for Youth (counseling for youth involved with the courts); Westchester County Office of Criminal Justice Planning; Westchester County Department of Probation; municipal Bureau of Youth Services (efforts to prevent juvenile delinquency)	Juvenile Law Education Project (concerned with improving the quality of legal services available to juveniles); Lawyer Referral Service; Victims Assistance Service of Westchester (assistance for victims of crimes)
Education	Greenburgh 11 Union Free School District (municipal special education program for emotionally disturbed youngsters); New Rochelle Youth Employment Service (municipal employment counseling program in the public school system); local community school boards (responsible for primary and secondary schools)	Educational Opportunity Center of Westchester (free remedial education for low-income people); Ferncliff Manor (education and training for the severely retarded); Literacy Volunteers of Mt. Vernon (tutoring and teaching English as a second language); New York School for the Deaf

TABLE 6.1   THE ABCS OF SOCIAL WELFARE AGENCIES   (*continued*)

Service Area	Public	Private
Employment and Unemployment	New York State Commission for the Blind and Visually Handicapped (vocational rehabilitation services); New York State Department of Labor (employment offices); New York State Education Department and Office of Vocational Rehabilitation	Westchester Hispanic Coalition (employment training and placement primarily for Hispanics); Senior Personnel Placement Bureau (employment service for elderly people who want to work); Urban League of Westchester (job placement assistance primarily for blacks)
Family Counseling	Westchester County Department of Health (parenting counseling); Westchester County Department of Social Services (financial and other resource management counseling); Mt. Vernon Diversion and Counseling Program (municipal personal and family counseling service)	Family Service of Westchester; Catholic Charities Family and Children's Services; Center for Family Learning; Guidance Center of New Rochelle (services to strengthen all aspects of family life); Northern Westchester Shelter (for victims of domestic violence)
Health	Westchester County Medical Center (in- and outpatient services); Westchester County Department of Health (health information, screening, inoculations); Veterans Administration Hospital (medical service for veterans)	Nursing homes; hospitals; American Cancer Society; Red Cross; Burke Rehabilitation Center (rehabilitation services for those with physical limitations)
Income Maintenance and Meeting Basic Needs	Department of Social Services (public grant and in-kind programs); Social Security Administration (local offices for public social insurance programs); New York State Division of Housing and Community Renewal (housing assistance)	Salvation Army (food and housing assistance); Freedom Gardens for the Handicapped (low-cost housing); Cortland Emergency Food Bank; Meals-on-Wheels (home delivery of meals for the home-bound elderly)
Mental and Physical Limitations	Westchester County Department of Community Mental Health (diagnostic and counseling services); Westchester County Medical Center (inpatient and outpatient care); New York State Office of Mental Retardation and Developmental Disability (group homes; inpatient services; information and referral); New York State Commission for the Blind and Visually Handicapped (planning services for the blind and visually limited)	Four Winds Hospital (psychiatric hospital); Community Based Services (rehabilitation for the developmentally disabled); Young Adult Institute (group homes for the mentally retarded); Harlem Valley Psychiatric Center (outpatient treatment); North East Westchester Special Recreation, Inc. (therapeutic recreation for the developmentally disabled)
Recreation	Municipal departments of recreation; Westchester County Department of Parks, Recreation, and Conservation (county recreation facilities); municipal Offices for the Aging (day care, meals, information, transportation, recreation)	Neighborhood House (recreation for the elderly and the disadvantaged); Boys Clubs; Don Bosco Community Center; YM/YWCA (recreation and continuing education programs); Westchester/Putnam Special Olympics (athletic program for the disabled)

TABLE 6.1 THE ABCS OF SOCIAL WELFARE AGENCIES *(continued)*

Service Area	Public	Private
Retirement	Department of Social Services (public grant and in-kind programs); municipal and county Offices for the Aging (information, day care, recreation, meal programs, advocacy); Social Security Administration (public insurance programs)	American Association of Retired People (advocacy, information); Visiting Nurse Service (home health care); Volunteer Service Bureau (telephone reassurance, volunteer opportunities); nursing homes
Substance Abuse	Municipal Youth Advocate Programs (prevention and early identification of youth at risk); municipal Drug Abuse Prevention Councils (information); Veterans Administration Hospital (in- and outpatient treatment for veterans who are substance abusers); Westchester County Department of Community Mental Health (substance abuse counseling)	Daytop Village (drug rehabilitation); Alcoholics Anonymous (rehabilitation of alcoholics); Halfway House of Westchester (group home for recovering alcoholics); National Council on Alcoholism (information, training); Renaissance Project (drug counseling and information)
Workplace	New York State Department of Labor, Unemployment Insurance Division (operates state unemployment insurance program) and Job Service Division (employment service to provide training and help in finding jobs)	Union benefit programs; health, pension, and other benefits provided by employers; employer-run day care centers

Source: Westchester Human Services Directory, Westchester Community Service Council, Inc., 1984.

needs or problems (retirement, for example), and that they provide several types of benefits (income maintenance is a major one). In more formal terms, we can see that resources are organized into programs that are administered by agencies. *A* **social welfare program** *is an organized procedure for distributing social welfare resources to targeted recipients.* The social security retirement program, for example, distributes retirement income to eligible people who are 62 or older.

Social welfare agencies *are formal organizations whose function is to administer social welfare programs so that they effectively and efficiently meet people's needs.* You can see, then, that the formal social welfare system works by making resources available to people in the form of programs administered by agencies.

We are so accustomed to hearing about agencies and programs that we sometimes take their existence for granted. However, resources exist only if programs are created to make them available. Furthermore, the way programs are designed very much affects the resources provided. For example, unemployment insurance generally lasts for 26 weeks. No further benefits are paid after that time *whether or not the recipient has found a new job*. Or consider education. Free public education is provided through high school, *but not above that level*. Because there is no free education beyond high school, many people in the United States are denied access to higher education. Similarly, those who are unable to find work within the limited period of time covered by unemployment insurance receive no further benefits from the formal system.

Regardless of the structure of the program, potential clients must be able to find out about it if it is to be effective. As we saw in Chapter 1, the complexity of the system, and the fact that services are delivered by such a large number of agencies, can create difficulties. As a result, some communities have issued directories of social welfare agencies to help people find the programs they need. Others have established information and referral agencies to perform a similar function. And there is always the phone book. However, all of these methods can be problematic. What listing do you look for in the phone book? Where do you obtain a community directory, and what do you do if your community doesn't have one? How do you find out if your community has an information and referral service, and what do you do if it does not?

DEALING WITH THE ORGANIZATIONAL COMPLEXITY OF THE SYSTEM

If your first step as a potential user of social welfare services is to identify and locate the agencies and programs appropriate to your needs, the second is to grapple with the organizational complexities of the agencies involved. If you were seeking assistance from the New Hanover County Department of Social Services in North Carolina, for example, you would walk into an agency organized in the manner depicted in Figure 6.1.

Whatever assistance you are seeking, perhaps food stamps, will be but one service provided by an agency that administers many kinds of programs. Your task, therefore, will be to make contact with the proper social welfare worker. Once you have done so, the help you receive will depend in part on the rules of the organization. However, it will also depend on your worker's interpretation and application of the rules, and his or her skill and competence in filling out the forms correctly, meeting submission deadlines, and straightening out any problems that might arise.

But the situation is more complicated still. The local agency to which you go for help is likely to be part of a much larger network. For example, the New Hanover Department of Social Services is part of the larger state-wide North Carolina Department of Social Services. Further, many of the programs administered by that agency originate with and are at least partially funded by the federal government's Department of Health and Human Services (HHS). As Figure 6.2 suggests, HHS is a very complex agency.

In case you are wondering, your request for food stamps is ultimately dependent on the activities of the Office of Family Assistance in the Family Support Administration of the federal Department of Health and Human Services (HHS). The state and local departments of social services which administer

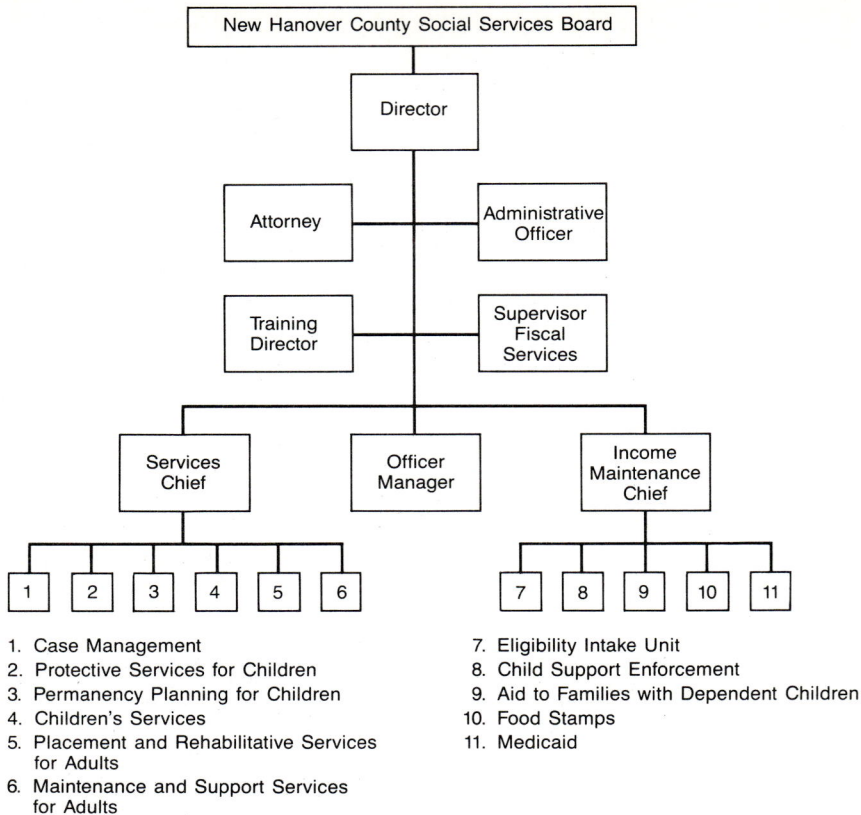

1. Case Management
2. Protective Services for Children
3. Permanency Planning for Children
4. Children's Services
5. Placement and Rehabilitative Services for Adults
6. Maintenance and Support Services for Adults

7. Eligibility Intake Unit
8. Child Support Enforcement
9. Aid to Families with Dependent Children
10. Food Stamps
11. Medicaid

FIGURE 6.1   Organization of the New Hanover Department of Social Services. (Courtesy, New Hanover County Department of Social Services, Wilmington, N.C., F. Wayne Morris, Director.)

the food stamps program are carrying out policies established there. Just as the competence of the social welfare worker affects the resources you receive, so do the activities of the directors of local and state agencies. The success of their efforts in advocating for programs helps determine the ones that will be available to you and the resources they will provide.

The agency most concerned with social welfare programs at the federal level is HHS, whose major function is the delivery of social welfare services. Other federal agencies, however, are also involved with social welfare. The Department of Agriculture is responsible for a number of nutrition and supplemental food programs, as well as training and employment programs for youth and the elderly (the Job Corps, for example). The Department of Commerce's social welfare responsibilities include assistance to minority businesses, while the Department of the Interior administers training and employment programs for youth, the national parks (recreational services), and the Bureau of Indian Affairs (which provides a range of social welfare services for the American

Department of Health and Human Services

Executive Assistant to the Secretary	Secretary	Deputy Under Secretary
	Under Secretary	
Executive Secretary	Chief of Staff	

Office of Assistant Secretary for Management and Budget

Office of Assistant Secretary for Legislation

Office of Assistant Secretary for Personnel Administration

Office of Assistant Secretary for Public Affairs

Office of Consumer Affairs*

Office of Human Development Services
Administration on Aging
Administration for Children, Youth and Families
Administration for Native Americans
Administration on Developmental Disabilities
Office of Coordination and Review

Public Health Service
Centers for Disease Control
Food and Drug Administration
Health Resources and Services Administration
National Institutes of Health, Alcohol, Drug Abuse and Mental Health Administration
Agency for Toxic Substances and Disease Registry

Health Care Financing Administration
Office of Executive Operations
Office of the Associate Administrator for External Affairs
Office of the Associate Administrator for Management and Support Services
Office of the Associate Administrator for Operations
Office of the Associate Administrator for Policy

Social Security Administration
Office of Systems
Office of Field Operations
Office of Hearing and Appeals
Office of Operational Policy and Procedures
Office of Assessment
Office of Management, Budget and Personnel
Office of the Actuary
Office of Central Operations
Office of Policy

Office of General Counsel

Office of Assistant Secretary for Planning and Evaluation

Office for Civil Rights

Office of Inspector General

Family Support Administration
Office of Family Assistance
Office of Refugee Resettlement
Office of Child Support Enforcement
Office of Community Services

Regional Directors

Region	Headquarters
I	Boston
II	New York
III	Philadelphia
IV	Atlanta
V	Chicago
VI	Dallas
VII	Kansas City
VIII	Denver
IX	San Francisco
X	Seattle

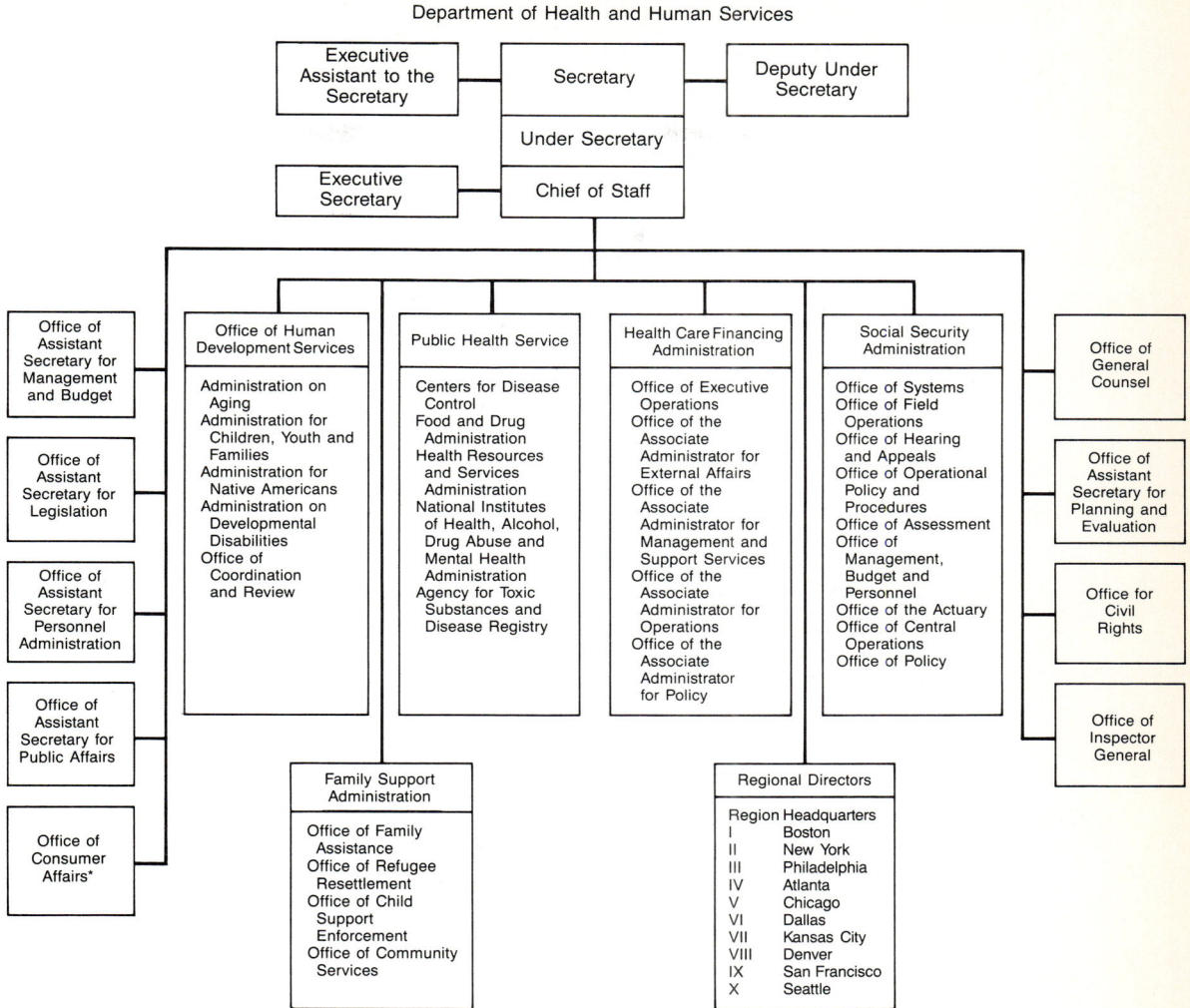

*Located administratively in HHS but reports to the President.

FIGURE 6.2 Organization of the Department of Health and Human Services. (Office of the Federal Register. National Archives and Records Administration. 1986. *1986/87 United States Government Manual.* Washington, D.C.: U. S. Government Printing Office, p. 856.)

Indian population). The Department of Justice is the federal agency responsible for civil rights and a variety of criminal justice programs. The Department of Education oversees educational policy and educational enrichment programs, and the Department of Labor offers extensive employment-related assistance (the unemployment insurance program, state employment offices, and so on).

This is but a brief overview of the many social welfare programs provided by the federal government. Many additional programs exist at the state and local levels, and you will want to investigate the particular set of public programs and resources available in *your* state and community.

To summarize, we have seen that social welfare resources are organized and delivered through programs which are themselves administered by agencies. It is sometimes difficult to identify programs and locate agencies. Even when one has established contact with an agency, the agency's organization and functioning can influence the effectiveness and way in which its programs operate. Since individual agencies are frequently part of larger networks, their actions and policies are shaped at least in part by decision-making at these higher levels.

A final point about the relationship between resources, programs, and agencies is that there are often multiple programs and agencies that address the same problem. For example, consider Figure 6.3, which depicts the way in which the Red Cross and the government work together in the event of a disaster.

You can see from Figure 6.3 that relief efforts in the case of a community disaster involve many agencies, of which the Red Cross is but one. Others include the government agencies responsible for such services as child welfare, income maintenance, and the police. Many private agencies not included in Figure 6.3 would undoubtedly also respond (churches, for example). Since each agency has its own programs and its own policies, there is ample room for duplication of services and confusion among those receiving help. Nevertheless, people affected by a disaster would no doubt welcome as much help as they can get.

Our example returns us to a topic we have addressed several times already: the relationship between public and private agencies (the Red Cross is a private agency). We see once again how the public and private sectors interact, sometimes providing similar services and sometimes services that are different but complementary.

We have also seen that public agencies tend to be larger and more complex (remember the organization charts above). However, notice that the Red Cross, a private agency, is also large and complex. Like many government agencies, it has a national office and local branches. The flow of policy and programs from the center out to the local units is similar to that from the Department of Health and Human Services in Washington to state and local departments of social services. However, we should remember that some private agencies, a skid row gospel mission for example, are quite small. And you will recall that whether large or small, private agencies are directly accountable to their sponsors rather than to the public.

UNDERSTANDING SPECIFIC SOCIAL WELFARE PROGRAMS

There are countless social welfare programs, each addressing one or more particular needs. No one can master the details of all of them. It is possible, how-

WHEN DISASTER STRIKES

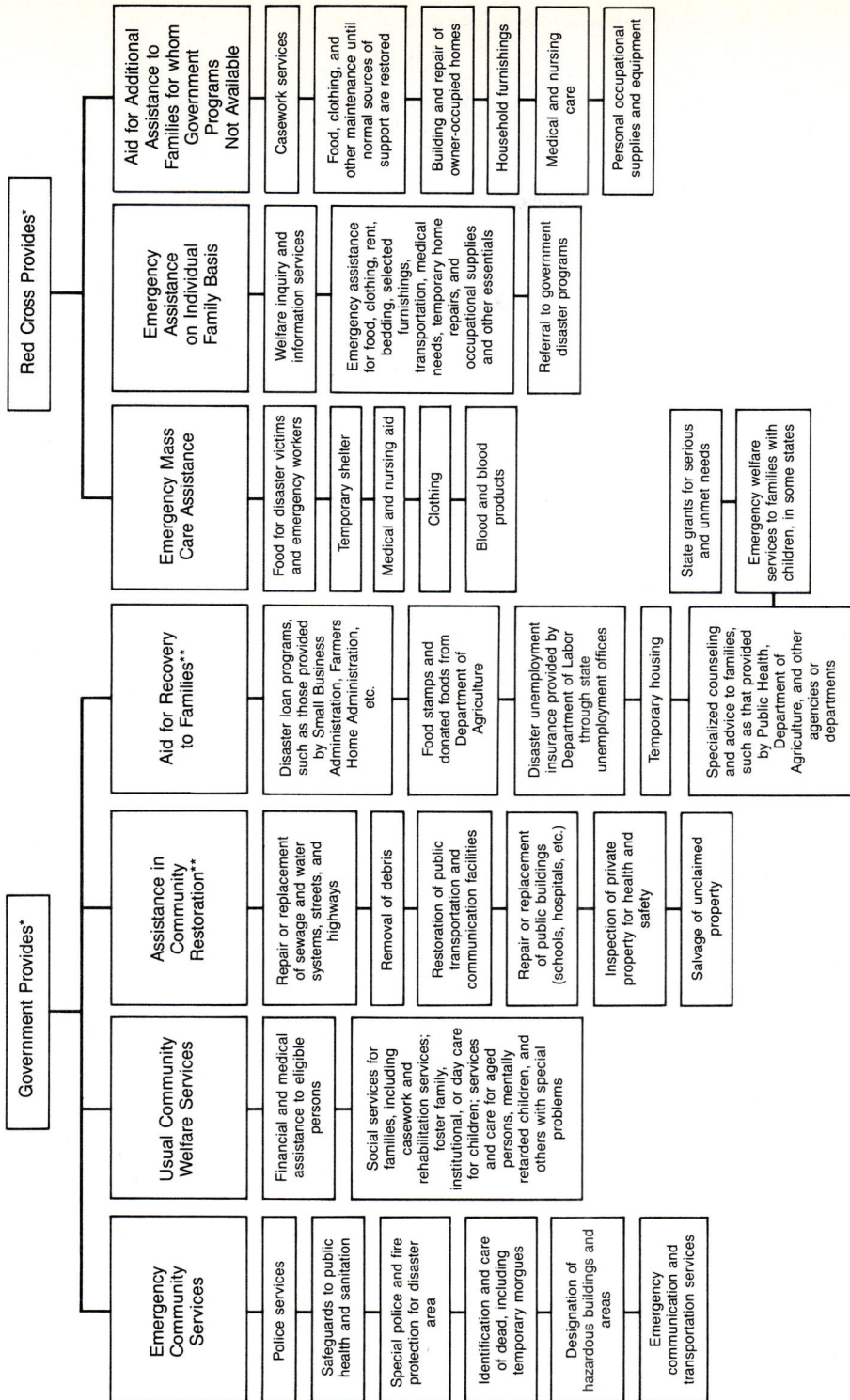

Government Provides*

- **Emergency Community Services**
  - Police services
  - Safeguards to public health and sanitation
  - Special police and fire protection for disaster area
  - Identification and care of dead, including temporary morgues
  - Designation of hazardous buildings and areas
  - Emergency communication and transportation services

- **Usual Community Welfare Services**
  - Financial and medical assistance to eligible persons
  - Social services for families, including casework and rehabilitation services; foster family, institutional, or day care for children; services and care for aged persons, mentally retarded children, and others with special problems

- **Assistance in Community Restoration****
  - Repair or replacement of sewage and water systems, streets, and highways
  - Removal of debris
  - Restoration of public transportation and communication facilities
  - Repair or replacement of public buildings (schools, hospitals, etc.)
  - Inspection of private property for health and safety
  - Salvage of unclaimed property

- **Aid for Recovery to Families****
  - Disaster loan programs, such as those provided by Small Business Administration, Farmers Home Administration, etc.
  - Food stamps and donated foods from Department of Agriculture
  - Disaster unemployment insurance provided by Department of Labor through state unemployment offices
  - Temporary housing
  - Specialized counseling and advice to families, such as that provided by Public Health, Department of Agriculture, and other agencies or departments
  - State grants for serious and unmet needs
  - Emergency welfare services to families with children, in some states

Red Cross Provides*

- **Emergency Mass Care Assistance**
  - Food for disaster victims and emergency workers
  - Temporary shelter
  - Medical and nursing aid
  - Clothing
  - Blood and blood products

- **Emergency Assistance on Individual Family Basis**
  - Welfare inquiry and information services
  - Emergency assistance for food, clothing, rent, bedding, selected furnishings, transportation, medical needs, temporary home repairs, and occupational supplies and other essentials
  - Referral to government disaster programs

- **Aid for Additional Assistance to Families for whom Government Programs Not Available**
  - Casework services
  - Food, clothing, and other maintenance until normal sources of support are restored
  - Building and repair of owner-occupied homes
  - Household furnishings
  - Medical and nursing care
  - Personal occupational supplies and equipment

*The chart shows how distinct and yet how closely related are the responsibilities of Red Cross and of government in natural disasters.

**Some of these programs are activated only after a Presidential Declaration of a major disaster. Federal disaster assistance is coordinated by the Federal Emergency Management Agency (FEMA).

Red Cross and government are both needed to perform disaster functions.

FIGURE 6.3   The operation of multiple systems when disaster strikes. (*Your Community Could Have a Disaster.* 1979. American Red Cross pamphlet.)   **193**

ever, to devise a general approach for understanding whatever programs may be of interest. You will find this approach useful for finding out more about any program that you or someone you know may need to know more about. It will be particularly useful if you become a social welfare professional, for familiarity with the programs that provide services in your field of practice will be an important part of your work.

The following three-step process can be applied to any social welfare program:

1 *Identify the type of program you need.* Is it an income maintenance program, one to strengthen family integrity, services for personal development and enrichment, or a program to empower people? The problem you are trying to resolve may require more than one of these types of programs, but it is important to begin by identifying each of the services needed individually. Later you can worry about coordinating the benefits received from different programs.

2 *Identify the service area or areas most likely to be a source of the type of program you are seeking.* If the problem with which you are dealing concerns a school-age child, for example, you may wish to begin by contacting the child's school system. Counseling and other services for troubled families are available from a variety of sources. Depending on the type of problem involved, you might need to contact an employer, a child welfare agency, or even a criminal justice agency. In other words, after identifying the type of problem you are confronting and the type of user involved, target your search for programs to those that deal with the appropriate types of problems and clients.

3 *Make use of a consistent framework to analyze and understand the programs you locate.* Because there may be many programs to explore, you may find it difficult to decide which are likely to be most useful. If, however, you use a consistent framework to analyze each program, you will find it easier to identify those which are relevant to your needs. Used as a checklist, the following set of questions will help you identify and understand the programs most likely to be useful to you for any given purpose.

• *What is the program's purpose?* What type of need is the program designed to meet? Does it, for example, help people to obtain better health care, provide them with more money, better housing, more education, or assistance in finding a job?

• *What are the program's eligibility requirements?* **Eligibility requirements** *are the conditions that must be met before people qualify to receive benefits from a social welfare program.* Who qualifies to receive the program? Is there an age requirement, an income limit, a requirement that the degree of disability be certified, an employment history requirement, or any other specific requirements?

• *What benefits does the program provide?* **Social welfare benefits** *are the actual resources a particular social welfare program provides to users.* In the case of a health care program covering the cost of treatment associated with certain illnesses, you would want to ask exactly what illnesses are covered.

Similarly, when dealing with a financial aid program, you would need to know how much aid was provided and for how long. Only by asking the appropriate questions can you determine exactly what help people should expect to receive. Keep in mind too that benefits from one program are often insufficient to meet one's total needs. As a result, people often have to make use of several programs.

• *What agency or agencies are responsible for the administration of the program?* Knowing this tells you where to go to apply for benefits and provides an indication of the procedures that may be involved. If it is a federal program, for example, there are likely to be well-defined appeals procedures in case benefits are denied. Such procedures may not exist if the program is privately run. Remember too that the structure and organization of the agency itself can affect the effectiveness of the program and the efficiency with which benefits are provided.

• *In what manner are benefits provided?* How do benefits reach people? Is a check sent through the mail? Does it come automatically every month, or is it necessary to reapply each time? Are the benefits payable to other parties, such as hospitals and physicians, or are they paid to the client who is then responsible for paying these other parties? Do you have to wait in line to receive a meal, or is it delivered to your home? It is important to ask such questions in order to be certain the benefits are provided in such a way that the client can actually use them.

The method by which benefits are provided can sometimes be troublesome. Benefit checks mailed to those living in rundown housing in crime-ridden neighborhoods are sometimes stolen. Having the check deposited directly in the client's bank account makes sense in such cases—provided, of course, the client has a bank account. (Unfortunately, many poor people do not have enough money to maintain an account.) Some homeless people are reluctant to go to shelters because they fear they will be robbed or assaulted. Elderly people may not have the strength to go to the location where free food is being distributed and wait in line. Ensuring that resources actually get to people is a major concern for clients and social welfare professionals. In order for this to occur, not only must the resources be available, but people must know about them and realistically be able to obtain them.

Now let's apply this framework to some specific social welfare programs. We'll begin with a few of the most important public social welfare programs in the United States, move on to a private program, and then to a program in Sweden. The goal is to help you understand how to apply the framework and demonstrate its usefulness. In the process, you will become acquainted with the specifics of several representative social welfare programs.

Medicaid

Source   New York State Department of Social Services. 1985. *Medicaid: How New York State Helps When Illness Strikes*. Albany, N.Y.: New York Department of Social Services.

Purpose A public in-kind grant program that pays the medical expenses of low-income people.

Eligibility People who receive public assistance; people who receive Supplemental Security Income (SSI); others whose income and assets are below specified maximums. (In the case of a one-person family, for example, assets—excluding a home, automobile, and personal effects—cannot exceed $2,850 and annual income cannot exceed $4,700.) These are broad guidelines; specific details are available from local departments of social services.

Benefits Covers inpatient and outpatient hospital services; laboratory services; care in nursing homes; home health care; care by physicians, dentists, and ophthalmologists; hearing aids; treatment in psychiatric hospitals and other mental health facilities; care in facilities for the disabled; family planning services; early periodic screening, diagnosis, and treatment for children under 21 years of age; drugs and necessary medical equipment; physical, occupational, and speech therapy; private duty nursing.

Administration This is a shared federal and state program, with both levels contributing funds and establishing program rules and regulations. In 1985, the federal share was $21.7 billion, the state share $17.8 billion. Many of the more important program requirements and characteristics originate at the federal level. The program is administered at the federal level by the Health Care Financing Administration of the Department of Health and Human Services (HHS), at the state level (in New York) by the Division of Medical Assistance of the New York State Department of Social Services with local social services districts throughout the state. (Other states have a similar state agency.)

Delivery of Benefits Benefits are obtained by applying at the local social services department office, filling out an application, having an interview, and providing proof of income, assets, and age. When approved for the program, users receive a Medicaid card which must be shown whenever services are provided. Continued eligibility to receive benefits must be periodically reestablished.

Payment is made directly to the individual or organization providing the health care. Participating physicians and health care facilities must agree to accept the benefit levels established by the program. Many services must be approved in advance by state health officials in order to be eligible for payment. There is an appeals procedure for applicants who believe they have been improperly found ineligible for coverage or users who are dissatisfied with the handling of their benefits.

Aid to Families with Dependent Children or AFDC ("Welfare")

SOURCE *Social Security Programs in the United States.* 1988. Washington, D.C.: U. S. Government Printing Office, pp. 51–54; Welfare bill's radical goals would take years. 1988. *The New York Times,* October 2, p. 20.

Purpose   A public grant program to provide financial help for needy families with children. AFDC provides benefits to children who are deprived of the financial support of their parents due to death, disability, absence from the home, or unemployment. The level of benefits provided varies from state to state and is determined by the gap between the family's actual income and the income required for a minimum standard of living as determined by the state involved. The program is designed to bridge the gap between the two income levels, but many states provide grants that only partially close the gap.

Eligibility   Benefits are payable for needy dependent children who live in the home of a parent, whose family's gross income is less than 185 percent of the state minimum standard, and whose family's assets are less than $1,000, excluding a home, car (the value of the family car cannot exceed $1,500), and personal items of limited value. Recipients who are classified as employable must register for work or training under the Job Opportunities and Basic Skills (JOBS) program; recipients must agree to allow the child support enforcement agency to enforce child support payment obligations by absent parents.

Benefits   Payments vary by state. In December 1986, the average benefit nationwide was $358 per family or $122 per recipient. Persons who qualify for AFDC usually qualify for other income maintenance programs such as Medicaid and food stamps.

Administration   Administration and financing are shared by the federal, state, and local governments. Federal funding is determined by a complex formula that is related to the per capita income in each state. Generally speaking, the design of this program in any given state is heavily influenced by state requirements which must, however, conform to broad federal guidelines. The program is administered at the federal level by the Office of Family Assistance in the HHS and at the state level by the state agency given responsibility for the program. In New York, the state agency involved is the Department of Social Services, which administers the program through its local offices.

Delivery of Benefits   Payments (checks) are usually mailed directly to AFDC recipients each month. There is an application procedure similar to that described above for Medicaid. There is also a similar appeals procedure.

Aid to Families with Dependent Children was revised by federal legislation enacted in 1988. Among the changes resulting from this legislation were an increased emphasis on providing job training and education and a strengthening of the procedures for collecting child support payments from absent parents. Employment-related restrictions on child care and medical benefits were eased so that newly employed families can remain eligible for these important benefits until they become more economically independent. Although labeled as "welfare reform" when passed, the 1988 revisions have not changed the fundamental character or operation of the AFDC program.

Old Age Insurance ("Social Security")

SOURCES *Social Security Programs in the United States.* 1986. Washington, D.C.: U.S. Government Printing Office, pp. 7–18, and "Personal Earnings and Benefit Estimate Statement," Social Security Administration, March 8, 1989.

Purpose A public insurance program to supplement the income of workers and their families after the worker's retirement. The program assumes that retirees will have other sources of income in addition to social security benefits.

Eligibility Eligibility begins at age 62. Recipients must have been employed in positions covered by this social insurance program (about 95 percent of workers are employed in such jobs), and they must have contributed for a specified period of time. Generally speaking, ten years of contributions are required, time being measured in credits. (In 1989, $500 of covered wages earned one credit, but a maximum of 4 credits can be earned in any one year.)

Benefits Benefits are based on the worker's average covered earnings computed during the period in which he or she could reasonably have been expected to work prior to retirement. Retirement benefits replace approximately 41 percent of covered earnings for people who have been employed for the maximum period of time stipulated, whose earnings were equal to the national average, and who retired at age 65. Benefits are lower for those who retire at age 62, and higher for those who defer applying for benefits beyond age 65. In January 1989, the average benefit paid to retired workers was $546. Benefit levels are indexed to the national cost of living (that is, benefits increase in proportion to increases in the cost of living). Any income from employment while receiving social security may reduce the amount of benefits until age 70, after which full benefits are received regardless of current income. A small death benefit is also provided.

Administration This is an entirely federal program administered by the Social Security Administration in the Department of Health and Human Services. The Internal Revenue Service in the Department of the Treasury is responsible for collecting social security payments from workers and employers. There are local Social Security Administration offices which process applications and answer questions.

Delivery of Benefits Proof of age must be provided when applying for benefits, which is usually done through one's local social security office. Once declared eligible, retirees receive benefits on a monthly basis for the remainder of their lives.

Big Brothers/Big Sisters of Yonkers (New York), Inc.

SOURCE *Big Brothers/Big Sisters of Yonkers.* 1988. Yonkers, N.Y.: Big Brothers/Big

Sisters of Yonkers, Inc.; *Westchester Human Services Directory. 1984. White Plains, N.Y.: Westchester Community Services Council, p. 12.*

Purpose   A private program that provides combined volunteer and professional assistance to high-risk youth from single-parent families. It seeks to prevent juvenile delinquency and serious behavioral or emotional problems, rehabilitate children manifesting problems, and strengthen family life. It also offers therapeutic groups for parents and youth, summer camp scholarships, and after-school recreational programs. Furthermore, it provides interested adults with an opportunity to work as volunteers with young people.

Eligibility   Local youth must be between the ages of 7 and 14, from a single-parent family or otherwise troubled home, and judged to be at risk for developing behavioral or emotional problems. Volunteers must demonstrate evidence of maturity and emotional stability, have good interpersonal skills with youth, and be reliable.

Benefits   Youth are matched with an adult volunteer with whom they spend time on a regular basis doing whatever enriching or recreational activity they both enjoy; professional counseling services are provided to youth and their families; volunteers receive professional supervision and training; therapy groups are run for parents and youth; and after-school recreational programs are provided, as are some summer camp scholarships.

Administration   This is a member agency of a national organization, Big Brothers/Big Sisters of America, and has its own board of directors. The agency raises a portion of its own funds. The remainder is provided from outside sources, including the United Way of Westchester (a private fund-raising group), the Yonkers Bureau of Youth Services (a municipal agency), and the New York State Division of Criminal Justice Services. All services are provided free of charge to clients.

Delivery of Benefits   Both volunteers and those seeking assistance must apply at the agency. Once approved, adult volunteers and youth are matched. They set their own time and place for meetings. Appropriate professional counseling and other services are automatically offered to program participants.

Retirement Insurance (Sweden)

SOURCES   Social Insurance in Sweden. 1986. Stockholm: The Swedish Institute, booklet; *The Economic Situation of Swedish Households*. 1984. Stockholm: The Swedish Institute, printed information sheet; *Useful Information on Social Security*. 1984. Stockholm: Forsakringskasseforbundet, booklet.

Purpose   A public social insurance program to provide income to workers upon retirement.

Eligibility   All Swedish citizens are eligible for the basic pension (Folkpension); those who have employment income in excess of the base amount or "pensionable income" (23,300 krona in 1986), receive a supplementary pension (ATP). Income greater than seven and one-half times the base amount is not considered when calculating the supplementary pension.

Benefits   The basic pension, which is reviewed each year and adjusted to keep up with changes in the cost of living, was 22,368 krona per year (96 percent of the base amount), or 36,581 krona for a husband and wife (157 percent of the base amount) in 1986. (By comparison, the average Swedish family with two earners working in white-collar jobs earned 88,800 krona per year in 1984.) Persons who receive only the basic pension also receive a municipal housing allowance and a pension supplement of 11,184 krona. Those eligible for a supplementary pension (ATP) receive a pension equal to 60 percent of their average pensionable income. This amount will vary according to their income history. They may also qualify for a municipal housing allowance. (Remember too that health care is essentially free in Sweden.)

Administration   The retirement insurance program is operated by the National Social Insurance Board, and is delivered through a network of regional social insurance offices. It is a completely national (federal) program. In 1984, 24 percent of the funding for the basic pension came from tax monies and 76 percent from payments made by employers. The ATP pension is funded entirely from employer monies. Decisions about benefits can be appealed to the Insurance Court.

Delivery of Benefits   Benefits are paid monthly, and retirees must apply for the program. Once approved, they are eligible for the rest of their lives.

LET'S REVIEW

This chapter has sought to give you a practical understanding of social welfare programs in the United States. These are organized into service delivery areas like child welfare, criminal justice, health, counseling, and others. In each area, we have examined the general kinds of services provided and discussed examples of the public and private agencies that provide them.

The relationship between social welfare resources, programs, and agencies was also highlighted in this chapter. Programs are ways to organize resources that people need, and they are delivered through agencies. The operation of agencies in turn influences how effectively services are delivered. Agencies can, as you know, be public or private, and are found at three levels—national, state, or local. In many areas, services are provided by a combination of public and private agencies and programs, as is illustrated by community disaster relief, which is jointly provided by the Red Cross and a large number of government agencies. Likewise, the delivery of many services involves the interaction of agencies at different levels (as with the relationship between federal and state agencies in the case of AFDC, for example).

The chapter concluded with a general framework encompassing program purpose, eligibility requirements, benefits, administrative structure, and the method of benefit delivery. Designed for analyzing social welfare programs and identifying those most likely to be useful for any given purpose, the framework was then applied to several representative programs, including Medicaid, Aid to Families with Dependent Children (AFDC), Old Age Insurance ("Social Security"), Big Brothers/Big Sisters of Yonkers, and retirement pensions in Sweden. I hope you will find this simple framework helpful in analyzing any social welfare program.

This chapter concludes the first major section of the book. Thus far we have been focusing on social welfare as a concept, as a response to human and social needs, and as the provision of resources to address those needs. You should now understand what social welfare is, why it is needed, how it developed, and the types of resources it provides. Starting in the next chapter, we will examine the relationship of social welfare to other parts of society. As you learn more about this interaction, you will be preparing yourself to address the final question posed in this book: What might be the future role of social welfare?

CHAPTER OUTLINE

WHAT TO EXPECT FROM THIS CHAPTER

LEARNING OBJECTIVES

SERVICE AREAS

  On the Street in Sollentuna, Sweden: A Comprehensive
    Approach to Care

  Child Welfare

  Counseling

  Community Development

  Criminal Justice

  Education

  Employment and Unemployment

  Family Services

  Health

  Income Maintenance and Meeting Basic Needs

  Mental and Physical Limitations

  Polish Cooperatives for the Disabled

  Recreation

  Retirement

  Substance Abuse

  The Workplace

RESOURCES, PROGRAMS, AND AGENCIES

DEALING WITH THE ORGANIZATIONAL COMPLEXITY OF THE SYSTEM
UNDERSTANDING SPECIFIC SOCIAL WELFARE SYSTEMS
  Medicaid
  Aid to Families with Dependent Children or AFDC ("Welfare")
  Old Age Insurance ("Social Security")
  Big Brothers/Big Sisters of Yonkers (New York), Inc.
  Retirement Insurance (Sweden)
LET'S REVIEW

STUDY QUESTIONS

1 Prepare a list of the areas in which social welfare services are delivered (child welfare, health, etc.). Under each heading, list the relevant services that you have received at some time in your life. Then attempt to identify the specific program through which these benefits were provided, the agency responsible, and whether the agency involved was public or private. Finally, write a one-page summary of your impression of the service delivery system based on your own experience. (Note: You will probably need to check with others—parents, friends, etc.—to complete this assignment.)

2 Find out if your community has a directory of social services. If so, obtain a copy and browse through it. If not, use your local phone book to identify as many social welfare agencies as you can. Then prepare a brief (one paragraph or so) evaluation of the adequacy of the social welfare resources available in your community.

3 Select a specific social welfare program that interests you (a program for abused spouses, for example, or one for substance abusers). Visit the agency that administers the program and obtain all the information you need to apply the general program analysis framework described in this chapter. After doing so, identify at least one need you feel the program is not meeting.

4 Interview a classmate to discuss her or his experiences with any single social welfare program (a hospital, for instance, or a school program). Try to determine what led the person to seek help and how he or she found out about the program in question. Ask him or her to evaluate the effectiveness of the services received, and her or his personal feelings about the experience. (Was it easy or hard to find out about the program and actually obtain the service? Was he or she treated well? Did the services meet the original need?) Then write a one-paragraph statement describing what you learned from this exercise.

5 Two of the current major problems in our society are homelessness and AIDS. Choose either problem, and then prepare a list of all the services likely to be of use to those experiencing the problem. Within each service area, identify the programs and agencies in your own community that would be especially useful to those with the problem you have selected. (For example, people suffering from AIDS need health care. What health programs and facilities exist in your community that would be useful for AIDS victims?) Remember, though, that AIDS and homelessness are complex problems. In addition to health care, AIDS victims, for example, might need counseling, income maintenance assistance, recreation, help for a substance abuse problem, and so on.

KEY TERMS AND CONCEPTS

eligibility requirements
mental illness
mental retardation
parole
physical limitations
pre-retirement planning
probation

prosthesis
social welfare agencies
social welfare benefits
social welfare program
social welfare resources
substance abuse

SUGGESTED READINGS

Encyclopedia of Social Work, 18th ed. 1987. Silver Spring, Md.: National Association of Social Workers. A basic reference for studying the social welfare system in America. It utilizes a social work perspective, but includes useful information about the structure of services and types of services. Includes a helpful statistical supplement.

Kahn, Alfred, and Sheila Kamerman. 1976. *Social Services in International Perspective.* Washington, D.C.: U.S. Government Printing Office. An interesting and important comparison of nonfinancial social welfare services in eight societies, including the United States. The overall structure of services and service delivery approaches are briefly described.

Kamerman, Sheila, and Alfred Kahn. 1976. *Social Services in the United States.* Philadelphia: Temple University Press. An excellent summary and analysis of nonfinancial social welfare services in the United States. It describes services, service delivery approaches, and issues in service delivery.

Social Security Programs in the United States. 1986. Washington, D.C.: U.S. Government Printing Office. Describes in some detail public social insurance and means-tested programs (grant programs), as well as programs for special groups like veterans. A basic reference for anyone wanting to understand these programs—their history, benefits, and eligibility criteria.

U.S. Department of Commerce. Bureau of the Census. *Statistical Abstract of the United States.* 1987. Washington, D.C.: U.S. Government Printing Office. A compendium of data about the United States, including public social welfare programs (benefit levels, number of users, breakdown by geographical area, characteristics of users, and so on).

REFERENCES

Anderson, Sandra. 1987. Alcohol use and addiction. In the *Encyclopedia of Social Work,* 18th ed. Silver Spring, Md.: National Association of Social Workers, pp. 132–142.

The Educational and Rehabilitation Centre for Disabled People (1986). Mimeographed pamphlet published by the Centre, 05-510 Konstancin-Jeziorna, Gasiorowskiego 12/14, Poland.

Employers offer aid on child care. 1988. *The New York Times,* January 17, p. 25.

Encyclopedia of Social Work, 18th ed. 1987. Silver Spring, Md.: National Association of Social Workers.

Fernandez, John. 1986. *Child Care and Corporate Productivity.* Lexington, Mass.: Lexington Books.

Kahn, Alfred, and Sheila Kamerman. 1976. *Social Services in International Perspective*. Washington, D.C.: U.S. Government Printing Office.

Kamerman, Sheila, and Alfred Kahn. 1976. *Social Services in the United States*. Philadelphia: Temple University Press.

Mikulski, Jerzy. 1987. *Rehabilitation Services in the Polish Cooperatives of Disabled Persons*. Warsaw: Research Center of Central Union of Invalids' Cooperatives.

Nelson, Harold. 1983. *Poland: A Country Study*. Washington, D.C.: U.S. Government Printing Office.

Quinn, Jane. 1988. A crisis in child care. *Newsweek,* February 15, p. 57.

Roffman, Roger. 1987. Drug use and abuse. In the *Encyclopedia of Social Work,* 18th ed. Silver Spring, Md.: National Association of Social Workers, pp. 477–487.

Ruggie, Mary. 1984. *The State and Working Women*. Princeton, N.J.: Princeton University Press.

Sheahan, John. 1987. *Patterns of Development in Latin America*. Princeton, N.J.: Princeton University Press.

Social Security Programs in the United States. 1986. Washington, D.C.: U.S. Government Printing Office.

U.S. Department of Commerce. Bureau of the Census. *Statistical Abstract of the United States*. 1987. Washington, D.C.: U.S. Government Printing Office.

CHAPTER 7

HOW DOES SOCIAL WELFARE RELATE TO THE REST OF SOCIETY?

WHAT TO EXPECT FROM THIS CHAPTER

This chapter explores the relationship between social welfare and the other major social institutions: the family, education, religion, the political system, and the economic system. Each of these institutions performs one or more important functions for society. The family, for example, provides an environment for the birth and rearing of children who will become the adults of the future, enabling society to perpetuate itself. People's ability to perform their various roles within any given social institutions, however, depends to a large degree on the availability of certain basic resources. Parents, for example, need housing in which to raise their families, and workers need jobs.

Social welfare is itself a social institution. Its major function is to help the other social institutions perform more effectively. It performs this function in two major ways. The first is by providing resources that enable people to carry out their societal responsibilities. The provision of counseling services designed to improve parenting skills is an example. Second, it acts as a buffer between people and social changes that impair or alter the functioning of the other major social institutions, functioning, in effect, as the mechanism by which we respond to major social change. An example is social welfare's attempt to respond to the increasing need for adequate child care so more women can participate in the workforce (part of the economic institution).

This chapter systematically examines the relationship between social welfare and each of the other major social institutions. The emphasis is on how social welfare supports the functioning of each of the other institutions. The impact of social changes is also explored, as are the ways in which social welfare itself is affected by other social institutions.

The chapter then turns to the question of who benefits from social welfare. Analyzing the impact of social welfare on each of the major social institutions helps us see how pervasive it is in daily life. The wealthy, the middle class, and the poor all receive social welfare services. Collectively, society benefits by social welfare's emphasis on prevention rather than cure. Most important, the connection between society and each of its members is reinforced by social welfare's efforts to demonstrate that individual people matter. This strengthens the sense of community—one for all and all for one—that holds society together.

At the conclusion of this chapter, you will have an understanding of the web of relationships between social welfare and its societal context. However, these relationships are constantly changing and being renegotiated. The next chapter will discuss some of the reasons why social welfare is controversial. For now, though, let's put the controversial aspects of social welfare aside and focus on a description of its connections with other parts of society.

LEARNING OBJECTIVES

After completing this chapter you should be able to do the following:

1 List six major social institutions of society and define the social functions of each.

2 Identify at least five resources provided by social welfare that help families function more effectively.

3 List and briefly describe at least three social changes affecting the family to which social welfare has responded.

4 Briefly discuss how racism, sexism, ageism, and homophobia influence family functioning and the need of its members for social welfare resources.

5 List at least three resources provided by social welfare that help the educational institution function more effectively.

6 List at least three ways in which the educational institution reduces the need for social welfare services.

7 Briefly summarize the relationship between the religious institution and social welfare.

8 Describe how the political institution influences societal decision-making about social welfare.

9 Identify at least three ways that social welfare increases the ability of people to participate in the political process.

10 List at least three ways that the economic institution affects social welfare.

11 Provide examples of at least three social welfare programs that address problems created by the operation of the economic institution.

12 Identify at least one social welfare program that serves the wealthy, one that helps the middle class, and one that is targeted to the poor.

13 List at least three ways that social welfare contributes to social cohesion.

SOCIAL WELFARE AND OTHER SOCIAL INSTITUTIONS

You will recall that social welfare was defined in Chapter 1 as "a major unit of society that is socially approved and that is intended to help individual people as well as society itself. This occurs by organizing the distribution of resources and the activities of people...." As a social institution, social welfare shares certain characteristics common to all social institutions. It has been approved by society, it helps individuals and society function more effectively, it distributes resources, and it organizes activities. The family, for example, is the socially approved structure that is intended to promote intimacy, reproduction, economic success, and successful child rearing.

Social institutions perform their tasks most effectively when there is basic agreement about the importance of their tasks, and when the resources needed to perform those tasks are available. As an example of the importance of consensus and resources, consider the current controversy over the role of the family in sex education.

At one time, responsibility for all types of education—including sex education—rested with the family. With the growth of free public education, however, the family's responsibilities in this area gradually decreased. In due course, responsibility for basic and technical education was largely transferred to the schools. This was not necessarily true for certain other types of education, however, including sex education, where the absence of a consensus on the proper locus of responsibility—the school versus the family—has resulted in extensive debate.

Sex education is today a controversial area. It used to be that children learned about sexuality from their parents, siblings, and friends, supplemented by whatever they could learn on their own or from experimentation. Many now argue, however, that this is insufficient given the high cost to society of inadequate education in this area. While some have continued to defend the family's right to control the information made available to its members—and especially those who are children—in this highly personal area, critics began pointing to the rising incidence of teen pregnancy and out-of-wedlock births. More recently, a continuing increase in the incidence of sexually transmitted diseases, especially AIDS, has added fuel to the critics' arguments.

Kamerman (1985:11), for example, notes that approximately 500,000 babies a year are born to adolescents in the United States, almost half of them out of wedlock. Many of these children are raised in poverty, especially those born to black families, where 60.1 percent of all children are born out of wedlock (Bernstein, 1988). Such children are exposed to an increased risk of intravenous drug use, which is associated with poverty, and thus to one of the primary sources of AIDS infection in the United States—the sharing of contaminated needles. The AIDS infection, once it occurs, can be spread through sexual contact. Thus, the high incidence of teen pregnancy suggests that many teenagers are practicing sex without adequate safeguards to avoid either pregnancy or the AIDS infection.

Even without the risk posed by AIDS, the cost of caring for a poor, out-of-wedlock child is fearsomely high in lost potential, family disorganization, and medical costs. When AIDS enters the picture, the toll in money, pain, and personal and family stress is multiplied.

Perhaps inevitably, society's response to these developments has been to seek to educate people about responsible sexuality through the media and the educational system. The responsibility for sex education no longer rests with the family. This, however, is a controversial development, particularly for those who feel that only within the family can a full appreciation of sexuality's role as part of the complex web of human aspirations and responsibility be adequately communicated.

Whatever your views on the proper place for sex education, the issue illustrates the relationship between consensus, resources, and the ability of social institutions to function effectively. The current lack of consensus about sex education raises many difficult questions. Should parents teach their children about sex or rely on the school to do it? Are parents adequately informed about subjects like AIDS, and, if not, how can they be informed? How fair is it to the children involved that some schools have sex education programs and others do not?

Given the current uncertainty as to who knows what about sex, and who ultimately should be responsible for sex education, it is difficult to develop effective strategies for attacking problems like teen pregnancy and sexually transmitted diseases. One result is an inadequate level of resources for providing sex education, whether in the home or at school. Instead, the social welfare system is left to cope with increasing numbers of problems resulting from sexual activity.

Even as social welfare seeks to help other social institutions perform their functions, it may itself be changed in the process. Its own role, for example, may be expanded to include new responsibilities such as sex education. The societal consensus underlying such an expansion may also serve to strengthen society's commitment to social welfare. In the next section, we will focus on the interaction between social welfare and each of the other major social institutions. Doing so will help us understand social welfare's role, not only in the lives of individuals, but in the larger society.

SOCIAL WELFARE AND THE FAMILY

The family is one of the major institutions of society, one with which we are all familiar but do not often stop to define. There are, in fact, many definitions of the family. For our purposes, we will define the **family** *as a social group com-*

THE HUMAN FACE OF SOCIAL WELFARE 12

A New Approach in Sex Education

Most teen-age mothers are unmarried high-school dropouts. But as a student at the New Futures School, an Albuquerque public school for girls who are pregnant or have babies, Angela can keep up with her eighth-grade classes while her daughter Crystal plays in the New Futures nursery....

One of every eight babies born in the United States has a teen-age mother, and more than a fifth of the 478,000 teen-agers giving birth every year have already had at least one child.

One expert in teen-age pregnancy said the idea of day care in schools was slowly taking hold because it helps the young parents and because other pupils who work in child care can get a lesson in how hard it can be.

"It used to be that a lot of people opposed day care in the school, saying it would make it too attractive for girls to get pregnant," said Karen Pittman, of the Children's Defense Fund, an advocacy group in Washington. "On-site day care may actually be a deterrent to teen pregnancy, and it certainly helps teen-agers learn about parenting."

Such programs are aimed at helping the infants as well, particularly those like the one at New Futures that add counseling and care for girls while they are pregnant. The babies of teen-age parents face a greater likelihood of low birth weight and other medical problems and are more likely to grow up in poverty, drop out of school and become teen-age parents themselves.

Breaking the cycle is difficult....

Nationally, 23 percent of all teen-age mothers have another baby within two years of their first, and 43 percent have another baby within three years. But at [this school], the repeat pregnancy rates are lower....

"Preventing that second child is what it's all about," said Marian Wright Edelman, president of the Children's Defense Fund. "If you can delay that next baby, you can stop that teen-ager from messing up her whole life"....

Students are required to spend time working in the school's three nurseries, getting practical experience in diapering, feeding and bathing babies even before their own child is born. There are childbirth classes, and courses in child health, infant development, the care and raising of toddlers and children's literature....

Mary, who got a part-time secretarial job at a construction company through the school's job-training programs, says she has become scrupulous about birth control since coming to New Futures. "Now, I will not miss a pill," she said. "I will not, I will not. I'm going to graduate and I'm going to work."

The New Futures School in Albuquerque, New Mexico helps its students become more responsible parents and understand better the relationship between sexuality, personal aspirations, and economic success. The school's holistic approach goes well beyond the biology of sex to approximate the ideal of sex education as it might, but does not always, take place within the family. This innovative program illustrates how social welfare services can substitute for or supplement the functioning of other social institutions.

From Tamar Lewin. 1988. More teen-agers take their babies to school. *The New York Times,* March 15, A1ff. Copyright (c) 1988 by The New York Times Company. Reprinted by permission.

posed of adults of both sexes, at least two of whom carry on socially approved sex relations, and their children, if any. Its functions include regulating sex behavior, child bearing and child rearing, providing for the economic and emotional needs of its members, and socializing children to become successful participants in society. These activities are basic to the healthy development of individuals, as well as for the survival of society.

Industrialization has had a substantial impact on the structure of the family and the ways that families perform their social functions. This is true in all of the societies we have been examining in this book, although less so in nations such as Mexico that are still only partially industrialized. The large extended families common in agricultural societies have generally become small nuclear units that are better adapted to urban life. Smaller families are also more suited to an economic environment where wages are used to purchase goods and services. As families have shrunk in size, their daily interactions involve primarily spouses and their children, usually few in number. Other relatives are less likely to share the same household, and even elderly parents may be expected to live in their own homes.

Indeed, our whole concept of the family is changing. Its traditional basis is the marriage bond and blood ties between married people and their children and kin. However, *the functions of the family may also be performed within households, composed of people who are not married or related or in single-person households*. In other words, the **household** is an important locus for the provision of family functions, even in those instances where the household is not composed of family members as traditionally defined.

Consider the elderly. As married partners age, their children frequently marry and establish their own homes. If one of the elderly parents dies or has to be placed in a nursing home, the other is left alone. Under these circumstances, unrelated elderly people sometimes choose to live together to share costs and companionship, and to provide mutual support. Relationships with other family members usually continue—calls and visits to the children and grandchildren, and contact with the spouse who is not living at home. But the fundamentals of daily life take place in a household which does not meet the traditional definition of a family.

This kind of household life is also common among other groups. Gay and lesbian people who are neither married nor biologically related often live together in stable, long-term relationships. People with mental or physical limitations may spend much of their lives in group homes that can meet their specialized needs more effectively than can their biological families—or "families of origin." In such cases, the household provides daily physical and emotional care, although contact is often maintained with the biological family as well.

Family units are not always stable over time. Between 1970 and 1985, the proportion of the U.S. population that was married fell from 71.7 to 63.0 percent, while the divorced percentage of the population increased from 3.2 to 7.6 and the percentage of single people rose from 16.2 to 21.5 (U.S. Department of Commerce, Statistical Abstract, 1987:38). As we might expect given these data, the number of family households increased by 15.7 percent between 1970 and 1980, while the number of nonfamily households (including single-person households) increased by 77.7 percent (U.S. Department of Commerce, Statistical Abstract, 1987:42). These changes have had a significant impact on the nature of family life. For example, about 10 percent of all children in the United States today live in families composed of one step-parent and one birth parent (Collins, 1985), while 23 percent live with only one parent (Kamerman, 1985:10).

The purpose of this discussion is not to minimize the family's importance. It is instead intended to suggest that households are important because they perform a function similar to the family. For this reason, they are highly relevant to an examination of the needs that have resulted from changes in the nature of the family and social welfare's response to them.

The Impact of Broken Families

When families dissolve, their members are affected in a variety of ways. Children often feel rejected and guilty, believing that they somehow caused the divorce. Spouses (including unmarried partners) may be angry and fearful about their future well-being. The economic consequences of divorce can be substantial, especially for women who even now generally are given the responsibility for child care, and most especially women who are members of minority groups (Kamerman, 1985:9–11). Creating conditions that allow children to maintain contact with both biological parents is another concern.

Social welfare provides a range of services to address the changing needs of broken families and households. Many child welfare services, including income maintenance programs, programs designed to prevent child abuse and neglect, foster care, adoption services, and parenting skills programs, are available to help people deal with the strains caused by divorce or single parenthood. So too is a range of family and personal counseling programs designed to help adults and children cope with the feelings of loss, anger, and anxiety that often accompany divorce and remarriage (*Social Work,* 1987). Finally, job training and placement services sometimes provide assistance to those who need to seek employment as a result of divorce and remarriage.

Meeting the Needs of Dependent Members

As increasing numbers of parents work outside the home, many families and households find it difficult to arrange suitable care for their children or elderly members. Because of the number of people affected, the need for child care is currently a highly visible issue (Fernandez, 1986; Kamerman, 1985:10–11; Quinn, 1988; Ruggie, 1984:182–294). Clearly, access to quality child care that provides a healthy and safe environment for the child is critical for many families and households. And for some children, child care programs provide opportunities for stimulation and growth that supplement the limited opportunities available through the family because of poverty, single parenthood, or other factors.

The needs of elderly family and household members are less visible than those of children. In the United States, where the elderly are responsible for their own care, little attention is paid to the number of grown children who are called upon to aid their elderly parents. Yet the financial strain, time pres-

THE HUMAN FACE OF SOCIAL WELFARE 13

Have Toys, Will Travel

It is 10 o'clock on a Saturday morning and the parade of the children is beginning at Houston Intercontinental Airport.

Here comes 12-year-old Scott Craiger, skateboard hung rakishly over knapsack, on his regular filial pilgrimage from Wilmington, Delaware, where he lives with his mother, to spend the summer with his father in San Angelo, Texas. "I've been flying alone since I was 5," he says with aplomb.

Next comes tousle-haired Alvin Devore, 11, bound from Cleveland to visit his father in Irving, Texas.

At airports all over the country young children, clutching favorite toys and dolls, are traveling alone in record numbers....

The airlines say the surge in young frequent fliers is a product of two unrelated facts of modern American life: the growing number of divorced couples and several years of airline deregulation, which has brought fares down and made flying nearly as routine as taking the bus.

While the young passengers require much special attention, the airlines welcome the business.... "They are the passengers of the future, and we want them to have a good experience the first time they fly" [said a long-time flight attendant].

[Several airlines] have set up special supervised lounges for children at major hubs [which may include] television, toys, games and snacks to keep children occupied while awaiting connections.... [One airline] deals with about 300 unaccompanied children each day [at Houston's airport], and at Denver's [airport]... about 450 to 500 children a day....

Industry officials say they expect about half a million unaccompanied children [during the summer of 1986], normally the heaviest period for such travel. Most of the children, they say, are shuttling between parents separated by divorce or jobs. The main such divorce routes are along the heavily traveled corridor between Boston and Washington, and between cities such as Houston and Dallas in Texas and San Francisco and Los Angeles in California....

The Federal Government has no rules governing unaccompanied children....

Not all children relish flying alone. It often means a frightening separation from parents, and flight crews find themselves playing child psychologist. (A flight attendant) recalls a 6-year-old girl who was being sent to live with her father and who did not want to leave her mother. The girl began to cry hysterically in flight, and the attendant tried to assure her about the new family awaiting her. Ultimately, (the flight attendant), using a common maneuver, calmed the child by deputizing her to hand out the peanuts during beverage service.

———

There are many statistics to demonstrate the impact of divorce on children, but sometimes it is the little things that provide the most insight. A glimpse into the lives of children who commute between separated parents by air is such an experience. It also illustrates how external factors like technology (the modern jet airplane) and economics (airline deregulation and the desire of the airlines to woo children who will be the travelers of the future) can shape people's lives—in this instance, enabling children to maintain contact with separated parents who live many miles apart.

sures, and emotional burdens imposed on both parties by the reversal of the parent-child relationship are considerable. Degenerative illnesses that impair the elderly's ability to care for themselves only increase the difficulties, as does the limited availability of affordable and appealing long-term care facilities for the elderly.

While the social welfare system in the United States does include a network of public and private child care facilities, the number of spaces available is insufficient to meet current demand. In addition, the costs involved are beyond the reach of many families and households. Gradually, however, we are seeing an expansion in the availability of child care as a result of cooperation between social welfare agencies and the business community. Among the several strategies that have emerged as a result of this cooperation are company subsidies to reduce the cost of child care, the provision of child care facilities within the workplace, and increased use of flexible work hours and job sharing to make it easier for parents to care for their children.

Programs to help families and households care for the elderly are less well developed. Income maintenance programs such as "Social Security" and the Supplemental Security Income program are useful. Medicare and Medicaid also provide some coverage when medical care or home-based health care services are needed. A variety of social agencies provide counseling services to help families manage interpersonal stress, and identify and plan for needed care (Tonti and Silverstone, 1985). The availability of an increasing range of residential facilities for the elderly may also reduce pressure on families whose adult members must work and have little time to care for aged parents or grandparents. Finally, the increasing use of pre-retirement planning in the workplace also helps families and households plan for the care of their elderly members (Monk, 1985).

Housing and Poverty

An increasing number of families in the United States is becoming poor and homeless, and this is a growing source of concern. From 1970 to 1984, the number of middle-income families declined from 53.4 percent to 43.9 percent, while the number of low-income families increased by 16 percent (Iatridis, 1988:12). In addition, from 1979 to 1987 the poorest 20 percent of the population experienced a 9.8 percent decrease in amount of family income, while the richest 20 percent had a 15.6 percent increase (Tolchin, 1989). In the United States, the top fifth of the population accounts for 42.8 percent of the total income, whereas the comparable figure for Sweden is 37 percent and for Mexico, 64 percent (Muller, 1988:54). The distribution of income in the United States is, therefore, less equal than that in Sweden (the least unequal) but more equal than in Mexico. And, as in the past, minority families in the United States continue to experience the highest rates of poverty (Bernstein, 1988.)

Increasingly, as the cost of housing rises and the supply of low-cost housing decreases, poverty is accompanied by homelessness. For example, in

ON THE STREETS IN WARSAW, POLAND

The Day Care Center for the Elderly located in the Mocatow neighborhood of Warsaw illustrates Poland's efforts to employ a comprehensive and integrated approach to the provision of social welfare services. Housed in the same building with the Mocatow Social Services Center, the Center for the Elderly provides its members with access to social workers and other social welfare personnel.

Polish law requires that the elderly be cared for by their families. For this reason, most public facilities provide care and recreation only during the day when family members are working. However, elderly who have no families or who are homebound are eligible for in-home or residential care. All of these services are free, as is medical care. The elderly also receive a pension sufficient to provide a minimal standard of living.

The Mocatow Center serves about fifty neighborhood residents and has a warm, personal feeling. There are many more women than men, a result of the demographic reality that women generally live longer than men as well as the heavy military casualties suffered by Poland during World War II. There are several rooms that accommodate a variety of activities. The largest is a living room with armchairs and sofas. Here the seniors chat, watch television, and participate in activities they enjoy such as knitting, embroidery, or painting.

Their handiwork is displayed, and much of it is quite beautiful. There is also a room where medical care is provided and another for the preparation of simple meals and snacks. Finally, there is a quiet room with lounging chairs where the members can nap or rest.

Occasionally there are trips or guest speakers. These seem much appreciated and enjoyed by the seniors. The Mocatow Center has its own scrapbook that chronicles the activities and even the deaths of its members. Pictures, descriptions of events, and eulogies to the dead are included, and they are proudly displayed and discussed with visitors.

As with much of the Polish social welfare system, the day care center accomplishes much with very little. It is a simple but comfortable facility, characterized more by a warm sense of companionship than by extensive facilities. Its small size and neighborhood location help those who attend to feel welcome and integrated into the group. It reduces the burdens of employed family members (remember that in Poland most people work) by providing care during working hours. This center demonstrates how social welfare services can help the family perform its functions and at the same time encourage familylike interactions among its clients.

November 1987 there were 871 homeless families with 1749 children in relatively affluent Westchester County, New York. Of these families, 673—with 1,323 children—were being temporarily housed in motels until permanent housing could be found (Westchester County Department of Social Services, 1987). Estimates of the total number of homeless people nationwide range from 250,000 to 2 million (Iatridis, 1988:11), and concern is growing that increasing numbers of the homeless are families with children.

Poverty has always been a major concern of the social welfare system. Among the many social welfare responses to poverty are income maintenance programs such as AFDC (Aid to Families with Dependent Children), the several programs established by the Social Security Act of 1935, and a variety of other programs that provide some degree of income support—food stamps, school nutrition programs, Medicare and Medicaid, and others. Housing needs, on the other hand, are addressed by relatively few programs. As the federal monies available for housing have decreased in recent years, public housing programs have been cut back substantially, and housing allowances provided by AFDC have become increasingly inadequate. For example, the monthly housing allowance for a family of four receiving AFDC in Westchester County, New York is only $390 and very little, if any, housing is available at this price (Cupaiuolo, 1988).

Housing is central to the functioning of the family, and its absence is associated with many other needs. Studies show that the homeless, in addition to needing a place to live, are likely to need substantial medical and psychiatric care (Sauber et al., 1988:116). Homeless children face special problems in the areas of education, self-image, physical safety, and socialization. In an effort to meet some of these needs, a range of special programs has been developed. These include mobile medical vans, roving teams of medical and social work personnel who go into the community to provide assistance to people on the street, and efforts to resolve the often thorny territorial disputes between school districts over responsibility for educating children from homeless families.

The limited effectiveness of the social welfare system in meeting the needs of homeless families reflects the degree to which this issue is tied to more fundamental social problems. What Iatridis (1988:11–12) calls a policy of "underdevelopment" has contributed to such problems as high unemployment rates—especially among the urban poor—inadequate health care, surprisingly high illiteracy rates, inadequate welfare payment levels, and a dwindling stock of decent low-cost housing. These factors combine to force many families into poverty and out of decent housing. Attempts to meet the immediate needs of homeless and poor families are important, but an enduring solution to their problems will require a change in social policy.

Meeting the Personal Needs of Family and Household Members

Recent data show that there have been some important shifts in how and when people establish family or household units. Increasingly, the tendency is to defer marriage. For example, the marriage rates per thousand for single women aged 15 to 44 declined from 140.2 in 1970 to 102.6 in 1980. In addition, between 1974 and 1983 the age at which women marry increased by about 2 years (*The New York Times*, 1986). While this suggests that at least some women may be deliberately choosing to marry later, it is also true that deferring marriage tends to decrease the probability a woman will ever marry, a consequence that may or may not be intended (Greer, 1986).

One factor in these changes is the increased desire—often reinforced by necessity—on the part of women to work and have a career outside the home. Women who work outside the home have less time and energy to devote to a family than those who do not. At the same time, however, women today are also more willing to have children without being married than in the past (Kantrowitz et al., 1985). Modern birth control techniques and reproductive technology have given women an increased range of choices with respect to parenting and marriage.

These choices open up many new possibilities. People may choose to live alone, to live with someone in a nonmarital relationship, or to marry. In each case, children may or may not be present. What emerges is an array of family and household types, each of which offers a different solution for meeting the needs of its members.

One of the purposes of social welfare then is to help people make appropriate choices that they can live with successfully. Among the services it provides to help them do so are marital counseling, family planning, nonfamily support networks, personal counseling, preparation for independent living, training in parenting skills, and income maintenance programs. These services attempt to strengthen the ability of the unit involved, whether family or household, to function effectively, and to link it to other structures that offer needed physical and emotional resources.

The Family as an Aid to Social Welfare

The centrality of the family in people's lives makes it vitally important to the social welfare system as well. There are two principal reasons for this. The first is the family's ability to control the incidence of problems. People reared in strong, healthy families are likely to perform their social roles effectively and to possess a sense of personal well-being. They are highly likely to avoid self-destructive behavior, be productive members of the workforce, and form strong, healthy families (or households) themselves. In so doing, they will avoid problems such as substance abuse, family violence, inadequate performance in the workplace, and alienation. In a sense, the social welfare system is constantly trying to put itself out of business by helping people and systems to function well on their own. Successful intervention at the family and household level is an important part of this strategy.

The second is that the family can assist the social welfare system by strengthening society's commitment to social welfare. It is within the family that most people learn many of their values. As they grow into adulthood, they live in family and household units that also develop and transmit values. When the values taught in the family include the importance of helping others function more effectively, people are more likely to support the allocation of resources to social welfare. In this sense, to the degree that social welfare is successful in strengthening the family as a major social institution, it can strengthen itself.

SOCIAL WELFARE AND EDUCATION

The **educational institution** *performs three major functions in society: socialization, preparing people to participate in the workforce, and promoting racial and ethnic integration.* Let's look at each in turn.

Socialization

Socialization *is the process of social learning through which we come to internalize culturally approved ways of thinking, feeling, and behaving.* In the United States, children receive a considerable amount of their socialization in educational settings. All children in this country are to attend school from age 5 or 6 until age 16 or 17. In addition, many children spend additional time in other educational settings such as nursery school, programs of religious or language instruction, or courses in music, dance, or other arts and crafts.

The importance of schooling goes well beyond the course content. It is in school that we learn much about how to get along with others, following instructions, how to learn, and assessing our own abilities in comparison to others and in relation to organizational expectations. All of this helps prepare people to succeed in their adult lives by increasing their ability to work in cooperation with others.

Ideally, the skills and attitudes taught in the educational institution are consistent with those taught in the family, another highly significant socializing structure. Ideally too, the family prepares its members for school and reinforces the values taught there, including the value of education. There are, unfortunately, many instances where this does not occur. Some families, those with vision- or hearing-impaired children, for example, may lack the training and experience necessary to socialize their children appropriately. Other families, especially those with problems, teach their youngsters values and behaviors considered undesirable by society in general. The school system then faces the problem of reorienting the student toward the values and behavior considered desirable by society. The type of tensions that result are illustrated by the case of James Diggs.

Preparing for Work

In addition to socializing students, schools also teach them knowledge and skills useful for the job market. Since a wage is essential for survival in industrial societies, preparation for meaningful and well-paying work is terribly important. Some of this learning occurs in families, but increasingly it is the province of the school.

There are several reasons for this. The first is the increasing complexity and specialization of knowledge and skills. Another is the fact that most adults work outside the home where their children can neither observe what they do nor easily acquire their skills. A third factor is the increasing reliance on academic degrees and other credentials as a prerequisite for many jobs. James Diggs, for example, needs a high school diploma to be a policeman. It is increasingly difficult to qualify for many jobs in the absence of the appropriate educational degrees or credentials.

THE HUMAN FACE OF SOCIAL WELFARE 14

The Battle for James Diggs

James Diggs...comes from a troubled and impoverished family, from a neighborhood where drugs offer the constant temptation of escape and quick money, and he has poor academic skills....

Those who share James' background are at high risk of dropping out—a description that applies to about 75 percent of those who enter New York City's schools....

"They come from communities where poverty is the norm," [said a school official] "where the presence of drug and alcohol abuse is commonplace and where the likelihood of living with a single parent and several brothers and sisters gives them more reasons not to go to school than to go. What is remarkable is that young people who come out of those circumstances get through...."

James slouched low in his seat in class one day in November. He rarely took off his calf-length gray parka, and that day was no exception. He was depressed, he said, as he showed a visitor a newspaper article about a homeless, 20-year-old mother.

"It makes me feel bad," he said.

His reaction to the article was instructive. In the next three months, as James talked about his experience at school and home, he was jarred by homelessness, and ultimately, the fear of becoming like the people he read about, or who surrounded him. That fear kept him in school.

At 17, an age when many have graduated, James...was midway through his sophomore year. His support system was tenuous at best. His father died when James was 9 years old, and his mother died four years later. "When my father died the house just went down," he said.

Two of his older brothers are in prison, one for murder, the other for robbery. A twin brother is handicapped and lives with his grandmother and two sisters....For the time being, James lives alone. His grandmother threw him out last year when he quit school, and a friend's parents have lent him a small apartment....

[James enrolled in an alternative school for dropouts.] James says he battles constantly to stay out of trouble and in school....He sold food at concession stands at sporting events,...but wanted a job that kept him occupied every night....Part of the reason, he said, was that too much free time might lead him to involvement with drugs....

[Speaking about classes at the school, James's teacher said] "Some socialization goes on....The whole world is really enemy territory to them [the students]. Almost all of them have low skills and so they act out in class...."

James [has] no trouble connecting the value of a diploma with his future. He wants to be a police officer and to do that, he needs to graduate.

As the fall term went on, however, it became clearer that there was a gap between James's desire to finish and his will to attend classes. From November to the end of January, he missed 18 days and finished the term by completing only one and a half credits out of five.

"I look out in the morning," when it is raining and cold, he said, "and I think I ain't going to go. You know, we don't have anyone behind us telling us to go."

James Diggs's experience clearly illustrates how both the family and the school serve as socializing agents. Ideally, the lessons the two impart will be complementary, but for many people this is not the case. James Diggs is such a person. What he has learned at home does not reinforce what the school is trying to teach him, and the family is ill-prepared to support his efforts to internalize the values and goals imparted in the classroom. The social welfare system has tried to respond to James's need by creating a modified school that can compensate for the family's weaknesses. However, the inherent difficulty of the task is apparent from James's ongoing struggle.

Promoting Racial and Ethnic Integration

The socializing and skill-building functions of education are especially important for members of minority groups. There are two reasons for this. Many come from cultures outside the United States. Their families are poorly prepared to teach them how to succeed here, so it becomes the school's task to do so. In addition, many members of minority groups are poor. For them, education is a way to qualify for better-paying jobs so that they can move out of poverty. Unfortunately, education alone is often insufficient to prevent them from facing discrimination. Nevertheless, educational credentials help minority group members to succeed.

Education is an important way to integrate persons from different racial and cultural backgrounds into American society. Today, as in the past, the United States is a multicultural society, although today's immigrants are increasingly from non-Western societies. Evidence of the multicultural nature of the U.S. population appears in Table 7.1, which contains a breakdown of the major ethnic groups in Los Angeles in 1983.

Although we often tend to lump similar ethnic groups together by using labels such as Hispanic or Asian, each group is unique. Each has a distinctive language or dialect, distinctive cultural beliefs and behavior patterns, and distinctive attitudes toward life in their new country (Castex, 1988; Gould, 1988). Common exposure to the educational process makes possible meaningful interaction with members of other ethnic groups and of the larger society.

The multicultural nature of American society encompasses groups such as blacks and Hispanics that have been here for many years but that still experience unusually high rates of poverty and discrimination. For members of these groups, education continues to be an important route out of poverty. Despite

TABLE 7.1 THE RICH ETHNIC MIX IN LOS ANGELES: 1983

Group	1983 population	1970 population
Mexicans	2,100,000	822,300
Iranians	200,000	20,000
Salvadorans	200,000	*
Japanese	175,000	104,000
Armenians	175,000	75,000
Chinese	153,000	41,000
Koreans	150,000	8,900
Filipinos	150,000	33,500
Arab-Americans	130,000	45,000
Israelis	90,000	10,000
Samoans	60,000	22,000
Guatemalans	50,000	*
Vietnamese	40,000	*

*Fewer than 2,000
Source: *Time Magazine,* June 13, 1983, p. 22.

this, the number of black and Hispanic high school graduates enrolling in college actually declined from 1976 to 1985 (Fiske, 1987). In addition, members of these groups continue to be underrepresented in professional education programs (*College Board News,* 1985). As the case of James Diggs suggests, the effects of poverty and discrimination are felt early, often offsetting any potential benefits from education in the lives of those from poor or minority backgrounds.

One of education's functions, then, no matter how imperfectly performed, is to promote social integration by teaching people from minority groups how to function successfully in the dominant cultural environment. In addition, education helps all members of society to understand and respect each other. It does so by teaching *positive values,* including the importance of respecting cultural differences and living in peace with others. Schools also provide *knowledge* about different cultures—what others do, why they do it, and the contribution each group makes to society. Finally, schools provide a setting in which people from different groups interact so that abstract learning is reinforced by day-to-day contact. This is one of the reasons why school integration has been such an important issue in the United States.

Social welfare attempts to assist the educational institution in many ways. Some of these efforts take place within the schools. Among these are counseling services for students and their families; programs that provide information about drugs, alcohol, pregnancy, and crime; and educational programs designed to meet the needs of exceptional students (the gifted, those with limitations, students with behavior problems, and others). Such programs entail a variety of educational approaches designed to engage and motivate students, such as bringing in guest speakers from the business world to talk about work opportunities, cooperative programs where students alternate between work and school, work-study programs that pay students while they study, college and career placement programs, and others. Finally, social welfare's basic message—that people matter—reinforces the educational institution's efforts to socialize people in such a way that they can lead more satisfying and productive lives.

Similarly, the activities of the educational institution strengthen social welfare. As we have seen, educated people are more likely to be successful in the workplace and thus less likely to need income support programs and related services. Then too, ideally, as with the family, the values taught by the educational institution are supportive of social welfare. An understanding of common human aspirations and needs and the wonderful diversity of human life helps people to value themselves and others. This sense of shared experience often leads people to help others and to believe that helping is an important part of social life. Finally, for those who do, there are educational programs that prepare them to become professional helpers.

SOCIAL WELFARE AND RELIGION

Religion *as a social institution helps people relate to the unknown.* Religion grapples with questions about the fundamental nature of human existence, the meaning of death, and our responsibility, both as individuals and as a society, for the world in which we live. For many, religious beliefs provide answers to these basic questions. In addition, organized religious life provides a sense of community to its members, as well as guidelines for behavior in everyday life.

Many believe that religion is less significant in people's lives today than in the past. However, if we use church attendance as an indication of religious commitment, this is not true of the United States, where church attendance has been generally steady for Protestants, Catholics, and Jews since 1975 (Hunt and Greeley, 1987). What does seem to have emerged is an increased tendency for individuals to challenge or reinterpret church doctrines with which they are uncomfortable. This appears to be especially true among Catholics, where formal church positions may not be as influential in guiding people's behavior as in the past, particularly with respect to issues such as premarital sex and birth control. Nevertheless, Americans continue to exhibit a strong belief in basic religious values.

Religion and religious values play a significant role in many aspects of society, including politics. In the United States, for example, the fundamentalist Protestant minister Pat Robertson was a serious candidate for the Republican presidential nomination in 1988. In Poland, a predominately Catholic nation, the Catholic Church continues to be a powerful institution through which Poles who dislike the ruling Communist government can express their discontent. The church in Mexico, also a Catholic country, plays a somewhat more traditional role, encouraging family life and discouraging birth control. Ironically, religion plays the least significant role in Sweden, the only country among the four discussed in this book that has a state religion—Lutheranism.

In contrast to the family and education, religion has more of an impact on social welfare than vice versa. Since the earliest days of social welfare, many social welfare services have been delivered under religious auspices. This is still true today. Among the services commonly provided through or by religious groups are informal care for the poor and the homeless, counseling, and a variety of other helping services.

Of particular significance for social welfare is religion's emphasis on the value of human life and the right of each person to be treated with love and respect. Such values encourage a sense of a human community in which people have responsibility for their neighbors. This sense of caring and of community responsibility is the bedrock upon which social welfare is built. Religious teachings that reinforce it are important, especially in the face of the continuing challenge from more economically motivated views that seek to limit society's commitment to social welfare.

The exchange between religion and social welfare is not all in one direction. Social welfare does aid the religious institution in some ways. Public social welfare programs, for example, often contribute to the support of private church-run programs by contracting with them, as in the example of the New York City foster care program discussed in Chapter 4. Also, just as religion reinforces social welfare values, so social welfare strengthens religious values. The social welfare system provides opportunities for people to operationalize their religious commitments by working as volunteers or professionals. It is also common for religious groups to join social welfare activists in advocating for legislation that better meets people's needs.

SOCIAL WELFARE AND POLITICS

Politics, like social welfare, is a universal phenomenon. *The major function of a* **political institution** *is to ensure an orderly process for societal decision-making, and to provide a workable structure for enforcing rules and laws.* Political systems take a variety of forms. Most provide for some degree of citizen participation, usually in the form of elections in which citizens select leaders to represent their interests. Political systems differ greatly from society to society on a variety of matters, including (1) the extent to which governmental and economic planning is centralized; (2) the ability of powerful groups to control elections and dominate the policy process; and (3) the ability of citizens to vote in a free and informed manner.

Social welfare performs two major functions that affect the political institution. The first is empowering citizens to participate in the political process so that they can express and advocate for their needs. While this generally occurs within the framework of the existing political structure, on occasion it is the structure itself that people want to change. Empowering citizens is a multifaceted effort that includes educating people about issues and the way in which the political system works, and helping them develop the skills needed to seek social change through collective action.

A second way in which social welfare influences politics is by seeking to monitor and protect people's rights. One way in which it does so is by encouraging the enforcement of existing laws protecting rights and advocating the passage of laws needed to protect rights that have not yet received legal protection. Because such activities are in and of themselves often insufficient, other approaches must be utilized. These include litigation and direct action to encourage those violating people's rights to stop doing so voluntarily. To this end, the social welfare institution employs a variety of tactics, including the negotiation of procedural and structural changes within businesses and other organizations, educating people about the effects of their discriminatory behavior, boycotting those who do discriminate, and organizing other forms of collective protest.

To be sure, these efforts do not ensure that all people will be treated fairly. Examples of continued inequity in the treatment of minority groups and others can be found in all of the countries discussed in this book, including the United States. Equal treatment for all is, nonetheless, a declared goal of the social welfare institution.

Social welfare seeks to achieve its goals in the political process in a number of ways. Personal counseling programs help people recognize their needs, develop the strength and skills to express and advocate for them, and identify opportunities to seek their goals. Community action agencies conduct voter registration drives, are involved in community education efforts, and promote collective action. Legal aid services employ litigation to challenge discrimination or exclusion from the political process. In addition, social welfare agencies and professions actively lobby, provide testimony during lawsuits, and participate in organizational and governmental policymaking.

The Effects of Politics on Social Welfare

The political institution also has powerful effects on social welfare. We have seen that the availability of public sector services depends on decisions made in the political arena. Without legal authorization and the funding needed to support them, such services cannot exist. The priorities established through the legislative and budgeting processes strongly influence the extent to which human needs are recognized and addressed through the social welfare system. The federal budget proposed for fiscal year 1989 by the Reagan administration would have reduced the federal budget for housing and community development by $2 billion and the funds available for subsidized housing from $7.9 billion to $6.9 billion (*Washington Social Welfare Legislation Bulletin,* 1988:1). These proposals, coming at a time of widespread calls for increased funds to address the housing needs of the homeless and the poor, can be seen as an effort to reduce still further the federal government's responsibility for housing.

It is through the political process that a society establishes its priorities. When social welfare issues are on the whole ignored, as occurred during the Reagan administration, society's commitment to meeting human needs is in effect called into question. A continuing effort to identify needs, as well as access to the resources required to address them, are vital to the functioning of the social welfare system. A reduction in society's efforts to enhance the lives of its members is likely only to produce an increase in the extent of its members' human needs. Sadly, if the social environment is sufficiently uncaring, even an increase in such needs may not prompt the allocation of more resources to social welfare.

SOCIAL WELFARE AND THE ECONOMIC INSTITUTION

The **economic institution** *is concerned with the production, distribution, and consumption of goods and services.* At its heart are work, wages, and the class divisions that result from the unequal distribution of wealth. People's access to income and other economic resources is determined by at least five factors: (1) their family of origin; (2) their educational level; (3) their genetically endowed abilities; (4) the structural characteristics of the workplace that determine the type and quantity of available jobs; and (5) discriminatory social and organizational policies that channel particular groups of people in certain directions. Taken as a whole, the economic institution produces the resources available to achieve society's goals, as these are determined by the political institution.

ON THE STREET IN CRACOW, POLAND

On the university campus in Cracow, Poland, there is a tremendously moving monument to eighty-five distinguished professors who were among the first residents of Cracow to be arrested and killed when the Nazis invaded the city during World War II. In addition to serving as a memorial to these scholars, it is testament to the power of social welfare in politics. The Nazis feared the power of knowledge and its ability to mobilize people to resist political oppression. They knew that eliminating Cracow's leaders would reduce the probability of organized resistance.

Today, Polish intellectuals continue to struggle with their proper role in the political system. The imposition of martial law in 1981, effectively suspending civil rights and opportunities for collective action, led to an exodus of Poles from their homeland. Although martial law has since been revoked, Poles continue to emigrate because of a lack of confidence in the political system and its inability thus far to solve Poland's serious economic problems. It is estimated that about 100,000 Poles, most of them young, emigrate each year, this out of a total population of approximately 37 million. Among the emigrants are about 10 percent of all Polish university graduates (Tagliabue, 1988).

Many Polish intellectuals struggle continuously with the issue of whether to go or stay. As academics, they often have access to the resources and the connections outside Poland needed to leave. However, they also recognize the importance of their leadership role in efforts to improve the political system. A prominent Polish sociologist, for example, recently conducted research that demonstrated people did not believe the government-run health service, although free, was meeting their needs. In addition, she studied the alternative health care organizations that were created because of people's dissatisfaction with the existing national system. Her research led to an acknowledgment of the inadequacies in its health care system by the government and governmental encouragement of the development of alternative systems (Diehl, 1988).

Others have exercised leadership outside the government. Some intellectuals have chosen to work with citizen groups, providing them with information and helping them devise strategies to advocate for change. Polish university professors who teach social work, social welfare, and social policy, for example, recently banded together with social welfare practitioners to form an association of Polish social workers. This group provides an opportunity for social welfare professionals to develop self-help strategies, to build a network of colleagues able to work together to solve problems in the government-controlled social welfare system, and to present an organized voice for seeking improvements in social welfare services.

For many of these professionals, leaving the country would be the easier and more comfortable option. Their wages are relatively low, and daily living conditions in Poland can be difficult. That they choose not to do so is only in part because of their pride as Poles and their commitment to their culture. It is also because they realize their departure would make political and social change all the more difficult for those who remain behind. In their decision, we can better appreciate social welfare's role in the political institution.

Work is central to life in industrialized societies (Ran and Roncek, 1987:360). It provides most people's primary source of income, as well as a sense of identity. One of the most frequently asked questions when we meet someone new is, "And what do you do?" Since wages are so important, workers seek to maximize them. Employers, of course, try to keep their payroll costs as low as possible. In the United States, political intervention in this struggle between workers and employers is relatively rare. In social democracies such as Sweden, on the other hand, unions are active participants in the political system where they advocate for the needs of workers (Esping-Andersen, 1985:10). In socialist nations such as Poland, wages are generally controlled by the government.

Wages are essential to the production and consumption aspects of the economic institution. In industrial societies, a salary provides an important incentive for people to work. Their work makes the production of goods and services possible and rewards workers with wages that enable them to be consumers. What is produced is consumed because people have the income to purchase it, and income most often comes from wages. It can also come from other sources, such as investments, an inheritance, or social welfare income maintenance benefits, but the income of most people is dependent on wages. Therefore, work enables production to take place and at the same time makes possible the consumption of what is produced.

Problems occur when people cannot find work. At first, it is an individual problem for the worker involved since he or she is, in all probability, dependent upon work for income. As unemployment increases, however, production is also affected because unemployed workers can consume less, and production must, therefore, also decline to meet reduced demand. For this reason, high levels of unemployment become a corporate and societal problem. If society provides social welfare benefits to the unemployed so they can survive, the problem becomes even larger. The money for such benefits is needed precisely when government income from individual and corporate income taxes is being reduced.

Full employment is an important goal of most industrialized societies. The achievement of this goal, however, is not totally within the control of any single society in today's world. All countries import and export goods and services. The balance between the money spent to purchase imports and the income earned from the sale of exported goods greatly affects levels of employment. The automobile industry in the United States is an excellent example. When U.S. consumers buy imported cars, domestic manufacturers must reduce their production so they are not producing more cars than they can sell. Building fewer cars requires fewer workers, resulting in increased unemployment in the U.S. automobile industry. This would not happen if foreign autos were not imported, or if the value of American cars being exported roughly equaled the value of those being imported.

The relationship between the economic values of a nation's imports and exports is called the **trade balance** *or balance of trade. When a country's imports exceed exports, the result is a* **trade deficit.** This is currently a serious problem in the United States. Many developing countries have a similar problem, but the effects are more severe for them because of the more fragile condition of their economies (Sheahan, 1987).

There are several employment-related problems in the United States at the present time. In 1987, unemployment stood at 6.0 percent of the workforce, down from a peak of 9.5 percent a few years earlier. However, with 7.3 million people unemployed, it is still a substantial problem (Uchitelle, 1987). In addition, this figure hides some troubling additional concerns. Data indicate that about 6 million people, called "discouraged workers," have given up even trying to find work because they have been chronically unsuccessful (Uchitelle, 1987). An additional nearly 18 million people work less than half the year and earn annual incomes of less than $10,000, well below the poverty level (Uchitelle, 1987).

Another problem is the increasing use of temporary rather than permanent workers. These are workers hired on a full-time but temporary basis, who are usually paid less and receive fewer benefits than regular full-time workers (Uchitelle, 1988). Even part-time workers are suffering because of the low level of the minimum wage. Currently set at $3.35 an hour, it translates into a weekly income of only $134 and an annual income of $7,000 for a full-time worker, well under the poverty level (Levitan and Shapiro, 1986). We can see, then, that in the United States there are a number of problems facing both unemployed workers and those who are working under poorly paid or uncertain conditions.

Finally, there is the problem of discrimination. As we have noted at several points, one of the goals of the social welfare institution is to eliminate discrimination in the larger society. That minority groups continue to face such discrimination in the workplace is amply documented by the data in Table 7.2. Despite many years of public attention, the problem of discrimination continues to affect many American workers. As the data in the table indicate, men continue to earn more than women, and whites earn more than blacks or Hispanics.

The reliance of the United States on a free-market system makes unemployment or underemployment both likely and relatively acceptable. The determination of the number of workers needed at any given time is left to the marketplace so that the workforce expands or contracts in response to market conditions.

Not all societies take this approach. National policy in Sweden calls for full employment, and in 1984 when unemployment in the United States was 7.4 percent, it was only 3.1 percent in Sweden (Zimbalist, 1987:23). As a socialist

TABLE 7.2 COMPARATIVE EARNINGS IN THE UNITED STATES

Category	Mean annual earnings	Percent of white males
White males	$28,159	100.0
Black males	19,949	70.8
Hispanic males	19,692	69.9
White women	$17,253	61.2
Black women	15,459	54.8
Hispanic women	14,576	51.7

Source: National Commission on Working Women (1985).

nation, Poland has no official unemployment. Everyone who wants a job is guaranteed one. In these two systems, economic planning is used to regulate the labor market so that jobs are created as necessary and people are kept employed. These societies attempt to manage the labor market in such a way as to control the level of employment rather than allowing the workforce to be controlled by the market.

Whatever the type of economic system, it is assisted by the social welfare institution. In the United States and Sweden, the social welfare system provides income maintenance programs to help support those who are unemployed or do not earn an income adequate to meet their needs. Job training and job placement programs provided by the social welfare system also seek to reduce employment-related problems. By actively preparing people for employment, the educational system helps to minimize unemployment, especially in Sweden (Ruggie, 1984:143–181). Certain other social welfare services, notably those related to child welfare, health care, and housing, are useful in dealing with the unhealthful emotional and physical conditions associated with low income that may, therefore, accompany unemployment (Wyers, 1988).

Personal counseling programs can and do help those who have become discouraged and may have dropped out of the workforce. As we have already noted, stress increases the probability of dysfunctional behavior. This is true of unemployment as well. In a modern wage-based economy, unemployment can breed feelings of panic and humiliation, feelings that personal counseling can help counteract.

The practice of linking many benefits, such as health care, to full-time permanent employment—a common pattern in the United States, Mexico, and, to a lesser degree, Poland—contributes to the vulnerability of workers in the societies involved. When this is the case, part-time and temporary workers often fail to qualify for benefits. A further complication is that, even when workers are eligible for benefits, the value of the benefits provided has in many cases declined in recent years as employers have attempted to lower costs by reducing benefits or by requiring workers to share in the cost of any benefits provided (Freudenheim, 1985). In the first instance, workers' benefits and the protection they provide are reduced. In the second, workers' disposable income is reduced. In either case, the workers' situation has worsened.

The tools available to social welfare for addressing these problems include political action and litigation. Unions and other groups have filed suits to obtain increased protection for workers. In addition, social welfare groups have sought such legislative changes as an increase in the minimum wage and, in the United States, national health insurance so that people do not have to rely on the workplace for health protection. While an increase in the minimum wage seems probable, health coverage for all is still a distant goal.

Another economic area of some concern to social welfare is consumer protection. In a free-market economy where people are free to buy whatever they want and can afford, there is often a staggering proliferation of products. Many are dangerous (firearms) or unhealthful (cigarettes, liquor, large amounts of

THE WORKER STUMBLES: A COMPARISON OF SWEDEN AND THE UNITED STATES

The difference between benefits that are work-related and those that are not is illustrated in the following realistic account of the resources provided to two workers and their respective families confronting similar situations in Sweden and the United States.

The situation is the following: A 45-year-old researcher with two teenage children and a spouse who is employed by a consulting company becomes permanently disabled because of alcoholism and related medical problems. The spouse, like the worker, is also employed outside the home in a full-time professional-level position. The strains on the family result in a nervous breakdown for one of the two teenage children. Both the worker and the teenager have to be hospitalized, the worker several times for serious medical complications related to alcoholism. In such a situation, what resources are available to this family?

As we shall see, the resources available in Sweden and the United States are quite different. In Sweden, government disability, pension, and health programs provide nearly comprehensive protection for workers and their families. Benefits in the United States are much less comprehensive and tied to employment, leaving workers much more vulnerable.

Sweden

In Sweden, the researcher, once diagnosed as suffering from chronic alcoholism, is declared disabled and begins receiving a monthly government disability payment. This money, along with the spouse's income, ensures the family's continued economic security. Hospital care for both the researcher and the teenage child is free, while the cost of longer-term medical and psychiatric care and prescriptions is minimal. The family's only medically related expenses are a very small set fee for each of the first ten visits to the doctor and the first ten prescriptions. Thereafter, all medical care and prescriptions are free. The researcher's spouse makes use of the 5-week annual vacation to which all Swedes are entitled by law to help care for the researcher and the teenage child. In addition, the spouse is able to use paid sick leave as needed to deal with any additional family crises.

As a result of the benefits available to Swedish workers, the family's lifestyle is preserved while its disabled members struggle to reestablish themselves.

Should the researcher's disability become permanent, both spouses, upon reaching retirement age, will still receive their individual government pension based on their own work history. Thus the researcher's interrupted earnings will not reduce the spouse's pension.

United States

As in Sweden, the researcher is diagnosed as suffering from chronic alcoholism and determined to be eligible for disability benefits from the government. This, along with the spouse's income, protects the family's economic security to some degree. The disabled worker qualifies for health insurance through the employer's private plan. Under this plan, the family is reimbursed for 80 percent of the cost of all medical and hospital care, but receives no reimbursement for prescription costs. Fifty percent of the cost of the teenager's psychiatric care is covered by the spouse's health insurance plan provided by the spouse's employer. This plan, however, limits hospitalization coverage to 30 days and outpatient treatment to 1 year. The spouse's employer also provides 2 weeks' paid vacation and 12 days of sick leave that the spouse is able to use during the course of dealing with the family's medical crises.

As a result of its circumstances, the family amasses large medical and drug bills that force severe economies in its lifestyle. A second mortgage is used to help pay the medical bills, and the second child has postponed graduate school to work and help support the family. Throughout the crisis, the amount of time the spouse is able to spend with ill family members is limited by the amount of the available vacation time and sick leave.

Should the researcher's disability become permanent, the family's retirement income will be reduced because the working spouse's pension will be tied to the worker's now-interrupted work history.

sugar, salt, or other additives in food). Others do not work well, or do not perform as advertised. Unethical sales and advertising practices are sometimes employed to trick people into purchasing items they do not really want or need, or into purchasing needed goods at artificially high prices.

Social welfare attempts to prevent such problems through consumer education programs and by seeking legislation that protects consumers. In addition, legal aid programs help consumers seek redress when they have been exploited by producers, distributors, advertisers, or salespeople.

The Impact of the Economic Institution on Social Welfare

The economic institution has very powerful effects on social welfare. The rise of the modern welfare state has been linked with the productivity made possible by industrialization. The extensive social welfare programs we take for granted are costly. In 1981, for example, Sweden spent 33.4 percent of its gross domestic product on public social expenditures, while the United States spent 20.8 percent (Zimbalist, 1987). Mexico is a good example of a nation whose struggling economy is unable to support such an extensive social welfare network. Even Poland, which has a comprehensive public social welfare system, is finding it difficult to find the resources necessary to provide adequate housing for its citizens.

In the United States, where there are fewer public programs than in many other societies, private philanthropy is important. We have seen that the wealth generated by the economic system is not equally distributed. Many wealthy people contribute considerable sums to various social welfare programs. This provides a valuable supplement to the public social welfare system. Such large-scale charitable giving is only possible because of the tremendous productivity of the economic system.

SOCIAL WELFARE FOR ALL

An examination of the relationships between social welfare and each of the other major social institutions helps us to understand how it touches the life of everyone. This can happen in a very personal way, as when a middle-class, middle-aged gay man becomes ill with AIDS and requires medical care and emotional counseling. In all probability, his employer's health insurance plan will pay for much of the care that he needs. Or consider the wealthy industrialist who develops a drinking problem, or discovers that the wife of his adult son is being battered by her husband. A variety of social welfare agencies stand ready to help in these situations, even though those needing help are not poor. Social welfare serves everyone, those who are economically secure as well as the homeless family or the unwed teenage mother with no income.

Social welfare is a pervasive part of our society, indeed of all societies. It helps families with parenting and personal problems, aids students in obtaining needed financial or emotional help, assists communities in averting potential conflicts, and helps workers find employment. By touching everyone in a society, social welfare also has a larger cumulative effect. When problems arise, the social welfare system provides channels for people to express their needs, to seek help, and to advocate for change in an orderly way. Destructive social conflict is frequently avoided when people feel that their basic needs are being met.

Social welfare's impact upon all members of society takes at least three forms.

The prevention of problems. Social welfare services supplement the efforts of other social institutions to prevent problems. One of the clearest examples of this is education, where social welfare programs increase the likelihood that people will be able and willing to attend school and thus increase their prospects for becoming self-sufficient adults. By preventing problems, social welfare reduces the expenditures otherwise needed to cure them, reduces the pain experienced by people who have them, and makes life more pleasant for everyone. For example, many people find it troubling and unpleasant to encounter homeless, alcoholic, or mentally ill people on the street. Programs that provide housing and rehabilitation for those who are in need not only help the homeless and potentially homeless, but make life more pleasant for the average citizen as well.

Reinforcing the link between people and society. Social welfare is tangible evidence that society cares for its members. When we pay our taxes we sometimes question the value of doing so. But when we see that our money improves life in some tangible way, our commitment to society itself is likely to increase. Most of us feel good when we see a disabled child helped to obtain schooling, or a battered child receiving the physical and emotional care that he or she needs. Such incidents make us realize that sometimes people are helpless, and that we have a collective responsibility to come to their aid. Social welfare helps us to do this.

Asserting that people matter. A fundamental principle of social welfare is that each individual deserves a decent, satisfying life. Each life is precious, and each is to be nurtured. The needs of organizations or even society itself must never be allowed to thoughtlessly crush individuals. This goal is sometimes elusive in daily life, but social welfare's commitment is a firm one. It is important that there be a clear, steady, insistent voice in society with this message. Everyone benefits as a result.

Linking people and society, preventing problems, and asserting that people matter all result from the interplay between social welfare and the other institutions of society. It is through these institutional structures that helping is made possible on a daily basis. It is also through them that social welfare seeks to influence the decisions that will shape the future.

LET'S REVIEW

This chapter began by reintroducing the concept of a social institution first discussed in Chapter 1. Social institutions, we reminded ourselves, are socially approved, perform identifiable social functions, distribute resources, and organize activities. The major social institutions are social welfare, the family, education, religion, and the political and economic institutions.

The main focus of the chapter was on how social welfare relates to each of the other social institutions. Particular attention was paid to how social welfare helps each institution perform its major social functions. The ways in which social welfare is itself influenced by the other social institutions were also explored. It was noted too that changes in the other major social institutions often create new needs to which social welfare attempts to respond.

The chapter concluded with a brief examination of how everyone benefits from social welfare. Rich and poor, men and women, no matter what race or ethnicity, everyone's life is touched—usually in a positive way—by the social welfare institution. Improved personal functioning and strengthened social cohesion are the goals of social welfare's efforts to make society more responsive to the needs of its citizens.

If social welfare is so useful and if everyone benefits from it, you may wonder why so few people seem satisfied with the current social welfare system. There are any number of reasons. It turns out that many of its successes are viewed by some people as failures. In addition, people who benefit from its services refuse to acknowledge that they are doing so. Then, too, social welfare is not always effective, and many focus on its failures rather than its successes.

In this chapter we have emphasized the positive aspects of social welfare's interaction with the rest of society. Now we are ready to explore social welfare's possible negative consequences for society. We will do so in the next chapter.

CHAPTER OUTLINE

SOCIAL WELFARE AND RELIGION

SOCIAL WELFARE AND POLITICS
   The Effects of Politics on Social Welfare
   On the Street in Cracow, Poland
SOCIAL WELFARE AND THE ECONOMIC INSTITUTION
   The Worker Stumbles: A Comparison of Sweden and the United
      States
   The Impact of the Economic Institution on Social Welfare
SOCIAL WELFARE FOR ALL
LET'S REVIEW

STUDY QUESTIONS

1 Write your own definition of social welfare as a social institution. Be sure that your definition takes account of all of the major characteristics exhibited by all social institutions. Then provide a specific example of each of these characteristics as exhibited by social welfare.

2 Interview and record the answers of at least three people to the following two questions: (a) What do you believe are the most pressing needs of the contemporary American family? (b) What do you believe society should do to meet these needs? Compile a list of the needs mentioned and briefly indicate what you believe society should do about each.

3 This chapter discussed the positive aspects of religion and social welfare. Can you think of any negative interactions? For example, some feel that social welfare programs that promote birth control undermine religious beliefs. Others feel that fundamentalist religious beliefs increase problems by oppressing certain groups, especially women, children, and minorities. What are your thoughts about these issues, and any others you can identify?

4 Research the current literature on technology and the workplace. What kinds of changes are predicted concerning the number and types of workers who will be needed in the future? What kinds of problems can you foresee if these predictions prove accurate? How do you believe the social welfare institution should respond to these problems?

5 This chapter makes the point that everyone benefits from social welfare, both at the personal level and in terms of a better-functioning society. Do you agree with this? Can you identify aspects of your own life that have been improved because of social welfare? Can you think of people you know whose lives have not been improved? Prepare a summary of your personal views on the value of social welfare to society as a whole.

KEY TERMS AND CONCEPTS

economic institution
education institution
family
household
political institution

religion
socialization
trade balance
trade deficit

SUGGESTED READINGS

Clarke-Stewart, Alison. 1977. *Child Care in the Family*. New York: Academic Press. A study of the needs of children in families and the factors that determine whether those needs are met. The author discusses and recommends several policies designed to strengthen families, and argues on behalf of her view of the proper role of social welfare in improving child care.

Esping-Andersen, Gøsta. 1985. *Politics Against Markets*. Princeton, N.J.: Princeton University Press. Analyzes the development of social democracy in Sweden, Norway, and Denmark, and explains why it has been a crucial factor in the development (or decline) of social welfare programs in those countries. A heavily historical work that nonetheless clearly illustrates the relationship between the political, economic, and social welfare institutions.

Graycar, Adam, ed. 1983. *Retreat from the Welfare State*. Sydney, Australia: George Allen & Unwin, Ltd. An edited collection of articles that examines why social welfare programs are under attack in Australia. The contributors focus on people's perceptions of how social welfare has or has not contributed to the strengthening of social institutions.

Gutmann, Amy, ed. 1988. *Democracy and the Welfare State*. Princeton, N.J.: Princeton University Press. An edited work that explores current issues in the relationship of social welfare to the other institutions of society. It thoughtfully examines the influence of social institutions on the value base of social welfare in a democratic society like our own.

Social Work. 1987. 32, no. 1 (January–February) is entirely devoted to issues of helping families adjust to divorce and related problems.

REFERENCES

Bernstein, Richard. 1988. 20 years after the Kerner Report: Three societies, all separate. *The New York Times,* February 29, p. B8.

Castex, Graciela. 1988. The creation of "Hispanic": Social myths and objective realities. Paper presented at the Annual Program Meeting of the Council on Social Work Education, March 8, Atlanta, Georgia.

Chavez, Lydia. 1988. Crisis over dropouts: A look at two youths. *The New York Times,* February 16, p. B1ff.

Clarke-Stewart, Alison. 1977. *Child Care in the Family*. New York: Academic Press.

College Board News. 1988. Black educational gains endangered by social, economic, and policy trends. *College Board News,* Spring, p. 1ff.

Collins, Glenn. 1985. Remarriage: Bigger ready-made families. *The New York Times,* May 13, p. B5.

Cupaiuolo, Anthony. 1988. Lecture to the Westchester Division of the National Association of Social Workers, January 21, New York Hospital, White Plains, N.Y.

Diehl, Jackson. 1988. Poles plan capitalist cure for health system. *The Washington Post,* June 6, A1.

Esping-Andersen, Gøsta. 1985. *Politics Against Markets*. Princeton, N.J.: Princeton University Press.

Fernandez, John. 1986. *Child Care and Corporate Productivity*. Lexington, Mass.: Lexington Books.

Fiske, Edward. 1987. Colleges open new minority drives. *The New York Times,* November 18, p. B6.

Freudenheim, Milt. 1985. Company expenses for retirees soar. *The New York Times,* September 9, p. A1ff.

Gould, Ketayun. 1988. Asian and Pacific islanders: Myth and reality. *Social Work,* 33, no. 2 (March–April):142–148.

Graycar, Adam, ed. 1983. *Retreat from the Welfare State.* Sydney, Australia: George Allen & Unwin, Ltd.

Greer, William. 1986. The changing women's marriage market. *The New York Times,* February 22, p. 48.

Gutmann, Amy, ed. 1988. *Democracy and the Welfare State.* Princeton, N.J.: Princeton University Press.

Hunt, Michael, and Andrew Greeley. 1987. The center doesn't hold: Church attendance in the United States, 1940–1984. *American Sociological Review,* 52 (June):325–345.

Iatridis, Demetrius. 1988. New social deficit: Neoconservatism's policy of social underdevelopment. *Social Work,* 33, no. 1 (January–February):11–15.

Kamerman, Sheila. 1985. Children and their families: The impact of the Reagan Administration and the choices for social work. Proceedings of the Werner and Bernice Boehm Distinguished Lectureship in Social Work. New Brunswick, N. J.: School of Social Work of Rutgers University.

Kantrowitz, Barbara, et al. 1985. Mothers on their own. *Newsweek,* December 23, pp. 66–67.

Levitan, Sar, and Isaac Shapiro. 1986. The minimum wage: A sinking floor. *The New York Times,* January 16, p. A23.

Lewin, Tamar. 1988. More teen-agers take their babies to school. *The New York Times,* March 15, p. A1ff.

Marriage rate hits low mark. 1986. *The New York Times,* May 8, p. C11.

Monk, Abraham. 1985. Preretirement planning programs. In Abraham Monk, ed. *Handbook of Gerontological Services,* New York: Van Nostrand Reinhold Company, pp. 322–340.

Muller, Edward. 1988. Democracy, economic development, and income inequality. *American Sociological Review,* 53 (February):50–68.

National Commission on Working Women. 1985. Pay Equity—A Fact Sheet. Flyer printed by the commission, 1325 G. Street, N.W., Washington, D.C., 20005.

Quinn, Jane. 1988. A crisis in child care. *Newsweek,* February 15, p. 57.

Ran, William, and Dennis Roncek. 1987. Industrialization and world inequality: The transformation of the division of labor in 59 nations. *American Sociological Review,* 52 (June):359–369.

Reinhold, Robert. 1986. Have toys, will travel: Children fly alone. *The New York Times,* June 21, p. 1.

Ruggie, Mary. 1984. *The State and Working Women.* Princeton, N.J.: Princeton University Press.

Sauber, Robert, et al. 1988. Medical and psychiatric needs of the homeless—a preliminary response. *Social Work,* 33, no. 2:116–119.

Sheahan, John. 1987. *Patterns of Development in Latin America.* Princeton, N.J.: Princeton University Press.

Tagliabue, John. 1988. Emigrant flow from Poland worries regime and church. *The New York Times,* February 14, p. 18.

Tolchin, Martin. 1989. Richer get richer and poorest poorer in 1979–87. *The New York Times,* March 23, pp. A1ff.

Tonti, Mario, and Barbara Silverstone. 1985. Services to families of the elderly. In Abraham Monk, ed. *Handbook of Gerontological Services,* New York: Van Nostrand Reinhold Company, pp. 211–239.

Uchitelle, Louis. 1987. America's army of non-workers. *The New York Times,* September 27, section 3, p. 1ff.

———.1988. Reliance on temporary jobs hints at economic fragility. *The New York Times,* March 16, p. 1ff.

U.S. Department of Commerce. Bureau of the Census. 1987. *Statistical Abstract of the United States 1987.* Washington, D.C.: U.S. Government Printing Office.

Washington Social Welfare Legislation Bulletin. 1988. The President's Budget for FY 1989. vol. 30, issue 28 (February 22). Published by the Social Legislation Information Service, Washington, D.C.

Westchester County (N.Y.) Department of Social Services. 1987. Number of Homeless Families, Children and Singles: November 1987. Mimeographed, December 1.

Wyers, Norman. 1988. Economic insecurity: Notes for social workers. *Social Work,* 33, no. 1 (January–February):18–22.

Zimbalist, Sidney. 1987. A welfare state against the economic current: Sweden and the United States as contrasting cases. *International Social Work,* 30, no. 1 (January):15–29.

8

WHY IS SOCIAL WELFARE CONTROVERSIAL?

WHAT TO EXPECT FROM THIS CHAPTER

At first glance, it might seem strange that helping others would be controversial. After all, we learn from the time we are children that we should be nice to others, and that we should be helpful when we can. But as we grow older, we learn that helping is more complex than we thought. When confronted with a series of people seeking handouts, should we feel an obligation to help them all? Are we even certain that giving them money will help them? Or are we instead worsening their problem with alcoholism, drug use, or just plain laziness? We may even be putting our own safety at risk. Is that hitchhiker standing beside a seemingly disabled car actually in need, or a criminal who will rob us if we stop to offer help?

These are troubling questions not just for individuals but for society. What types of assistance are truly helpful? When should we refuse to give aid because giving it will actually be damaging? We don't really know the answers.

In part, the difficulty is that we lack the data that would tell us what kind of help works and what kind does not. There is another difficulty, however. The answers to these questions involve values. Our decisions about when to give help and what to expect in return are very much reflections of our values. Some are willing to dispense birth control because their goal is to stop out-of-wedlock births. Others agree with the goal, but disagree with the means. Still others feel that people should be free to do whatever they want as long as they are willing to accept the consequences. And yet others focus on the children born out of wedlock—should they be the victims of their parents' behavior? As you can see, there are many ways to look at helping, and that is why it is controversial.

This chapter will examine some of the major controversies that surround social welfare. *Note that our goal is to understand issues, not to find answers.* There are no simple answers to these controversies. There are only positions that reflect different people's views as to what is right or effective. Social welfare will probably always be controversial because most people have strong and often ambivalent feelings about helping. So as you proceed through this chapter, don't look for answers. Instead, open yourself to new ways of thinking about the issues.

LEARNING OBJECTIVES

At the conclusion of this chapter, you should be able to do the following:

1 Identify three basic questions about the provision of help in society that provoke controversy and debate.

2 Explain why helping has an impact on both individuals and society.

3 List at least two moral effects of helping on individuals and two on society.

4 List at least two financial effects of helping on individuals, and two on society.

5 Use the analytical framework presented in this chapter to identify the impact on individuals and society of at least two social welfare programs.

6 Discuss the significance of the difference between meeting people's immediate need and helping them to become more self-sufficient.

7 Define welfare capitalism.

8 Define privatization and discuss its advantages and disadvantages.

9 Explain why dependency is a controversial issue in social welfare.

10 State your own position about the value of social welfare in society.

11 Explain in your own words why social welfare is controversial.

WHO SHOULD BE HELPED?

In Chapter 1 we explored three basic questions: Who should be helped? What kind of help should be provided? How much help is appropriate? These, we concluded, were important questions, but difficult to answer. We return to them here, but from a somewhat different perspective. We wish now to focus on the *results* of helping, and we turn first to the question of who should be helped.

The Domestic Policy Association (1985:9) has identified three basic responses to the question of who should be helped. The first is that the social welfare system should provide adequate benefits to everyone. We call this the *comprehensive* or *universal approach*. The second is that welfare programs should focus on the truly needy, providing relatively little assistance to those able to care for themselves. We call this the *focusing on the most needy approach*. The third is based on the belief that "...the welfare state is inherently inefficient, a threat to personal freedom, a strategy that undermines the very sense of community it is supposed to embody" (Domestic Policy Association, 1985:9). Proponents of this, the *conservative approach,* argue that public social welfare efforts should be reduced to a minimal level while encouraging alternative private approaches such as greater reliance on the family, charity, and measures designed to stimulate overall economic growth and thus reduce the number of poor people.

There is, therefore, more than one response to the question of who should be helped. Let's examine these three positions in terms of their results.

A Framework for Analysis

In order to compare the impact of these approaches, we will employ a simple analytic framework based on the notion that there is not one but several types of impacts to be considered. Any approach to providing services is going to have a separate impact on *those who receive benefits* and on *society*. These impacts in turn are of at least two types. One is the *moral impact* that may alter people's values, thinking, and behavior in ways that are either desirable or undesirable.

Second, there is a *financial impact* on people and on society. Clearly the provision of assistance has an impact on the resources available to the person or persons receiving help. It also has an impact on society. Social welfare is costly. It employs social resources that once expended on social welfare cannot then be used for other purposes. Thus, the decision to devote certain resources to social welfare often means forgoing other possible purchases. On the other hand, successful helping efforts can provide a variety of benefits to society. These too have economic value.

Before applying this framework to the question at hand, let's consider an example—farm price supports. Farm price supports have been used in the United States and several European nations as a means of helping farmers. Under a price support program, the government either agrees to buy surplus farm products from the farmer or pays farmers for agreeing to produce less than they otherwise could. (Be sure you understand why farm price supports are social welfare programs.) What are the moral and financial impacts of such a program on farmers?

The potential moral impacts are several. One possible impact is to encourage farmers to cheat. Farmers might, for example, be tempted to overstate their productive capacity in order to maximize the payments they receive from the government. Another possible outcome is that they might become cynical about being paid *not* to work instead of *for* working. On the other hand, they might also respond with appreciation to a program that provides them with an alternative source of income under difficult market conditions.

On the financial side, there is little doubt that the price support program enhances the financial position of farmers, at least in the short term. On the other hand, if it were possible for farmers to sell everything they could produce on the open market, they might well earn more than the price support program pays them.

And what about the impact on government? Farm support programs place it in the morally questionable position of paying people not to work. This could easily generate resentment among those who are instead paid for what they *do* produce—which is to say most other people. Some might also wonder about the difference between paying farmers not to work and payments to recipients of public assistance, many of whom also don't work. Paying farmers not to produce has, in addition, moral implications in a world where people are starving.

Among the financial impacts on society of such programs are the costs to taxpayers. Is it, in fact, justifiable to buy and store excess production at great expense to the taxpayer? Farm price support programs are expensive. But would not the social and financial costs of allowing farmers to go bankrupt be even worse, especially if long-term implications include the potential loss of the nation's ability to produce enough to feed its own citizens?

We turn now to a similar analysis of our three alternative approaches to deciding who will be helped.

The Comprehensive or Universal Approach

Among the social welfare systems discussed in this book, Sweden's is the best example of a system based on a comprehensive or universal approach. The Swedish answer to the question of who should be helped is, ''Everyone.'' In Sweden, all citizens are provided with a comprehensive range of services including health care, housing, unemployment protection, child care, retirement pensions, maternity benefits, and free education (through the university level).

The Swedish approach has several goals. One is to improve the overall health and productivity of the population, a goal that has most certainly been met if judged in terms of such commonly used standards as infant mortality, average life span, incidence of poverty, and unemployment rates (Zimbalist, 1988). A second goal is to create an educated and motivated population that can adapt to changes in the workplace and will ensure Sweden's economic competitiveness. This, too, is within reach in Sweden, as indicated by its low unemployment rate (Zimbalist, 1988:48). The third goal is social cohesion, a general commitment by the members of the society to its existing political and economic structure based on satisfaction with the society's quality of life and a belief that it should be preserved. The political dominance of the Social Democrats for most of the past 60 years offers strong evidence of the existence of such a consensus in Sweden (Esping-Andersen, 1985:106–113).

Sweden's approach to social welfare has helped create a society in which people are fundamentally healthy and generally satisfied with the quality of their lives. The result has been a stable and economically productive society. Thus, the financial impact on individuals and on society has been positive in many ways. It is, however, a costly approach when viewed in purely financial terms. Sweden spent over 33 percent of its gross domestic product for public social expenditures in 1981 (Zimbalist, 1987:18). Similarly, the cost to individuals is also high. National income tax rates in Sweden range from 4 to 50 percent of personal taxable income to which are added local income taxes that add an additional 30 percent on average (Swedish Institute, 1986).

The moral impact of the Swedish approach is less readily identified. On the whole, Swedes seem to value their social welfare system, and it does not appear to have substantially reduced people's feelings of personal responsibility or initiative (Heckscher, 1984:102–123). However, Swedish social planners are nevertheless watching carefully for a variety of potentially negative effects. One is the possibility that a comprehensive system may reduce the extent to which people care for themselves. Another is a potential reduction in the use of natural (informal) helping networks, while a third is a possible reduction in the frequency with which people volunteer to help others (Ording, 1987).

We noted in Chapter 7 that an extensive social welfare system depends on a productive economy (Heckscher, 1984:105) which in turn is in large part dependent on favorable economic and political conditions, both domestic and international. A nation's economic strength is also affected by social welfare's effectiveness at preparing domestic workers for a changing and increasingly complex workplace. What we do not know is how a country with a comprehensive social welfare system would react to a sustained decrease in economic resources. Would everyone's services be reduced, or would programs for less needy groups be cut first?

Given the brevity of our experience with a truly comprehensive approach to social welfare, it is also not clear how durable an experiment systems like the current one in Sweden will prove to be. How will future generations react to it? Heckscher (1984:160–180) notes that the successes of such an approach may yield the unrealistic expectation that all social problems will be eliminated. Another concern is that generations that grow up without ever having experienced poverty will be unwilling to continue to support such a strategy. Lacking firsthand experience with the problems such a system is designed to prevent, they may react only to its cost. Thus, the future of comprehensive approaches to social welfare is somewhat uncertain, although there is little question, in the Swedish case at least, about its current effectiveness in meeting the needs of individuals and of society.

ON THE STREET IN STOCKHOLM, SWEDEN

The Kronan District Health Care Center is in a lower-middle-class neighborhood of Stockholm, whose residents it serves. It is reasonably representative of other similar centers which are scattered throughout the city.

One part of the center deals exclusively with the health care needs of infants and children. The services it provides include prenatal care that begins with a visit by nurses from the center to the pregnant mother in her home. During the course of her pregnancy, they check her health and that of her fetus, hand out brochures, and provide instruction in infant and child care skills. When the new mother and child return home, there are further visits to check on the family. Later, when she is able to do so, the mother brings her baby to the center once a week to be weighed, measured, and tested.

The center is not large, and it has a cozy, personal feel. The rooms where infants and children are examined are decorated with colorful mobiles and pictures. The mothers and their children obviously develop a close relationship with the staff. During a visit to the Kronan District Center, I observed one mother chatting easily with the nurse and handling her own baby as it was being weighed and measured. The baby was calm and content and clearly accustomed to the staff and the surroundings.

After 6 months the mother is asked to bring her child once each month and then, after the child is 2, once or twice a year. When the child begins school, the center sends its records to the school where the resident nurse takes over the child's care. Although not all parents make full use of them, these services are available to all Swedes, regardless of income, education, or other characteristics.

In talking with another mother, this one with grown children, it became clear she believed the system worked well and found it valuable. She had, for example, taken advantage of an option available to all working parents to reduce their work week in order to have more time at home with their children. In her case, she now worked 6 hours a day instead of 8. (Her salary was adjusted, of course.) In general, Sweden's social welfare system provides parents with time off from work so that they can meet their children's health and education needs.

On the whole, while she wished the taxes were not so high, the mother found the social welfare services provided very helpful. For example, her family received 485 krona per month from the government toward the cost of day care for her child. Since the actual cost was about 600 krona, she had to pay only about 115 krona out of her monthly salary of about 10,000 krona. (Her husband, whose salary was higher than hers, was also employed.)

Observing the Swedish social welfare system in action, it is evident that it is used by virtually everyone. The services are provided in an appealing way, and they seem to be effective. Still, there is some regret that such a system is so costly. However, when asked directly, the Swedes with whom I talked felt that the system was worth the cost.

Focusing on the Most Needy

A second approach for deciding who should be helped is to focus on the most needy. This is a residual approach that focuses on helping those clearly in need. Programs based on such an approach are usually means-tested; that is, they require people to demonstrate their eligibility for benefits according to specific criteria. These programs distribute benefits on a selective rather than a universal basis.

A useful example of this approach is the social security retirement program here in the United States. Under this program, receipts from a special social security tax on workers' incomes are deposited into a fund from which retirement benefits are paid. However, the amount of income subject to this tax is limited. Thus, people who earn income in excess of the limit (currently approximately $45,000 a year) pay no social security tax on their income above that amount. Conversely, people earning less than the current limit will pay social security taxes on their entire income. Thus, someone currently earning less than $45,000 per year will pay social security taxes on his or her entire income while someone earning $100,000 will pay only on the first $45,000; the remaining $55,000 will not be taxed.

On the benefit side, the benefits received reflect the amount paid in. Thus, someone whose average annual income was well in excess of the amount subject to the social security tax would receive the same level of benefits as another worker whose income simply equaled the taxable amount. The amount paid in by the two workers would, after all, have been equal even though the first had a much higher income than the second.

This seems a fair arrangement until we consider that the worker with the smaller income would probably have had much less opportunity to save money than someone with a higher income. The question then becomes whether both *need* the same benefits? Both are being treated fairly in the sense that, having both paid in the same amount, they will receive equal benefits. But they are not being treated fairly in the sense that one's need may be greater than the other's. Consider the example of high-ranking corporate executives. As Table 8.1 illustrates, for many corporate chairpeople, social security retirement benefits seem beside the point. Their incomes eliminate any need for the retirement benefit that social security is intended to provide.

Our example raises, in fact, a number of issues. Should everyone be treated equally even though they may have different needs? And should social welfare programs be designed to include even those who are not needy?

Most Swedes, one suspects, would answer "Yes" to these questions. In Sweden, social welfare is a right of citizenship and thus available to all. One of the benefits of this approach is that it is thought to reduce the reluctance of the

TABLE 8.1   WHO NEEDS SOCIAL SECURITY? PERSONAL INCOME FOR CHAIRPEOPLE OF SELECTED MAJOR CORPORATIONS

Company	1984 salary and bonus	Total earned*
United Technologies	$1,557,620	$4,241,179
Mesa Petroleum	4,223,077	4,223,077
IBM	1,034,390	3,841,334
Sears	1,481,250	2,088,720
AT&T	1,098,026	1,126,359
Citicorp	678,367	834,867

*Total includes value of stock options exercised in 1984, and the company's contribution to the executive's savings plan during the same period.
Source: Berg (1985:D1)

wealthy to support a social welfare system since they too are eligible for and receive benefits. In addition, the Swedish system is designed to respond to special needs in two ways. The first is via a strongly progressive tax system that requires those who have high incomes to pay proportionately more in taxes. The system is, therefore, most heavily funded by those most able to pay. Similarly, the system provides supplemental benefits for those who are especially needy. Everyone is eligible for basic benefits, but those who need more are eligible for more, as was noted in the description of Sweden's pension system in Chapter 5.

The United States approach is, of course, far less comprehensive and much closer in principle to "focusing on the needy." It combines a few basic universal services (like the social security retirement program) with a much larger number of residual, means-tested programs.

The financial impact of this "mixed" approach, in which some programs are universal—or almost so—and most are not, has caused some to raise serious questions about its effectiveness. Expenditures for the relatively few universal programs are four-and-a-half times larger than for those that are means-tested (Domestic Policy Association, 1985:16). The most expensive programs are Medicare and pensions for veterans, neither of which is means-tested, and the social security retirement and disability programs, which are only partially so. Proponents of targeting services for the most needy decry this as a waste of money, and ineffective in meeting the needs of those who are most helpless. Why, for example, give money to wealthy retirees or to wealthy veterans? Such a question becomes more prominent during periods of economic austerity. When resources are limited, shouldn't as much as possible of those allocated to social welfare go to those who are most in need?

But here too it is important to consider the moral and financial impact of an approach that focuses exclusively on the needy. To be sure, under such a system the poor would probably receive increased benefits. But how will we decide who is, or is likely to become, truly needy? Retirees are a good example. Even those with substantial incomes during their working life may have their savings depleted by illness or nursing home care. Is it fair to require that they exhaust all their resources—to become poor—before they qualify for help? (This, by the way, is precisely what happens to those who wish to qualify for Medicaid, a means-tested program.) It is easy to imagine that there are many people who are marginally secure economically and thus considered too well off to qualify for aid. Many of these, however, may not be sufficiently wealthy to weather an illness-related economic crisis or to pay for long-term institutional care.

Society, too, might experience gains and losses should the system be changed to focus only on the truly needy. Social welfare costs would undoubtedly be more easily controlled. Further, to the extent that the assistance provided to the poor was increased to a level that raised their income above the poverty line, some at least might find it far easier to break the poverty cycle and become self-sufficient. Thus, the number of truly needy people might gradually shrink, saving money and, over the long run, averting the waste of much human potential. On the other hand, means-tested programs involve application procedures that are cumbersome and expensive to operate, and fraud is an ever-present possibility. Increasingly too, social welfare would become much more closely linked to the poor and needy, increasing the stigma associated with it and possibly decreasing people's willingness to pay for it. The result could easily be a "we" and "them" mentality, with those who primarily pay for assistance attributing highly negative personality and behavioral characteristics to those who receive it.

We can see, then, that, even though it might reduce the financial costs of social welfare, the moral costs of an approach that "focuses on the needy" might well be very high. The question is, which of these potential impacts is more important? Undermining a society's general commitment to helping and creating a society divided into the "haves" and "have nots" is risky. The resulting society could be similar to Mexico's highly stratified society in which the wealthy have little contact with the poor, and often use their power to limit social welfare services. Nor are the consequences likely to be beneficial for those being helped, who are likely to come to see themselves as less worthy than others.

Limiting the Role of Social Welfare

There is a third approach to the question of who should be helped. Generally viewed as the most conservative of the three approaches, it is based on the belief that while helping is a worthwhile goal, the current social welfare system actually hurts people rather than helping them. Proponents of this approach generally argue that the public social welfare system has become too large and that public social welfare services should be reduced (Murray, 1984).

Proponents of reducing the social welfare system assert that it discourages people from working and taking responsibility for themselves. Fullinwider (1988:262) notes that citizenship is "...a set of habits and attitudes that may be affected positively or negatively by welfare services....The way welfare is delivered and received can teach good or bad civic lessons. It can foster or undermine social responsibility." One of the problems with public social welfare, then, is that many of the programs involved, notably means-tested programs which pay reduced benefits as the recipient's income increases, discourage people from working, especially those whose earning potential is relatively low (Domestic Policy Association, 1985:26–27). Further, these critics argue, public assistance becomes a way of life for many recipients who then focus on how to get the most from the system rather than becoming independent and self-reliant.

What are the moral and financial impacts of such an approach? Proponents cite numerous advantages in both areas.

In the moral realm, advocates of the conservative approach believe that reducing public services will increase people's sense of responsibility toward

THE HUMAN FACE OF SOCIAL WELFARE 15

The Mayor Hits the Streets

...I asked her how she liked the apartment.

She said, "It's wonderful." And it is. I asked her where she lived before. She said she'd been living in one of the welfare hotels. I asked her how long she had been there. "Five years," she replied.

I was shocked....

I said, "Five years—and we [referring to the city's welfare department] never offered you an apartment?"

She said: "Oh no, Mayor. Of course you did. Your people showed me 19 apartments."

"Why didn't you take one?"

"I didn't like any of them. Either they weren't located in nice buildings or nice neighborhoods, or they weren't in the [part of the city] I wanted to live in."

Again I was shocked. Here was a person who was bringing up her children under difficult, squalid circumstances in a welfare hotel and she'd turned down 19 apartments until she got the one she wanted. I thought to myself, people who are part of the working poor, and who are perhaps either doubled up or living in substandard housing would be furious if they knew they'd been denied the opportunity to take one of those 19 apartments this woman had turned down.

Something has gone wrong when people on public assistance have more choices than people who are making it on their own. However, when I sought to place restrictions on the number of apartments any recipient could turn down, welfare advocates denounced me....

When rights without responsibilities become the order of the day, we encourage a social breakdown that will harm us in ways yet unimagined. There is a limit to what government can and should do in a democracy. No city or state can be expected to protect adults from themselves. If that is the course we choose for our society, then nothing can protect us from each other.

_____

The preceding words were written by Edward Koch, the Mayor of New York City. The issues he raises about the moral impact of social welfare on people are important ones. He questions the extent of society's responsibility for people's well-being, and the right of the needy to decide what type of help is acceptable. Do you think that this mother's choices indicate that the social welfare system has damaged her moral integrity, or can you suggest other reasons that explain why she acted as she did? Do you agree with Mayor Koch that this woman exercised "rights without responsibilities?"

From Edward Koch. 1988. Welfare isn't a way of life. *The New York Times,* March 4, p. 27. Copyright © 1988 by The New York Times Company. Reprinted by permission.

each other. They point to the widespread concern that the availability of formal social welfare services reduces the use of informal helping systems. When people know that formal services are available, they may be less likely to make use of their natural helping networks. This issue has been raised not only in the United States, but in Sweden, Poland, Mexico, and many other societies as well.

Conservatives are also concerned that when people believe the needs of others are being met by the formal system, they may assume less personal responsibility for helping others. Centralized fund-raising programs like the

United Way, for example, give contributors the sense that they have already done their share. Believing this, they may be less likely to give money to a beggar on the street, or perhaps even to help their neighbor. The very nature of formal helping networks creates a distance between the helper and the person being helped.

There is a larger moral concern here as well. Conservatives also worry about the loss of community that accompanies reliance on large-scale governmental programs. Such programs are often remote from and poorly understood by the average person, who is left only with the vague impression that social welfare needs are somehow being met, a certain unease as to whether the money is being well spent, and a belief that by paying taxes he or she has done all that is required. Rather than developing a sense of community—one for all, and all for one—conservatives believe large-scale public services promote a reluctance to become further involved with a system that seems too large and too complicated and has been essentially imposed on them from above. This loss of community is a recurring theme in the findings of Bellah et al. (1985) and is often cited by conservative critics of the current social welfare system (Domestic Policy Association, 1985:29–30).

Thus, those advocating a reduction in public social welfare services believe this approach will enhance the moral strength of the larger society and increase people's sense of personal responsibility for others as well as for themselves.

They also believe their approach will have a beneficial financial impact on both society and individuals. The current system, they argue, does financial harm both to those who help and those who receive help. As the cost of social welfare increases, so do the taxes and associated fees paid by people. As medical care expenses have increased, for example, both public (Medicare) and private medical plans have steadily increased their coinsurance requirements and the level of required deductible amounts, effectively transferring these expenses to policyholders and program recipients. These cost increases jeopardize the financial independence of economically marginal people. In addition, even those who can easily afford the additional expenses involved may nevertheless come to resent them, thereby weakening the societal consensus on the need for social welfare. For this reason, conservatives believe it is imperative to find ways in which to contain or reduce the costs of social welfare.

They also point out that the current system is not especially helpful to those it serves. The financial benefits provided enable many recipients barely to survive. We have seen in earlier chapters that income maintenance benefits are often so low that the recipient's income remains below the poverty level. Recipients are, therefore, unable either to improve their living conditions or obtain the economic toehold needed to move toward independence. Thus, current income maintenance programs tend to perpetuate poverty. Ironically, then, as the system grows it both alienates those who pay for it while disadvantaging those whom it is intended to help.

Those who advocate cutting back on social welfare also believe the cost of the system exceeds society's ability to pay (Domestic Policy Association, 1985:25–26). It becomes increasingly difficult to contain expansion of benefits, especially for entitlement programs such as social security that most people automatically qualify for. Inevitably, the costs of such programs spiral upward without regard to other economic factors and trends. The highly probable result, therefore, is that the tax revenues necessary to fund such programs will not keep pace with costs, with the further consequence that social welfare contributes to undesirable governmental budget deficits.

Finally, critics of social welfare argue that it utilizes resources that could be put to more worthwhile purposes. In particular, conservatives argue that such funds would be better invested in defense spending and in measures to increase the nation's productive capacity, such as research and development and plant modernization. This, of course, reflects a particular view of the relative importance of alternative public expenditures with which not everyone would agree. This is particularly true of defense expenditures. A Roper Poll in 1987 showed that over 60 percent of Americans favored spending more on the homeless, education, social security, health, and aid to the poor, while only 14 percent wanted more defense spending (*Newsweek,* 1987). In any case, conservatives argue that extensive welfare spending reduces the nation's economic competitiveness.

To summarize, each of the three approaches to deciding who should be helped raises a different set of issues concerning its moral and financial impact on individuals and society. A comprehensive approach is costly but maximizes opportunities for individual and social development. It may also, however, reduce people's self-reliance and willingness to make use of their informal support networks. Focusing on the needy, a more residual and selective approach, reduces costs but leaves unresolved the issue of deciding who is "truly needy." In addition, many taxpayers may resent supporting services that they feel do not benefit themselves. The conservative approach would reduce public social welfare expenditures still further in favor of increased public spending on other non-welfare-related activities. Implicit in this last approach is the assumption that informal support networks will be sufficient to meet people's needs.

Analyzing the three approaches in terms of their moral and financial impact on individuals and society helps to identify the issues associated with each.

WHAT KIND OF HELP SHOULD BE PROVIDED?

A second area of controversy in connection with social welfare is the question of what kind of help should be provided. There are four major issues that arise in this area. One is whether it is better to give people what they need or train them to provide for themselves. A second is the degree to which services should be provided through the marketplace rather than via the public sector. The third concerns the proper relationship between the formal and informal helping network and, most important, the question of which is preferable. Finally, there is the issue of the degree to which those who need help should be involved in planning and delivering services. In this section, we will look at each of these four controversial issues.

Giving Help Versus Developing People

There is a folk saying that goes something like this: "Give someone a fish and they can eat for a day; teach them to fish, and they can eat for a lifetime." It is a saying that captures the essence of the argument over the type of help social welfare should provide. The controversy that arises here is not over the ultimate goal of social welfare. Most people would agree that it is better to enable people to care for themselves than simply to provide short-term help. Difficulties are encountered, however, when programs are designed both to meet people's immediate needs *and at the same time* help them become self-sufficient.

At the heart of such controversies lies the question of whether recipients should be required to "earn" the benefits they receive, of whether they should be encouraged, or even required, to work. This controversy occurs because, in an industrial society, it is through work that most people earn the money they require to be independent. It is important to note, however, that money is not the only potential obstacle to self-sufficiency, particularly for groups such as the mentally ill and those with mental or physical limitations. As with the poor, the fundamental question is how to help such people on a day-to-day basis while at the same time preparing them to be as independent as possible. We will return to these two groups after first looking at the poor.

Over the years, there has been a recurring controversy over proposals that the poor be required to earn their benefits. *The name given to plans which require people who receive public assistance to work in return for their benefits is* **workfare** (Gueron and Auspos, 1987). Workfare seeks to achieve several goals. One is to enhance the self-respect of the aid recipient. Instead of receiving a handout, he or she can legitimately claim to have earned the aid provided. A second objective is to provide him or her with the opportunity to learn a variety of useful work skills. A third is to reinforce the social cohesion of the society by providing those who receive help with the sense that they are contributing something in return (all for one, and one for all). Finally, workfare is designed to reduce the cost of aid by providing society with tangible goods and services in return for the money it spends on social welfare.

While all of these goals are legitimate, the way in which some workfare programs attempt to accomplish them are open to challenge. Critics of workfare object, for example, to requiring single parents to work in return for their public assistance checks. They note that this deprives poor children of the opportunity to be cared for by their parents, an opportunity that society generally declares all children should have. Similarly, these parents are denied the pleasures of child rearing that the more affluent can enjoy because they do not have to work. There is the further problem that because of factors such as poor health, poor education, and minority background—characteristics commonly associated with poverty—many of the poor have limited work skills, a limited ability to work, and must further contend with discrimination, which limits the number and type of positions open to them (Hochschild, 1988:177–178). Many are, in fact, unable to work because of either physical or mental illness or limitations. Most qualify for only the most menial jobs where they will learn and earn very little.

Finally, a major objection to workfare is that it creates a pool of low-paid workers who compete in the job market with other workers who are not receiving any financial assistance. It is for precisely this reason that Polish cooperatives for the handicapped, discussed earlier, are granted the exclusive right to produce certain types of products, thus ensuring that their output does not compete with that of other workers who depend on their wages.

Many of the same issues apply to workfare for the physically or mentally limited and the mentally ill. Many are employed in **sheltered workshops,** *special facilities to train and employ the mentally ill and those with mental or physical limitations who would not be able to compete successfully in the regular workplace.* Critics have argued that such arrangements exploit the workers involved—who are usually paid extremely low wages. Further, the net effect of such operations has been criticized as taking jobs away from other workers. For these people and many of the disadvantaged poor as well, training is critical. Without it, the probability of long-term employability is very low. Yet training is costly. When these costs are added to the costs of the financial benefits provided, the total may seem burdensome. Although most recognize that it is far more economical over the long run to train people for independence, even if this means increased costs in the short term, this is not always a politically popular strategy (Hochschild, 1988:177). In a democratic system, proposals that involve higher initial costs in order to obtain future savings can be difficult to explain to voters.

Underlying much of the controversy about work and training is the fear of laziness. There is a prevailing belief that people will avoid work if at all possible. Studies consistently show that this is not true, that people would prefer to work if they can support themselves by doing so (Morris, 1986:46–53; Perales, 1983). Nevertheless, the myth endures, and is reinforced when instances of **welfare cheating** occur, *in which people lie about their true situation in order to qualify for social welfare benefits.*

As long as we fear that people who receive assistance are uninterested in caring for themselves, it will be difficult to resolve the ''spend more now in order to realize future savings'' versus ''spend only what you must'' dilemma. There will continue to be a reluctance to commit the funds necessary to change the conditions that create dependency. Training is costly, and changing the social and environmental conditions that are handicapping people requires a strong and sustained societal commitment. Yet, without such a commitment the cumulative impact of need and disadvantage will continue to prevent many people from becoming full and productive members of society. We will continue to give people enough to survive but not enough to thrive.

The Role of the Marketplace

As we have already seen, one of the purposes of the modern welfare state is to strike a balance between the marketplace and social welfare. The purpose of social welfare is not to compete with or supplant the market, but to redress its imbalances and thus complement its operation over both the long and short run. "The aim (of the modern welfare state) was to abolish injustices and hardships to the common people which appeared to accompany the capitalistic system...the market economy should be preserved, but with modifications introduced in the interests of social justice" (Heckscher, 1984:ix). There is, nonetheless, a continuing controversy over the proper relationship between the two.

At the crux of this debate is the issue of control. Shall the market be subordinate to the social welfare system or vice versa? Implicit is the assumption that the two sectors are in competition with one another. And clearly, in some sense, this is true. We have already seen that government expenditures for social welfare, and the taxes required to pay for them, effectively preempts the use of these monies for other purposes, thus affecting the workings of the market. In addition, private providers of services, especially those that are for profit, compete with the public sector.

Many of the issues involved in this ongoing controversy come to the fore in the current debate over **privatization,** *the transfer to the private sector of services previously provided by the public sector.* Privatization is seen by its advocates as a way to make service delivery more efficient and effective by reducing the size and power of large governmental social welfare bureaucracies. Reducing the cost of public services is attractive to those who feel that taxes are too high, a concern even in an advanced welfare state like Sweden. The provision of competing services is seen as desirable because it offers users a choice and because competition encourages the agencies involved to offer more efficient and appealing services.

Critics of privatization point to a number of drawbacks (Abramovitz, 1986). They raise first the fundamental question of whether money spent on social welfare should go to pay profits, or, more dramatically, should we allow for-profit agencies to make money on people's misery? Another issue is whether the cost of for-profit services is higher than those provided through the public or nonprofit sectors? If so, these costs may tend to exclude those who are most needy but least able to pay for help, leaving the public sector with the burden of serving those who are most needy and least able to pay. Allowing the for-profit agencies to "skim off the cream" makes the public sector appear to be less efficient, when in reality it is being left to deal with the most difficult

THE HUMAN FACE OF SOCIAL WELFARE 16

Down in the Valley

In 1964 President Lyndon Johnson declared America's first war on poverty with a battery of laws to improve education and attack hunger and disease, from urban ghettos to the remote, gritty valleys of Appalachia. If Johnson could witness what is happening in his native Texas today, however, he would surely shudder—perhaps as Antonio Gonzalez's 10 children do every winter. The Gonzalez family lives in the lower Rio Grande valley in a cramped, dark and drafty three-room shack. Their home is in a *colonia* (neighborhood), an unincorporated rural subdivision. They have no heat or sewage system, and when it rains the colonia's rutted dirt roads and yards flood so badly that children must wade through a stew of water and raw sewage to get to the school buses. Even in the dry, 100-degree heat of spring, kids have the wheezing cough of poverty.

That cough echoes up and down the U.S. border with Mexico, a poverty belt more desperate than even Appalachia. The heart of the squalor is in the lower Rio Grande valley, now the poorest region in the United States. In "the Valley," as it is known, Gonzalez and up to 250,000 other American citizens live in more than 400 rural slums. Unemployment in the colonias runs as high as 50 percent, water supplies are fouled and chronic diseases are rampant. Schools in the Valley's three main counties are hopelessly overcrowded. In short, the conditions in the colonias are the worst America has to offer. And the population is increasing so rapidly that studies predict it will double by the year 2000. Until recently the crisis was all but ignored, in large part because officials in Austin and Washington viewed the Valley as just another part of Mexico.

Like most of the colonia residents, Gonzalez is a first-generation Mexican-American whose parents came to the United States in search of opportunity. In the beginning they bought cheap plots from wealthy landlords, putting $10 down and paying the balance in monthly install-

ments of $25. County officials ignored the explosive growth of the unrecorded subdivisions. Before long the landlords were supplanted by large-scale developers who charged more in return for less land and even more primitive services.

Gloria Costilla's two-room home in El Dora has dirt floors and wall-to-wall beds—for herself, her husband and eight children. Unable to afford either the $200 meter installation fee or the developer's monthly water-supply bill of $14, she resigned herself to rising each dawn and hauling eight 10-gallon buckets from a neighbor's house. One day in April open sores broke out on her seven-year-old son Roberto's face and arms. The same thing happened to her husband. Finally Texas Rural Legal Aid attorneys took the Costillas to a doctor and paid for the visit. The family learned, after El Dora's water was tested, what caused the infections—the water was contaminated with fecal matter. "In some cases the water is so bad that even using it for bathing can make people sick," says Evonne Charboneau, a Legal Aid lawyer.

Doctors in the valley work overtime controlling basic illnesses normally seen only in developing countries. Their patients' lack of education and the high cost of medicine make health care a Sisyphean task. Diabetes, for instance, which can be easily controlled, frequently causes blindness and limb loss in the Valley.

FUNDING CUTS

Yet last year Congress froze the appropriations that support the seven federally funded health clinics in the region. And the National Health Service Corps, the federal program that supplies 85 percent of the health centers' doctors, was abolished by the Reagan administration. In the meantime, there are waiting lists of 1,000 patients at the clinics.

Most of the people who live in the colonias do not have health insurance, and there is widespread ignorance about Medicaid. Only 3.5 percent of the colonia residents use Medicaid. As a result, many colonia dwellers depend on the Valley's private hospitals, where profits are important. These hospitals usually demand a deposit: cold cash, a lien on a patient's truck or, as was the case at one hospital, a patient's silver belt buckle.

The fertility rate in the colonias is estimated at twice the national average, and infant mortality is high. Ten percent of the nation's out-of-hospital births occur in Hidalgo and Cameron counties, which contain only two-tenths of 1 percent of the nation's population. If pregnant women receive prenatal care, it is usually not until they are well into pregnancy, and often ill mothers give birth to babies with a variety of sicknesses and disorders. For example, a disproportionate number of colonia babies are born partially deaf from middle-ear infections.

Though school is a haven—most children get their only decent meal of the day there—few make it beyond the ninth grade. Many children of migrant farmhands miss the beginning and end of the school year, and the overall dropout rates are pushing 50 percent.

Local and State governments are gradually facing up to hardship in the Valley. In March, after all but ignoring the colonias for 20 years, the Hidalgo County commissioners issued regulations that they hope will effectively bar the establishment of any new colonias. But local officials say there is little money to ease the plight of existing settlements. It was not until three years ago that state officials even acknowledged the desperation in the Valley. Two weeks ago Texas provided a $4.1 million, low-interest loan to the city of Pharr to install sewage lines for 5,000 families who live in Las Milpas and Lopezville colonias. But such measures barely put a dent in the colonia problem. According to a recent study by the Texas Water Development Board, it would take 30 years and at least $200 million just to bring clean water and sewage lines to all 400 of the existing colonias.

REPUBLICAN BUSINESSMAN

Until very recently the federal government seemed oblivious to the squalor and poverty in the Valley. But when Assistant Surgeon General David Sundwall visited the border last December, he was so shocked by the conditions there that he immediately authorized a Border Health Initiative to provide money for health projects. But there is only $2 million in the BHI pot, and that money must be stretched from Texas to California. Doctors fear that state funding for health care may shrink because of Texas's severe fiscal crunch.

"It's like we live in a forgotten land down here," says Iris Hernandez, executive director of the Hidalgo County Health Care Corporation. Antonio Gonzalez, who has worked as a migrant laborer since he was 10, has one great hope: "I tell my children, 'This is not life, you must get an education and get out.'" But the colonias are prisons of poverty from which few have managed to escape.

Limited education, poor housing, low employability, and minority status often accompany poverty. Taken together, these factors make it very difficult for the poor to change their situation. The families described above who live in Texas' Rio Grande Valley, now considered the poorest region in the United States, need many resources if they are to become healthy and economically self-sufficient. Do you think that society is ready to make the commitment to do more than simply enable them to survive at their current level?

and costly problems while the for-profit sector services those whose needs are least extensive and whose ability to pay is greater.

An additional concern is that the needy are sometimes not very effective participants in the marketplace. They may lack the information needed to compare and evaluate the quality of services available from competing sources, or, as is often the case, the transportation or money necessary to make use of the services they might prefer.

Finally, some critics worry that shifting responsibility away from the public sector undermines the societal commitment to social welfare. If so, and if the private sector proves unable or unwilling to perform the social welfare role some believe it should perform, a greatly reduced public sector may be unable to meet the demands placed upon it by the private sector's failure. In addition, a devalued and poorly funded public sector can be expected to deliver shoddy services, while those who must make use of the system will be considered second-class citizens.

Privatization is especially controversial because it incorporates two rather different ideas. On the one hand, the purchase of service arrangements involved are similar to traditional relationships between the public and private nonprofit sector in which the public sector contracts for the delivery of services as discussed in Chapter 4. In general, these have worked well. Similar arrangements involving for-profit private services are a different proposition. The relationship between the two types of agencies can be expected to be more competitive. For-profit agencies may, for example, want to shift the least profitable users to the public agencies. Further, the question remains as to the implications of a profit-making approach to meeting human need for society's commitment to social welfare.

On the other hand, there is little doubt that the public sector can become so large that it is impersonal, rigid, and inefficient. It can also become so powerful that it exerts unwelcome influence and control over people's lives, as some feel has happened in Sweden. Societies based on centralized social planning, as in Poland and Sweden, are of course more accepting of a larger role for the public sector. Societies that view such a role for the public sector as inappropriate, the United States for example, continue to push for more private involvement with social welfare. Perhaps, however, the two types of societies will each learn from the experiences of the other. If so, it may be that a new role will emerge for the marketplace in the provision of social welfare services.

Developing Informal Support Networks

Is it better to provide help informally or on a formal basis? There is still considerable controversy over this issue (Gilbert, 1986:254). Many decry the family's diminished role in meeting the needs of its members, seeing in this change a deterioration in our sense of moral responsibility. Replacing natural care givers such as the family and the local community with large, rigid, and impersonal public and private agencies is seen as detrimental to the quality of help provided and as undermining important interpersonal relationships. Others disagree, believing that the institutionalization of social welfare is indicative of a stronger commitment by individuals and society to helping others.

The controversy is a particularly difficult one to resolve because most modern industrial societies now rely much more heavily than in the past on formal helping, a result of social and economic changes associated with industrialization. Gilbert (1986:254) summarizes some of these changes that together have diminished the family's ability to function as a center of care-giving. The increased life expectancies of the elderly and disabled, resulting from medical advances, have placed an increased burden on other family members. Further, there are an increasing number of families headed by a single adult or in which both adults work outside the home. In such families, there is often no adult available to provide other family members with personal care during working hours. Similar problems exist at the community level where the above factors combine with high rates of geographic mobility to greatly reduce the amount of time most people have for volunteer work and other civic activities, including interpersonal helping (Bellah et al., 1985).

As we saw in Chapter 4, the relationship between formal and informal helping is close and important. However, changes accompanying industrialization have fundamentally altered the ability of informal structures to meet people's needs. In the tension that exists between individual freedom and government control, people are often reluctant to give more power than is absolutely necessary to the government. Whether in Poland, where the state is very powerful, or in the United States, where individual freedom is much valued, modern society continues to seek an optimum balance between informal and formal helping systems.

Involving People in Decision-Making

What should be the role of those who receive services in social welfare decision-making? There is, of course, their role in the political process, which most would agree is important. Even here, however, theory and reality diverge. Those who are most needy are also least politically active. Therefore, much of the planning for services that they receive is done by others. The Community Action Programs created as a result of the 1964 Economic Opportunity Act represented a major effort to alter this situation (Kramer, 1969). The results, however, were politically controversial as the newly enfranchised community boards came into conflict with more established players. In addition, the heady experience of political involvement sometimes led to confrontation rather than productive dialogue. As a result, there have been many fewer efforts in recent years to involve users of services in social welfare decision-making, and the issues involved continue to be controversial.

Another form of involvement, one briefly mentioned earlier in this chapter, is allowing people to choose the services they want from among a range of alternatives. Proponents of privatization assert that it does exactly this. Competition between doctors, for example, allows those who are ill to choose a physician who provides the best type of care. Indeed, the idea of national health insurance is vigorously resisted by those who see it as eliminating this choice. Similarly, those who support proposals to give parents educational vouchers that would be good at any school, public or private, argue that this would provide people with choices and improve the quality of education by stimulating competition among school systems.

The right of people to determine their own fate is a deeply held value in the United States. Allowing people to choose the social welfare services they want is consistent with this goal. However, there are also problems with its implementation. The presumed benefits of being able to choose among suppliers can only be realized if two assumptions apply. The first is that people are sufficiently knowledgeable to recognize differences in quality of service, and will then be able to select those of the highest possible quality. Taking the example of medical care, this is unlikely for three reasons. One is that people may respond to the quality of interpersonal caring rather than to the quality of medical care. Another is that the increasing complexity and specialization of medical care make it extremely difficult for average citizens to know what constitutes good care. The third is that people are often frightened when they are ill. Thus, their usual ability to think and reason may be seriously impaired.

A second assumption is that people will have access to several possible suppliers. However, this may not be the case. Again, using the example of doctors, there may well be no more than a few, perhaps only one, located nearby. (This is especially true in rural areas.) Or the patient may have limited mobility due to age, disability, or lack of transportation. Further, patients with health insurance may have only limited freedom of choice as a result of constraints imposed by the insurer. Not all doctors, for example, will accept Medicare reimbursement levels as full payment. Patients who cannot afford additional fees are, therefore, limited to those physicians who will accept Medicare payment levels. Similar objections can be raised with respect to other service areas.

A third form of involvement is *participation in the actual delivery of services*. A common label for such participation is **self-help.** Self-help greatly increases the user's role in the helping process. By assuming some responsibility for acknowledging problems, and participating with others who also have the problem in efforts to find solutions to them, people become far more involved in their own care. Organizations such as Alcoholics Anonymous use self-help extensively. However, most types of services can be delivered in ways that encourage people to be more active in helping efforts. For example, changes in lifestyle can be as important as medication in solving many medical problems. While the physician can prescribe medicine, it is up to the patient to control lifestyle.

We can see, then, that people can be involved in social welfare decision-making in at least three different ways—at the planning stage, in choosing a supplier, and in service delivery. Each type of involvement raises its own set of issues. Planning involves some degree of power, a commodity about which there are always strong feelings. Choice involves knowledge and access, variables that are related to other resources such as education and money, that are presently unequally distributed. Participation in service delivery requires that social welfare personnel be able to accept input from others and that people are motivated to participate.

HOW MUCH HELP IS NEEDED?

Let's take a moment to review. So far, we have looked at two major questions that make social welfare controversial: Who should be helped, and what kind of help should they get? We have seen that there are many different answers to these questions. The differences involved reflect underlying differences in values having to do with social and individual responsibility and the proper use of resources. Now we will turn to the third and last controversial question: how much help should be given?

We all know that some people need help over an extended period, and that others are only temporarily impaired. For example, we expect children to need help for many years and recognize that those with physical limitations may require aid all their lives. However, those who are unemployed are generally thought to have a temporary problem. As a result, programs designed to help children and the disabled often provide services over a relatively long interval while programs designed to alleviate unemployment provide services for a much shorter period. One frequent source of controversy, therefore, is the length of time over which services *should* be provided, particularly when problems that are generally thought to be short-term in nature prove to be long-term instead.

We have already seen that fostering dependency is an undesirable outcome of helping. It is undesirable to make someone who has what ought to be a short-term problem dependent on a program intended to solve long-term needs. Much of the controversy surrounding the Aid to Families with Dependent Children program has to do with precisely this issue.

Underlying the controversy is the sense that the inability to support one's family *should* be a relatively short-term problem. If decent-paying jobs or adequate day care are needed, these needs *should* be met fairly quickly. Similarly, if job training is the issue, this too *should* be a relatively short-run problem. When these needs are not met quickly—or simply not met at all—aid recipients are likely to wonder whether they will ever become self-sufficient. At this point, a program intended to address a short-term need begins to perform a different function. Since the program is poorly designed for this new function, it is not likely to be very effective. In addition, by placing recipients in a long-term dependent position, the helping effort may actually harm them.

The point has been made many times in this book that social welfare seeks to work closely with the other institutions of society. However, social welfare's working relationship with other social institutions is not always as close as it should be. In part, this is because it takes time for any system to change.

When an economic problem arises—increased unemployment, for example—there is usually a delay before the problem is recognized and appropriate solutions are implemented. The most vulnerable groups in society are especially at risk in this process. They are, for example, the groups most likely to experience unemployment first and most often. Therefore, they are the groups most damaged by delays in developing programs to address new types of unemployment problems.

Over time, a chronic cycle of employment and unemployment can erode a family's resources. In addition, it is very discouraging. Over time, all too chronic unemployment can easily become a source of despair and hopelessness rather than a short-term need for a job. For those so affected, job placement programs alone will be insufficient. Such workers need more than a paid position. They require retraining and counseling to bolster their self-confidence and motivation as well as their work skills. Unfortunately, these services may not be available.

Even if these auxiliary services do exist, other problems arise that outsiders may not understand. If an aid recipient needs a job and a new McDonald's opens nearby, why not apply?

There may be several reasons. For one thing, the salary may be lower than the income provided by public assistance which is already at or below the poverty level—plus Medicaid health coverage would be lost. Further, the job is also unlikely to be interesting or to offer any chance for stability or advancement. Also, in all probability the worker will have held countless similar jobs during earlier economic upswings, only to lose them with the next recession. Under these circumstances, the worker may well choose to remain on public assistance.

To many, this will seem an inappropriate use of that program. Citizens whose taxes support such programs may be angered that their money is going to support unemployed adults rather than providing short-term help to poor families with needy children. To them, it may seem that the worker who refuses to take an available job is lazy. To the unemployed worker, things may seem quite different. Remaining on welfare rather than accepting the low-paying, dead-end jobs they are often offered may seem perfectly sensible. Indeed, in the absence of effective programs designed to meet their long-term needs, they may well see it as the best choice available.

To many, such reasoning is difficult to accept. In their view, it is up to the individual to exhibit the tenacity and energy required for self-improvement, to save every penny, to seek out every opportunity. Many comforts must be sacrificed in order to make progress possible. Any job should be acceptable. Any apartment should be welcome. Any help should be gratefully received. The only help anyone should need is short-term help. If people really took advantage of their opportunities, they would be able to make it on their own.

This is the realm of the famous welfare Cadillac. People who feel this way believe many welfare recipients are not willing to help themselves. They believe that they want everything given to them, and expect to have what others have without working for it. They reject jobs (like the one at McDonald's) and apartments that they don't like (as in Mayor Koch's encounter with the welfare mother described earlier in the chapter). When they do get money, so the story goes, they spend it on televisions and cars, fancy clothes and drugs. Many tax-paying citizens become very angry at "welfare cheats" and believe that they do not deserve help.

No doubt some people lie about their needs and accept money for which they don't qualify. On the other hand, plenty of otherwise law-abiding citizens cheat on their income tax and defraud insurance companies with bogus claims. Cheating, whether by the rich or the poor, is wrong. However, it is unlikely that it will ever disappear from the ranks of either group. Precautions to prevent cheating are taken. Fraud rates among welfare recipients are actually quite low, in part because states with high error rates lose federal funds. Most people want to work and prefer to be independent. Yet this remains a difficult goal for many.

The cumulative effects of disadvantage lead to long-term dependence and despair. Instead of driving welfare Cadillacs, most poor people face deprivation on a daily basis. The occasional instance of cheating that makes the newspapers angers people, and appropriately so. The solution, though, is not imposing more and more controls to stop cheating. It is instead reforming social structures so that systematic disadvantages are eliminated. In the words of Hochschild (1988:177–178), "Solving the problem of cumulative inequalities, however, would require a coordinated attack on racial discrimination and poverty and political powerlessness...." Until this occurs, we can anticipate that the disadvantaged will be forced into long-term dependency.

DEVELOPING POSITIONS

By now you may have a better understanding of why social welfare is controversial only to realize that this poses a problem for you. What should *your* position about these issues be? The objective of this section is to help you develop your own informed positions on these issues.

Most of us feel more comfortable when we have taken a position about issues. However, I would encourage you to retain some flexibility and openness about social welfare. You can, for example, be in favor of certain goals and still disagree with programs designed to achieve them. Just because you believe social welfare in general is good doesn't mean that you have to agree with everything that is done in this area. Indeed, one of your responsibilities as a citizen is to identify social welfare policies or programs where change is needed, and then work for those changes however you can—by voting for candidates who support your position, participating in relevant community activities, and so on. But you want to be sure to have a clear objective in mind—the creation of a specific program or the passage of a particular piece of legislation, for example. The important thing is to have reason to believe that the

THE HUMAN FACE OF SOCIAL WELFARE 17

Ramona Parish

Like many other single mothers, I am on welfare. I have received Aid to Families with Dependent Children ever since I divorced my husband six years ago. Living on government aid does several things to people. It destroys their pride and dignity; it makes them dependent on a system that penalizes them for being willing to work. I am not lazy and I want to work. But at this time the best I can hope for is a minimum-wage job that would only undermine my attempts to get ahead. Instead of just being poor, I would become one of the nation's working poor. I cannot survive on $3.35 per hour with three children, without regular child-support payments or health insurance. So I live on AFDC and often feel guilty because I take advantage of this system and its services. But I'm also made to feel ashamed because I cannot pay for things with my own hard-earned money.

To the People behind Me on the Grocery-store Line

You have helped me feel guilty. You chip away at what little pride I have left by snickering to others when I use my food stamps, at the same time commenting loudly about an abuse of taxpayers' dollars. It is because of such comments that I shop in a town 15 miles away, and even there my face reddens with shame.

To All Landlords

Some of you believe that because I receive welfare I have no pride in my home or my surroundings. Many times I've called on the phone to ask about a rental and, sight unseen, been turned down when I mention I receive AFDC. I know you have heard that most welfare people will destroy your home and are completely unreliable in paying the rent on time. It doesn't matter if I have excellent references from previous landlords or that I can have the rent payments sent directly to you. On the other hand, there are some of you who will rent only to welfare. You like having the money sent to you from social services. You don't care what condition your apartment is in because if I complain about needed repairs (windows that won't open, doors with broken locks), you tell me: "So? Move out." Because there are only a few of you who will rent to AFDC, your apartment will not be empty long.

To My Ex-husband

In the past six years I have asked very little from you. Although I appreciate the bags of "used clothing" you sent when I asked if you could help with school clothes, I would have preferred if you had sent child support. Why should I have been the one who was embarrassed when your father stopped by and gave our son a pair of tennis shoes and each of our two daughters $10? You should be the one who is embarrassed—more help from you could make a difference in the way our children live. I make sure they have all their basic needs met, but I get tired of telling them, no, they can't have things they want because I don't have the money.

To My Children

I did not intend to raise you on welfare. Bear with me a few more years, for I am trying to make a bad situation better. All of you kids have complained about having to apply for the free-lunch program. I know how ashamed you must feel when you're singled out in the classroom as a free-luncher, and the hurt caused by whispers among your friends that you're poor and your mother is on welfare. I'm sorry for the things I can't afford. But my biggest apology is for the groceries and boxes of toys you saw delivered to the house four years ago by the Old Newsboys organization. Tears still come to my eyes when I think of the question you each asked so innocently, "Mom, I thought people collected these for the poor who can't afford food and toys for the holidays." Little did you know, we were one of the poor. Since that day my pride has not allowed me to accept any more gift baskets.

To All Doctors and Dentists

Would my hysterectomy which was done three years ago when I was only 28 have been so urgent if I hadn't had Medicaid to pay for it? Could I have avoided having to take estrogen every day for the rest of my life? Although I had a choice of whether to have the surgery or not, I believe scare tactics were used. I wonder if some professionals take advantage of Medicaid recipients because women on AFDC are seen as uneducated and are expected to believe what they are told? And would that explain why so many AFDC women have lost all their teeth? After several extractions—six teeth lost in the six years on AFDC with three more to go soon—I find it difficult to chew my food properly. It's a standard joke now that I'm always the last one to leave the table; in reality, I'm too embarrassed to tell people that dentists suggest pulling teeth because Medicaid won't pay for root canals and crowns....

To All Social-service Case Workers

When I am willing to help myself and work, why do you take everything away? Can't you at least let me keep the food stamps and medical insurance until I'm above the poverty level? Without these benefits I cannot make it, so I stay on the soaring welfare rolls. I don't want a free ride, but I do need a lift.

To Whom It May Concern

Do not feel pity for me. I don't want it. I have been given an abundance of self-worth these past two years. Enrolling in college and getting an education is my key to a future without AFDC. Managing a full-time class load, 20 hours a week on a work-study program, and being a mother hasn't been easy, but I've survived. Every time I cash my work-study check, I get back a piece of my pride. I still use my food stamps in another town, but at the same time I use dollar bills that I have earned myself. With each passing semester my head lifts a little higher. What I could use is a smile of understanding and words of encouragement and support. With help, not hindrance, I will make it.

———

Ms. Parish discusses in a very articulate way many of the issues we have been examining. On the one hand, some people would question the wisdom of her divorce, saying that if she could not support herself she should have stayed married. Others recognize that a bad marriage may be far more damaging than welfare over the long run.

In her efforts to become self-sufficient, Ms. Parish has experienced problems with the economic system (employment and housing), the social welfare system (inadequate benefits), and social stigma in her community. Her plea for understanding from her children is especially touching, because they, too, have suffered from being on welfare.

Ramona Parish hopes that her enrollment in a program to become a legal secretary will enable her finally to break the welfare cycle for her family. Is this a realistic option for less intelligent and less articulate welfare mothers? What alternatives do these women have?

change sought will help to resolve the problem with which it is intended to deal.

Another point to consider is that your perspectives will change over time. As you have different kinds of experiences, you will understand issues in different ways. Your attitudes toward workfare, for example, may be quite different when you are a parent with children under your care than it was before you had parenting responsibilities. After an especially stressful period in your life, your perceptions of why people sometimes stop trying to be self-sufficient may be altered. What this means, of course, is that our experiences and cultural backgrounds affect the way in which we view situations. Minorities who experience discrimination on a regular basis feel differently about it than those who do not. To some—a woman looking for a desirable job, a black family seeking a good school for their children, or a gay man considering the risks involved in taking an AIDS test—the problem of discrimination looms much larger than it does to those who are less likely to encounter it and consequently feel more in control of their lives.

You can also expect that you will have strong emotional reactions to many social welfare issues because they involve our values as well as our intellect. As an educated person, you will want to use your analytical skills, to obtain as much data as you can about issues before making up your mind. But also try to be in touch with your own feelings and see if you can understand their origins. Often, we have been taught values and have never really thought much about them. Our personal experiences are also a rich source of feelings and perceptions. Whatever their source, try to be aware of what you feel and why. Ex-

---

AVOIDING DEPENDENCY: THE SWEDISH APPROACH

Sweden's strategy for avoiding long-term dependency is built around education and employment. Other supportive services, such as virtually free health care and subsidized housing, help. Fundamentally, however, the problem is not addressed by giving people welfare checks, although these are available to those who need this type of help. Rather, the focus is on efforts to prepare people for self-sufficiency.

Education is a critical component of Swedish society. Education at all levels is free. It is also highly diversified, with many types of vocational and other specialized education available through full- and part-time programs. Education is also much valued. There are even home-study programs on the public radio stations. In addition, Swedes value data for problem-solving purposes, so people are oriented toward using knowledge to plan and make decisions.

Swedish high schools make a concerted effort to prepare students for the job market. As part of their studies, students spend time working in positions that provide them with first-hand business experience and a sense of what different types of jobs are like. They are not paid for this; it is considered part of their learning. This helps them to identify possible career options which can then be pur-

sued through appropriate educational programs (all of which are free).

The Swedish political system and Swedish values provide further additional help. The goal of equality for all people—men and women, immigrants and native Swedes—is diligently pursued. Substantial efforts are made to ensure that all types of education and all jobs are open to both men and women. The educational system instructs immigrants in their own language, and the social welfare system provides services on a similar basis. The goal is to help integrate immigrants into Swedish society as quickly as possible, enabling them to become full-fledged and productive citizens. Labor unions play a significant, formal role in political decision-making, and full employment is a declared societal goal. Swedish social policy derives from a mandate to involve people in productive work that makes self-sufficiency possible, and that mandate is reflected not only in the substance of policy but the social and political structures that implement it.

To be sure, Sweden's aspirations sometimes outstrip its abilities to achieve them. However, the Swedish approach to self-sufficiency offers an interesting model for other societies to consider.

amine your feelings within the context of the knowledge you possess and see if you can find a point at which there is a comfortable fit.

Don't avoid taking positions about social welfare controversies. Your positions may sometimes be challenged. However, unless people become truly involved with these issues they will not receive the attention and action they deserve. Whether in the political arena, the family, churches, schools, or social welfare agencies, the issues raised by social welfare must be aired, debated, and understood. Controversy can be healthy as long as it leads to socially productive discussion and action.

Finally, seek to understand the implications of your positions. If you believe that many recipients of public assistance are cheats and don't deserve what they get, you will probably not want to plan on a career as a social worker. If you feel strongly that society does not spend enough on social welfare programs, you might want to consider working as a lawyer or running for political office. If you have a commitment to helping people develop their capacity to become healthy, self-sufficient adults, working in education would make sense. In other words, try to align your daily activities with your positions about social welfare issues so that you are not constantly in a position where your ideas conflict with your behaviors.

In the end, controversies are troublesome because they have no easy answers. For each of the issues discussed in this chapter there are valid opposing viewpoints. Facts can help. We know that most unemployed people would rather work than receive public assistance. But facts alone don't solve the dilemmas. If someone wants to work but can't find a job, how hard must they search before they have explored every "reasonable" possibility? Do they have to accept physically dangerous or very-low-paid work? (Recall Ms. Parish's views.) These, you see, are value-related issues for which there are no factual answers.

Many of the controversies about social welfare are of this sort. They embody fundamental values about human nature and the proper relationship between society and its members. They are issues that have been argued throughout human history, and they will continue to provoke argument for the foreseeable future. Your job is not to resolve them. Rather, your task is to understand them and to have the courage and the sensitivity to form your own positions.

LET'S REVIEW

Our discussion of why social welfare is controversial in this chapter has been organized around three questions: Who should be helped? What kind of help should be given? How much help is appropriate? In each case, we have seen that there are different points of view about whether social welfare is helpful or not. These differences reflect differences in values as well as varying interpretations of data related to the costs and benefits of social welfare.

In examining the controversy over who should be helped, we employed an analytic framework that focused on the moral and financial impact of social welfare on individuals and society. This framework was used to highlight the different impacts of three major approaches: providing services to all (the comprehensive or universal approach), to just the most needy (the residual approach), or to as few people as possible (the conservative approach). We also highlighted the importance of economic factors in deciding who to help. Furthermore, we saw that, however well intended, helping sometimes has negative consequences for recipients.

Our discussion of the controversies surrounding what kind of help should be provided centered on four issues. Assistance can aim at solving an immediate problem, or it can prepare people to become self-sufficient. The central role that work plays in this process was highlighted. The appropriateness of the marketplace as a possible locus for the delivery of services was discussed. We also returned to the question of the proper relationship between formal and informal helping networks. The section ended with a consideration of whether and how people should be involved in planning, choosing, and delivering social welfare services.

The last question, how much help should be provided, was explored by looking at short- and long-term helping and their relationship to dependency. We saw that one of the inadvertent results of the failure of short-term programs can be long-term dependence. The chapter ended with a discussion of the importance of our taking informed positions on these controversial issues.

This chapter concludes our discussion of the basic concepts, structure, and functioning of the social welfare institution. I hope that by now you feel comfortable with your understanding of our large and complex social welfare system. It is knowledge that will prove very useful, no matter where your life takes you in the years to come.

Now only two chapters remain. Chapter 9 discusses the activities of social welfare professionals, a topic of particular interest if you are considering such a career, but helpful also to anyone who makes use of the services the social welfare system provides—which is to say, virtually everyone. Finally, Chapter 10 examines the future of social welfare with a particular focus on likely developments during the next few years.

CHAPTER OUTLINE

STUDY QUESTIONS

1 In the course of conversation at a party someone you have just met expresses his or her opinion that there are too many "welfare cheats." How would you respond? Would you try to steer the conversation to some other topic? Would you present facts? Would you express your own opinion? In general, how do you think you would feel in this situation?

2 Select a social welfare service that you have received. (Don't forget such things as student grants, health care, tax breaks, and so on.) On a piece of paper, make two columns, one headed "financial" and the other "moral." Then list as many of the effects as you can that the service has had on your life, separating them into financial and moral. For example, if you were awarded a student grant that made it unnecessary for you to work, what has been the effect on your sense of independence? Or perhaps you received the grant but continued to work so that you could buy the car you have always wanted. How has this affected you? Try to be as thoughtful and honest as you can.

3 Survey the content of your local paper over the past several years and find as many articles as you can that discuss your community's reactions to social welfare. What issues have been raised? What positions were adopted by various groups, especially the poor and members of minorities? How were the issues resolved? Summarize your findings and interpret their meaning for the social welfare institution.

4 Work is becoming a reality for more and more people. Try to list as many effects of this as you can. For example, as work becomes more necessary, what happens to those who cannot work, or who become unemployed? What about the family—who will be available to provide care for children or for sick or elderly members? In what ways is work a source of problems as well as a solution to problems?

5 Take a few sheets of paper and write a short essay describing your positions on the three controversies discussed in this chapter: Who should be helped, what kind of help should be provided, and how much help is appropriate? Take some time to think carefully about your positions, using the suggestions provided in this chapter. Then exchange your essay with a friend. How similar are your views? Why do you think this is the case?

KEY TERMS AND CONCEPTS

privatization
self-help
sheltered workshops

welfare cheating
workfare

SUGGESTED READINGS

Block, Fred, et al., eds. 1987. *The Mean Season*. New York: Pantheon Books. An edited volume featuring essays written from a liberal and even radical point of view, this book explores the moral and financial impact of cutbacks in social welfare during the Reagan administration. A provocative counterpoint to the conservative point of view expressed by Murray (see below).

Marmor, Theodore, and Jerry L. Mashaw, eds. 1988. *Social Security in Contemporary American Politics*. Princeton, N.J.: Princeton University Press. This collection of essays examines current issues about America's social security legislation, including retirement, disability, and medical care benefits. The controversial aspects of these programs are described, along with possible future directions.

Murray, Charles. 1984. *Losing Ground*. New York: Basic Books. The most thorough presentation to appear in recent years of the conservative approach to social welfare. It attempts to show how increased social welfare services are financially irresponsible, ineffective, and morally damaging.

Ryan, William. 1976. *Blaming the Victim,* rev. ed. New York: Vintage Books. This powerful book explores many of the most popular myths about people in need. It argues that society must take responsibility for social problems and the individual crises that they create.

Schumacher, E. F. 1973. *Small is Beautiful*. New York: Harper & Row. Subtitled "Economics as if People Mattered," this book argues for changes in the economic system which would be more compatible with people's needs for participation, control over their own lives, and a sense of self-respect. An interesting and challenging alternative to current economic policies.

REFERENCES

Abramovitz, Mimi. 1986. The privatization of the welfare state: A review. *Social Work,* 31, no. 4 (July–August):257–264.

Bellah, Robert, et al. 1985. *Habits of the Heart*. Berkeley, Calif.: University of California Press.

Berg, Eric. 1985. Bulging executive paychecks. *The New York Times,* April 17, p. D1ff.

Block, Fred, et al., eds. 1987. *The Mean Season*. New York: Pantheon Books.

Domestic Policy Association. 1985. *Welfare: Who Should be Entitled to Public Help?* Dayton, Ohio: The Domestic Policy Association.

Esping-Andersen, Gøsta. 1985. *Politics Against Markets*. Princeton, N.J.: Princeton University Press.

Fullinwider, Robert. 1988. Citizenship and welfare. In Amy Guttman, ed., *Democracy and Social Welfare*. Princeton, N.J.: Princeton University Press, pp. 262–278.

Gibney, Jr., Frank. 1987. In Texas, a grim new Appalachia. *Newsweek,* June 8, p. 27.

Gilbert, Neil. 1983. *Capitalism and the Welfare State*. New Haven, Conn.: Yale University Press.

————. 1986. The welfare state adrift. *Social Work,* 31, no. 4 (July–August):251–256.

Gueron, Judith, and Patricia Auspos. 1987. Workfare. In the *Encyclopedia of Social Work,* 18th ed. Silver Spring, Md.: National Association of Social Workers, pp. 896–900.

Heckscher, Gunnar. 1984. *The Welfare State and Beyond.* Minneapolis: University of Minnesota Press.

Hochschild, Jennifer. 1988. Race, class, power, and the American welfare state. In Amy Guttman, ed. *Democracy and Social Welfare.* Princeton, N.J.: Princeton University Press, pp. 157–184.

Koch, Edward. 1988. Welfare isn't a way of life. *The New York Times,* March 4, p. 27.

Kramer, Ralph. 1969. *Participation of the Poor.* Englewood Cliffs, N.J.: Prentice-Hall.

Marmor, Theodore, and Jerry L. Mashaw, eds. 1988. *Social Security in Contemporary American Politics.* Princeton, N.J.: Princeton University Press.

Morris, Robert. 1986. *Rethinking Social Welfare.* White Plains, N.Y.: Longman, Inc.

Murray, Charles. 1984. *Losing Ground.* New York: Basic Books.

New spending priorities. 1987. *Newsweek.* September 21, p. 7.

Ording, Jan. 1987. Material obtained in an interview with Mr. Ording, Head of the Division for Care of the Elderly, Economic Assistance and Social Care for Immigrants, of the National Board of Health and Welfare, on February 23.

Perales, Cesar. 1983. Myths about poverty. *The New York Times,* October 26, p. A27.

Price, Debbie. 1988. Just around the corner, a storeful of sympathy. *The New York Times,* March 13.

Ryan, William. 1976. *Blaming the Victim,* rev. ed. New York: Vintage Books.

Schumacher, E. F. 1973. *Small is Beautiful.* New York: Harper & Row.

Swedish Institute. 1986. *Texas In Sweden.* Stockholm: The Swedish Institute.

Zimbalist, Sidney. 1987. A welfare state against the economic current: Sweden and the United States as contrasting cases. *International Social Work,* 30, no. 1 (January):15–29.

————. 1988. Winning the war on poverty: The Swedish strategy. *Social Work,* 33, no. 1 (January–February):46–49.

CHAPTER 9

HOW DO THE SOCIAL WELFARE PROFESSIONS FUNCTION?

WHAT TO EXPECT FROM THIS CHAPTER

This chapter discusses the social welfare professions and their role in delivering helping services to people. It also examines the relationship between these professions and the informal helping network, which, as we have seen, is also an important source of social welfare services. The chapter concludes with a look at the opportunities for helping that are available to all of us.

An understanding of the structure and function of the social welfare professions is useful in several ways. First, it completes our picture of social welfare as a social institution. An examination of how helping professions have developed can help us better understand how society operationalizes its helping role and how closely linked social welfare is to the other institutions of society. We will see that there is competition and overlap among the social welfare profes-

267

sions, a situation we might expect in a market-oriented society that limits centralized government planning and control. Finally, if you are considering a helping career, you will find this overview of the helping professions particularly useful.

This chapter will increase your understanding of the institutional components of social welfare by bringing together many of the issues discussed earlier. The next chapter, which is the last, moves in a different direction. Rather than examining the past or the present, it looks to the future. What is the role of social welfare likely to be in the years ahead? For now, though, let's focus on the people and the professions who deliver helping services today.

LEARNING OBJECTIVES

At the conclusion of this chapter, you should be able to do the following:

1 List four major characteristics of a profession, and apply them to a social welfare profession of your choice.

2 Distinguish between licensing, legal certification, registration, and professional certification as they are used in social welfare.

3 List at least five social welfare professions, and briefly describe the function of each.

4 Give an example of a generalist role and a specialist role in one of the social welfare professions.

5 Distinguish between professional and volunteer roles in social welfare, and discuss how they interact.

6 List at least five ways in which ordinary people can become involved in societal helping efforts.

7 Define the difference between a profession and a job.

THE FUNCTIONS OF THE HELPING PROFESSIONS

All the helping professions share the goal of helping people and institutions to function more effectively so that people's lives are enhanced and social cohesion is strengthened. Each profession approaches this task from its own particular vantage point. We will see that each profession trains its members to be skillful and effective providers of particular kinds of services. However, they also work together so that the distinctive services provided by each type of professional fits together into a holistic helping effort.

The Generalist Approach

When a profession attempts to address all of the needs that people experience in problematic situations, it is using a **generalist approach.** Some professions, such as social work, are by their very nature generalist. Social work adopts a holistic view of the interaction between people and their environment, seeking to improve this relationship by strengthening the individual's ability to function independently, modifying the environment, or both. Social workers, therefore, provide a variety of services, including personal counseling, political advocacy, organizing community groups, family therapy, counseling in personal financial management, and so on. A generalist approach, therefore, is one which involves using a variety of skills to intervene at any and all levels required to ensure that *all* the elements of the problem are addressed.

Consider the example of a social worker employed in a senior citizen center who one day observes that one of the women who comes regularly to the center often has bruises. Through skillful counseling, the worker discovers that the elderly woman lives with her son and his family, and that she is subject to emotional and physical abuse. Furthermore, her son has forced her to sign over most of her assets to him, limiting her ability to move out. Employing a generalist approach, the worker might define the types of assistance needed to solve the problem as including all of the following:

1 Legal help to protect the elderly woman's assets and rights.
2 Medical care to treat her injuries.
3 Psychological help to address her emotional trauma.
4 Counseling to help her plan a safe and secure future for herself.
5 Housing assistance to help her locate an affordable place to live that will be appropriate for her physical abilities and social needs.
6 Contact with other community social agencies and professional groups to explore the problem of elder abuse as a social problem, and to plan appropriate community and legislative action.
7 Counseling with the family to help them participate in finding solutions to the problem.

In this example, the social worker involved employs a generalist approach to identify all the elements of the problem and the measures needed to address them. Obviously, however, one professional working alone cannot provide all the services listed above. For this reason, a generalist often becomes a **case manager,** *a professional who oversees the provision of a variety of specialized services to ensure that they are delivered in a fashion that represents an effective response to the whole problem.* The generalist approach allows a professional to focus on the whole problem while breaking it down into its component parts so that each can be addressed by professionals with specialized expertise. This assures that the users of services receive help in ways that address all relevant aspects of their problem and contribute to an overall sense of well-being.

The Specialist Approach

An alternative but complementary approach to that of the generalist is the specialist approach. *The **specialist approach** utilizes professionals with specialized training to solve particular problems.* We are all familiar with medical specialists to whom our family practitioner refers patients with problems that require specialized treatment, such as kidney disease, hearing loss, or cancer. Specialists have extensive training in a particular area, which makes them highly qualified to treat problems within that area.

Some professions utilize both generalist and specialist approaches. Physicians are an excellent example. All physicians are specialists in the sense that they only treat problems involving people's physical health. However, some doctors specialize much more than others. Family practitioners concern themselves with their patient's overall health, referring problems that lie outside their immediate competence to other physicians who specialize in a particular branch of medicine or type of disease, such as oncologists who treat cancer. In such cases, responsibility for all aspects of the patient's care other than the problem that led to the referral is generally left to the family practitioner, whose approach is a generalist one. Medicine, therefore, is an example of a profession in which we find both generalists and specialists.

Both the generalist and specialist approaches are also employed in social work. All social workers are trained as generalists, and many function in this capacity. However, many others, particularly those with graduate-level training, also develop specialties that become their primary area or mode of practice. Psychiatric social workers, for example, work in mental health or private practice settings where they provide counseling and related psychiatric services. However, since the social work role almost always includes some case management responsibilities, even highly specialized social workers are likely to provide a mix of generalist and specialist services.

Generalists and specialists serve complementary functions. People need help with their particular problems, help that the specialist is uniquely qualified to provide. However, to be effective help must be integrated into people's daily lives so that the fabric of their existence is maintained.

Future Prospects

A recent effort to project the growth of jobs in various occupational areas between 1984 and 1995 yielded the results for the helping professions reported in Table 9.1.

The data in Table 9.1 suggest there will be a continuing need for social welfare professionals. The increasing complexity of modern society poses problems for those whose education, age, or physical or mental capacities limit their ability to function independently. Families continue to struggle with such consequences of social change as larger numbers of working parents and single parents, high divorce rates, and high levels of stress that damage marital and parent-child relationships. The continuing growth in the elderly population will require increased services to maintain and enhance the quality of their lives. In addition, there is increasing concern over environmental and economic problems, while the longstanding problems of racism and sexism continue to disadvantage large numbers of people. All these and more suggest a continued need for social welfare and its professions.

TABLE 9.1 PROJECTED GROWTH FOR SOCIAL WELFARE PROFESSIONS: 1984–1995

Profession	Percent increase in jobs
Social work	
Social workers	22
Physical health	
Dieticians and nutritionists	26
Physical therapists	42
Physicians and surgeons	23
Registered nurses	33
Mental health	
Psychologists	22
Education	
Kindergarten and elementary school teachers	20
Secondary school teachers	5
Law	
Lawyers	36

Source: The New York Times (1986). Based on Department of Labor Statistics for November 1985.

The resurgence in the number of applications to schools of social work during the mid-1980s in this country (Wilkerson, 1987) suggests that society may be recognizing this need. Perhaps, as some feel, a growing awareness of social problems such as AIDS and homelessness has increased people's interest in helping careers. Another factor may be disappointment with jobs that provide little human contact, seem to make little difference in people's lives, or that are financially rewarding but not personally enriching. For all of these societal and personal reasons, then, it is likely that the social welfare professions will continue to grow.

THE NATURE OF PROFESSIONS

Professions are vocational fields with very special characteristics (Hall, 1968). Professionals, like other workers, have jobs and, in many cases, an employer. (Professionals may also be self-employed.) However, the professional's primary commitment is to the profession itself rather than to the employer. (Notice that here we are using the term "profession" to refer to a type of occupation, not how well people do their work. It is common to speak of people who do their jobs very well as being very "professional." In this sense, anyone can be professional. This is not the sense in which we are using the term, however.)

Professions share four important characteristics. However, as has been noted by Khinduka (1987:682) "... professionalism is not an either-or phenomenon. Instead, the attributes of a profession constitute a continuum, and professionalism should thus be viewed as a scale...." With that caution in mind, let's examine the four characteristics of a profession.

Professions have specialized knowledge and skills. Most professions involve mastery of a large body of specialized knowledge that requires extensive education. Lawyers, for example, undergo 3 years of graduate-level training in legal precedent, existing law, and legal procedures. Most professional training involves practicums in which students apply their knowledge in an effort to develop practice skills. Only those who master the required specialized knowledge and skills qualify for professional membership.

Consider the example of social work. Many people feel that social work is just common sense. Those who call social workers "do-gooders" are, in effect, suggesting that social workers are guided primarily by good intentions rather than specialized knowledge or skills. Those who hold this view believe social work consists of sympathizing with others, filling out forms, and giving advice.

In reality, professionally trained social workers must master a large body of knowledge about all aspects of human and social functioning. This includes the life span, theories of personality development, elements of intergroup dynamics, the political process, and existing social welfare programs. In addition, they have very specific problem-solving skills. Of special importance are the skills required to relate effectively to others, to understand and utilize the special skills of members of various ethnic and lifestyle groups, to identify problems and the resources needed to solve them, to help people implement changes in lifestyle and behavior, and to evaluate the results of helping efforts. People who are not trained as professional social workers lack this knowledge and these skills.

Like social work, each of the helping professions has a distinctive knowledge base, values, and set of skills that make its members uniquely capable of performing helping activities.

Professions have a code of ethics. Professions place the value of human life and human dignity ahead of the profit motive. Because they address situations in which human rights, physical and emotional well-being, fundamental human relationships, and even life itself are at stake, great care is taken to protect users of services. The professional code of ethics is a major means by which this protection occurs. *A **code of ethics** is a profession's set of standards concerning the ethical behavior of its members. All members are expected to be guided by this code in their professional activities.* Each profession has its own code, but all are grounded in similar beliefs; the value of human life, a respect for the right of people to control their own lives, and a commitment always to strive to help others rather than to enrich or promote oneself.

A professional code of ethics protects users from exploitation by professionals or the agencies for which they work. A code also extends protection in the form of guaranteeing that information will be kept confidential, that people will be treated with respect, fairness, and equality, and that they will retain control over decision-making about their own lives. Finally, a code of ethics protects the user's right to receive competent services. Social work's code of ethics is illustrative.

SUMMARY OF THE MAJOR PRINCIPLES OF THE SOCIAL WORK CODE OF ETHICS

1 The social worker's conduct and comportment as a social worker
  a *Propriety.* The social worker should maintain high standards of personal conduct in the capacity or identity as social worker.
  b *Competence and professional development.* The social worker should strive to become and remain proficient in professional practice and the performance of professional functions.
  c *Service.* The social worker should regard as primary the service obligation of the social work profession.
  d *Integrity.* The social worker should act in accordance with the highest standards of professional integrity.
  e *Scholarship and research.* The social worker engaged in study and research should be guided by the conventions of scholarly inquiry.
2 The social worker's ethical responsibility to clients
  a *Primacy of clients' interest.* The social worker's primary responsibility is to clients.
  b *Rights and prerogatives of clients.* The social worker should make every effort to foster maximum self-determination on the part of clients.
  c *Confidentiality and privacy.* The social worker should respect the privacy of clients and hold in confidence all information obtained in the course of professional service.
  d *Fees.* When setting fees, the social worker should ensure that they are fair, reasonable, considerate, and commensurate with the service performed and with due regard for the clients' ability to pay.
3 The social worker's ethical responsibility to colleagues

  a *Respect, fairness, and courtesy.* The social worker should treat colleagues with respect, courtesy, fairness, and good faith.
  b *Dealing with colleagues' clients.* The social worker has the responsibility to relate to the clients of colleagues with full professional consideration.
4 The social worker's ethical responsibility to employers and employing organizations
  a *Commitments to employing organizations.* The social worker should adhere to commitments made to the employing organizations.
5 The social worker's ethical responsibility to the social work profession
  a *Maintaining the integrity of the profession.* The social worker should uphold and advance the values, ethics, knowledge, and mission of the profession.
  b *Community service.* The social worker should assist the profession in making social services available to the general public.
  c *Development of knowledge.* The social worker should take responsibility for identifying, developing, and fully utilizing knowledge for professional practice.
6 The social worker's ethical responsibility to society
  a *Promoting the general welfare.* The social worker should promote the general welfare of society.

Source: Adapted from NASW code of ethics. 1987. In *Encyclopedia of Social Work*, 18th ed., vol. II. Silver Spring, Md.: National Association of Social Workers, pp. 952–956.

Professions practice self-regulation and are granted autonomy. Professions claim the right and responsibility to monitor the behavior of their members. This makes them self-regulating and autonomous, meaning that control over the behavior of their members primarily occurs within the profession rather than from outside. You will recall that professions have a specialized knowledge base and that their practice is guided by their code of ethics. As a result, outsiders lack the knowledge to evaluate the work of professionals. For example, only those with medical training are likely to be able to evaluate whether a surgical procedure was competently performed.

Professionals accept the responsibility to monitor the behavior of their members to ensure ethical and competent behavior. Thus, professions operate with relatively little external control because, they argue, society can trust them to regulate themselves.

Of course, society does not grant professions complete autonomy. There are laws and procedures regulating certain aspects of professional behavior (King, 1988). One is the issuance of licenses. **Licensing** *is the legal control of the use of a title and the practice of a profession.* For example, only those licensed as physicians can call themselves by that title and can practice as physicians. Anyone who does either without the proper license is subject to arrest.

A somewhat less extensive form of regulation is certification. **Certification** *is the legal control of the use of a title only.* Those without certification as psychologists may not use that title in states where psychologists are certified. However, since only the title is protected, anyone can do what psychologists do just as long as they don't call themselves psychologists.

Society grants professions considerable autonomy, in part because of their commitment to helping and to high standards of competence and ethical behavior. On the other hand, as we all know, professionals are not perfect. In spite of their good intent, they too sometimes make mistakes. When this occurs, they may be sued, providing clients with a type of protection and society with a limited form of control. For the most part, though, professions regulate their own behavior.

Professions have their own associations. A professional association serves two major functions. One is to provide its members with a source of professional identity. It does so by providing a variety of services aimed at promoting professional growth and strengthening a sense of professionalism among its members. Most professional associations publish journals to disseminate research findings, set standards for professional education programs, lobby on behalf of the profession's interests in the political arena, and develop and implement a code of ethics. In addition, they may offer professional liability insurance, publish newsletters or other informal publications that focus on professional issues and news of the profession, and even offer study trips designed to contribute to professional enrichment.

A second function of professional associations is to promote and protect the profession's interests. This involves a variety of activities including political action and the use of media. Professional associations also seek to influence legal regulations affecting the profession and to develop internal procedures such as registration for regulating professional practice. **Professional registration** *is a list of names of people who have met specified professional standards.* It should be emphasized that registration does not have legal status, whereas licensing and title certification do. The National Association of Social Workers, for example, maintains separate lists of members who have registered as either Clinical Social Workers or as members of the Academy of Certified Social Workers. Those listed have all met registration requirements established by NASW. However, registration with NASW does not in and of itself provide the workers involved with legal standing in the same sense that a licensed or certified social worker has standing in the forty-one states that have one or the other procedure (*NASW News,* 1987).

To summarize briefly, we have seen that a profession has four distinctive characteristics: a specialized knowledge and skill base, a code of ethics that includes a commitment to service, a considerable degree of autonomy that includes self-regulation, and a professional association. Now we will look at some of the major helping professions. Each has all of the characteristics of a profession as described above, and each provides particular kinds of social welfare services.

MAJOR HELPING PROFESSIONS

There are many helping professions and many possible ways to classify them. We will examine the following professions and professional areas: social work, the physical health professions, the mental health professions, education, and the legal profession. Together these groups provide the majority of the workers involved in the delivery of social welfare services.

Although highly diverse in function and makeup, these professions share the common goal of improving the functioning of individuals and social institutions. While each group performs a particular specialized function or set of functions, their members are often called upon to work together in order to help people effectively. Similarly, they often cooperate in efforts to improve the social welfare institution through the political process. Nevertheless, we will also see that disputes sometimes arise over territorial boundaries, especially those concerning which profession should provide certain kinds of services to particular groups of people.

Social Work

Perhaps the single profession most closely identified with social welfare is social work. **Social work** *is a profession that uses a generalist approach to help people singly and in groups meet their survival and developmental needs.* According to government figures, there were approximately 443,000 social workers in the United States in 1980 (Scheurell, 1987:82).

Social workers often function as case managers, coordinating the delivery of a variety of services that together help people better meet their needs. Some social workers work in organizations or agencies that specialize in a particular service area such as hospitals, schools, or mental health clinics. Others work in organizations such as family service agencies or public departments of social services that offer a broad range of services to a varied clientele.

Social work's approach to the delivery of helping services has three distinctive characteristics:

An emphasis on problem solving. Social workers employ a systematic problem-solving process in carrying out their work. Consisting of a series of

steps, this process begins by involving the prospective user in the helping process, moves on to an assessment of needs and resources, and then to the development of a plan for resolving the problem. The resulting plan is then implemented and the results evaluated, after which the helping relationship either
ends or new plans are developed as necessary.

A systems focus. People live in groups of many kinds and sizes—families,
friendship groups, communities, organizations, bureaucracies, and social institutions, all of which may be viewed as systems. All of these systems affect the
conditions under which people live and their responses to the social and physical environment. Social workers consider these various systems in their assessment, planning, and intervention-related activities so that the problem-
solving process takes account of all relevant resources and obstacles. *This
focus on the many groups in which people live and the way in which these
groups affect people's lives is called a* **systems approach.**

An awareness of human diversity. Social workers work with many kinds of
people who differ in terms of gender, age, race, ethnicity, culture, lifestyle,
physical and mental abilities, socioeconomic status, education, religion, and so
on. Social workers are trained to respect, understand, and make use of these
distinctive characteristics in the problem-solving process.

Table 9.2 summarizes the goals and activities of social workers as described
in a recent study.

Social workers are found in a wide range of settings, such as public departments of social welfare, hospitals, family centers, schools, and mental health
centers. Some are self-employed, preferring to set up their own private practice in a manner similar to many physicians and lawyers. Social workers work
with all kinds of people, and are themselves sometimes stigmatized because of
the low status of many of the people to whom they provide services—a group
that includes the poor, substance abusers, unwed mothers, abusive adults, and
members of minority groups. Social work salaries vary widely, but a 1987
study by the National Association of Social Workers, the major professional
association, reported an average income of $27,800 among its members
(*NASW News,* 1987:1).

TABLE 9.2 THE GOALS AND ACTIVITIES OF SOCIAL WORKERS

Goal	Practice roles
Develop needed resources	Planner, policy and procedures developer, researcher
Maintain and enhance existing resources	Administrator and manager, consultant, supervisor, teacher and trainer, team manager
Link people with resources	Advocate, arbitrator, broker, case manager, mediator and negotiator, make referrals
Provide direct services to people	Work with individuals, groups, families, and communities

Source: Adapted from Lister (1987:385).

THE STATUS OF SOCIAL WORK: A FOUR-COUNTRY COMPARISON

The four nations that we have been using for comparative purposes in this book—the United States, Mexico, Poland, and Sweden—share some interesting similarities in the status of social workers.

Most social workers in the four countries are women. Relative to the standards of their respective societies, they receive modest salaries, and many feel they are relatively powerless to influence social policy. In spite of varying degrees of formal commitment to equality for women within their societies, many also feel that their low pay and lack of power reflect lingering sexism. Many social workers in all four societies also believe that human values are considered less important than economic issues by those in power.

There are, however, also differences in the beliefs of social workers in these four countries as to why members of their profession are not more highly valued and better rewarded. Social workers in Mexico and Poland tend to cite the presence of a certain degree of political repression as the likely explanation. Social workers in the United States are more likely to blame their profession's lack of

status on the conflict between capitalist and humanitarian values. Sweden seems to suffer from an ambiguous stance toward social work. On one hand, the value of social work to individuals and the society as a whole is widely recognized. On the other hand, there is a certain resentment of the high cost of the social welfare system. This ambivalence seems to translate into relatively low prestige and income for social workers.

The United States offers both baccalaureate and graduate-level training for social workers. Social work training in Sweden and Mexico is primarily carried out at the baccalaureate level, although a few graduate programs also exist. Most social work practitioners in Poland receive their training through 2-year technical programs, equivalent to our associate degree. Compared to the U.S. curriculum, social work programs in our other three nations include more time in agency-based field practicums and more classroom emphasis on the impact of political and economic systems on social welfare. Private practice by social workers is virtually unknown in Mexico, Poland, and Sweden.

The Physical Health Professions

There are many kinds of physical health professionals. In 1980, the two largest such groups in the United States were nurses (1,086,355) and physicians (373,782) (Scheurell, 1987:798). Other important groups of health professionals include dietitians, physical therapists, dentists, opticians, and anesthesiologists.

Several of these professions can be further broken down into a variety of more specialized subfields. Physicians, for example, may be further subdivided into specialists in such fields as family practice, gynecology, oncology, surgery, ophthalmology, and many others. Nurses, too, often specialize. One result of specialization in the medical profession is that family practitioners often function as case managers. In some cases, however, this function is performed by social workers who cooperate with medical professionals to oversee the delivery of a comprehensive physical health care plan.

Because it is so diverse, it is difficult to generalize about the work of medical professionals (see Table 9.3). Many, especially physicians, work in private or group practice settings. Health care is highly valued in the United States, and many health care professionals can expect to earn high salaries. For example, in 1985 the average salary for physicians in the United States was $106,300. For dentists in group practice it was $59,000, and for those in specialty practice $100,000 (*Occupational Outlook Handbook,* 1988:127,131).

TABLE 9.3   ACTIVITIES OF PHYSICAL HEALTH PROFESSIONALS

Medical diagnosis
Prescription of medication or treatment
Emergency first aid
Trace communicable diseases
Home care for the homebound
Dental treatment and surgery
Health education
School health services
Convalescent center care
Speech correction
Eye treatment and corrective lenses
Public health planning
Performing medical tests

Source: Based on Scheurell (1987) and other sources.

Other medical professionals, such as nurses, are not so well paid. The average annual earnings of full-time registered nurses in 1986 were about $23,900 (*Occupational Outlook Handbook,* 1988:152). In the case of physical therapists, average starting salaries in 1982 were approximately $20,000 per year and increased to approximately $40,000 for experienced therapists in private practice (*Careers Magazine,* 1984:19). The rise in **health maintenance organizations (HMOs),** *organizations that provide comprehensive medical care for a set, prepaid fee,* has tended to bring large numbers of medical personnel under corporate umbrellas where their salaries are generally less than in private practice.

Mexico, Poland, and Sweden provide free or low-cost medical care to their citizens. Medical professionals in these societies are generally less well paid than in the United States, where most medical care is provided on a for-profit basis. In societies which offer free or low-cost medical care, there is often a two-tier health care system consisting of the public system and a much more costly private system. In such cases, medical professionals in private practice are likely to earn far more, and the quality of private care is thought to be better. Generally speaking, although medicine tends everywhere to be a highly regarded profession, its status is less high in those societies where the public health care system predominates than in those with a primarily private system of health care.

The Mental Health Professions

Four professions specialize in providing help to people with psychological needs: psychiatry, psychology, psychiatric nursing, and psychiatric social work (Scheurell, 1987:659). It should be noted, however, that psychiatric nursing and psychiatric social work are specialties within the larger nursing and social work professions discussed above. Psychiatry is a branch of medicine,

TABLE 9.4   INDICATORS OF MEDICAL CARE IN FOUR SOCIETIES

	Mexico	Poland	Sweden	United States
Number of people per physician†	2,136	541	506	549
Number of people per hospital bed†	863	134	67	171
Infant mortality rate (1983)*	52	19	8	11
Life expectancy (1983)*	66	71	78	75

Sources: *Data from *The World Bank Atlas 1986.* 1986. Washington, D.C.: The World Bank, pp. 8–9.
†*Data for all countries except Sweden from *Statistical Abstract of the United States 1987,* Washington, D.C.: United States Government Printing Office, p. 822. The data are for the following years: Mexico, 1974; Poland, 1982; the United States, 1980. Data for Sweden are for 1981 and are from Richard Mayne, ed. 1986. *Western Europe.* New York: Facts on File Publishers.

and psychiatrists have medical as well as mental health training. As a result, they can prescribe medicine, whereas other mental health professionals cannot. In 1980 there were over 31,000 psychiatrists, nearly 91,000 psychologists, more than 48,000 psychiatric nurses, and over 96,000 psychiatric social workers (Scheurell, 1987:659–663).

Fees tend to reflect the differing levels of training. In 1985, the average fee for a 50-minute private session was $90 for psychiatrists, $65 for psychologists, and $50 for psychiatric social workers (Goleman, 1985). These mental health professionals often work collaboratively. Psychologists or social workers who have private practices may have a professional relationship with a psychiatrist who helps with diagnoses, prescribes medication when needed, and provides consultation services. Of course many psychiatrists, psychologists, and psychiatric social workers are employed in agencies such as mental hospitals and mental health centers. Psychiatric nurses are primarily employed in these settings.

Education

Teachers are by far the largest professional group in the field of education. In 1980, there were close to 4 million kindergarten, primary, secondary, and

TABLE 9.5   ACTIVITIES OF MENTAL HEALTH PROFESSIONALS

Diagnosis and evaluation of mental illness
Individual and group therapy
Testing and measurement of psychological functioning
Care in mental hospitals and mental health clinics
Family and marital therapy
Predischarge planning and postrelease follow-up
Counseling
Supervision of mental health aides
Behavior modification
Community mental health education

postsecondary teachers in the United States (Scheurell, 1987:266), and an additional 18,000 special education teachers who work with those with special learning needs. There were also close to 500,000 educational administrators, almost 147,000 of whom were educational and vocational counselors. In addition, there is a large number of paraprofessionals who work as teacher's aides and child care workers.

Some teachers specialize in a particular subject area or the learning needs of particular students. At the secondary and higher levels, teachers usually have specialized training in particular subject areas. Other teachers are trained to work with special populations, such as the retarded, learning disabled, emotionally disturbed, or autistic. Teachers generally have to have state or local certification to hold regular teaching positions. Pay scales vary tremendously, in part because most teachers are employed by local school districts. However, in 1985–1986 public secondary school teachers averaged $26,080 a year (*Occupational Outlook Handbook,* 1988:122). In general, teachers in higher education earn more than their elementary or secondary level counterparts, but this is not always true.

Education provides a good example of the continuum of professionalism. Many of those who teach are not trained as teachers. For example, many in-service, community education, and art courses are taught by people who are experts or practitioners in the subject area but have not been trained as teachers. The need for professional qualifications and certification is, in fact, sometimes challenged by those who lack such credentials but are employed in a teaching capacity. This can pose a problem for the profession.

This is particularly likely to occur when nonprofessionals employed in a teaching capacity perform poorly. In such cases, the public at large may fail to recognize that the individual involved is *not* a trained professional, with the result that his or her poor performance has an adverse effect on people's opinion of the education profession. It is the desire to prevent situations of this sort that explains why professions are often so protective of their titles, functions, and training procedures.

The Legal Profession

Many people would probably not consider the law a helping profession. Certainly the commercial transactions that account for a significant proportion of the profession's activities are often wholly unrelated to social welfare. Nonetheless, the law helps people to meet their needs in a variety of important ways. Members of the legal profession make important contributions in such areas as civil rights, consumer protection, child welfare, and the enforcement of legal contracts affecting families and individuals.

Lawyers and judges dominate the legal professions. In 1980 there were over 490,000 lawyers and over 27,000 judges in the United States (Scheurell, 1987:372,429). Attorneys work in a variety of settings including government agencies, private practice, and Legal Aid offices that provide free or low-cost legal help to those unable to afford a lawyer. Judges preside over the public and administrative court systems. As such, they are invariably public officials but the majority are appointed rather than elected to office.

The salary of attorneys employed in the private sector is likely to be much higher than that of their counterparts in government or legal aid work. Starting salaries for attorneys in private industry averaged nearly $31,000 in 1986, while their most experienced counterparts earned over $101,000 (*Occupational Outlook Handbook,* 1988:87). Those employed in the public sector earn much less (see "The Human Face of Social Welfare" below).

The wide range of activities open to lawyers means that involvement in helping people is very much a matter of individual choice. Attorneys are generally free to choose an area of practice, and the available choices range from work in a Legal Aid agency through corporate law. Whatever the attorney's area of practice, he or she will be subject to professional standards. However, whereas the Legal Aid attorney is clearly involved in social welfare, the corporate attorney is generally not.

The same choices exist in other professions. In selecting an area of practice, doctors can choose to help those who are needy or to enter an area of practice such as cosmetic surgery where their clientele is primarily the wealthy. The medical profession, like the law, encompasses a range of activities, some of which are directly related to social welfare goals and others which are not. For the members of many of the professions described here, involvement with the social welfare institution is a matter of individual choice rather than professional affiliation.

THE ROLE OF THE PARAPROFESSIONAL

Not all of the people who work in social welfare are professionals. Many are paraprofessionals. **Paraprofessionals** *are persons with work experience or specialized training who are generally trained to assist professionals but do not themselves have professional training and credentials.* Among the types of paraprofessionals in social welfare are mental health technicians, health aides, social work aides, substance abuse counselors, recreational therapists, and teacher's aides. Paraprofessionals perform important service delivery activities, but they have not had the training required for professional certification or licensing.

The manner in which paraprofessionals are sometimes used in social welfare has raised the issues of sexism and racism. Many paraprofessionals are minority women, for whom professional education has been an unrealistic goal given their economic resources and life situation. Lacking professional status, they have been less well paid and their positions are among the first to be eliminated during budgetary cutbacks. In addition, the pattern of generally white, often male, professionals supervising minority women has seemed all too representative of discriminatory social patterns in the larger society.

THE HUMAN FACE OF SOCIAL WELFARE 18

A Do-Gooder Lawyer

The following account is by a father who is reminiscing about his son's career as an attorney. It captures the social welfare dimensions of the law profession, as well as some of the societal ambivalence about doing good versus being economically successful.

On March 13 my son won his first case in federal court. He was 26 years old, and I was damn proud of him, but by then he'd changed my point of view. Frankly, I despaired when he turned down a $66,000 job with a Wall Street law firm—that's what they were paying highly ranked law-school graduates in June of 1986. Chris chose instead to work for the Legal Aid Society's Office for the Aging in Brooklyn, N.Y.

It shouldn't have been a surprise. One summer I got him a job with the firm of Cravath, Swaine & Moore, where he worked on the massive IBM antitrust case. He was unimpressed. Despite the modest stipend, he preferred working for the Center for Constitutional Rights, with the likes of William Kunstler. Or for the NOW Legal Defense and Education Fund. Or for the Connecticut Legal Services—for nothing.

I suppose other fathers of sons who have chosen to do good instead of well can understand my concern. I paid $80,000 for his undergraduate and graduate education (he still has $10,000 in student loans to repay). And the rejection of a high-salaried job seemed to me, a man born in the Depression year of 1934, an affront to common sense. Add to that my dislike of the idea of government helping community groups sue the government. All in all, I was troubled about my son's future.

But there was another lesson to be learned from the 1930s—indeed from some 1,900 years before that. If I was so down on do-gooders, Chris asked, where did this Christianity stuff that I and William F. Buckley profess fit in?

The case my son won in federal district court was one of those Simon Legree situations regularly created by the U.S. Department of Health and Human Services. Chris represented an 86-year-old man who had been refused a much-needed supplement to his social security because he owned a house. But the house was uninhabitable. Vandals reduced it to a pile of junk after its owner was hospitalized. Even so, a social-security administrative judge said, it was a house. Had not Chris and his colleagues brought the suit, that ruling would have prevailed.

Chris spends an enormous amount of his time in Brooklyn's housing court, a place a reporter once described as seething with anger, potential violence and marginally ill people. He thinks the reporter underplayed the chaos. He says the courtroom makes the station house in "Hill Street Blues" look orderly. It is hardly a place where his clients would stand a chance without a smart, dedicated and well-trained advocate.

These are some of the people I'm talking about:

A 70-year-old widow whose landlord presented her with a lump-sum bill for $4,000 after he discovered that for seven years he had been charging her less than he could have under New York's complicated rent-control program. When she couldn't pay it, he brought eviction proceedings against her, even though she had always paid the monthly rent she was charged.

A 64-year-old terminally ill woman received a 72-hour eviction notice after a proceeding against her. She had no knowledge of the lawsuit; therefore she had not opposed it, and a default judgment had been entered against her.

In this last case, the issue was nonpayment of rent, and Chris's client didn't have the money to pay it. His job was not only to represent her in court but to go to the city's welfare department for an emergency grant that would keep her from becoming homeless. Often, just a few hundred dollars can save the city the cost of a welfare hotel where the charges can be $20,000 a room or more a year.

Chris's workweek frequently begins on Sunday. One recent Sunday he went to the office to write a brief for an elderly Russian woman. Despite the fact that she rented her apartment from a relative, she was eligible for a housing benefit, but the statute of limitations required a Tuesday filing. On Monday a sympathetic secretary agreed to stay late to type the brief. Chris's client arrived still later and the document was read in Russian so she could understand what she was signing. He left his office at 10 P.M.

He made his filing deadline on Tuesday. He also stopped off in Brooklyn's housing court where he met with a client who refused to sign a lease that Legal Aid had painstakingly negotiated for him. The man had agreed to it, thus ending a dispute with his landlord that threatened him with homelessness. But Chris couldn't persuade him to sign it. The client's daughter couldn't get him to sign. Only Chris's supervisor, who had worked on the man's legal problems for four years, was able to overcome his suspicion.

Back at his office, Chris found a message to call another client, who told the secretary she couldn't remember her own phone number. At that moment, my son says, he envied a female acquaintance who took a job like the one he turned down. It wasn't the work she described; she hates it. And it wasn't the money; he says he gets along just fine on $29,749. But he figured that her clients probably sign the leases they have agreed to and know their own phone numbers. That flash of regret passed and he looked up his new client's phone number....

From James Lamb, Jr. 1987. My son, the do-gooder. *Newsweek,* November 16, pp. 14–15. Copyright (c) 1987, Newsweek, Inc. All rights reserved. Reprinted by permission.

As a result, some schools have developed programs designed to help talented paraprofessionals obtain additional training. The most common such programs are the 2-year Human Service Programs that offer an associate degree. For many workers, these programs have served as a stepping-stone to baccalaureate or even graduate-level training in one of the social welfare professions.

Declassification

The availability of a growing workforce of skilled paraprofessionals has presented a tempting opportunity for many social agencies suffering from budget cutbacks. That opportunity took the form of **declassification,** *the lowering of the credentials needed to perform specified tasks*. By declassifying positions that had heretofore been held by professionals, and then hiring paraprofessionals to fill these positions, public agencies could both respond to political pressure from paraprofessional groups and save on salaries. As a result, many public agencies did precisely this, declassifying positions to make them available to paraprofessionals.

Declassification itself is not necessarily undesirable. It becomes so when the qualifications necessary for a particular position are determined by the desire to save money or are a response to political pressure. The qualifications needed for any position should be the result of a careful analysis of the tasks to be accomplished. Some tasks are appropriate for paraprofessionals, some for entry-level professionals, and others for more experienced professionals. Ensuring that the qualifications established for each position within a given agency or organization are appropriate to the tasks to be performed is a goal still being sought by professions such as social work and teaching.

OTHER PEOPLE WHO DELIVER SOCIAL WELFARE SERVICES

Having examined the structure of several major helping professions, let's turn to others involved in helping people. We have seen at many points in this book that not all social welfare services are provided by professionals. Among the nonprofessionals who are important to the delivery of helping services are those involved in natural helping networks and volunteers.

Natural Helping Networks

As you already know, natural helping networks are comprised of people who help others in the course of their day-to-day activities. Family members, friends, colleagues at work, and neighbors are often part of such networks. Sometimes the help provided is purely spontaneous, as when a neighbor offers to babysit so that you can respond to an unexpected situation. Other such helping efforts are more planned. Neighbors may form a carpool to transport children to and from school, or people who work together may form a support group to discuss work or family-related stresses.

Natural helping networks result from the interpersonal bonds formed among small groups of people due to common family ties, shared interests, or a sense of community. The efforts of those involved are frequently not viewed as part of a helping network but rather as simply part of being a good neighbor or a good friend. The desire to help in such cases arises from a personal commitment to people one likes and cares about, not from a larger sense of societal obligation. Within such networks there is often a sense of mutual responsibility; those providing help often believe that others would in turn help them if the need arose.

Although informal, natural helping networks are vital to successful daily living for most people. They are also critical for maintaining a society's sense of cohesion and mutual responsibility.

Volunteers

Volunteers perform a more formal helping role because they work within some type of organized social welfare program. The program itself can be fairly loosely organized, such as a church-run soup kitchen. But inherent in the volunteer role is a formal commitment to perform certain functions at certain times within some organized structure. The use of volunteers is usually seen to have three major benefits: (1) Social welfare programs are better able to provide services to people, (2) people's needs are met more effectively, and (3) the volunteers themselves derive satisfaction and personal growth from their work.

Some organizations rely very heavily on volunteers. The Red Cross, for example, uses more than 1.4 million volunteers nationwide in such settings as community health clinics, child-care centers, and hospitals, during blood drives, in disaster situations, and others (American Red Cross, 1984:9). The volunteers are trained and perform under the supervision of social welfare professionals. Their contribution is an important one. Without the help of volunteers, the Red Cross could not provide the services it does.

Volunteering, then, is a second level of personal helping. It is more formal than the helping in natural helping networks. It is also more directly linked to a larger sense of responsibility for the well-being of others than is participation in a natural helping network, since volunteers often help people they are unlikely to know on a personal basis.

Cooperation between Professionals and Others

Professionals and nonprofessionals work together in many social welfare programs. An excellent example of such a program is Elderplan, a nonprofit experimental program to help the elderly remain independent as long as possible (Freudenheim, 1986). Similar in function to a health maintenance organization, it provides both social and medical services. Its purpose is to provide physical health, mental health, and personal care services that supplement those provided by the elderly person's natural helping network, especially family and friends. It is designed to work in conjunction with the natural helping network, stepping in only to assist with needs that exceed the network's resources.

Ideally, the Elderplan pattern would be the norm in social welfare programs, that is, the efforts of professionals would be designed to supplement the natural helping network and the work of volunteers (Miller, 1985). This is not always easy. In some cases, it can be difficult for professionals even to determine who the members of the client's natural helping network are. Some of these people may be reluctant to become involved with professionals. It may frighten them, and they may not think of their own activity as "helping." The amount of time and effort required to identify and make contact with these people may strain the resources of often overworked professionals.

Volunteers are generally more accessible and the results of working with them more predictable. Even so, issues can arise. Unless adequately trained by the agency, volunteers may make mistakes that take time and effort to correct. Further, the task of figuring out how to help volunteers function effectively and make the best use of their skills is itself a time-consuming task.

In spite of these problems, the contributions to social welfare of each of the groups we have discussed—natural helping networks, volunteers, paraprofessionals, and professionals—are significant. Each has a special role to play. Natural helping networks are best suited to providing relatively limited types of help needed in daily situations. Volunteers provide a personal touch and valuable extra hands in often hard-pressed social welfare agencies. Paraprofessionals bring a special combination of skill, motivation, and life experience to the helping situation. Professionals have the special knowledge, skill, and commitment required to plan and deliver the services that make large-scale helping possible. Working together, each group contributes to the strengthening of society's commitment to interpersonal caring and helping.

FINDING A PLACE FOR YOURSELF IN SOCIAL WELFARE

The Responsibility for Helping

The extent of our responsibility for helping others is something each of us must decide for ourselves. That decision will, in turn, determine much of our behavior toward others. If we believe that we are responsible for others, we will be far more likely to attempt to help than we will if we believe other people should care for themselves. The choice is ours. Although clearly written from the point of view that people should feel a sense of responsibility for others, this book also reflects another basic social welfare value—people have the right to make their own decisions.

Opportunities to Help

If you are one of those who feel a responsibility for helping others, you may wonder how you can act upon your belief. People sometimes don't know how to go about helping others. Actually, opportunities to help surround us. They range from involvement with our own natural helping networks through the decision to enter a social welfare profession. Let's look a little more closely at this spectrum of opportunities.

Day-to-day situations in which we can be helpful abound. Remember that helping is not always written with a capital ''H'' and does not always involve a dramatic or life-threatening event. There are countless small opportunities to help others. Giving directions to a stranger, taking a moment to listen to someone momentarily frightened by the loss of her or his money, smiling at a friend who seems glum, touching a family member to let them know you care, all these and more are examples of helping. To be sure, you may someday happen upon an automobile accident where you can aid someone who is seriously injured, but you are more likely to spend most of your days with people buffeted by the stresses of daily life. Reaching out to others in small ways is very much a part of helping. We should also not overlook the fact that helping can be done by contributing money or other needed goods. Sometimes people feel they are too busy, under too much pressure, or too shy to reach out to others personally. For such people, contributing to programs run by others is a useful and legitimate alternative to personal involvement. Community fund-raising efforts such as the United Way provide excellent opportunities to help in this way. Although the satisfactions involved are different from those provided by more personal helping, giving is a significant expression of one's commitment to the well-being of others.

Many people prefer to focus their helping activities on those to whom they feel a special commitment. Family members may devote extraordinary time and energy to the care of a child with physical or mental limitations, for example. These efforts may include involvement with support groups run for parents of children with special problems, fund-raising activities to support research or expanded services, and activities run by social agencies for children like theirs.

A similar pattern of involvement is often found among groups whose members share a characteristic that makes them a target of discrimination. Some blacks are particularly active in efforts to help other blacks, while gay and lesbian people are apt to be especially attracted to activities designed to help members of their own group. This kind of group cohesiveness has historically been an important impetus for the development of social welfare services.

Another possible avenue for involvement with social welfare is to advocate for people's rights. Often this begins with increased self-awareness and greater personal strength. For example, it has been difficult to get men and women to understand how sexism affects their own lives. Once understood, it is not easy for many people to develop the strength to refuse being treated in a sexist manner. However, it is the cumulative effect of people standing up for their rights that increases the likelihood of social change. The civil rights movement initi-

---

ON THE STREET IN CUERNAVACA, MEXICO
The Olga Tamayo Home

Tucked in the shadow of a large hospital in a busy section of Cuernavaca is a one-story modern white building. Called the Olga Tamayo Nursing Home, it is an interesting example of how one person can contribute to the well-being of others through a financial donation.

The home was built with money donated by the Mexican artist Rufino Tamayo, famous for his public murals depicting historical themes connected with the country's Indian heritage and its Revolution. Tamayo's money created the facility, which is named in honor of his wife, and the government now runs it. It is part of the social welfare structure available to government workers or, in the case of the Olga Tamayo Home, retired government employees.

What the artist's donation made possible is a lovely facility serving fifty-five residential elderly people and sixteen day users. It has a staff of 125, and provides comprehensive services to meet the needs of its clients—housing, medical care, therapy, recreation, and so on. Residents share double rooms, each with its own patio and small garden. The public areas include a spacious and airy dining room, lounges, and a large auditorium. In addition, there are facilities for medical care and therapy. It is located in an area where the elderly can walk to shopping if they wish.

Mexico's economic difficulties have limited the public sector's ability to meet the nation's social welfare needs. In such an environment, initiatives by private citizens, such as Rufino Tamayo, provide resources that would otherwise be unavailable. Although the needs of many Mexicans remain unmet, such contributions are nonetheless beneficial to the social welfare system.

ated by blacks illustrated this in a powerful way. Since respecting people's rights is so basic to social welfare, any progress in this area strengthens the entire social welfare institution.

In a democracy, being an informed participant in debates and decision-making about social welfare is another way to help. In order to do so effectively, you must first have a basic understanding of social welfare issues. As we have seen, these often involve sensitive and sometimes painful value-related questions that many would rather not examine closely.

In dealing with such questions, the natural tendency is to fall back on one's assumptions and reject relevant factual information. This, however, only tends to perpetuate stereotypes that prevent the adoption of more effective solutions to social welfare problems. Progress in the area of social welfare requires an informed population that plays an active role in societal decision-making. When citizens don't participate in such decision-making, they permit others to determine social welfare policy (and many other aspects of social life).

Beyond informal helping and participation in social welfare decision-making, one can volunteer. As you have seen, becoming a volunteer involves a commitment to work within a particular social welfare agency or program. Aside from the satisfaction that comes from knowing you are improving the delivery of services, you will benefit from learning new skills and meeting new people. Volunteering can be a very rewarding experience.

Finally, you can choose to become a social welfare professional. If so, you will devote much of your time and energy to trying to improve people's lives, and to enabling them to better manage their own lives. The social welfare professions offer you many opportunities to work with others in whatever ways are most appealing. The opportunities to help, then, are boundless. No matter what kind of life you choose for yourself, you can include helping activities. Whether and how you wish to do so is your choice.

LET'S REVIEW

This chapter has focused on the helping professions. We began by looking at the common goals of helping professions—improving social functioning and individual well-being. These goals can be met most effectively through the combined efforts of professional generalists and specialists. The chapter then explored the meaning of a profession, emphasizing the difference between a job and a profession. The profession's specialized knowledge and skill base, its code of ethics, self-regulation and autonomy, and its reliance on a professional association were shown to be its major defining characteristics.

Five social welfare professions were briefly discussed so that you would have a sense of the activities and rewards of each. They are social work, the physical health professions, the mental health professions, education, and the legal professions. Some of the issues noted in passing included ways in which professions overlap and relate to each other, and the use of professional credentialing to protect title and function. The role of paraprofessionals and issues related to declassification were also addressed. The interaction of natural helping networks, volunteers, paraprofessionals, and professionals was shown to be of great importance for the creation of an effective comprehensive service delivery system.

The chapter concluded with an effort to personalize involvement in social welfare activities. For people who believe that we all share responsibility for the well-being of others, there is a broad spectrum of possible helping activities. These vary in scope in terms of whom we choose to help and the degree of formality involved in how we help. Nevertheless, all provide an opportunity to act out one's personal sense of commitment to others.

Where do we go from here? This chapter has perhaps given you some ideas where your own life might go in relationship to social welfare. But in the next chapter we'll try to take a broader look—where should society go?

CHAPTER OUTLINE

WHAT TO EXPECT FROM THIS CHAPTER

LEARNING OBJECTIVES

THE FUNCTIONS OF THE HELPING PROFESSIONS
    The Generalist Approach
    The Specialist Approach
    Future Prospects

THE NATURE OF PROFESSIONS
    Summary of the Major Principles of the Social Work Code of
      Ethics

MAJOR HELPING PROFESSIONS
    Social Work
    The Status of Social Work: A Four-Country Comparison
    The Physical Health Professions
    The Mental Health Professions
    Education
    The Legal Profession
    The Human Face of Social Welfare 18: A Do-Gooder Lawyer

THE ROLE OF THE PARAPROFESSIONAL
    Declassification

OTHER PEOPLE WHO DELIVER SOCIAL WELFARE SERVICES
    Natural Helping Networks
    Volunteers
    Cooperation Between Professionals and Others

FINDING A PLACE FOR YOURSELF IN SOCIAL WELFARE
    The Responsibility for Helping
    Opportunities to Help
    On the Street in Cuernavaca: The Olga Tamayo Home

LET'S REVIEW

STUDY QUESTIONS

1 Select one of the social welfare professions discussed in this chapter. Go to the library and research it, getting information about the training and education needed, the kinds of jobs available, the specific tasks involved, and salary levels. Then write a short paper describing your reactions to the information you have obtained. Focus on whether the profession is what you thought it would be, and how you now feel about it.

2 Visit an agency in your community that uses volunteers. Find out what volunteers do, and what kind of training and supervision they receive. Then make arrangements to interview a volunteer to find out what he or she likes and dislikes about the work. Also, try to find out the person's motivations for volunteering. To what degree is the motivation personal, and to what degree does the volunteer see the work as a contribution to the well-being of others?

3 Select a profession that interests you and contact its professional association (your instructor or the reference librarian can help you locate its name and address). Ask the association to send you the profession's code of ethics and a description of the services available to members. Compare this information with the information obtained by your classmates from at least one other professional association. What are the similarities and differences in this material? What do you think these similarities and differences tell you about the professions involved?

4 Write a one-paragraph statement explaining your current thinking about the responsibility you feel for helping others. If you feel such a responsibility, select one of the opportunities to help discussed in the chapter and write a short essay on how you could implement it in your own life.

5 Based on your personal experiences, do you think that professions effectively regulate the activities of their members? Give specific examples to support your position. Do you think that licensing of professionals is necessary and effective? Could you suggest additional or alternative strategies to regulate professional behavior?

KEY TERMS AND CONCEPTS

case manager
certification
code of ethics
declassification
generalist approach
health maintenance organizations
   (HMOs)

licensing
paraprofessionals
professional registration
social work
specialist approach
systems approach

SUGGESTED READINGS

Davies, Martin. 1981. *The Essential Social Worker*. London: Heinemann Educational Books. Although published in England, this book provides a realistic sense of what it is like to be a social worker in any society. It presents a good balance between personal, organizational, and structural issues that social workers face in their work.

Guzzetta, Charles, with Arthur Katz and Richard English, eds. 1984. *Education for Social Work Practice: Selected International Models*. Washington, D.C.: Council on

Social Work Education. The articles in this book explore different approaches to educating and deploying social work professionals. They raise stimulating issues about the most effective strategies for training social welfare professionals, and about the most effective uses of such people in society.

Lubove, Roy. 1969. *The Professional Altruist*. New York: Atheneum Press. This classic study of the development of the profession of social work provides insight into the political, economic, and interpersonal factors that influence professions. It explores in some detail how professions support their claim to specialized knowledge and self-regulation.

Scheurell, Robert. 1987. *Introduction to Human Services*. Lanham, Md.: University Press of America. This book provides valuable data about the size, composition, and functions of the social welfare professions. It also includes important information about paraprofessionals and the ways in which paraprofessionals help support professional functioning.

U.S. Department of Labor. 1988. *Occupational Outlook Handbook*. Washington, D.C.: U.S. Government Printing Office. This government publication provides detailed information about all social welfare occupations including tasks performed, training required, salaries, and employment projections. It is an excellent reference for those interested in exploring specific social welfare careers.

REFERENCES

American Red Cross. 1984. *What You Should Know About Your Red Cross*. Pamphlet published by the American Red Cross.

Davies, Martin. 1981. *The Essential Social Worker*. London: Heinemann Educational Books.

Freudenheim, Milt. 1986. Health plan helps elderly to stay at home. *The New York Times,* December 27, p. 17.

Goleman, Daniel. 1985. Social workers vault into a leading role in psychotherapy. *The New York Times,* April 30, p. c1ff.

Guzzetta, Charles, with Arthur Katz and Richard English, eds. 1984. *Education for Social Work Practice: Selected International Models*. Washington, D.C.: Council on Social Work Education.

Hall, Richard. 1968. Professionalization and bureaucratization. *American Sociological Review,* 33 (February):92–104.

Helping hands are in short supply across the nation. 1984. *Careers Magazine,* 4, no. 2 (Fall):18–19.

Khinduka, S. K. 1987. Social work and the human services. In *Encyclopedia of Social Work,* 18th ed. Silver Spring, Md.: National Association of Social Workers, pp. 681–695.

King, Lisa. 1988. Certification, licensure, and legitimacy. *Footnotes,* 16, no. 1 (January):11.

Lamb, Jr., James. 1987. My son, the do-gooder. *Newsweek,* November 16, pp. 14–15.

Lister, Larry. 1987. Contemporary direct practice roles. *Social Work,* 32, no. 5 (October–November):385–390.

Lubove, Roy. 1969. *The Professional Altruist*. New York: Atheneum Press.

Miller, Pamela. 1985. Professional use of lay resources. *Social Work,* 30, no. 5 (September–October):409–416.

Mississippi passes licensure statute; total climbs to 41. 1987. *NASW News,* 32, no. 5 (May):9.

Pecora, Peter, and Michael Austin. 1983. Declassification of social service jobs: Issues and strategies. *Social Work,* 28, no. 6 (November–December):421–426.

Projections of popular jobs. 1986. *The New York Times,* March 23, p. 16W/C.

Scheurell, Robert. 1987. *Introduction to Human Services.* Lanham, Md.: University Press of America.

U.S. Department of Labor. 1988. *Occupational Outlook Handbook.* Washington, D.C.: U.S. Government Printing Office.

Wilkerson, Isabel. 1987. Schools of social work swamped by applicants. *The New York Times,* November 9, p. A17.

CHAPTER 10

WHAT IS THE FUTURE OF SOCIAL WELFARE?

INTRODUCTION

This chapter has a different purpose and structure than those you have already completed. Its purpose is to share with you my thinking about the future of social welfare in the United States. In other chapters, I have tried to be generally neutral about issues, seeking instead to provide you with an overview of the basic facts about social welfare, particularly in the United States. Now you are ready to begin formulating your own positions about social welfare and its future. Remember that social welfare is about choices. With your new knowledge, you are ready to make informed choices.

To help you think about these choices, this chapter will discuss a variety of issues and concerns that seem to me to be important to the future of social welfare. We will identify ongoing and emerging social concerns, explore how the social welfare system itself can be strengthened, and develop a clear vision about what social welfare's future role should be.

Because this chapter is based on my perspectives rather than commonly accepted theory and data, it will take the form of a dialogue between us. Unfortunately, the limitations of a book format will make the dialogue one way. It will, therefore, be up to you to identify and sort out your own reactions as you go along. And if, upon conclusion, you'd like to write and engage in a real dialogue, I would be delighted to hear from you. You can write to me at Iona College, 715 North Avenue, New Rochelle, New York 10801. In any case, I hope the following discussion stimulates you to develop your own ideas and your own plans for action.

ENDURING SOCIAL CONCERNS

In talking about his life living as a runaway on the streets of San Francisco, a teenager said, "That's what street life is like. You learn to survive. But you also learn not to care if you don't" (Axthelm, 1988:66). For me, his comment captures the essence of why we must continue the struggle to solve social problems. As a social welfare professional, I deeply respect the strength that people exhibit. Even when faced with terrible living conditions and little hope, most people continue to seek better lives. However, underlying such efforts there is often a desperation and a feeling of worthlessness that translates into a fatal alienation. Under such conditions, the conventional rules may seem irrelevant. What reason is there not to commit suicide, or even awful crimes against others? What does it matter?

Social problems do take a toll, and a dreadful one. People's lives are diminished or destroyed. Society is disrupted by the behavior of those who no longer care, or are so damaged that they cannot function in acceptable ways. Our society continues to suffer from serious problems, some of them long-standing and others more recent. In this section, I would like to discuss briefly those problems that I believe most need serious attention in the years ahead.

Poverty and Other Effects of Injustice.

The paradox of entrenched poverty amidst plenty in the United States continues to haunt the lives of millions of people. Government figures reveal that, in 1985, 33.1 million people, or 14 percent of the population, were below the poverty level* (Statistical Abstract, 1987:442). These same figures also show a widening gap between the incomes of the rich and the poor, as Table 10.1 demonstrates.

The data in Table 10.1 suggest that the wealthy receive an increasing share of the nation's income. Other indicators confirm this. In 1986, for example, "...the top 10 percent of income receivers owned 85 percent of publicly traded stock, 92 percent of mutual bonds, 72 percent of all other bonds, [and] 80 percent of mutual funds....Families in the top 1 percent of the income dis-

---

*In 1989, The official United States government poverty level was $5,960 per year for a single person, or $12,100 for a family of four. The poverty level represents the minimum income needed to meet people's minimal basic needs, such as food, shelter, and clothing.

TABLE 10.1   THE DISTRIBUTION OF INCOME IN THE UNITED STATES

Income group by quintile	Percent ot total money income		
	1960	1975	1984
Lowest fifth	4.8	5.4	4.7
Second fifth	12.2	11.8	11.0
Third fifth	17.8	17.6	17.0
Fourth fifth	23.7	23.9	24.4
Highest fifth	40.7	40.7	42.9
Top five percent	15.7	15.4	16.0

Source: Summer Rosen, David Fanshel, and Mary Lutz, eds. 1987. Face of the Nation 1987. Statistical Supplement to the 18th edition of the *Encyclopedia of Social Work.* Silver Spring, Md.: National Association of Social Workers, p. 16.

tribution held 19 percent of all assets and 34 percent of financial assets''
(Rosen et al., 1987:13). Inequality of income is, therefore, increasing in the
United States, not decreasing.

Further, poverty continues to afflict certain groups much more than others.
Blacks, some Hispanic groups, and female-headed families comprise a disproportionate share of those living in poverty. So too do rural residents, who are
also more frequent victims of poverty than the population as a whole
(McCormick, 1988). The poverty problem for women has become so serious
that it now even has a name: the feminization of poverty (Bane, 1988; Pearce,
1978). Of all the groups that have traditionally suffered from poverty, only the
elderly have made substantial progress in improving their economic situation
over the past few decades. Table 10.2 documents the differential incidence of
poverty.

TABLE 10.2   POVERTY IN THE UNITED STATES

Group	Percent of group members in poverty			
	1960	1970	1980	1985
Total population	22.2	12.6	13.0	14.0
People age 65 and over	NA	24.6	15.7	12.6
Black people	55.1*	33.5	32.5	31.3
Black people in families headed by women	70.6*	58.7	53.4	53.2
Spanish origin people	NA†	21.9‡	25.7	29.0
Spanish origin people in families headed by women	NA†	57.4‡	54.5	55.7
White people	17.8	9.9	10.2	11.4
White people in families headed by women	39.0	28.4	28.0	29.8

*Data are for the year 1959 instead of 1960.
†Data not available for this group for this year.
‡Data are for the year 1973 instead of 1970.
Source: U.S. Bureau of the Census, *Current Population Reports,* Series P-60, no. 154. Money Income and Poverty Status of Families and Persons in the United States: 1985 (Advance Data from the March 1986 Current Population Survey. Washington, D.C.: U.S. Government Printing Office.

The effects of poverty are well known. These include stunted physical growth, psychological stress, social isolation, alienation, and increased risk of disease and violent death. We also know that poverty can become entrenched in communities and families, and that the costs of current programs that maintain the poor represent a continuing drain on society's financial resources. Yet, as great as the cost of these programs may be, the social costs of our failure to end poverty—the wasted lives and the contributions forgone—are far greater still. Only if we are prepared to address seriously its systemic causes will we be able to help people break out of the patterns that perpetuate poverty.

In my opinion, it is increasingly important that we make this effort. As we have seen, the distance between the poor and the wealthy in the United States is increasing. We are becoming a polarized society with an increasing number of very rich, an increasing number of very poor, and a shrinking middle class.

This polarization is troublesome. We know from observing other societies all over the world that the most common result of polarization is crime and alienation. Once poverty is seen as inevitable and unchangeable, those who are poor have little incentive to respect societal norms. Instead, they can only attempt to survive in whatever way they can, giving little concern to a future that may or may not exist. In response, society becomes increasingly repressive and uncaring, seeking only to stop crime by whatever means are necessary and to separate those who are well-off from the unpleasant realities of life as experienced by the poor. The potential result of polarization is a widening gulf between socioeconomic classes and an erosion of society's commitment to human life and social justice (Butterfield, 1988).

Efforts to reduce or eliminate poverty must be linked with changes in all the institutions of society (Hochschild, 1988). This is a large and politically sensitive task. History has shown that those who benefit from the existing social system are often reluctant to change it (Weir et al., 1988). This certainly seems to be true in the United States where it has been extremely difficult to obtain the cooperation of those groups such as unions and corporations whose assistance is needed to open up meaningful employment opportunities for the poor. In addition, conflicts between racial, ethnic, and socioeconomic groups have taken their toll at the community level where schooling and many other social welfare services are delivered. Providing the poor with access to quality education is a powerful tool for moving them into the mainstream of society (Sheahan, 1987:23–48). Unfortunately, the public education system in the United States has increasingly come to reflect economic divisions rather than helping to reduce them.

Poverty continues because we allow it to. The unequal way in which it affects different groups is also something we allow. There is no doubt that the perpetuation of these patterns weakens society. Indeed, in my opinion, our society's economic vitality and productivity is increasingly being impaired by poverty and discrimination. People who are ill, alienated, uneducated, or addicted are rarely effective participants in an urbanized, high-tech society.

Solving such problems will require a new consensus about the importance of human life and social justice. It will also entail painful and controversial decisions to redistribute resources and opportunities from those who are most privileged in our society to those who are at its fringes. This is one of the goals of the social welfare system, but its realization will require a fundamental change in the distribution of income and other resources, a change we have yet to make (Douglas, 1989). Eliminating poverty and increasing social justice will require very different choices than those we have made in the past. It is less clear how we can motivate people to choose such a new path.

The Struggling Family

The American family occupies a place in mythology that does not reflect its current reality. We expect it to perform many social functions that are not realistic in today's world. The family has become primarily an economic unit, generating the income its members need to survive and thrive. High divorce rates, the increasing number of single-parent families, and the smallness of today's families make it increasingly likely that all adult members of the family—and an increasing number of the children—will work outside the home. Inevitably, this results in less time for family members to be together and attend to one another's social and emotional needs.

The declining ability of the family to meet the nonfinancial needs of its members has left these needs either unmet, or transferred the responsibility for meeting them to other social institutions such as social welfare. Among the more pressing of these needs are day care for children, care for the elderly, health care, and programs designed to prevent and control destructive behavior like crime, substance abuse, irresponsible sexual activity, and family violence. We have, as yet, devised no consistent or comprehensive social policy to address these family-related issues. Sadly, we have not even been able to agree on something as noncontroversial as pregnancy and child-rearing leaves for working women. It is little wonder that more controversial issues, such as family violence, remain in limbo.

It is clear, I believe, that the family cannot solve the problems it faces without help. The stresses faced by single parents and working parents are simply too great for them to handle both their own needs and those of other family members effectively. The current piecemeal approach to the provision of services is not working. Some families obtain the help they need. Many others do not. Too often, and for too many families, the all-too-predictable results include divorce, abandonment, violence, mental illness, or poverty. Thus does a failure to provide needed services result in a whole new set of family-generated problems for society.

Contributing to the family's difficulties in recent years has been a wave of corporate mergers and bankruptcies that has resulted in workers losing their jobs or being moved geographically. The job-related stresses involved inevitably spill over into family life. While some employers now offer social welfare services to their workers, the services offered are quite limited in scope and their availability sporadic (Cohn, 1988). Unfortunately, it is the poorest paid and most unskilled workers who are least likely to be served. These circumstances, coupled with the relative lack of success enjoyed by unions in protecting the rights of workers, has made the workplace far less effective as a provider of social welfare services in the United States than in many other societies.

There is little reason to believe that the family will be less important in the future, or that it will function more effectively if conditions remain the same. It is caught up in economic forces that are beyond its control but which powerfully affect its members. Thus, the question becomes one of society's willingness to develop a social policy that explicitly supports family life. It is ironic that the family is held so dear in the United States, while at the same time it is being left to fend for itself. What we need, I believe, is a family policy that includes at a minimum: guaranteed health insurance for everyone; affordable, quality child care that is available to everyone who needs it; and employment policies that provide women with time off to have children and that allow all parents to devote time to child-rearing at critical periods in the child's development.

It is difficult to say whether such a policy will soon become reality. Models for such a policy can be found in other societies, and there is currently a widespread concern about the state of the family that may encourage the emergence of a new policy. Still, there is a pervasive reluctance in our country to allow the government to intrude on the privacy of the family in any way. We are, it seems, faced with a choice between policies that would strengthen the family—at some risk of violating our traditional view of the family's right to privacy—or allowing a continuation of the problems that are an all-too-common feature of life in many American families.

Future Demographic Changes

Any attempt to assess future social welfare needs must take account of demographic trends. Several of these apparent trends are particularly important.

The first of these is the increasing proportion of elderly in our society. Demographers project that this pattern, which is common to most western industrialized societies, will continue (see Table 10.3). Its implications for future welfare needs are significant. As people live longer, they have increased need of services in the areas of health, housing, financial, and personal care.

Another demographic trend likely to affect future welfare needs is the growing proportion of minority families in the population. Between 1970 and 1980, the Hispanic population in the United States increased by 61 percent compared with a 9 percent increase for the population as a whole (Kincannon, 1983:4). Given the relative youth of the Hispanic population and its higher average birthrate, this trend is likely to continue (Rendon, 1985:13). Government projections are that Hispanics will comprise about 9 percent of the United

TABLE 10.3   CARING FOR THE ELDERLY: A COMPARATIVE VIEW

	Mexico	Poland	Sweden	United States
Percent of population 65 or over in 1980	3.1	9.8	15	11.3
Primary responsibility for the elderly	Family	Family	Society	Self and/or Society
Elderly covered by public retirement insurance	Some	Most	All	Nearly all
Appropriate housing available for the elderly	Little	Limited	Extensive	Some
Value of the elderly in society	Respect	Respect	Respect	Tolerance

Source for numerical data: Demographic Yearbook 1985. New York: The United Nations.

States population in the year 2000, up from 6.4 percent in 1980 (*Statistical Abstract,* 1987:16). Similarly, the black proportion of the population is expected to increase from 11.8 percent in 1980 to 13.2 percent in 2000 (*Statistical Abstract,* 1987:16). If current immigration patterns continue, other minority groups are likely to grow in size and importance as well.

If the growing minority proportion of the population is to be successfully integrated into American life, new and different types of social welfare services will have to be developed. If members of minority groups are not to continue to be disadvantaged in terms of employment, income, and educational opportunities, they must be provided with culturally appropriate services that make effective use of natural helping networks. Such services must be accompanied by modifications in our societal values so that different ethnic groups are viewed as valuable contributors to society rather than as potential threats to an entrenched social order.

Finally, much of the future need for welfare services will be determined by society's response to the needs of women. As we have seen, an increasing number of women are single parents, divorced, or unmarried. We have also seen that female-headed families are more likely to be poor, and that women are disadvantaged in terms of employment opportunities and income. Yet women continue to bear the primary responsibility for child-rearing and are increasingly important in a gradually shrinking workforce. The role of women in society is too important to continue institutional patterns that impede their ability to function. Social welfare must continue to play an important role in advocating for women's needs.

The Impact of World Issues

In spite of the fact that the United States has always been a multicultural society, the great diversity in the cultural backgrounds of today's immigrants, as well as the fact that many of them are from nonwestern cultures about which most Americans know little, are creating new problems. These are accentuated by the parochialism of many Americans who assume that all Spanish-speaking people are alike, and who similarly lump together people from many different Southeast Asian cultures. These stereotypes make it difficult to understand the different needs of each group, and to respect the fact that many of these groups have long histories of distrust and even conflict with each other. If the United States is to maintain its tradition as a haven for oppressed groups, it must develop more sensitivity to the differences among them so that more appropriate responses can be developed.

Unlike the years of the American frontier when the opportunities available seemed limitless, today's immigrants face resentment from citizens who feel the newcomers threaten their jobs and economic security. This fear is heightened by anxiety over the decline in the domestic manufacturing industry resulting from a great increase in the importation of low-cost goods from developing nations. Together, the influx of immigrants and imports leads many to question whether America's borders should be so open. To resolve this issue, we must clarify the balance between our current commitment to meeting the economic needs of our own citizens and that of helping new immigrants and refugees.

The economic pressures facing many Americans deserve attention. As noted earlier, these pressures are having a powerful effect on family life, and also have the potential to create considerable intergroup hostility, as residents come to fear immigrants who threaten their jobs. The tendency of large multinational corporations to purposefully shift jobs out of the United States while importing cheaper goods for sale under their label only worsens the problems facing American workers. A more rational approach to economic planning and its relationship to employment is needed, so that groups are not forced to fight each other to survive in the workplace. Nor should existing standards of work, pay, and benefits be changed without careful assessment of the impact on worker motivation, standards of living, and social problems.

The United States is a major player in the world economic system. It is a major participant in international lending, and American-controlled multinational corporations are active throughout the world. This economic power can be used for a variety of purposes. It can, for example, be used to help other societies solve their economic problems and encourage the spread of social justice and individual freedom. The United States has, however, been ambivalent about assuming this role. The choice to be made here is one between maximum profit and democratic social development, for the two are often incompatible. In the long run, helping other nations to develop in a way that minimizes social problems will, I believe, prove the least expensive alternative, reducing the probability of having to deal with large numbers of refugees, dictatorships that become hostile toward us, and requests for massive financial aid.

The difficulty here is one that has been widely acknowledged, namely that of helping an investment-oriented capitalist system overcome its preference for short-term profits over long-term gains and to recognize that some activities that yield corporate profits are costly for society. The earth's resources are finite. How to regulate the use and consumption of these resources while still permitting free enterprise to flourish is a question of increasing importance in each of our four societies. Of the four, the United States seems the most reluctant to develop and implement plans that would regulate the use of non-renewable resources. Indeed, the trend in recent years has been in favor of deregulation. Change will have to occur if we are to share resources more equitably with others, and if our economy is to compete effectively against the economies of other societies where long-range planning is a way of life.

Rebuilding Moral Commitments

Large industrial societies find it difficult to maintain a sense of common purpose and destiny. As work and leisure activities become increasingly specialized, society fragments into groups whose members know little about each other and find it difficult to perceive shared interests. The resulting sense of social isolation is often reinforced by special-interest radio programs, TV shows, and print media designed to appeal to different groups. Portable stereos with earphones enable people to share the same physical space, yet to be in quite different emotional and cognitive worlds. VCRs encourage people to remain at home rather than attend the theater, sports events, or other types of entertainment outside the home where they would be surrounded by others.

The family has also tended to fragment as its members pursue their own individual goals. Parents who work outside the home have less time for each other and for traditional parenting roles. Children have more freedom to select their own activities, and to conceal their activities from their parents. An increasing number of American adolescents hold part-time jobs while attending high school, leaving them with little time for family life. Increasingly too, the elderly live independently, often far from other family members. And if they must instead be placed in a residential treatment facility, their contact with other family members and with young people is often restricted.

Capitalism itself can also be alienating and fragmenting. The goal of economic success is not always compatible with human needs. The increasing centralization of economic power through mergers and buyouts has made workers and consumers more vulnerable to the policies and decisions of a few large corporations. At the same time they have less input into the formulation of policies that have a real impact on their lives. The stresses that result affect many people in negative ways. Exhausted by worry and overwork, they may want to go home and simply watch television rather than participate in family activities. Others seek a sense of well-being and purpose by pursuing self-gratification regardless of its effects on others. Still others withdraw into self-protective emotional shells, or strike out against even more vulnerable family members.

The alienating tendencies within modern society are strengthened by unethical activities by governmental and corporate leaders. Scandals in the government, on Wall Street, in corporate boardrooms, and among evangelists all undermine the belief that individual sacrifice and interpersonal cooperation are necessary for societal well-being. It can easily seem that the only way to succeed is to cheat, and that power is to be used for one's own purposes. Observing the self-enriching activities of many influential people, ordinary citizens can easily conclude it is foolish to allow ethical principles to stand in the way of personal gain.

Indeed, the government's role as overseer of other major social institutions has been eroded in the past few years. Deregulation, privatization, and a markedly less vigorous level of enforcement of civil rights legislation have together marked a significant reduction in the government's traditional role as protector of people's rights. As the government retreats, the market's sphere of influence grows and public scrutiny is reduced. Yet, as the social domain of the market expands, the most vulnerable members of society tend to be ignored or excluded because of their economic and social powerlessness.

To be sure, the government cannot solve all problems. Its role as a moral force is critical, however. Public officials must model ethical behavior and demand it from leaders in the corporate, financial, and religious fields. In a modern society, only the government can ensure the overall quality of the conditions under which its people live and work, regulate the relationship between consumers and the market to protect the weak, and fund the educational infrastructure required to create an informed and skilled workforce.

The government must also take leadership in reaffirming the value of people. This can only occur if the impact on people becomes a factor in all governmental decisions, including decisions that affect the relationship between the public and private sectors. The conditions under which people live must allow and encourage them to act out the values that nurture human life. What are needed are policies that strengthen family life rather than divide family members, and that strike a better balance between short-term economic gains and the long-term development of our most valuable resource, people. In the long run, it is a society's sense of moral commitment and common purpose that either holds it together or allows it to disintegrate.

Improving Social Welfare Service Delivery Systems

Effective social welfare services require adequate resources. Resources affect the way services are delivered, whether they are used, and the effectiveness with which they accomplish their intended purposes. If we wish to improve the effectiveness of the social welfare system, improvements will be required in a number of areas.

Personnel Service delivery is heavily dependent on the people who provide the services. They must be properly trained, their work loads must be realistic, and their working conditions must contribute to maintaining their motivation and sense of professional purpose.

This is not always the case. Programs are sometimes staffed by people who lack the proper training, as when agencies hire paraprofessionals rather than professionals to save money. Too often, workers struggle with unrealistic work loads that make any attempt to bring about needed changes wholly impractical. And some social welfare personnel work in agencies where their privacy and even physical safety are problematic, or they receive salaries far below the level appropriate to their level of training and work responsibilities.

Access   If services are to be used, they must be accessible. Unfortunately, social welfare services are sometimes located where they are physically inaccessible to people, especially those who must rely on public transportation. Access can be affected by other considerations as well. Lengthy, confusing, or complicated application procedures can reduce access. So too can the way in which potential users are treated. If they are made to feel uncomfortable, unwanted, or misunderstood, or if they perceive they are being treated disrespectfully, incompetently, or in a discriminatory or culturally insensitive manner, they are far less likely to make use of the services involved. Unless services are physically, emotionally, culturally, and financially accessible, they will not be used.

Policies   One of the major shortcomings of the social welfare system in the United States is a fragmentation of services that makes it difficult or impossible to address many needs in a coherent or holistic manner. The continuing scarcity of adequate child care, for example, undermines other programs that attempt to provide employment training for single parents. In addition, as we

---

MAXIMIZING ACCESS TO SOCIAL WELFARE FOR IMMIGRANTS LIVING IN SWEDEN

Sweden has taken a number of unusual steps to ensure that social welfare services are accessible to immigrants. A concerted effort is made to reduce the economic, cultural, emotional, and geographic barriers to participation in Swedish society, including the social welfare system. Among the major elements of that effort are:

1 Free Swedish language instruction.
2 240 hours of leave at full pay to study Swedish.
3 Several hours of native language instruction per week in their own community for all children from preschool through secondary levels.
4 Grants to fund the publication of Swedish literature in other languages and the purchase of foreign literature by local libraries.

5 Funding to assist the ethnic press.
6 Grants to fund national immigration organizations to help members maintain their ethnic identity and provide a vehicle for the public expression of that identity.
7 A policy that all aliens who have resided in Sweden for at least 3 years may vote and run for local and regional office.
8 A policy that all applicants for services have the right to receive help from social welfare agencies in their native language, and a program of courses to train interpreters for this task.

Source: Immigrants in Sweden. 1984. Stockholm: The Swedish Institute.

noted in our earlier discussion of income maintenance programs in this country, services that provide inadequate levels of assistance can make people more rather than less dependent. To be effective, a social welfare system must provide integrated services that neither conflict with one another nor create additional problems.

Applying this standard, we can identify several specific social welfare policy needs in the United States:

• The public social welfare system should be expanded to cover the *basic* needs of *all* citizens. Such an approach would be consistent with that taken in most other western industrialized nations and would involve the creation of several new programs. Chief among these would be a new health care program. A comprehensive program to provide all Americans with free or low-cost quality health care is long overdue. The current system of private health insurance linked to employment is insufficient. It leaves many without coverage of any sort, including the unemployed, most part-time workers, and those whose employers do not choose, or are unable, to provide coverage. Further, many medical expenses are not included, and the claim procedures are costly, cumbersome, and slow. The medical insurance plan for the elderly, Medicare, is also incomplete, expensive to operate, and complex. It is especially inadequate for those who need nursing home care.

• More must be done to strengthen families. A coherent family policy that will meet the needs of children, working parents, and young adults attempting to start families is badly needed. There is a particularly pressing need for a national policy regarding parental leaves for working parents during pregnancy and thereafter as well as a great need for improved child care.

• Income maintenance benefits must be improved. Benefit levels that leave recipients mired in poverty are counterproductive, as are the disincentives to independence that are built into many existing income maintenance programs.

• The quality of public education is also a major concern. The low quality of the education provided to many of the poor and members of minority groups impedes their personal development and greatly limits their opportunities to become economically self-sufficient. Consideration should be given to providing free higher education and specialized adult education programs. Improved access to education will make for a better-educated, more versatile, and more productive workforce, and will reduce the number of people restricted to low-paying, dead-end jobs.

• More must be done to address the needs of the elderly that are not currently being effectively addressed. The elderly comprise an increasing percentage of the population, and it is important that they not be isolated from productive roles in society. While their overall economic position has improved, many of the elderly still live alone and in poverty. The extended custodial care provided by nursing home facilities is frequently of poor quality and unaffordable. Senior citizen centers provide needed day care and recreational services, but the link between these and home-based programs is often weak.

Indeed, many of the available home-based services are expensive, fragmented, and riddled with problems. More and better services that can complement the efforts of family members must be made available for the elderly if the family is to continue to serve its elderly members.

Summary

As we have frequently discussed, social welfare is closely linked to the other institutions of society. Decisions made within these other social units have a powerful effect on the nature and quality of social welfare programs. A more effective social welfare system will require stronger support from the rest of society. It would include increased resources, a stronger role for the public sector in overseeing and coordinating the whole service delivery system, and new and improved programs in many areas of social life.

Beyond this, there is a need for changes within the social welfare institution itself, a topic to which we now turn.

CONTEMPORARY ISSUES WITHIN SOCIAL WELFARE

In this section, we will explore four issues concerning the internal structure of social welfare that will influence its future ability to meet people's needs and contribute to societal well-being. While each of these issues has implications for the larger society, our concern here is with their effect on social welfare itself. Let's now look at each of these four issues in some depth.

Reassessing Universal and Selective Approaches

As we have seen, the social welfare system in the United States is atypical in its extensive use of selective, residual programs. Like Poland and Sweden, most other industrialized societies employ more comprehensive or universal approaches. Selective programs not only complicate service delivery and pose difficulties for recipients of services, they also undermine public support for social welfare itself. They tend to stigmatize social welfare as an activity that serves the poor and others who are "failures."

By contrast, universal programs make it easier for people to perceive social welfare as a positive influence that enhances everyone's life. Rather than being a drain on societal resources, social welfare becomes a way to improve productivity and the overall quality of social life.

Universal services can also be funded in more acceptable ways. In Sweden, for example, all cash benefits received from social welfare programs are treated as taxable income, thus helping to fund the programs involved while simultaneously diminishing the perception that the recipient is receiving a handout. When everyone pays and everyone benefits, social welfare becomes a natural part of daily life for all. It is less likely to be seen as an irritant by those who feel they pay to support "deadbeats," while never themselves receiving any benefit from their payments; perceptions that, however inaccurate, nevertheless influence behavior. Under a more universal system, it is easier to justify a sharply progressive tax that transfers a larger proportion of program costs to the wealthy. For example, the top federal income tax rate for individuals in Sweden is 50 percent compared to 33 percent in the United States.

Providing multiple levels of benefits is another means by which universal systems can be strengthened. In Sweden, for example, many programs provide two levels of benefits: basic and supplemental. Basic benefits are provided to everyone, supplemental benefits to those with special needs.

Such an arrangement has at least two advantages. Providing basic benefits to everyone attests to society's interest in the well-being of all citizens and contributes to a stable, productive societal structure. By making supplemental benefits available to those with special needs, society both acknowledges those needs and its obligation to help those who are more vulnerable. In Sweden, for example, all elderly receive a basic pension while those with special physical or economic needs also are given special housing allowances to supplement their pension. Everyone receives some benefits while those with special needs receive special help, thus strengthening the society's sense of community.

Whatever the specific strategies involved, the move from a selective to a universal system of social welfare would strengthen the U.S. social welfare system. The stigma associated with a selective approach would be greatly reduced, thereby lessening resentment against social welfare professionals and those they serve. Such a move would provide social welfare with more opportunities to participate in societal decision-making and reduce its need to defend itself and those it serves from critics who emphasize the inefficiencies inherent in our present system.

Focusing on Competence

Effective helping can occur at many levels, as we have seen. Sometimes the deep caring and natural skills of family and friends are enough to enable people to cope with or solve their problems. When these resources are unavailable, or when they are insufficient, the formal social welfare system becomes important. We must ensure that those who work in this system are competent for the tasks they will be performing. This means developing education and training systems that combine the knowledge, values, and skills needed to produce effective helpers. Although the training for different groups of workers will differ in purpose and content, there should be no difference in the caring and quality involved.

It has often been difficult to gain recognition for the fact that effective helping requires education and training. This results in part from sexist attitudes about nurturing roles. Traditionally assigned to women, they were seen as "natural" or "instinctive" parts of the maternal role. As a result, helping activities are still dominated by women and are thought by many not to need specialized preparation. This kind of thinking is reinforced by the attitude that helping is all heart and little intellect. Such attitudes display little awareness of the training, ability to analyze problems, and intellectual demands required of professional helpers.

I believe that all social welfare personnel should be educated and trained to be competent practitioners. Competence must, of course, be defined in terms of the tasks to be performed. Volunteers, paraprofessionals, and professionals perform different tasks requiring different levels of knowledge and skill. Their training requirements should, therefore, reflect these differences, although all should be thoroughly schooled in the values that guide social welfare practice, their meaning, and their application.

Once trained, each of the different types of professional helpers should be assigned tasks appropriate to their level of preparation. The inappropriate use of personnel is illogical, counterproductive, and wasteful. It is unreasonable to expect people to do well at tasks for which they are unprepared.

The social welfare professions can do their part to improve competence by avoiding unproductive turf battles. These only serve to confuse the public and the decision-makers whose responsibilities involve an understanding of the proper roles for each profession. In addition, professional education and training programs must be strengthened so that the public has confidence in the preparation of those who complete them.

At the organizational level, agency and program administrators should resist the tendency to base personnel requirements on cost rather than competence. They must be willing to advocate for additional funds when needed, and to create ways in which to make use of personnel with competence of different types. The current tendency for social welfare administrators to have business backgrounds, but sometimes little or no practice experience, limits their ability to understand the importance of competence and related issues. We must never lose sight of our responsibility to ensure that people in need will be served by those competent to help them with their problems.

Working for Environmental Change

Helping individuals solve their personal and collective problems is a major function of social welfare. However, it cannot be the only one. The environment in which people live affects their behavior in powerful ways. It serves either to support or impede people's efforts to live healthy, satisfying lives. Therefore, part of the task of social welfare is to help create an environment conducive to healthy living.

That effort must concern itself with both the physical and social environments. Factors in the physical environment such as water quality, air pollution, and ground contamination affect people's physical health. Similarly, the quality of people's lives is influenced by a variety of factors in the social environment including the physical and organizational features of the workplace, discrimination, economic pressures, inadequate neighborhood services, poor housing, violence, and a lack of respect for human life. Without a healthy environment, social welfare will be continually addressing problems whose only long-term solution involves environmental change.

Bringing about such changes will often involve the political process. Governmental decision-making has a major effect on the conditions under which people live. It is the government which determines how resources will be used, creates legislation affecting people's rights, reaffirms values and behaviors that respect human life, and establishes the parameters within which the business community operates.

One way for the social welfare professions and professionals to influence that process is through their own direct participation. This is reasonable and legitimate. However, it is also important for them to involve the network of social agencies and users of services in such efforts. This is especially important at the state and local levels where many decisions are made that affect daily life.

In addition to the decisions of government, the environment is also deeply affected by the decisions of many other large organizations. These decisions too should be monitored. Large corporations, for example, make many decisions that together affect working conditions, resources available for charitable purposes, and the level of economic investment in the community and the larger society. The decisions of multinational corporations affect people and living conditions here and in other nations. Social agencies themselves make policies that influence the services delivered and their effectiveness.

Political participation and monitoring the decisions of large organizations are only two of the possible ways to influence the environment. Boycotts of organizations that exploit people, and peaceful protests such as sit-ins, rent strikes, and letter-writing campaigns have also been effective tools for change. Less peaceful strategies are also available, but there are many problems associated with their use.

An important tactic for bringing about environmental change is mobilizing people for social action. Although necessary, it is seldom easy. Many social welfare workers do not recognize the importance of this part of their work and feel uncomfortable with social action. In addition, users of social welfare services often feel disenfranchised because of their limited education, minority status, or fear that political or social action will lead to the loss of their benefits. They may also feel hopeless about the potential for change, or intimidated by feelings of powerlessness and confusion about systems that are strange to them.

In spite of these obstacles, the social welfare professions must continue to promoté social change that enhances human functioning. An active role in such efforts promotes feelings of hope and empowerment, and strengthens social welfare's role in society. Passivity breeds a sense of helplessness as problems multiply beyond the resources of helping systems.

The ultimate goal is for the social welfare institution to be an active participant in social planning so that the environment of the future is one that promotes healthy and satisfying human life. This is most likely to occur if helping professionals actively seek such a role and are tireless in their monitoring of decision-making that affects social welfare. Understanding the importance of solidarity with those they serve is also essential for developing a coalition powerful enough to bring about change.

Rewarding Social Welfare Professionals

Effective social welfare delivery systems demand competent personnel. Recruiting and retaining such people depends on providing them with rewarding and meaningful careers. People considering a social welfare career usually find intrinsic satisfaction in helping others, and this motivation is a powerful incentive. However, one's occupation is also a source of prestige and the income needed to obtain desired resources like cars, housing, travel, and entertainment. Even those who would find a social welfare career personally rewarding must realistically consider whether such work will enable them and their loved ones to enjoy a comfortable and secure life.

The attractiveness of any career depends on its income potential, working conditions, and the esteem in which it is held by society. Many people have rejected a social welfare career because they viewed the pay as inadequate. Those who have pursued such a career have often done so because, as women or members of minority groups, they have had less access to higher-paying careers. As barriers to education and employment have slowly begun to fall, members of these groups are also seeking positions in higher-paid professions or in the business world. Increasing salary levels and enhancing the value attached to a career in social welfare are essential if the social welfare professions are to attract competent people.

Another issue is working conditions. Social welfare personnel who feel overworked and underappreciated are likely to become alienated, discouraged, and ineffective (Simpkin, 1983:45–112). When the stress and disappointment become intolerable, people change jobs. Many nurses, for example, have abandoned their profession in recent years because of poor working conditions and inadequate salaries. Teachers too sometimes find that the stresses involved in public school teaching are difficult and unrewarding. These include fears for their personal safety, inadequate instructional materials, and unmotivated or unprepared students. And all social welfare personnel find it tiresome and discouraging to continually have to justify the value of their work in response to attacks in the media and expressions of doubt from friends and acquaintances (Wells, 1989:169–178).

Here in the United States we are fond of financial solutions to problems, but money alone will not deal with the problems confronting our social welfare system. To be sure, increasing salaries will help to attract and retain competent workers. Most of the problems discussed above, however, are not primarily financial. Designing social welfare positions that allow workers to utilize their helping skills and increasing society's perception that social welfare is important are goals that do not entail large expenditures of money. To be sure, some small outlays may be involved, but fundamentally such goals require new administrative arrangements and opportunities to enhance the public image of social welfare. Such changes are important to the future strength of professional and paraprofessional social welfare occupations. Their health is in turn essential to more effective service delivery in tomorrow's world.

WHY WE CAN'T AFFORD TO FAIL: NATIONAL AND INTERNATIONAL PERSPECTIVES

The success of social welfare is important for the world's future. From a national perspective, the costs of social problems are too high. We must not continue to spend many billions of dollars for prisons where inmates spend years of idleness. We must not continue to lose people to AIDS and other preventable diseases. We must not allow people to become so mired in poverty that they are unable to be productive citizens. We must not lose young people to drugs and to lives of ignorance because they drop out of school. We must not continue to waste the abilities of women and members of other minority groups. We must not continue to lose the contributions of our elderly citizens whose productive lives are prematurely ended by poor-quality health and custodial care.

Resources should instead be used to prevent problems and enhance human functioning. Does it really make sense to focus our energies and resources on short-term solutions to problems, knowing that they will occur again and again? Doesn't it make more sense to see human development as a long-term investment, much as we see economic development? Unless we do, the costs will continue to escalate and the conditions under which people live will worsen. To be sure, investing in human development will itself prove costly. Over the long run, however, the result will be a healthier and more productive society.

If we fail to invest in people, we may come to deeply regret our decision. A stratified society in which the very wealthy and those who live in poverty with little hope of escape coexist is a dangerous mix. In today's world, where affluence is flaunted in the media, and where the media report new accounts of white-collar crime in business and government almost daily, I believe we have to expect that those who are disadvantaged will become increasingly restless. If having money and the things it buys bring social acceptance, they too will want to be part of the mainstream. If crime works for others, why not for them? If the rich and famous have so much, they won't miss a little that is stolen. Ultimately, those who feel totally alienated and helpless may come to believe they have little to lose by simply taking what they want. Current patterns of street and violent crime suggest that this mode of thinking is gaining acceptance.

We have much to learn in this area from the experience of other countries where there are vast socioeconomic differences between classes. In most such societies with large numbers of poor and uneducated people, crime and harshly repressive efforts to control it are common. These are the conditions under which military rule and dictatorships flourish. Once these patterns are established, it is very difficult to break them or to reestablish democracy. While this may not yet be a likely scenario in the United States, we must realize that the decisions we make about social welfare today have implications for the polarization of social classes in the future. This in turn will affect the future of American democracy and our capitalistic economic system.

The issues involved are ones with international implications. As a multicultural society, the United States is host to large numbers of immigrants from societies where poverty and dictatorships are common. An effective social welfare system is critical to their integration into our society. If we fail to help them become productive citizens, they will either require costly long-term assistance or will resort to crime to survive.

Increasingly too our country's ability to remain a world economic leader depends on an educated and flexible workforce. Unless the social welfare and business communities work together more effectively in the future, we will fall further behind in our ability to compete in international markets. This is, of course, an issue that also involves economic and social planning. Devising policies that key social welfare services to conditions in the workplace and governmental fiscal practices will require creative thinking and close cooperation among the major social institutions of American society. For a model of how such cooperation can be achieved, we can look to Sweden.

Finally, we need to recognize that America's continued ability to provide leadership in the world community will depend on its commitment to human values. We have long been vulnerable to accusations that we allow and perpetrate at home the very civil rights abuses we have sought to prevent abroad. Our international economic policies and the practices of our multinational corporations have sometimes contributed to the creation of unhealthy living conditions in underdeveloped nations, not to mention the maintenance of dictatorships. The scandal of widespread homelessness amid affluence in the United States leads others to question our commitment to social justice and human well-being. The success of the social welfare system's efforts on behalf of the most vulnerable and oppressed among us is vital to the legitimacy of our claim to moral leadership in the world community, and our support for the well-being of people everywhere.

CONCLUSION

I hope that this chapter has convinced you of one thing: that social welfare is central to the future of our society and its role in world affairs. We must be concerned with the social welfare institution itself because its success requires a strong moral and financial base. We must improve the linkages between social welfare and the other institutions of society if we are to move toward a

ON THE STREET IN GOTHENBURG, SWEDEN

When I entered a gift shop in Gothenburg, I was greeted and offered assistance by a young woman. Her knowledge of the store's merchandise turned out to be limited, but she was able to obtain any needed information from the other clerk, an older woman.

When paying for my purchases, I asked the more experienced woman if the other was her daughter. She laughed and said not. She then explained that the clerk who had waited on me was a high school student who, as part of her studies, spent several weeks in the workplace to learn about different types of jobs and the work skills required. All Swedish young people do this during their schooling.

This is one example of Swedish coordination of education and labor policies. Sweden believes that education is essential if its workers are going to participate effectively in a rapidly changing and increasingly complex workplace. Skilled workers will in turn enable Swedish businesses to be efficient and effective competitors in the world economy. The goal is to maintain a high level of productivity so that Sweden can continue to fund its impressive network of social welfare services.

Education in Sweden prepares students for the world of work in other ways as well. All types and levels of education are free. In addition to the usual academic curricula, there are well-developed vocational and continuing education programs. All Swedish students learn English as well as Swedish in school, and they are encouraged to study other languages as well. The public radio stations even have instructional programs to teach listeners popular languages such as French and German.

Even child care centers are designed to contribute to the productivity of the workforce. These programs, which provide day care for all children of preschool age, are intended to give women equal access to the job market. This not only helps provide women with equal opportunity in the workplace, it also results in a larger workforce of higher quality.

And the children themselves are not ignored. Child care centers do not attempt to teach children to read and write. This takes place when the children go to school. Instead, they are taught social skills—how to get along with others, follow instructions, and be patient. These are skills that come in handy in the workplace, and are useful in many daily living situations as well.

We can see, then, how Sweden coordinates social welfare policy (education, in this case) with labor policy. This type of integrated planning helps to ensure that social institutions work together to achieve societal goals.

future with fewer problems and more opportunities for all. The success of these efforts will affect not only our own future but that of the world community as well.

Now, as you conclude your reading of this book, I hope that you feel good about what you have learned. The facts you have acquired will be useful in your own life, and in the lives of those you love. For some of you, this knowledge will also be useful in your work. You should now have a better understanding of how society works and social welfare's role in the larger social fabric. Finally, you are now aware of some of the issues that will shape our future.

As you think further about what you have learned, I hope you will realize how many opportunities you have to affect the future. Knowledge is power, and my final hope is that you will use your knowledge to make the world of today and tomorrow better for everyone.

CHAPTER OUTLINE

INTRODUCTION

ENDURING SOCIAL CONCERNS
   Poverty and Other Effects of Injustice
   The Struggling Family
   Future Demographic Changes
   The Impact of World Issues
   Rebuilding Moral Commitments
   Improving Social Welfare Service Delivery Systems
      Personnel
      Access
   Maximizing Access to Social Welfare for Immigrants in Sweden
      Policies
   Summary

CONTEMPORARY ISSUES WITHIN SOCIAL WELFARE
   Reassessing Universal and Selective Approaches
   Focusing on Competence
   Working for Environmental Change
   Rewarding Social Welfare Professionals

WHY WE CAN'T AFFORD TO FAIL: NATIONAL AND
INTERNATIONAL PERSPECTIVES
   On the Street in Gothenburg, Sweden

CONCLUSION

STUDY QUESTIONS

1 What do you consider the most serious issue facing the United States in the years ahead? How can the social welfare institution help to resolve it?

2 Go to the library and locate the most recent census data for your community (the reference librarian can assist you). Examine the data from 1960 to the present and identify as many demographic changes as you can—the number of elderly people, for example, or the population of minority group members. Briefly discuss the impact on the social welfare system in your community of each change you identify.

3 Interview a social welfare professional in your community. Learn as much as you can about the aspects of the position involved and the working conditions that your respondent finds most frustrating. Find out how your respondent handles these frustrations.

4 Interview one of your local legislators concerning the problems facing your community that the legislator views as most pressing. Ask your respondent to discuss how the social welfare system can help solve these problems.

5 Research the current employment, education, and housing situation in Mexico. Compare your findings with similar data from the United States. Then briefly discuss how the two countries can help each other solve these problems.

REFERENCES

Axthelm, Pete. 1988. Somebody else's kids. *Newsweek,* April 25, pp. 64–68.

Bane, Mary Jo. 1988. Politics and policies of the feminization of poverty. In Margaret Weir et al., eds. *The Politics of Social Policy in the United States.* Princeton, N.J.: Princeton University Press, pp. 381–396.

Butterfield, Fox. 1988. New Yorkers grow angry over aggressive panhandlers. *The New York Times,* July 28, p. A1ff.

Cohn, Bob. 1988. A glimpse of the "flex" future. *Newsweek.* August 1, pp. 38–39.

Douglas, Jack. 1989. *The Myth of the Welfare State.* New Brunswick, N.J.: Transaction Books.

Hochschild, Jennifer. 1988. Race, class, power, and the American welfare state. In Amy Guttman, ed. *Democracy and the Welfare State.* Princeton, N.J.: Princeton University Press, pp. 157–184.

Kincannon, C. Lewis. 1983. *Condition of Hispanics in America Today.* Washington, D.C.: U.S. Government Printing Office.

McCormick, John. 1988. America's third world. *Newsweek.* August 8, pp. 20–24.

Pearce, Diana. 1978. The feminization of poverty: Women, work, and welfare. *Urban and Social Change Review* (February):28–36.

Rendon, Armando. 1985. *Nosotros.... We.* Washington, D.C.: U.S. Government Printing Office.

Rosen, Sumner, with David Fanshel and Mary Lutz, eds. 1987. Face of the Nation 1987. Statistical Supplement to the 18th edition of the *Encyclopedia of Social Work.* Silver Spring, Md.: National Association of Social Workers.

Sheahan, John. 1987. *Patterns of Development in Latin America.* Princeton, N.J.: Princeton University Press.

Simpkin, Michael. 1983. *Trapped Within Welfare,* 2d ed. London: Macmillan.

Sosin, Michael. 1986. *Private Benefits.* New York: Academic Press.

Tobin, James. 1988. The future of Social Security: One economist's assessment. In Theodore Marmor and Jerry Mashaw, eds. *Social Security in Contemporary American Politics.* Princeton, N.J.: Princeton University Press, pp. 41–67.

Weir, Margaret, et al. 1988. Understanding American social politics. In Margaret Weir, et al., eds. *The Politics of Social Policy in the United States.* Princeton, N.J.: Princeton University Press, pp. 3–35.

Wells, Carolyn Cressy. 1989. *Social Work Day to Day,* 2d ed. White Plains, N.Y.: Longman, Inc.

GLOSSARY

Adoption   The permanent removal of a child from the natural parents and legal transfer of custody to the adopting parents.

Almshouses   Residences established under the Elizabethan Poor Law in which those in greatest need lived and were cared for.

Biopsychosocial whole   The unity of people's biological, psychological, and social selves.

Block grants   Federal grants to states that are earmarked for a specific social welfare purpose but are accompanied by relatively few guidelines regarding program design and implementation.

Case manager   A professional who oversees the provision of a variety of specialized services to ensure that they are delivered in a fashion that represents an effective response to the whole problem.

Case services   Personal social services meant to help those with personal maladjustments, problems, illness, or other difficulties.

Certification   The legal control of the use of a title.

Charity   Help donated to others by individuals and private organizations.

Charity Organization Societies   Social welfare agencies established in the latter part of the 1800s that utilized a "scientific charity" approach to studying the needs of individuals and families.

Child welfare   Programs that seek to improve the quality of parenting that children receive.

Code of ethics   A profession's set of standards concerning the ethical behavior of its members. All members are expected to be guided by this code in their professional activities.

Common human needs   Needs shared by all human beings that are basic to human survival and development.

Contracting   The practice of hiring private agencies to implement specified public social welfare activities and deliver certain services in return for payment from public funds.

Day care The supervision of children during hours when working parents cannot care for their children or want them to be in a supervised program with other children.

Declassification The lowering of the credentials needed to perform specified tasks.

Deinstitutionalization Removing the needy from residential facilities and placing them in the community where help can be provided in a less restrictive way more closely linked to community support systems.

Demographic changes Variations in the size, composition, and distribution of a population.

Disposable income The amount of income that people actually have available to spend.

Economic institution The social institution concerned with the production, distribution, and consumption of goods and services.

Education institution The social institution whose major functions include socializing children, preparing people for participation in the workplace, and promoting racial and ethnic integration.

Eligibility requirements The conditions that must be met before people qualify to receive benefits from a social welfare program.

Elizabethan Poor Law of 1601 Created the first system of national standards of social welfare which was administered at the local (parish) level.

Entitlements A right to a social welfare service.

Ethical behavior Behavior prescribed by a value.

Family The social institution comprised of adults of both sexes, at least two of whom carry on socially approved sex relations, and their children, if any. Its functions include regulating sex behavior, child-bearing and child-rearing, providing for the economic and emotional needs of its members, and socializing children to become successful participants in society.

For-profit private agencies Agencies that seek to make a profit from the delivery of services by maximizing income and reducing expenditures.

Formal helping An organized response to anticipated need that is provided by people who have had some type of training in the provision of helping services.

Foster care Interim care for children whose parents cannot currently provide it themselves.

Friendly visitors The workers (initially untrained) who did investigations for the Charity Organization Societies.

Generalist approach An approach to problem solving that attempts to address all of the needs being experienced by the people suffering from a problem.

Grant A monetary payment to people who have not previously contributed to the source of funds from which payments are made.

Halfway houses Small residential facilities in the community that provide treatment and supervision while at the same time allowing for more integration into ongoing community life.

Health maintenance organizations (HMOs) Health care organizations that provide comprehensive medical care for a set, prepaid fee.

Helpless A category of need used in the Elizabethan Poor Law that was comprised of those with a disabling condition over which they had no control.

Household A social unit formed by people who are not married or related, and that performs many of the functions of the family.

Houses of correction Facilities similar to prisons established under the Elizabethan Poor Law and to which workhouse residents were sent if they violated the rules. Houses of correction were also used for criminals, vagrants, and welfare cheats.

Human diversity   The biological, psychological, social, and cultural differences among people that affect the way their needs are expressed and satisfied.

Income maintenance programs   Social welfare services that attempt to ensure adequate financial resources for people.

Indenture   A type of social welfare service formalized by the Elizabethan Poor Law that placed orphans and children who had been removed from needy families in the homes of people who agreed to provide care in return for the child's labor.

Indoor relief   A type of social welfare service in which services are delivered in a residential facility rather than in the home of the recipient.

Industrial Revolution   The era in which machine power replaced human and animal power in the production process, generally said to have first begun on a large scale in England during the 1600s.

Informal helping   When people spontaneously seek help or offer it to others. It is usually provided by people who do not have any special training as helpers.

In-kind services   Programs that provide resources people need instead of money with which to purchase them.

Institutional view of social welfare   A view that emphasizes the preventive role of social welfare in modern industrial societies.

Involuntarily unemployed   A category of need under the Elizabethan Poor Law, comprised of those who had suffered some kind of misfortune.

Laissez-faire economics   An economic system based on the belief that an efficient and productive economy is best achieved by minimizing governmental intervention in economic activities.

Latent functions of social welfare   The less visible, and sometimes unintentional, effects of social welfare programs that often serve the special needs of powerful groups in society.

Licensing   The legal control of the use of a title and the practice of a profession.

Life span   The period from conception to death.

Life-span stages   Particular chronological periods in the lives of individuals that are associated with certain sets of social expectations about how needs should be met.

Manifest functions of social welfare   The visible and intended purpose of social welfare programs.

Mental illness   A mental disability in which cognitive and personality functioning is disturbed by biological or emotional factors.

Mental retardation   A mental disability resulting from abnormal or insufficient development of the brain.

New federalism   A policy initiated during the Nixon administration in which certain decision-making powers were returned to the state and local levels of government. A key element in the new federalism was the extensive use of revenue sharing and block grants.

Nonprofit private agencies   Agencies that use all of their resources to provide services.

Outdoor relief   Social welfare services provided in the homes of the helpless who were capable of managing on their own with some assistance.

Paraprofessionals   Persons with work experience or specialized training who are generally trained to assist professionals but do not themselves have professional training and credentials.

Parole   The practice of allowing prisoners to complete their sentences under supervision in the community after a period of imprisonment.

Participation of the poor   Involving poor people in planning for social welfare programs.

Personal social services Nonfinancial social welfare programs that enhance people's personal development and functioning.

Physical limitations The partial or total loss of the use of bodily organs, limbs, or other body parts.

Political institution The social institution aimed at ensuring an orderly process for societal decision-making, and providing a workable structure to enforce rules and laws.

Preretirement planning Helping people plan ahead so that they will be emotionally and financially prepared for retirement.

Private social welfare Social welfare programs funded by voluntary charitable contributions of individuals and private organizations, by fees people pay for the services they receive, or which are provided by funds spent by corporations to provide social welfare services for their employees.

Privatization The use of the private sector to provide social welfare services, often in addition to or instead of existing public services.

Probation Allowing convicted offenders to serve their sentence under supervision in the community instead of in prison.

Professional registration The process of compiling and maintaining a list of names of people who have met specified professional standards.

Prosthesis An artificial replacement for a limb or other bodily part.

Protestant ethic The belief, based in Protestant religious values, that work fulfills God's will and that those who do not work are sinners.

Public social utilities Services that are available to all members of society who might have a need for them.

Public social welfare Social welfare programs funded by tax monies or through income obtained from legally mandated programs.

Relative values Values that represent alternative ways of deciding what should be done. Different groups adopt their own preferred ways of acting as a result of their own cultural traditions and the life experiences of their members.

Religion The social institution that helps people relate to the unknown.

Residual view of social welfare A view in which the proper role of social welfare is seen as that of responding to breakdowns in the normal functioning of the market, the family, or the individual.

Revenue-sharing grants Federal grants provided to the states with nearly complete freedom in how the monies can be used.

Scientific method The use of empirical data to test hypotheses derived from theory.

Scientific philanthropy An approach to helping that involved the collection of empirical data concerning each person or family to be helped coupled with efforts to coordinate the help provided by different social agencies within the community.

Self-help The acquiring of information or the solving of one's problems without the direct intervention of professionals or experts, through independent reading or by joining or forming a group comprised of others who also have the problem.

Settlement houses Social welfare agencies established in the late 1800s, primarily to serve immigrants, that used community-oriented approaches to serving people.

Sheltered workshops Special facilities to train and employ the mentally ill and those with mental or physical limitations who would not be able to compete successfully in the regular workplace.

Social Darwinism The application of survival of the fittest thinking to humans (attributed to Herbert Spencer).

Social institution A socially approved system of values, norms, and roles that exists to accomplish specific societal goals.

Social insurance   A type of program in which participants make regular payments into a fund from which they receive benefits if the risk covered by the insurance occurs.

Socialization   The process of social learning through which we come to internalize culturally approved ways of thinking, feeling, and behaving.

Social order   The maintenance of predictable patterns of behavior.

Social welfare   A society's governmental and nongovernmental efforts to help its members function more effectively as individuals and as participants in organized social structures.

Social welfare agencies   Formal organizations whose function is to administer social welfare programs so that they effectively and efficiently meet people's needs.

Social welfare as a social institution   A major unit of society that is socially approved and that is intended to help individual people as well as society itself. This occurs by organizing the distribution of resources and the activities of people involved in helping activities.

Social welfare benefits   The actual resources provided to recipients of a social welfare program.

Social welfare program   Organized procedures for distributing social welfare resources to targeted recipients.

Social welfare resources   The services that people receive from the social welfare system which are intended to help them function more effectively.

Social welfare services   Actual resources provided to help people function more effectively in their environment.

Social work   The profession that uses a generalist approach to help people singly and in groups to meet their survival and developmental needs.

Specialist approach   An approach to problem solving that utilizes professionals with specialized training to solve particular problems.

Substance abuse   The excessive, uncontrolled, and injurious use of alcohol or drugs, including prescription or over-the-counter drugs.

Survival of the fittest   The process through which the best-adapted members of a species survive so that they can breed and thereby perpetuate themselves (attributed to Charles Darwin).

Systems approach   An approach to problem solving that focuses on the many groups in which people live, and the way in which these groups affect the lives of their members.

Trade balance   The relationship between the economic value of a society's imports and exports.

Trade deficit   The economic imbalance that results when the value of a nation's imports exceeds that of its exports.

Vagrants   A category of need used in the Elizabethan Poor Law that was comprised of those who lacked roots in the community.

Values   Preferred ways of believing that prescribe appropriate behavior (called *ethical behavior*).

Welfare cheating   When people lie about their true situation in order to qualify for social welfare benefits.

Workfare   The practice of making recipients of public assistance participate in work or training programs.

Workhouses   Residences established under the Elizabethan Poor Law that were used for the involuntarily unemployed and where basic needs were to be met in return for work.

Index

DATE DUE

JY 1 0 '98			
DE 1 7 '99			
GAYLORD 234			PRINTED IN U. S. A.